Welcome to San Andreas

Getting Around

There are lots of ways to get around in San Andreas; you can trek on foot, control almost any vehicle imaginable (see the Auto Trader chapter), or even purchase a ticket at any of the three major airports for a flight to another city. This option is available once you have safe access to the city to which you want to travel. If you try to swim to the next city before gaining safe entry, you gain a four-star Wanted Level (details below) until you leave and can lower the level in a city that welcomes you. Find the door with the yellow marker on the exterior upper levels of the Los Santos and San Fierro airports. The Las Venturas ticket machine is much easier to find since there's only one level.

Staying Out of Trouble

Wanted Level

The Wanted Level only appears below your weapon selection meter when you get into trouble. You can only get as high as a four-star Wanted Level in Los Santos, but a five-star level is possible once you access San Fierro, and even six when you visit Las Venturas. You can stay out of trouble to make a one-star Wanted Level go away, but beyond that you need to find Police Bribes (one bribe lowers the level by one star) and Pay 'n' Sprays (see our maps), complete the mission you are currently playing, get Busted, or Wasted. The latter two are not good options.

WANTED LEVEL CONDITIONS

WANTED LEVEL	LAW ENFORCEMENT
1 Star	If a cop sees you, he'll go after you.
2 Stars	Additional Police Cruisers join the bust.
3 Stars	Police Helicopter joins the mayhem.
4 Stars	SWAT with Mini-SMGs in Enforcers arrive and SWAT members repel from additional chopper.
5 Stars	Four FBI agents arrive in a Rancher packing MP5s.
6 Stars	Army is called in with Rhinos and Flatbeds full of Army men with M4s.

Stats

Stamina, Muscle, and Fat

The Stamina statistic reflects CJ's endurance when sprinting, swimming, and cycling. For more information on improving this stat and the muscle stat, see the Gyms section of this guide; for details on the Fat stat, see Restaurants—both in our Odd Jobs chapter.

Driving, Bike, Cycling and Flying

Driving stats increase as you drive vehicles. This improves the handling of all the vehicles you enter. The Bike skill increases as you ride motorcycles. The higher the stat, the less chance you have of falling off. Cycling skill increases as you ride bicycles (including stationary bikes at the Gyms). The higher the stat, the less chance you have of falling off; plus your bunny hops are higher and you can reverse at higher speeds without eating dirt. The Flying stat improves aircraft handling, and a pilot's license is given at 20%, granting you access to all the airports.

Respect

Respect enables you to recruit gang members, and is made up of a number of components:

RESPECT TYPE	RESPECT TOTAL CONTRIBUTION
Running respect	40%
Mission progression	36%
Territory under control	6%
Money	6%
Fitness	4%
Girlfriend progress	4%
Clothes	4%

RUNNING RESPECT BREAKDOWN	
ACTION	STATISTIC MODIFICATION
Killing a dealer	+ .005%
Killing a gang member	+ .5%
Killing a member of your gang	- .005%
A member of your gang gets killed	- 2%
Territory gained	+ 30%
Territory lost	- 3%

Recruiting Gang Members

You can recruit by pressing the Up on the D-pad while targeting a gang member. Once a gang is recruited, press Up on the D-pad again to call them to you; they will follow you and return fire if you get attacked. If you attack a target, the gang will do the same. If you attack an enemy gang member, your gang attacks any member of the gang you just attacked. Press Down on the D-pad to command the gang to stay put. To disband the gang, hold Down on the D-pad for a few seconds, or leave them far behind. The number of gang members the player can recruit is as follows:

RESPECT AMOUNT	NUMBER OF GANG MEMBERS
Above 1%	2
Above 10%	3
Above 20%	4
Above 40%	5
Above 60%	6
Above 80%	7

100 % Completion of San Andreas

To reach 100% completion of San Andreas, you must complete the tasks listed below—all of which is covered in this guide (and more)!

Completion of all game missions: This includes main story missions and prerequisite Odd Jobs.

Buying all the asset properties in the game: Zero RC Shot and Wang Auto; Verdant Meadows Airstrip.

Acquiring assets for all properties: Roboi's Food Mart, LS; Hippy Shopper, SF; Burger Shot, LV; Hunter Quarry, Bone County; Vank Hoff Hotel, SF; "RS Haul" Flint County.

Buying all save houses in the game

Painting all 100 Gang Tags

Photographing all 50 Photo Ops

Collection of all 50 Oysters

Collection of all 50 Horseshoes

GRAND THEFT AUTO SAN ANDREAS

CHAPTER 4: THE DESERT

CHAPTER 5: LAS VENTURAS

CHAPTER 6: RETURN TO LOS SANTOS

Weapons

WEAPONS SKILL UPGRADES

Your Weapon Skill increases with every accurate shot you land. Getting a high Weapon Skill increases your ability with weapons. View weapon skills by pressing the view stat button when holding the weapon in question. The skill level appears in the stat box in the bottom corner of the screen. You can also check weapon stats through the Stats menu. The Stats menu displays the weapon skill level and a label, such as "Poor," "Gangster," or "Hitman."

Gangster level is reached when skill levels fill 20% to 50% of the meter. All "Hitman" levels are reached when skill levels reach the maximum (100%). Your Weapon Skills improve in-between these milestones, as well.

Gangster Skill Level

This rule applies to the following weapons: Silenced Pistol, Desert Eagle, all Shotguns, Tec-9, Micro-SMG, MP5, AK-47, and M4.

When Gangster level is reached, you can move while in the aiming stance and your lock-on range, accuracy, rate of fire, and strafe speed increase.

Weapons (with skill levels) this rule does not apply to: Pistol

Pistol's Gangster Level Explained
The Pistol's Gangster level increases lock-on range, accuracy and rate of fire. You can already move while aiming and firing this weapon.

Hitman Skill Level

This rule applies to the following weapons: Silenced Pistol, Desert Eagle, Shotgun, Combat Shotgun, MP5, AK-47, and M4.

Hitman level is reached at maximum weapon skill (100%). This allows you to fire while moving. Lock-on range, accuracy, rate of fire, and strafe speed also improve.

Weapons (with skill levels) this rule does not apply to: Weapons held in each hand (see below).

Double Weapon Hitman Level

This rule applies to the following weapons: Pistol, Sawn-off Shotgun, Tec-9, and Micro-SMG.

You can wield two of the above weapons simultaneously and the lock-on range increases.

ARSENAL

The following weapons are categorized by weapon slots. CJ has 12 different weapon slots, which hold a particular class of weapons and items. You can only carry one weapon per slot, so if that slot is filled you must press the L1 button while standing over the weapon you want to add to the inventory. The old weapon in that slot is lost.

Slot 1: Hand

Weapons in this slot allow you to attack and block. To block, hold the target button to select a victim and press the block button to block.

Fist
No weapons, just the good ol' clenched fist.

Brass Knuckles
More damaging than the bare fist.

Slot 2: Melee Weapons

Weapons in this slot allow you to attack and block.

Baseball Bat

Katana

Knife

Shovel

Golf Club

Cane

Pool Stick

Nightstick

Chainsaw
Target select and press secondary button for single attack, the shoot button for brutal attack. Continue to hold the shoot button until CJ buries the chainsaw in the victim's gut.

Slot 3: Handguns

Every weapon in this slot has its own Weapon Skill. All Hitman Skill levels are reached at 100% Weapon Skill.

Pistol
Gangster Level reached at 10% Pistol Skill.

Desert Eagle
This is a very powerful handgun that must be held with two hands to control recoil. Almost twice as powerful as the Silenced Pistol. Gangster Level reached at 20% Desert Eagle Skill.

Silenced 9mm
The silenced pistol is not only good for keeping quiet, but it's also five times as powerful as the Pistol. Gangster Level reached at 20% Silenced Pistol Skill.

Slot 4: Shotguns

Every weapon in this slot has its own Weapon Skill. All Hitman Skill levels are reached at 100% Weapon Skill.

Shotgun
Gangster level at 20% Shotgun Skill

Combat Shotgun
This spaz shotgun is the most powerful Shotgun of the bunch. Gangster level reached at 20% Combat Shotgun Skill.

Sawn-Off Shotgun
This weapon is more powerful than the Shotgun at close range. Gangster level reached at 20% Sawn-Off Shotgun Skill.

Slot 5: Machine Pistols

The first two weapons below are in the "Machine Pistol" Skill category. All Hitman Skill levels are reached at 100% Weapon Skill.

Tec-9
The weakest of the Uzi-type weapons, but allows you to do Drive-bys. Gangster level reached at 10% Machine Pistol Skill.

MP5
The most powerful weapon in its category, the MP5 is the next best thing to having an AK. Gangster level reached at 30% MP5 Skill.

Micro-MP5
More powerful than the Tec-9, but can't touch the MP5. Gangster level reached at 10% Machine Pistol Skill.

Slot 6: Assault Rifles

Both weapons in this slot have their own Weapon Skill. All Hitman Skill levels are reached at 100% Weapon Skill.

AK-47
The AK-47 is a very powerful weapon with great accuracy at medium to long-range shooting. Gangster level reached at 30% AK-47 Skill.

M4
The M4 military weapon is top dog, although it's sometimes difficult to compare it to the AK-47. Gangster level reached at 20% M4 Skill.

Slot 7: Rifles

The weapons in this category have no upgrade ability and no auto targeting feature.

Country Rifle
A powerful and popular brand of rifle. With its long barrel comes extreme accuracy. You cannot move while shooting or aiming this weapon. Hold the targeting button for a targeting reticle.

Sniper Rifle
Hold the target button to raise the scope to your eye, Zoom in and out, and crouch for improved stability. You cannot move while shooting or aiming this weapon.

Slot 8: Heavy Artillery

The weapons in this category have no upgrade ability and you cannot crouch while wielding them.

Rocket Launcher
You cannot shoot this weapon without first pressing the target button to bring up the targeting box. Aim and press shoot to fire. You'll take damage if you shoot close objects.

Flame Thrower
Press the target button for a small round targeting reticle and burn baby, burn! Don't get too close to your own fire.

Heat-seeking Rocket Launcher
Press and hold the target button for auto-targeting until targeting reticle turns from green to red. Press shoot to fire a homing missile. The weapon only targets select vehicles and always the nearest vehicle in view. To force a lock-on on a different vehicle, aim away from the selected target and scope the desired target.

Minigun
This gun has no auto targeting, but you can pull up a targeting reticle to help your aim. This is one tough piece of hardware! Makes Swiss cheese of anything and everything.

Slot 9: Thrown Weapons

The weapons in this category have no upgrade ability and no auto-targeting; they're projectiles. The distance that these projectiles are thrown depends on how long you hold the Circle button—within reason.

Grenade
Explosive!

Molotov Cocktail
Poor man's grenade. Bottle of gas with a rag fuse.

Tear Gas
Tears up the eyes, prevents attackers from engaging, and can actually kill if you use enough. Has no effect on CJ.

Remote Satchel Explosive
Sticky bombs. Sticks to objects when thrown correctly. Switch to the remote control detonator and press shoot to set off.

Slot 10: Handheld Items

The items in this category have no upgrade ability. All have multiple uses.

Fire Extinguisher
Press the shoot button to shoot fire-retardant. Use the target button for a better view. Press the Right and Left Analog Stick to adjust your position and aim. Always target the base of the fire to put it out. Can also be used like sprayed tear gas to subdue enemies.

Camera
Hold target button to aim; zoom in and out. Press shoot to snap picture. Particularly handy for San Fierro Photo Opportunities. Recruit a gang; take their picture as they pose. Hand the camera to them and they'll take your picture!

Spray Can
Target and press shoot to spray green paint in face of the enemy to defeat them. Also used for tagging over rival gang tags.

Slot 11: Gifts

Flowers
Check our Unique Attractions maps to pick some pretty flowers. The ladies just love the surprise!

Mystery Items
See what other items you can find to give your girlfriends and fill this slot.

?

Slot 12: Apparel Items

Thermal Goggles
This makes warm bodies glow in the dark and allows you to see at night. To turn them off, you must scroll back to the Thermal Goggles.

Parachute
You can find these lying around San Andreas in the most unique places. You also receive these when jumping out of a plane after completing Pilot School. For more tips, see **Pilot School** in the **Odd Jobs** chapter.

AUTO TRADER

Cars, motorcycles, trucks, boats, planes, helicopters, government auctions, and more! We have everything you're looking for!

Pimp-out your ride at one of these fine Carmod shops around San Andreas:

TF = Transfenders   **⊕** = ArcAngels

SUVs & Wagons

Huntley
4-door luxury SUV. $40K. Great power and responsiveness. We dare you to go off-road with that sticker price. Export.

Landstalker
'92 SUV, fully loaded, no rollover worries!

Perennial
Vintage family wagon. For $8K we'll import one for ya!

Rancher
Nice compact yet heavy 2-door SUV. The Exporting guys from Easter Basin are knocking down our doors for this one. Come in today and take it home for $40K.

Regina
Station Wagon at its purest.

Romero
We know of one girl who digs this ride! Take it to Transfenders and see if they can breathe some life into it.

Solair
This year's Solair is beating the Stratum's high sticker price. We'll make an offer you can't refuse. We'll even throw in a coupon for Transfenders!

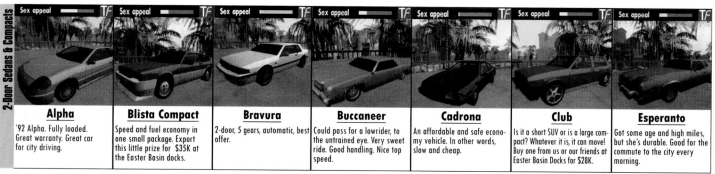

2-Door Sedans & Compacts

Alpha
'92 Alpha. Fully loaded. Great warranty. Great car for city driving.

Blista Compact
Speed and fuel economy in one small package. Export this little prize for $35K at the Easter Basin docks.

Bravura
2-door, 5 gears, automatic, best offer.

Buccaneer
Could pass for a lowrider, to the untrained eye. Very sweet ride. Good handling. Nice top speed.

Cadrona
An affordable and safe economy vehicle. In other words, slow and cheap.

Club
Is it a short SUV or is a large compact? Whatever it is, it can move! Buy one from us or our friends at Easter Basin Docks for $28K.

Esperanto
Got some age and high miles, but she's durable. Good for the commute to the city every morning.

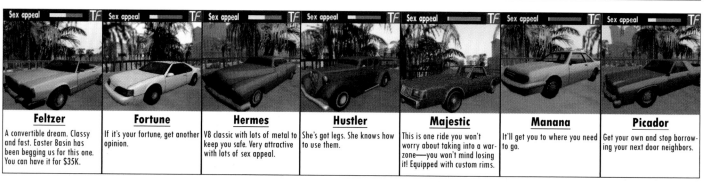

Feltzer
A convertible dream. Classy and fast. Easter Basin has been begging us for this one. You can have it for $35K.

Fortune
If it's your fortune, get another opinion.

Hermes
V8 classic with lots of metal to keep you safe. Very attractive with lots of sex appeal.

Hustler
She's got legs. She knows how to use them.

Majestic
This is one ride you won't worry about taking into a warzone—you won't mind losing it! Equipped with custom rims.

Manana
It'll get you to where you need to go.

Picador
Get your own and stop borrowing your next door neighbors.

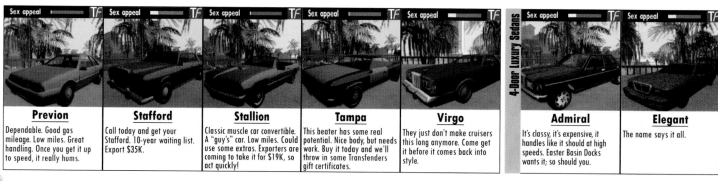

Previon
Dependable. Good gas mileage. Low miles. Great handling. Once you get it up to speed, it really hums.

Stafford
Call today and get your Stafford. 10-year waiting list. Export $35K.

Stallion
Classic muscle car convertible. A "guy's" car. Low miles. Could use some extras. Exporters are coming to take it for $19K, so act quickly!

Tampa
This beater has some real potential. Nice body, but needs work. Buy it today and we'll throw in some Transfenders gift certificates.

Virgo
They just don't make cruisers this long anymore. Come get it before it comes back into style.

4-Door Luxury Sedans

Admiral
It's classy, it's expensive, it handles like it should at high speeds. Easter Basin Docks wants it; so should you.

Elegant
The name says it all.

Emperor
King of the 4-door sedan. '99 model. New look but no advances in engine design.

Euros
A great affordable sports car. Extreme high speed and wonderful handling. Export and earn $35K.

Glendale
Nice vintage vehicle for cruises along the coastline.

Greenwood
Give her a chance and some time; she'll get up to speed after a while.

Intruder
4-door economy vehicle. Great for salesmen.

Merit
Good vehicle, nice acceleration, bad cornering unless you handbrake it! Transfenders will make it look nicer.

Nebula
This is your father's Olds-nebula. Pretty smooth ride when it's not moving between gears!

Oceanic
It's got some miles on it, but it refuses to go to the scrap yard. Cruise the beaches in style. Get your Oceanic today!

Premier
Smooth ride, looks great, girls dig it, makes you look responsible—come buy it.

Primo
Not the flashiest vehicle in our inventory, but this one will not disappoint the avid driver.

Sentinel
4-door luxury is just a phone call away. It's got class and speed! Exporters pay $35K for this vehicle, so act fast before it's gone.

Stretch
Drive through Carlton Heights in style. Handles great for its size. Come and get it now before the Export dock takes it off our hands for $40K.

Sunrise
Good name for such an enjoyable car...you'll want to drive it until the sun comes up. Handles nicely and has some power under the hood.

Tahoma
Grips the road, has great acceleration. Not bad, not bad at all. See if our buds at Transfenders can make it look more purdy.

Vincent
Nice look, good acceleration. What's the Vincent Price, you ask? Come in and we'll work something out.

Washington
'92 model. Brand spankin' new. May not be the sharpest one on the lot, but your significant other will like it.

Willard
Much like the movie: it squeaks and it's hard to get rid of.

Muscle Cars

Buffalo
"Have you seen this year's Buffalo?" Call Catalina in Fern Ridge for a test drive. Export $35K.

Clover
Yee-haw! This is the vehicle for you back road wanderers. Really kicks up the dirt!

Phoenix
Come and get the last Phoenix on the lot. If you're still sporting a mullet, we'll even make a special deal!

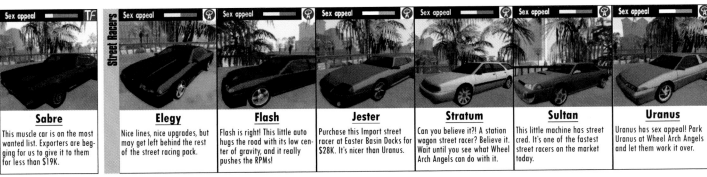

Sabre
This muscle car is on the most wanted list. Exporters are begging for us to give it to them for less than $19K.

Street Racers

Elegy
Nice lines, nice upgrades, but may get left behind the rest of the street racing pack.

Flash
Flash is right! This little auto hugs the road with its low center of gravity, and it really pushes the RPMs!

Jester
Purchase this Import street racer at Easter Basin Docks for $28K. It's nicer than Uranus.

Stratum
Can you believe it?! A station wagon street racer? Believe it. Wait until you see what Wheel Arch Angels can do with it.

Sultan
This little machine has street cred. It's one of the fastest street racers on the market today.

Uranus
Uranus has sex appeal! Park Uranus at Wheel Arch Angels and let them work it over.

High Performance Sports Cars

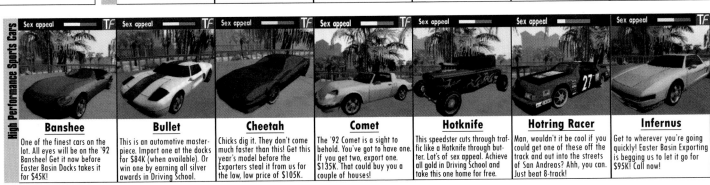

Banshee
One of the finest cars on the lot. All eyes will be on the '92 Banshee! Get it now before Easter Basin Docks takes it for $45K!

Bullet
This is an automotive masterpiece. Import one at the docks for $84K (when available). Or win one by earning all silver awards in Driving School.

Cheetah
Chicks dig it. They don't come much faster than this! Get this year's model before the Exporters steal it from us for the low, low price of $105K.

Comet
The '92 Comet is a sight to behold. You've got to have one. If you get two, export one. $135K. That could buy you a couple of houses!

Hotknife
This speedster cuts through traffic like a Hotknife through butter. Lot's of sex appeal. Achieve all gold in Driving School and take this one home for free.

Hotring Racer
Man, wouldn't it be cool if you could get one of these off the track and out into the streets of San Andreas? Ahh, you can. Just beat 8-track!

Infernus
Get to wherever you're going quickly! Easter Basin Exporting is begging us to let it go for $95K! Call now!

Super GT

Sex appeal

It's hard to let one go once you find one of these firecrackers, but Easter Basin will pay $105K to Export one. Earn one by getting all bronze in Driving School.

Turismo

Sex appeal

One fast puppy with sex appeal. This is an Easter Basin Import bonus vehicle. You can have it for $76K. What a steal!

Windsor

Sex appeal

Luxury, sport, and power in one elegant and affordable package. It's what everyone in Paradiso is driving. Import one when you can! $28K.

ZR-350

Sex appeal

The new ZR-350s are in! Get 'em while they're hot! If you can get your hands on one, export it. They can often be found in and around airports. $45K.

Heavy Trucks & Utility

Benson

Sex appeal

Leaving town? Leaving too fast to take stuff? If not, you need a moving van. Call us today.

Boxville

Sex appeal

Nope, this is not the one. Try looking for a black one for Burglary Missions.

Boxville (Black)

Sex appeal

Ahhh, yes. That's the one. Find three of these around San Andreas and begin a crime wave like never before seen in this state. Press R3 at night to begin Burglar.

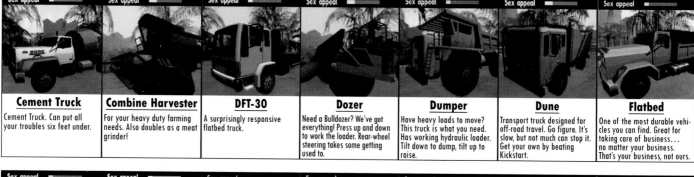

Cement Truck

Sex appeal

Cement Truck. Can put all your troubles six feet under.

Combine Harvester

Sex appeal

For your heavy duty farming needs. Also doubles as a meat grinder!

DFT-30

Sex appeal

A surprisingly responsive flatbed truck.

Dozer

Sex appeal

Need a Bulldozer? We've got everything! Press up and down to work the loader. Rear-wheel steering takes some getting used to.

Dumper

Sex appeal

Have heavy loads to move? This truck is what you need. Has working hydraulic loader. Tilt down to dump, tilt up to raise.

Dune

Sex appeal

Transport truck designed for off-road travel. Go figure. It's slow, but not much can stop it. Get your own by beating Kickstart.

Flatbed

Sex appeal

One of the most durable vehicles you can find. Great for taking care of business... no matter your business. That's your business, not ours.

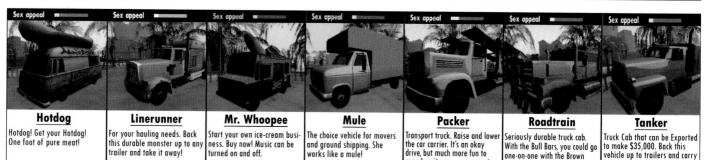

Hotdog

Sex appeal

Hotdog! Get your Hotdog! One foot of pure meat!

Linerunner

Sex appeal

For your hauling needs. Back this durable monster up to any trailer and take it away!

Mr. Whoopee

Sex appeal

Start your own ice-cream business. Buy now! Music can be turned on and off.

Mule

Sex appeal

The choice vehicle for movers and ground shipping. She works like a mule!

Packer

Sex appeal

Transport truck. Raise and lower the car carrier. It's an okay drive, but much more fun to speed up its ramps on a motorcycle!

Roadtrain

Sex appeal

Seriously durable truck cab. With the Bull Bars, you could go one-on-one with the Brown Streak. It hauls trailers, as well.

Tanker

Sex appeal

Truck Cab that can be Exported to make $35,000. Back this vehicle up to trailers and carry 'em away. Drive carefully or you'll lose your load.

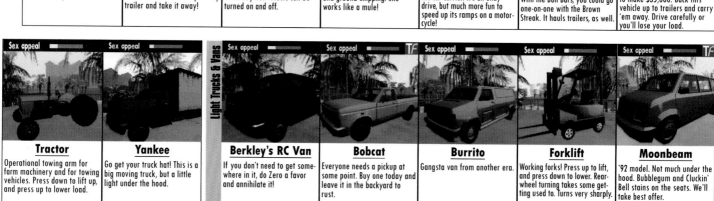

Tractor

Sex appeal

Operational towing arm for farm machinery and for towing vehicles. Press down to lift up, and press up to lower load.

Yankee

Sex appeal

Go get your truck hat! This is a big moving truck, but a little light under the hood.

Light Trucks & Vans

Berkley's RC Van

Sex appeal

If you don't need to get somewhere in it, do Zero a favor and annihilate it!

Bobcat

Sex appeal

Everyone needs a pickup at some point. Buy one today and leave it in the backyard to rust.

Burrito

Sex appeal

Gangsta van from another era.

Forklift

Sex appeal

Working forks! Press up to lift, and press down to lower. Rear-wheel turning takes some getting used to. Turns very sharply.

Moonbeam

Sex appeal

'92 model. Not much under the hood. Bubblegum and Cluckin' Bell stains on the seats. We'll take best offer.

Mower

Sex appeal

Next time she says, "Honey, will you go mow the lawn?" hop on this.

Newsvan

Sex appeal

The news starts here.

Pony

Sex appeal

New '92 model. Fully loaded, FM radio, new tires! Call now.

Rumpo

Sex appeal

Used van, decent tires, 40K miles, ignore the body in the back. Come and take it off our hands.

Sadler

Sex appeal

2-door pick-em-up truck.

Tug

Sex appeal

Airplane-tugging utility vehicle with a surprising level of sex appeal.

Sex appeal TF

Walton

Not a looker, but have the guys down at Transfenders see what they can do.

Sex appeal

Yosemite

When muscle is your number one priority, a Yosemite dually has unrivaled stability and performance.

Lowriders (Mod these at Loco Low Co.)

Sex appeal

Blade

2-door ragtop with no hydraulics. Go to Loco Low co. for help with your lowrider needs. Or, Export this vehicle for a quick $19K.

Sex appeal

Broadway

2-door ragtop lowrider with no hydraulics...yet. Use it to go Pimping. Take it to Loco Low Co. and see what they can make of it.

Sex appeal

Remington

12 cylnders under the hood. It's a gas-guzzler but it gets up and goes. No hydraulics, but you can get some at Loco Low Co. A $30K Export.

Sex appeal

Savanna

Convertible 4-door lowrider with no hydraulics. Loco Low can hook you up with that and much more.

Sex appeal

Slamvan

No hydraulics, but that can be rectified at Loco Low Co. Exporters are trying to get their hands on this one! Find at Jizzy's "Palace" under the Gant Bridge. $19K.

Sex appeal

Tornado

It's big, it's low, and it's powerful. Loco Low Co. is just waiting to get their hands on this one!

Sex appeal

Voodoo

Dreaming of a lowrider gang car? Not too popular with the ladies, but your homies will be envious. To get it cut and some hydraulics, take it to Loco Low Co.

Recreational

Sex appeal

Bandito

This dune buggy is not intimidated by any terrain. Import bonus vehicle. $12K.

Sex appeal

BF Injection

One of the best off-road vehicles available! Find one on the southern beach of Whetstone or beat Dirt-Track or buy ours for $15K.

Sex appeal

Bloodring Banger

Demolition at its finest. This can be yours if you survive the Blood Bowl!

Sex appeal

Caddy

Show up to the green in style in this, the latest '92 model golf cart. If you're not holding a melee weapon when you enter, you will be when you leave. Fore!

Sex appeal

Camper

This '92 model van/bus is a cool retro ride that can be Exported at Easter Basin. $26K.

Sex appeal

Journey

This small RV has it all for the weekend warrior. When you've had enough of the great outdoors, Export it for $22K.

Sex appeal

Kart

Go cart with insane cornering and one gear.

Sex appeal TF

Mesa

This popular off-road vehicle can be Exported. $25K.

Sex appeal

Monster

4-wheeling don't get bigger than this! This is a bonus Import vehicle that we'll let you have for $32K. Or you can win it by beating 8-track.

?

Personal Transport System

Rumored to be In development. Look for it after Green Goo at Verdant Meadows.

Sex appeal

Quad

Take a day off and go have some fun. Pick up a Quad and get off the pavement. Very stable for such a dangerous recreational vehicle.

Sex appeal

Sandking

Off-roading bliss is just moments away in this 2-door SUV.

Sex appeal

Vortex

Small hovercraft vehicle. Go on land or on sea. Import one when possible at Easter Basin Docks for $20,800.

Bikes

Sex appeal

BMX

Press and hold the hop button then release for bunny hop. Press the sprint button to pedal. Tap it repeatedly to sprint on the pedals. You can ring the bell.

Sex appeal

Lowrider Bike

Awesome sissy bar! We'll throw in some cards for the spokes if you pick one up today!

Sex appeal

Mountain Bike

A tough-built bike for off-road abuse. Press and hold the hop button then release for bunny hop. Press the sprint button to pedal. Tap it repeatedly to sprint on the pedals.

Sex appeal

BF-400

Crotch-rocket with optional windshield. Fly past those PCJ owners.

Sex appeal

Faggio

Come on now, that's pronounced Fah-jee-oh. Slow but stable and not something that you should drive to the girlfriend's house.

Sex appeal

FCR-900

A great bike. Export it for $10K. We have two models available. Get all silver awards in Bike School to make this yours.

Sex appeal

Freeway

Great sex appeal in the motorcycle class. Get your leather chaps and helmet! It's yours if you get all bronze awards at Bike School. $10K.

Sex appeal

NRG-500

The fastest bike available, bar none. Get all gold awards at Bike School for your very own NRG. Great to use for Unique Stunt Jumps.

Sex appeal

PCJ-600

Average racing bike, but still beats a car for getting through traffic. Used to be untouchable in its day. We're practically giving them away. Call now!

Sex appeal

Pizzaboy

Moped for Well Stacked Pizza delivery boys.

Sex appeal

Sanchez

Going off-road? Gotta have one of these. This is the best 2-wheel vehicle for getting across rough terrain. Exporters want it! $10K.

Sex appeal

Wayfarer

Very stable, very safe. For hog lovers who don't like bugs in their teeth.

Civil Servant & Transportation

Sex appeal

Baggage

Airport bag carrier.

Brown Streak Engine

If you can't afford the fare, highjack it! Take a ride around San Andreas. Use it to begin Freight Train.

Bus
Carry loads of homies! Get one today. Hope you have a large garage; you'll need it.

Cabbie
Use it to begin Taxi Driver. Steal one and make $12 bucks from cabby's stash.

Coach
Coach of a football team? Rockstar? Gangster with lots of backup? If this is you, come get this vehicle.

Freight
It's a train. It carries freight.

Sweeper
If you're looking for a quick getaway, run right past this one.

Taxi
Use it to begin Taxi Driver. Steal one and make $12 bucks in change from cabby's purse.

Towtruck

To lower the hook, press up. Back up to the front of a vehicle and press down to lift the vehicle. Drive away.

Trashmaster
It's more about chicken maggots than chick magnets.

Utility Van
We found this one out front! Come and get it soon.

Commercial/Government Auctions

Ambulance

Use it for Paramedic missions. Small amount of health given when entered. It's top heavy, so careful in sharp turns at high speeds.

Barracks
Use it to begin Vigilante. Very durable truck for the Vigilante mission, but you may find that it's too slow to keep up with the bad guys.

Enforcer

It's big, it's bad, and it's against the law to own one of these! Use it to begin Vigilante. Enter the truck and get full Armor—one time only.

FBI Rancher
It's big, it's bad, it's an FBI SUV! Working police radio still installed. Use it to become a weekend Vigilante!

FBI Truck

Durable all-terrain SUV, but has trouble catching speeders. Roof-mounted gun is for SWAT members only.

Fire Truck
Use it to begin Firefighter. Circle to use water cannon, Right Analog Stick to aim horizontally, Left Analog Stick to aim vertically.

HPV1000
Police motorcycle with Vigilante capabilities.

Patriot
It's not bulletproof, but it will get you through tough times. Very durable and great for off-road needs. Exporters are on their way right now to get this one for $40K!

Police

Police car. Use it to begin Vigilante missions. Enter for Shotgun and 5 rounds.

Ranger
2-door Police SUV. Use it to begin Vigilante missions. Enter for Shotgun and 5 rounds.

Rhino
RPGs can hardly stop this tank! Steal one during six-star Wanted Level or complete the game. Use it to begin Vigilante missions.

Securicar
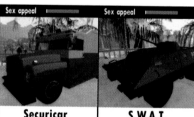
Durability when you need it the most!

S.W.A.T.
A small tank-like law enforcement vehicle that shoots water at rioters. Works just like the Firetruck's water cannon.

Aircraft

AT-400
Passenger jet airliner. Stay in coach and leave the flying to the real pilots. Go to the airports, purchase a ticket, and catch a flight to the next city.

Beagle
Medium-sized dual prop plane. Very light. Great for short runways. Non-retractable landing gear.

Cargobob

A weighty transport helicopter with a unique tail design. Looks military, but is harmless.

Cropduster

Single prop crop dusting plane. Look for one on the dirt road near a shanty in Bone County, north of Hunter Quarry. Non-retractable landing gear.

Dodo
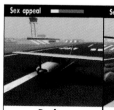
Dodo's latest model—comes with wings! Dodo Co. made great advancements this year.

Hunter
Use it for Vigilante Brown Thunder. Left Analog Stick is the flight stick. Win all gold in Pilot School to spawn one at Verdant Meadows Airstrip.

Leviathan
Appears in Verdant Meadows airstrip after **Up, Up, and Away.**

Maverick
Very stable and easy to fly. Carries four total passengers.

Nevada
Vintage dual-prop passenger plane. The price is still up in the air. Come make an offer. Only used in Whirly Bird race.

News Chopper
A smaller model of the popular Maverick, but with more speed and maneuverability.

Police Maverick

Law enforcement aircraft with no weapons and no Vigilante opportunity. But sure can rain hell from above when you're wanted!

Sex appeal ▬▬

Raindance

Large heli, little frills.

Sex appeal ▬▬

Rustler

Protect your clients from the air with this WWII fighter plane. Don't bail out without a parachute! All bronze awards will make this plane yours.

Sex appeal ▬▬

Seasparrow

Pontoon chopper with machine guns. For your land and sea needs. Call us today; we'll throw in a cheese grater!

Sex appeal ▬▬

Shamal

These private jets can be found parked near the aircraft control tower in LV International Airport. Fly like a dream.

Sex appeal ▬▬

Skimmer

It's a plane! No, it's a boat. It's a pontoon plane. Make water landings. Takes off from land, as well, if you have room.

Sex appeal ▬▬

Sparrow

From the Sparrow line. If you need guns, you'll have to upgrade to the Seasparrow. We think that may be too much chopper for you. Take this one.

Sex appeal ▬▬

Stuntplane

A single prop biplane. For flying tips, see Race Tournament Barnstorming. Get all silver awards in Pilot School to make this yours.

Sex appeal ▬▬

VTOL Fighter

This super jet is on the aircraft carrier in SF. Federal law prohibits us from showing a photo.

Sex appeal ▬▬

Boats

Coastguard

We guarantee if you buy one of these, you are not obligated to save drowning swimmers.

Sex appeal ▬▬

Dingy

Small inflatable boat with twin engines. Really moves!

Sex appeal ▬▬

Jetmax

This boat skips across the water and it can be yours if you win all gold awards at Boat School.

Sex appeal ▬▬

Launch

Attack boat with large yet unloaded machine gun mounted on the stern.

Sex appeal ▬▬

Marquis

An absolutely beautiful gift to yourself. Get all bronze awards at Boat School and this weekend getaway vehicle will be yours for the taking.

Sex appeal ▬▬

Predator

It's law enforcement transportation at its finest. No Vigilante, but you've got machine guns!

Sex appeal ▬▬

Reefer

Your basic fishing boat. For a higher-class cruiser, try the Tropic.

Sex appeal ▬▬

Speeder

Unmatched, unbelievable, under-the-sun, but never underwater. And Sexy! Come throw your money into the ocean and get this one-of-a kind speedboat.

Sex appeal ▬▬

Squallo

Nothing on or under the sea moves faster than a Squallo, except maybe a Speeder. Get this one by achieving all silver awards in Boat School.

Sex appeal ▬▬

Tropic

Now wouldn't your girl love a ride in this! Take the weekend off and do some traveling via San Andreas waterways.

RC Vehicles

RC Bandit

Zero's remote control race car.

RC Baron

Zero's RC biplane. Complete Zero's missions and fly one of these whenever you want! Just visit Zero's toy shop.

RC Goblin

Zero's RC chopper.

RC Tiger

Berkley's RC tank. "Curse you, Berkley!"

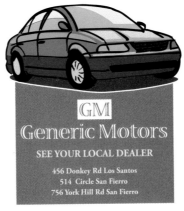

chapter 1
Los Santos

Los Santos, San Andreas... a bustling city that's equally cherished as it is corrupt; abundant and productive as it is vicious and malevolent. The millionaires and movie stars are as prevalent as the dregs and the gangbangers.

RESTAURANTS

Burger Shot	Marina	E4
Burger Shot	Mulholland	D5
Cluckin' Bell	East Los Santos	E6
Cluckin' Bell	Willowfield	E6
Cluckin' Bell	Market	E4
Well Stacked	Montgomery	C5
Well Stacked	Palomino Creek	C6
Well Stacked	Idlewood	E6

CLOTHING

binco	Ganton	E6
Didier Sachs	Rodeo	E4
Prolaps	Rodeo	E4
SubUrban	Glen Park	E6
Victim	Rodeo	E4
Zip	Downtown Los Santos	E5

POINTS OF INTEREST

LS Gym	Ganton	E6
Beach Gym	Santa Maria Beach	E4
Barber Shop	Playa Del Seville	F6
Barber Shop	Dillimore	D4
Barber Shop	Marina	E4
Barber Shop	Idlewood	E6
Off Track Betting	Downtown Los Santos	E5
Off Track Betting	Montgomery	C5
Tattoo Parlor	Idlewood	E5
Tattoo Parlor	El Corona	F6
City Hospital	Jefferson	E6
Suburban Hospital	Market	E5

Red Co. Hospital	Montgomery	C5
LS Police Dept.	Pershing Sq.	E5

• Mystery Weapon, Shotgun, Colt .45, Armor (x2)

Bomb Shop	El Corona	E5
LS Rail System	Unity Station	E5
LS Rail System	Market Station	E4
Loco Low Co.	Willowfield	F6
Transfender	Temple	D5
Ammu-Nation	Palomino Creek	D6
Ammu-Nation	Market	E5
Ammu-Nation	Blueberry	D4
Ammu-Nation	Willowfield	E6
24/7	Commerce	E5
24/7	Mulholland	D4
24/7	Ganton	D5
24/7	Little Mexico	E5

Safehouse

• Blueberry	$10,000	D4
• Dillimore	$40,000	D4
• Palomino Creek	$35,000	C6
• Mulholland	$120,000	D5
• Mulholland	N/A	D5
• Santa Maria Beach	$30,000	E4
• Verona Beach	$10,000	E4
• Jefferson	$10,000	E6
• Verdant Bluffs	$10,000	F5
• Ganton	N/A	E6
• Willowfield	$10,000	E6

 Bars/Clubs

HUNTER QUARRY

BLACKFIELD CHAPEL

RANDOLPH INDUSTRIAL ESTATE

LAST DIME MOTEL

ROCKSHORE WEST

FALLOW BRIDGE

THE MAKO SPAN

San Andreas Sound

FREDERICK BRIDGE

MONTGOMERY

MONTGOMERY INTERSECTION

HANKYPANKY POINT

HAMPTON BARNS

FERN RIDGE

RED COUNTY

Fisher's Lagoon

PALOMINO CREEK

BLUEBERRY

HILLTOP FARM

NORTHSTAR ROCK

DILLIMORE

RICHMAN

MULHOLLAND

MULHOLLAND INTERESECTION

LAS COLINAS

TEMPLE

VINEWOOD

GLEN PARK

LOS FLORES

DOWNTOWN LOS SANTOS

JEFFERSON

FLINT INTERSECTION

MARKET

EAST LOS SANTOS

EAST BEACH

RODEO

MARINA

LOS SANTOS

COMMERCE

GANTON

PERSHING SQ.

IDLEWOOD

WILLOW FIELD

PLAYA DEL SEVILLE

Los Santos Inlet

CONFERENCE

CITY HALL

LITTLE MEXICO

SANTA MARIA BEACH

VERONA BEACH

EL CORONA

VERDANT BLUFFS

LOS SANTOS INTERNATIONAL AIRPORT

F

OCEAN DOCKS

4   5   6

Security Services

WEAPONS

1. **Chainsaw** • The Panopticon • Beside west log shelter. • **D3**
2. **Shovel** • The Panopticon • Under back overhang of shanty in the logging site. • **D3**
3. **AK47** • Red County • Near Blueberry Acres outside the FleischBerg beer factory; north side. • **D3**
4. **Sawn-Off Shotgun** • Vinewood • Between buildings on movie lot. • **E4**
5. **Sniper Rifle** • Vinewood • Top of ramp at the Interglobal Television building. • **E4**
6. **Nightstick** • Vinewood • Security building at front of movie lot. • **E4**
7. **AK47** • Vinewood • Northwest corner of Movie Lot. • **E4**
8. **Micro SMG** • Ganton • Under bridge in flood control, short southeast walk from Mom's house. • **E6**
9. **Tec9** • Los Santos International Airport • Under LS International's raised freeway onramp, close to the parking lot. • **F5**
10. **M4** • Los Santos International Airport • End of runways between white and yellow striped ramps. • **F5**
11. **AK47** • Ocean Docks • In warehouse, behind steps to second floor. • **F6**
12. **Tear Gas** • Ocean Docks • Just inside warehouse. • **F6**
13. **Sawn Off Shotgun** • Ocean Docks • Inside train car. • **F6**
14. **Molotov** • Los Santos International • Just inside the fence. • **F6**
15. **Tec9** • Blueberry • Beside warehouse, opposite the spandex depot. • **C4**
16. **Pool Cue** • Blueberry • Outside the bar/restaurant on the corner. • **C4**
17. **Chainsaw** • Hampton Barns • In front of a shanty. • **C4**
18. **Shovel** • Fern Ridge • Just off road, next to trees • **D4**
19. **SMG** • Montgomery • Inside the yard on western side of partially burned building, behind the cement wall. • **C5**
20. **Satchel** • Montgomery • In alley between buildings. • **C5**
21. **Molotov** • Palomino Creek • On library roof (use roof access stairs). • **D6**
22. **Shovel** • Palomino Creek • In cemetery. • **D6**
23. **Sawnoff Shotgun** • Palomino Creek • Behind house with the single white garage door; on the back porch. • **D6**
24. **Country Rifle** • Red County • In backyard, by pool. • **D5**
25. **Tec9** • Mulholland • Behind posh house with two double door garages. • **D4**
26. **Cane** • Mulholland • Behind VINEWOOD sign. • **D5**
27. **Golf Club** • In front of the broadcasting tower, behind the VINEWOOD sign on the grassy hill. • **D5**
28. **Sniper Rifle** • Mulholland • On a balcony of the big house • **D4**
29. **AK47** • Mulholland • Behind Roboi's Food Mart (24/7 shop). • **D5**
30. **Molotov** • Mulholland • Setting next to diner. • **E4**
31. **Tear Gas** • Mulholland Intersection • Top of stairs of the opera house. • **E5**
32. **Cane** • Temple • Next to wall in middle of houses. • **E5**
33. **SMG** • Las Colinas • On large brick patio of posh house. • **E5**
34. **Grenade** • Las Colinas • Just inside fence by house. • **E6**
35. **Spray Can** • Las Colinas • Behind mobile home with porch addition. • **E6**
36. **Knife** • Market • Near loading bay behind strip of stores. • **E5**
37. **Parachute** • Downtown Los Santos • Rooftop helipad of tallest building in LS. Enter the building through the front door to warp to rooftop door. • **E5**
38. **Rocket Launcher** • Downtown Los Santos • Top of building, accessible only by aircraft or jet pack. • **E5**
39. **Sniper Rifle** • Jefferson • Roof of hospital. • **E6**
40. **SMG.** • Jefferson • Roof of Jefferson Motel • **E6**
41. **Colt 45** • Las Colinas • Where chain-link fence and stone wall meet. • **E6**
42. **Tec9** • Las Colinas • Next to fence on ledge above road. • **E6**
43. **Sawn Off Shotgun** • East Los Santos • Roof of the Pig Pen. Climb up on low north-eastern corner of the building to reach. • **E6**
44. **Molotov** • East Los Santos • In alley beside Rodriguez Iron Works building. • **E6**
45. **Micro Uzis** • East Beach • Top floor of parking garage. • **E6**
46. **Grenade** • East Beach • Third story of parking garage. • **E6**
47. **Cane** • Rodeo • In front of Didier Sachs. • **E4**
48. **Colt 45** • Santa Maria Beach • On a Santa Maria Beach lifeguard post. • **E4**
49. **Grenades** • Santa Maria Beach • Behind small, wooden building on the Santa Maria pier, behind pizza stand. • **E4**
50. **Silenced Pistol** • Conference Center • On the back steps of Conference Center. • **E5**
51. **Brass Knuckles** • Commerce • In alleyway beside Roboi's Food Mart (24/7 Shop), Courier Mission location. • **E5**
52. **SMG** • Unity Train Station, behind short white wall. • **E5**
53. **Katana** • El Corona • Behind wooden fence, behind 69cent (24/7 Shop), across from Unity Train Station. • **E5**
54. **Grenade** • Idlewood • Second floor walkway of 24-Hour Motel. Also near a tag location. Both accessed from parking lot in back. • **??**
55. **Chainsaw** • Willowfield • Near the piles of tires. • **E6**
56. **Brass Knuckle** • Ganton • Below overpass. • **E6**
57. **Shovel** • Ganton • In Ryder's Back yard. • **??**
58. **Chainsaw** • Ocean Docks • At the bottom of a stone pier near water level, behind the steps. • **F6**
59. **Desert Eagle** • Ocean Docks • Behind short cement wall and fence close to the shoreline, near the docks. • **F6**
60. **Colt 45** • Ganton • In backyard corner near road wall, behind Sweet's house. • **E6**
61. **Spray Can** • Ganton • Rooftop of Pawn Shop, behind Mom's house. Use short wall behind garage to reach garage top. • **E6**

PAY 'N' SPRAY

Idlewood • **E6**
Santa Maria Beach • **E4**
Temple • **D5**
Dillmore • **D4**

POLICE BRIBES

- **Verona Beach** • In alley. • **E5**
- **Ocean Docks** • Next to crates. • **F6**
- **Rodeo** • In parking lot. • **E4**
- **Montgomery Intersection** • Middle of dirt road. • **C5**
- **Mulholland** • Next to road. • **D5**
- **East Los Santos** • Through gap in fence to flood control. • **E6**
- **Ganton** • Through alleyway next to Discount Store. • **E6**
- **Las Colinas** • In sloping alleyway. • **E6**
- **Las Colinas** • Collected by jumping east down road • **E6**
- **Ocean Docks** • Top of bridge arch • **F6**
- **Market** • Under stairway between apartment buildings. • **E5**
- **Glen Park** • Archway under bridge. • **E5**
- **Vinewood** • In sloping back alley. • **E5**
- **Blueberry** • Alley between fence and building. • **D4**
- **Red County** • Next to water. • **D4**
- **The Panopticon** • On dirt road shortcut. • **C3**
- **Blueberry Acres** • On dirt road • **D4**

BODY ARMOR

- **NE Red County** • Between the stairways, on other side of San Andreas Sound. • **C6**
- **East Los Santos** • Under flood control overpass. • **E6**
- **Willowfield** • Behind building. • **E6**
- **East Beach** • Behind house. • **E6**
- **Willowfield** • Beside train tracks, between mound of scrap and crates. • **E6**
- **Las Colinas** • In yard. • **E6**
- **Verdant Bluffs** • Outside restaurant seating. • **E5**
- **Conference Center** • On walkway of building on corner of Conference Center and Verdant Bluffs. • **E5**
- **Pershing Square** • LS police locker room. • **E5**
- **Pershing Square** • LS police cell. • **E5**
- **Los Santos International** • Front of airport. • **F5**
- **Palomino Creek** • Between house and garage. • **C6**
- **Mulholland** • On top of the big house. • **D4**
- **Red County** • Top of ramp, next to double door. • **D4**
- **Ocean Docks** • Inside train car. • **F6**
- **Montgomery** • At corner of fences next to tree. • **C5**
- **Red County** • Between building and driveway. • **C4**

Unique Attractions

GANG TAGS

1. **Idlewood** • On the side of a large bridge. Part of Tagging Up Turf mission. • **E6**
2. **Idlewood** • On the front of a house. Part of Tagging Up Turf mission.• **E6**
3. **Idlewood** • On a brick wall in this back alleyway. Part of Tagging Up Turf mission.• **E6**
4. **East Los Santos** • On the corner wall of a Mexican food restaurant. Part of Tagging Up Turf mission.• **E6**
5. **East Los Santos** • Climb to the roof opposite of the Cluckin' Bell; it's on the wall. Part of Tagging Up Turf mission.• **E6**
6. **East Los Santos** • On the wall behind the Cluckin' Bell restaurant. Part of Tagging Up Turf mission. • **E6**
7. **Las Colinas** • South side of southern yellow house. • **E6**
8. **Las Colinas** • On the wall of the large apartment that overlooks the sea. • **E6**
9. **East Beach** • On the wall of the building opposite of Colonel Fuhrburger's house. • **E6**
10. **East Beach** • On the wall of the car park located behind the pedestrian overpass to the beach. • **E6**
11. **East Beach** • On the bottom floor of the multistory car park. • **E6**
12. **East Beach** • On the wall of a building just off the main road leading to the Los Santos Forum. • **E6**
13. **East Beach** • Behind the Body Armor in the back alleyway. • **E6**
14. **Los Flores** • Back garden opposite the vacant billboard. • **E6**
15. **East Los Santos** • On the wall by the crossroads. • **E6**
16. **East Beach** • On the "S"-shaped road in the central East Beach area. • **E6**
17. **Los Flores** • On the back alleyway wall in central Los Flores. • **E6**
18. **East Los Santos** • On a wall in the dark, crooked back alleyway. • **E6**
19. **East Los Santos** • In a crooked, narrow back alleyway. • **E6**
20. **East Los Santos** • On the side of some large brown steps. • **E6**
21. **East Los Santos** • Inside the tunnel on the wall of the car wash exit. • **E6**
22. **East Los Santos** • Behind the railings near the desolate shop's backyard. • **E6**
23. **East Beach** • On the wall of the Los Santos Forum. • **E6**
24. **Playa Del Seville** • OOn the wall that faces the beach; southeast of the Los Santos Forum. • **E6**
25. **Playa Del Seville** • On the wall of the house just opposite the Los Santos Forum. • **E6**
26. **Playa Del Seville** • On small wall in front of apartments. • **E6**
27. **Playa Del Seville** • On the wall of the basketball courts. • **E6**
28. **Ocean Docks** • On one of the bridge's support beams. • **F6**
29. **Playa Del Seville** • On a wall in front of some generators. • **E6**
30. **Ocean Docks** • On a street corner wall. • **F6**
31. **Ocean Docks** • Outside of the warehouse on a wall. • **F6**
32. **Willowfield** • On the side of a bridge in the flood control area. • **E6**
33. **Ocean Docks** • On the wooden wall near the docks. • **F6**
34. **Ocean Docks** • On the side of the flood control wall. • **F6**
35. **Willowfield** • On the side of the 98 cent store. • **E6**
36. **Willowfield** • On the side of the Sushi Man store. • **E6**
37. **East Beach** • Climb onto the roof of the eastern pacific house; it's on the wall. • **E6**
38. **Willowfield** • On the wall of the drive-thru restaurant. • **E6**
39. **Ganton** • On the side of the foundation of the overpass. • **E6**
40. **Ganton** • Behind the car park railings, on a wall. • **E6**
41. **Jefferson** • Inside the garage, on a wall. • **E6**
42. **Jefferson** • End of large church. • **E6**
43. **East Los Santos** • In the back alley of the desolate liquor store. • **E6**
44. **East Los Santos** • In an underground car park in the residential area, on a wall. • **E6**
45. **Las Colinas** • Inside of the train tunnel (used in "Catalyst"). • **E6**
46. **Las Colinas** • On the back of this house. • **D6**
47. **Las Colinas** • In-between these houses, on one of the walls. • **D6**
48. **Glen Park** • On a wall in this building's courtyard. • **E5**
49. **Las Colinas** • In the narrow alleyway. • **E6**
50. **Las Colinas** • On the wall on the bottom side of the zig-zag slope. • **D6**
51. **Jefferson** • On the side of the hotel in Jefferson featured in Reuniting the Families. • **E6**
52. **Jefferson** • On the fence in this back alleyway with garages. • **E6**
53. **Jefferson** • In narrow alleyway across from the park, on the brick wall. • **E6**
54. **Glen Park** • Under the bridge by the pond. • **E6**
55. **Glen Park** • On a wall in this narrow alleyway. • **E6**
56. **Glen Park** • On a fence in the corner of the skate park. • **E6**
57. **Jefferson** • On a wall in the hospital's garden. • **E6**
58. **Idlewood** • On the side of the 24-hour motel car park. • **E6**
59. **Willowfield** • On the side of the supermarket car park. • **E6**
60. **Idlewood** • In the alcove with the wire window. • **E6**
61. **Idlewood** • In the residential courtyard, on a wall. • **E6**
62. **Idlewood** • Side of the apartments in the residential area. • **E5**
63. **Idlewood** • On the wall in the shallow alcove of this building. • **E5**
64. **Little Mexico** • On the side of the building on the street corner. • **E5**
65. **Little Mexico** • On the side of the corner building. • **E5**
66. **Little Mexico** • On the wall down the side of this building. • **E5**
67. **Idlewood** • Climb to the roof of the car wash; it's on the back of the sign. • **E5**
68. **El Corona** • On the wall with lots of other graffiti. • **E5**
69. **El Corona** • On the side of this home, near the top level. • **E5**
70. **El Corona** • On the wall of a bar near the street corner. • **E5**
71. **El Corona** • On the side of the supermarket. • **E5**
72. **El Corona** • On the green fence. • **E5**
73. **El Corona** • On the side of this house. • **E5**
74. **Idlewood** • At the bottom of the flood control wall. • **E5**
75. **Pershing Square** • On the building opposite the large, town hall-like building. • **E5**
76. **Pershing Square** • On the side of the large, town hall-like building. • **E5**
77. **Commerce** • On the side of the building called "Regal". • **E5**
78. **Verona Beach** • On the balcony just past the top of the stairs. • **E5**
79. **Market** • At the base of the space-like building. • **E5**
80. **Downtown Los Santos** • Just past the food court, near the two trees. • **E5**
81. **Downtown Los Santos** • At the top of the long, crooked steps. • **E5**
82. **Mulholland** • On the northwest wall of the car park under the Mulholland Intersection. • **D5**
83. **Vinewood** • On the side of the small building on the street corner. • **D4**
84. **Temple** • On the wall of the building on the street corner. • **D5**
85. **Market** • At the base of the building on the street corner. • **E5**
86. **Market** • At the end of the first floor ledge of this building. • **E5**
87. **Market** • Climb to the top of the first floor roof of this building; it's on the back wall. • **E4**
88. **Marina** • On the wall near the wooden pier, at the bottom of the stairs. • **E4**
89. **Rodeo** • On the brick wall behind the large billboard. • **E4**
90. **Rodeo** • On the back wall of the Vinyl Countdown store. • **E4**
91. **Santa Maria Beach** • At the end of pier by the big wheel, on a back wall. • **E4**
92. **Santa Maria Beach** • At the base of the shop fronts on the beach. • **E4**
93. **Marina** • At the corner of the building leading to the beach. • **E4**
94. **Verona Beach** • At the base of the wall on the corner shop. • **E5**
95. **Verdant Bluffs** • Climb to the rooftop of the observatory; it's on a wall. • **E5**
96. **LS International** • On the southern wall of the control tower building. • **F5**
97. **LS International** • On a wall facing the top of the roof of the entrance to the tunnel. • **F5**
98. **Willowfield** • On the front of this house. • **F6**
99. **Downtown Los Santos** • At the base of the skyscraper. • **E5**
100. **Mulholland** • On the support beam of the spaghetti junction. • **D5**

UNIQUE STUNT JUMPS

1. **El Carona** • Jump going east onto the railway platform rooftop (use a PCJ). • **E5**
2. **Idlewood** • Jump south on the bridge structure. Drive fast between the railroad and trees to miss the tree near the jump. • **E6**
3. **Verona Beach** • Head north using the building's steps as a ramp; land on next building to avoid a spill. • **E5**
4. **Jefferson** • Drive north up the pedestrian walkway steps. Jump is possible on a bike or in a car. • **E6**
5. **Ocean Docks** • Drive approximately south by southeast over the mound of dirt behind the metal wall. Stop short of running into the next freeway wall. • **F6**
6. **East Beach** • Drive to the west up the pedestrian steps (it's an easy jump on an NRG). Clear the parking lot wall behind the steps. • **E6**
7. **Ocean Docks** • Drive south up the wooden ramp and land on the corrugated roof. This jump is possible in a variety of vehicles. • **F6**
8. **LS International** • Use the boarding ramp to get over the airport fence. • **F5**
9. **LS International** • Use the sign/ramp here and drive east. Clear concrete and red 06L-2 sign. • **F5**
10. **Ocean Docks** • Drive west up these steps and make it onto the adjacent building. • **F6**
11. **East Los Santos** • Head west up and over these steps; you must clear the railway tracks. • **E6**
12. **Market** • Jump east over the steps, over the roof, and land on the road. • **E5**
13. **East Beach** • Drive through the brick patio and through the hole in the stone wall, then jump far down to the street below without landing in the ocean. • **E6**
14. **Ocean Docks** • Drive north up the stairs and land in the street. • **F6**
15. **Ocean Docks** • Just south of the previous jump. Go south up the dock stairs. Again, avoid landing in the ocean. • **F6**
16. **East Los Santos** • Head to the west up the steps at basketball courts. • **E6**
17. **Mulholland Intersection** • Go north up the cement ramp on the freeway walkway. • **E5**
18. **Mulholland Intersection** • Drive south up the cement ramp on the freeway walkway. • **D5**
19. **Mulholland Intersection** • Jump the cement ramp underneath the freeway heading southeast and land in the parking lot. • **E5**
20. **Rodeo** • Go south up the small grassy knoll and land on the Yacht Harbor pier. • **E4**
21. **Vinewood** • To the west of the parking lot slope. Jump over the next rooftop and land on Sunset Road. • **E4**
22. **Commerce** • Drive north up the ramp out of the flood control trench. • **E5**
23. **Montgomery Intersection** • Jump off the dirt mound at the end of freeway heading west at the Mont. Int. • **C5**
24. **LS International** • Go west up the cement ramp between the airport and the ocean on the freeway prior to the underpass. • **F6**
25. **Santa Maria Beach** • From the beach, drive east up the steps underneath the promenade. • **E6**
26. **Red County** • Jump over bridge heading east into town. Jump is suitable with any vehicle. • **C6**
27. **Dillimore** • Jump this ramp heading south and land at least in front of the Gasso gas station or past the sheriff's office. • **D4**
28. **Palomino Creek** • Drive west over the broken bridge, as was the case with Catalina in the "Rob Bank" chase. • **C6**

OYSTERS

1. **Verdant Bluffs** • Near the entrance to the Bluffs Tunnel. • **F4**
2. **Mulholland** • Inside Doc G's pool. • **D5**
3. **Playa de Seville** • End of this Playa del Seville beach pier. • **E6**
4. **Ocean Docks** • Beside the most Southern Ocean Docks pier. • **F6**
5. **Ocean Docks** • Under the bridge, just East of Los Santos Airport. • **F6**
6. **Ocean Docks** • Under the docks bridge, situated on the small "island" part of the Docks. • **F6**
7. **Los Santos** • Just off the beach, West of Los Santos Airport. • **F5**
8. **Verona Beach** • Under Verona Beach Pedestrian Bridge. • **E4**
9. **Marina** • Under flood control bridge in the Marina area. • **E4**
10. **Santa Maria Beach** • South of the lighthouse at Santa Maria beach. • **F4**
11. **Glen Park** • Under park bridge in pond. • **E5**
12. **Fisher's Lagoon** • At the end of the pier, South West of Palomino Creek. • **D6**
13. **Frederick Bridge** • Underneath the middle of the Frederick Bridge, that connects Las Venturas to Los Santos. • **C6**
14. **Red County** • Under the bridge, North West of Palomino Creek. • **C6**
15. **Red County** • Under these 2 Red County bridges, just East of Blueberry. • **D4**

FLOWERS (8 of 40)

- **Las Colinas** • In flower bed, in front of house. • **D6**
- **Glen Park** • In park near water. • **D6**
- **Idlewood** • Next to Sprunk machine at gas station. • **E5**
- **El Corona** • In front yard of house. • **E5**
- **Verdant Bluffs** • Just in front of observatory. • **F5**
- **Verona Beach** • In front of Chili Dogs vendor. • **E5**
- **Mulholland** • Right next to road. • **D4**
- **Vinewood** • Just inside cemetery by a headstone. • **D4**

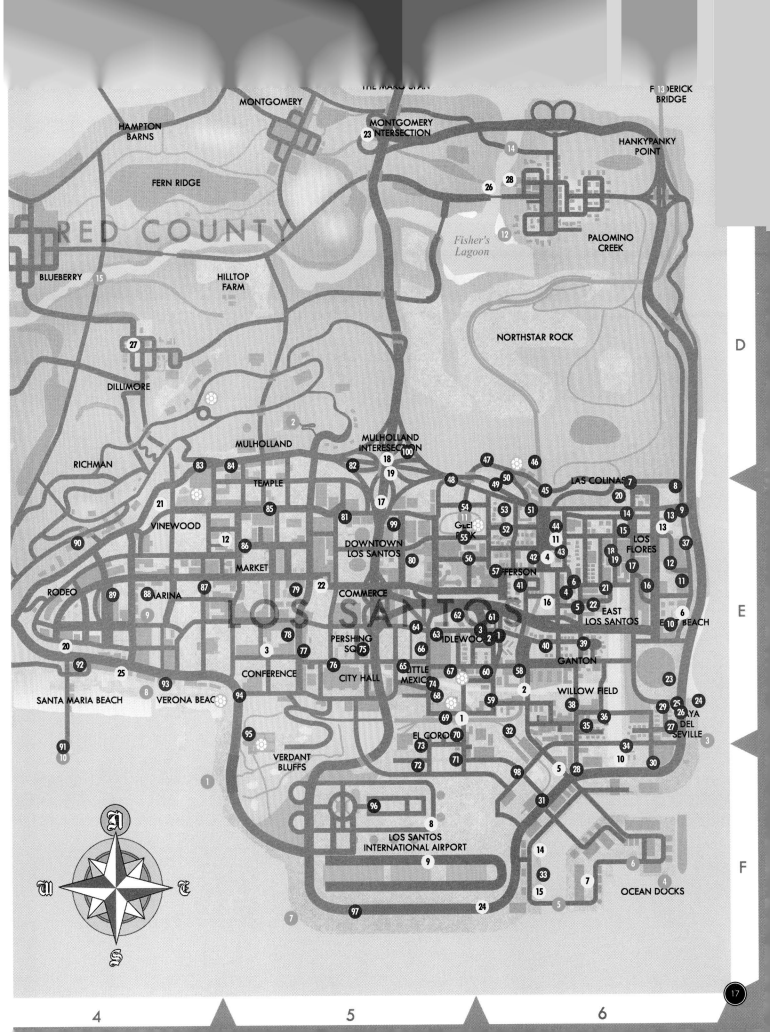

Five years ago Carl Johnson escaped the city, his past, and a life that was spiraling out of control. He abandoned Los Santos for Liberty City when his brother, Brian, met an early end. Unfortunately, recent gang violence also claimed his mother's life, forcing CJ's return to the city to attend the funeral... and to avenge her death.

En route from the Los Santos International Airport, CJ is welcomed by a couple of old acquaintances from his gangbanging past—corrupt police officers, Frank Tenpenny and Eddie Pulaski. They escort CJ into the squad car and drive him to the heart of Ballas territory (the unforgiving Ballas are gang rivals of CJ's gang, the Grove Street Families). Tenpenny and Pulaski dishonestly draw CJ back into their crooked game by linking him to a weapon used in a fresh cop killing.

You are Carl Johnson, you are unarmed and have just been dropped off in an alley in the middle of your rival gang's territory...

Noting Your Location

Whenever you enter a new area, its name appears briefly in the lower-right corner. As Tenpenny and Pulaski pull away and you gain control of CJ, note how "Jefferson," the neighborhood's name, appears onscreen.

THE BEGINNING STRAND

As its name suggests, this strand of missions introduces you to the story, some basic game elements, your 'hood, and a few of your homies.

In the Beginning

Gameplay Elements Introduced:
Using map blips, contact point locations, location of Grove Street Families and safe territories.

New Vehicle Introduced:
BMX bike

Directions

You begin the adventure on foot, in a Jefferson alley, with $350 in your pocket and no weapons—not a good combination when in hostile territory. For the moment, you are safe. You have time to check out the Pause Menu options and the San Andreas map. The Player Position in Jefferson and the "CJ" icon in Ganton are the most significant things to notice on the map at this time.

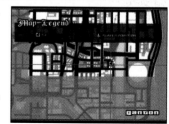

Approach the BMX bike (with the large, attention-getting blue marker cone above it) in the alley just ahead. Get on the bike and follow the roads leading to the "CJ" icon on the map. Several bike-riding tips appear onscreen as you pedal toward your destination. Do your best to read and ride at the same time. For more information on bikes, check out the *Auto Trader* section of this guide.

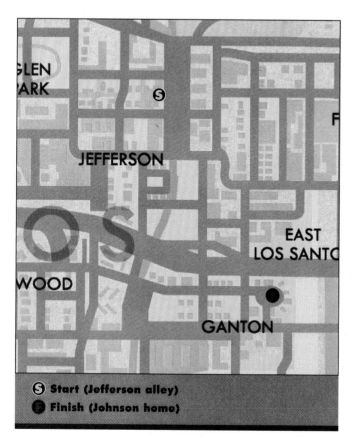

GLEN PARK

JEFFERSON

EAST LOS SANTO

WOOD

GANTON

Ⓢ **Start (Jefferson alley)**
Ⓕ **Finish (Johnson home)**

Secret Weapons

After you grab the BMX bike, exit the alley and go left around the corner to the red Jefferson Motel building. Climb the motel stairs to the roof and find a nice, gleaming MP5. Later, you can also find a some Body Armor and a Micro-SMG beneath the overpass bridge near Carl's Mom's House on Grove Street, plus a 9mm Pistol in a nearby backyard. Always check our **Security Services** maps for free weapon locations!

Sprinting & Pedaling

Just as you can now sprint faster (note that this is limited by Stamina), you can also pedal faster by applying the same method while riding a bike. When fast pedaling, CJ lifts off the seat and exerts some real energy onto the pedals for an incredible speed boost!

When you reach your destination, you find yourself in your old neighborhood. This is where the Grove Street Families reside—in a low-income housing cul-de-sac. Hop off the bike and walk into the red marker in front of your house to begin the first mission.

IN THE BEGINNING mission 2

Big Smoke

Gameplay Elements Introduced:
BMX riding and the new city, Los Santos.
Odd Job Opened:
BMX Challenge
Respect Gained:
3

CJ finds his mom's house plundered and trashed. As he sifts through memories, Big Smoke enters the backdoor, armed with a baseball bat. At first mistaking CJ for a based-up burglar, Big Smoke embraces his old pal and they take off to meet CJ's brother and sister at their mother's gravesite in Vinewood.

Big Smoke drives CJ to his mother's cemetery where he reunites with his big brother, Sweet; sister, Kendl; and fellow gang member, Ryder. The 5-year reunion is short-lived as family arguments return within seconds. Kendl leaves in a huff to see her boyfriend, Cesar, who Sweet does not approve of—an opinion based solely on prejudice.

As the remaining crew leaves the cemetery, the boys are subjected to a Ballas Drive-by, forcing them to the ground as Big Smoke's new car explodes into flames.

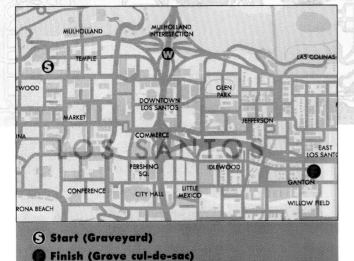

S Start (Graveyard)
● Finish (Grove cul-de-sac)
W Waypoint (Mulholland Intersection)

Directions

Follow Sweet

Follow the gang across the street to the line of BMX bikes. Your first objective is to stay close to Sweet, who is on the lead BMX. Sweet is indicated on the map as a blue square; a large blue cone marker appears above his head when he's in sight. Try to stay close; the Ballas are still on the hunt. New bike tips appear onscreen as you pedal after Sweet. Pedaling faster and bunny hopping are both introduced. Pedaling faster should be your primary focus.

If the Ballas in the Voodoo are giving you trouble, stop suddenly and drive behind their vehicle in another direction. If they drive beside you with guns blazing, try to lead them into hazards that force them to wreck. However, fast pedaling should keep you at a safe distance.

Sweet's lead ends under the Mulholland Intersection. After the short cinematic, Sweet draws the Ballas' attention off in one direction while the rest of the gang can make their escape. You are directed to follow Ryder, who now has the blue cone marker overhead and becomes the blue blip on the map.

Follow Ryder

Ryder leads you through alleys of Downtown Los Santos, across a BMX park, and onto the freeway. You reach a new Cycling Skill level while on this run.

Ryder takes the first exit ramp and follows the connecting road to your home in the Ganton cul-de-sac. In most missions, it is no longer necessary to come to a complete stop in the red markers. Drive through the marker to complete the mission. You earn Respect points at the end of the mission, but no monetary reward. Who'd you think would pay you for that?!

Sweet assumes you're leaving soon, but you inform him that you're going to stick around a while to see if you can help the gang get its grip back on the neighborhood. Ryder suggests you get some colors and a haircut.

NEW ODD JOBS AVAILABLE!

*Completing the **Big Smoke** mission opens access to the BMX odd jobs. For details on this, checkout the BMX section in our **Odd Jobs** chapter. The BMX Challenge is available from the beginning of the game, but you must increase your bike stat.*

between missions:
Stow Vehicles and Save Games

After the mission is complete, you can park vehicles or bikes in your house's attached garage and enter the house to save your progress. (Establishments with a yellow triangle marker floating in front of the door can be entered.) Walk into the save disc in the kitchen to save your progress. Doing so will advance time by six hours.

You can save a vehicle by parking it in the garage.

You can save your progress by entering CJ's house.

Wardrobe

Most save houses have a room with a wardrobe closet. Yours is empty at this time, since you have not yet purchased any apparel items. When you buy a new article of clothing, the old piece is sent to your wardrobe closet. Items you have purchased and that are available in your wardrobe are marked green in clothing stores, so that you know not to buy them. Enter the marker outside the closet to change into any of the apparel items purchased from clothing stores. You can also choose the "Remove" option and strip CJ down to his skivvies.

Ryder

Gameplay Elements Introduced:
Barbers, the Status menu, food shops, and reacquainting yourself with GTA driving.
Accomplice:
Ryder
Respect Gained:
3

Time for a gig with Ryder, who waits just next door. When you enter the red marker outside his house, you find him loading his gun in the kitchen. Ryder's upset with a local pizza place for covering up the Grove Families' tags. He invites you to go help teach them a lesson.

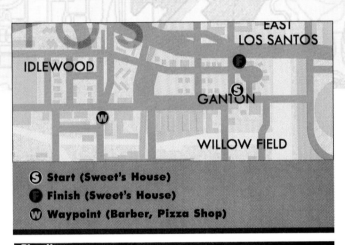

S Start (Sweet's House)
F Finish (Sweet's House)
W Waypoint (Barber, Pizza Shop)

Directions

Drive to the Barbers

Follow Ryder into his Picador and drive to the yellow blip on the map just a few blocks away. Stop in the red marker outside of Old Reece's Hair & Facial Studio. Walk through the door with the yellow marker to enter.

Reece's Barbershop

Enter the red marker and have a seat in the barber's chair. Select from Old Reece's cuts. When you find one you like, purchase the cut for the indicated price. Refer to the **Barbers** section in our **Odd Jobs** chapter for a list of available hairstyles by location.

Once outside, Ryder will comment on your choice of cut. You can safely assume that the more you pay for a cut, the higher your Respect and Sex Appeal stats will rise.

Enter Pizza Shop and Buy Some Food

When you receive your next objective (to eat), more tips appear onscreen. The Well Stacked Pizza Co. is directly across the street from Old Reece's shop. Cross the street and enter the restaurant.

Approach the counter, enter the red marker, and order some food. There are four different meals to choose from, each with a different price and varying amounts of food. These meals replenish lost health in proportion to the price of the meal.

After gobbling down the coronary delight, Ryder leaves his seat and holds the cashier at gunpoint. However, the pizza boy pulls a Shotgun from under the counter and returns the favor! CJ and Ryder run out of the joint with a new objective: Escape!

Get back in Ryder's Car!

Run back across the street to Ryder's vehicle and get away before the pizza boy plugs you full of Shotgun pellets. You can also gun down the foolish pizza boy (or run him over), if you've found one of the weapons hidden on the map.

Once out of Shotgun range, you can take your time plotting your course back to Ryder's house. Follow the yellow blip on the map. Enter the red marker in Ryder's driveway to complete the mission. More Respect is earned.

Ryder suggests heading over to Sweet's house, marked by the "S" on your radar map. Your brother is equally upset about the graffiti being covered up. Before you take the next mission, enter your house and save your progress. This is a good habit to get into.

Also note that this refills your Health and feeds you. It also advances the game by six hours. Lastly, note that you cannot save your game during a mission.

NEW MISSION STRAND OPEN!

Completing the Ryder mission opens up the Sweet strand and its first mission, Tagging Up Turf. To open the first mission, follow the "S" to Sweet's house, just down the street from Ryder's place.

 Cell Phone Call: Sweet

As you exit your house, your cell phone rings. It's Sweet on the other end. He informs you that the Seville Boulevard and Temple Drive Families that used to work together with the Grove Street Families have split apart. This means you should no longer assume that all thugs wearing green are friendly. Sweet ends with a warning: the split of the Families allowed the Ballas and Vagos to take over. You can skip cell phone calls, but you will miss important game details in doing so.

new mission strand
THE SWEET STRAND

✸ **Contact Point:**
Sweet's house on Grove Street in Ganton
⌗ **Total Respect Gained Throughout Strand:** 78

The Sweet mission strand introduces other gang members and integrates some training into the missions, enabling you to learn new skills while you complete jobs. Your mission contact is none other than your big brother, Sweet Johnson.

SWEET mission 1

Tagging Up Turf

🐾 **Gameplay Elements Introduced:**
Basic character movement and climbing
🔫 **Weapon/item Introduced:**
Spray Can
⌗ **Respect gained:**
3 (plus 5% per tag)
$ **Cash Gained:**
$200

PREREQUISITE NEEDED!

This mission is available only after you complete the Ryder mission from The Beginning strand.

Sweet and Big Smoke shoot hoops in the driveway. When CJ approaches, Sweet hands him a can of green spray paint and tells his brother to start re-tagging all the covered Grove tags in the neighborhood. This will send a clear message to enemy gangs. Then Sweet decides to join CJ. The Johnson boys are going to reclaim their old turf and take the fight to the Ballas!

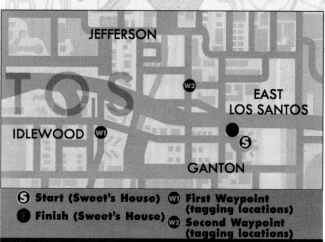

| ⓢ Start (Sweet's House) | ⓦ₁ First Waypoint (tagging locations) |
| ⓕ Finish (Sweet's House) | ⓦ₂ Second Waypoint (tagging locations) |

Directions

Drive to Idlewood

Enter Sweet's car and drive him to the yellow blip on the map. Park the car in the red marker near a freeway ramp in Idlewood. Sweet gets out of the vehicle and shows you how to spray over the purple Ballas tags.

This opens the Tagging Odd Job; Sweet just sprayed the first of 100 tags available in the game. Spraying over enemy tags earns you Respect points. For more information on this Odd Job and for the tag locations, see the **Odd Jobs** chapter of this guide. If you find a spray can before this mission, you can begin tagging.

Spray Over Ballas Tags

Sweet tells CJ to tag over two more "Front Yard Ballas" tags in the hood. Two green blips mark their location on the map. The closest tag location is directly across the street on the side of the green house. Go spray as directed and continue spraying until the complete Grove Street tag is painted.

The second Ballas tag is in the alley behind the green house. The tag is on the wall closest to the green house—it's difficult to spot without close inspection. (The Ballas tag is a dark purple that blends into the color of the brick.) Spray on the tag and you are instructed to return to Sweet's car.

Drive to East Los Santos

Drive Sweet to Ballas territory by following the yellow blip on the map into East Los Santos. Stop in the red marker near the red building with the interesting wall mural. (It's a Mexican food market called Lolita's.) CJ automatically exits the vehicle and Sweet takes off to tag another 'hood.

Find the Two Low Tags

Your next tag location is on the red building near the front door (circled on the screenshot). Spray over the tag until the Grove graffiti is complete, then head north past the interesting mural and turn right into the alley behind Lolita's. Two Ballas gang members await down the alley, near your next tag location.

A text message appears, informing you that Spray Cans can also be used as a lethal weapon. Use the spray can to defeat both Ballas, then paint over their tag on the alley wall.

Follow the Next Blip to Find the Next Tag

The next location is kind of tricky to find. Exit the alley and go around the Mexican restaurant to locate the red marker on the sidewalk—it's across the street, next to the C.C. Cabinets & Marble Tops shop.

Now follow the onscreen directions. Climb the small fence by facing it and pressing the climb button. Keep tapping the climb button to complete the climbing maneuver.

Next, climb over the larger fence at the end of the alley and turn left. Climb to the top of the small platform on the side of the building, then scale your way up to the rooftop of the Sign shop. (All three climbs are circled in this screenshot.)

Walk east along the edge of the rooftop and the small rooftop structure. The final tag is on the wall to your right. Spray over it and Sweet will pull up in the nearby street. Jump off the rooftop—very little damage is taken at this height—and enter the vehicle.

 Cell Phone Call: Officer Hernandez

CJ gets a phone call from Officer Tenpenny's partner, Officer Hernandez, warning him to stay in town.

Return to Sweet's House

Drive back to Ganton, following the yellow map blip into the red marker outside Sweet's house, to complete the mission. Sweet slides you 200 bucks to "get some beer or something." Head two doors down to your save house (The Johnson House) and save your progress in the kitchen. A spray can is now available in an upstairs bedroom for use in tagging activities.

SWEET mission 2

Cleaning the Hood

🎮 **Gameplay Element Introduced:**
Unarmed melee combat
🕴 **Accomplice:**
Ryder
🔫 **Weapon Obtained:**
Baseball Bat
\# **Respect Gained:**
3

the story

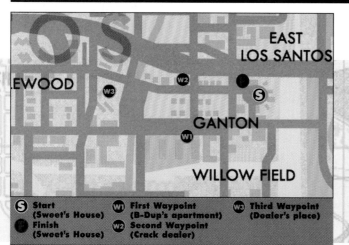

S Start (Sweet's House)
Finish (Sweet's House)
W1 First Waypoint (B-Dup's apartment)
W2 Second Waypoint (Crack dealer)
W3 Third Waypoint (Dealer's place)

Return to the red marker outside Sweet's house (indicated by the "S" icon on the map). Even though Grove Street Families are fighting back, the quality of the Grove soldiers is inferior. Grove Street is riddled with base and the old gang order no longer exists. Sweet wants the Family to force the dealers out of their territory and fly their flag once more, so everybody knows they're on the up.

Ryder joins CJ outside of Sweet's house. CJ wants to recruit a homey named B-Dup and his man Big Bear for the job of running the pushers out of the Grove Street hood.

Directions

Visit B-Dup's Crib

Ryder says B-Dup's place is just a few blocks away. Hop into the nearby Greenwood parked in the street and wait for Ryder to enter before taking off. Follow the yellow blip on the map to B-Dup's crib at the end of Grove Street.

A cinematic takes you and Ryder inside B-Dup's apartment. CJ and Ryder discover that B-Dup and Big Bear aren't the friends they used to be. Big Bear has become a base slave and B-Dup is treating him like dirt. CJ and Ryder leave disappointed, but even more motivated to correct the drug problem that has gripped the Family.

Beat Up the Crack Dealer

Get back into a car and follow the red blip around the block to the north. You'll find the crack dealer making a sale to one of the Grove Street homies in his front yard. Approach the dealer (the one with the red marker over his head). The

buyer usually runs off without confrontation. Beat the dealer to a pulp.

Melee Controls

Press and hold the lock on button to target the dealer. Press the special attack button while targeting to launch a special attack, and press the block button to block.

When the dealer lies lifeless on the ground, Ryder recognizes him as an ex-member of the Front Yard Ballas gang. He knows where he lives (just across the tracks in Idlewood). The boys decide to pay that crib a visit. Grab the Bat the dealer dropped.

Dealers usually carry around $2000. Killing them not only nets some quick cash, but it also raises CJ's respect in the hood. Dealers look the same way: they stand with their hands folded, looking for customers.

Find Crack Dealer's Crib

Drive Ryder to the yellow blip on the map. The dealer's place is a block away to the west in Idlewood. Drive into the red marker and enter the apartment with the yellow marker over the door.

Pummel the Dealer

A handful of Ballas OGs hang inside the crack den. Seconds later, the dealer enters the room with a baseball bat. Defeat the dealer to complete the objective, then get in some optional batting practice by

whacking the other gang members. Use the target-locking melee attacks to knock 'em dead.

Back to Sweet's House

Jack a car and make sure Ryder is with you, then follow the yellow blip back to Ganton and return to Sweet's crib on Grove Street. Drive into the red marker to complete the mission.

Drive-Thru

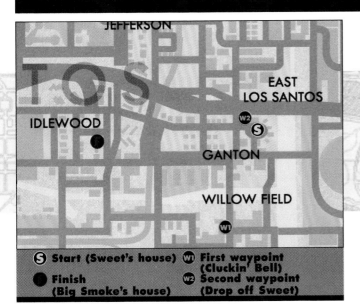

JEFFERSON

EAST LOS SANTOS

IDLEWOOD

W2

GANTON

WILLOW FIELD

W1

S Start (Sweet's house) **W1 First waypoint (Cluckin' Bell)**
● Finish (Big Smoke's house) **W2 Second waypoint (Drop off Sweet)**

⦿ Gameplay Element Introduced:
Passenger Drive-by
⦿ Accomplices:
Smoke, Ryder, Sweet
⦿ Cash Gained:
$200
⦿ Respect Gained:
5

Enter the marker outside of Sweet's crib to hook up with the boys as they exit the house. Big Smoke is hungry and talks the rest of the gang into getting a bite at the local Cluckin' Bell.

the story

Drive to the Cluckin' Bell Drive-Thru

Drive the gang a few blocks south to the yellow blip on the map in Willowfield. On the way, CJ inquires about his mother's death. Ryder comments that people saw a green Sabre speeding away from the drive-by that killed her. Pull into the red marker outside the Cluckin' Bell. This takes you to the restaurant's drive-thru lane.

As you exit the drive-thru window, Ryder spots a carload of Ballas heading toward Grove Street. The car whips around when they spot you.

Pursue Gang Car Before They Cap Your Homies!

Tear off after the Voodoo gang car. As you pull up beside the vehicle, your posse (minus Big Smoke, who is too busy eating) hangs out the windows and begins firing on the Ballas. The Ballas do the same, so it could be a draw if you're not careful.

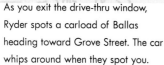 **Drive-By Controls**

To participate in a Drive-by shooting, you must have a submachine gun, such as an MP5 or Tec-9. Pull alongside your target and look left or right. Open fire by pressing the fire button.

If you find a Tec-9 or an MP5, you can contribute to your gang's offensive firepower. Otherwise, you need only to drive beside the gang car until your team disables the Voodoo. Before the burning Ballas ride can explode, back up to a safe distance to avoid collateral damage.

Kill the Ballas Gang Members

When their car explodes, surviving Ballas jump out and run. Chase them down in the car and ice them.

Drive Sweet & Big Smoke to Their Homes

Drive Sweet to his house, which isn't far away now. Once he's home, follow the yellow blip a few blocks west to take Smoke to his crib. Along the way, CJ questions why Big Smoke left the Grove. Smoke says he got some money from his aunt and bought a nicer place. Drive into the red marker outside his bungalow to complete the mission.

 Cell Phone Call: Sweet

The next time you exit your vehicle, you receive a cell phone call from your brother, Sweet. He says you're skinny and you should go get a gangsta's physique at the local gym. Take his advice and workout a bit to raise your Respect and Stamina. For more information on pumping up, refer to the **Gyms** section of our **Odd Jobs** chapter.

Nines and AKs

Gameplay Elements Introduced:
Firing the 9mm with the targeting system, and the advantages of crouching.

Weapon Obtained:
9mm Pistol

Respect Gained:
4

Head back to Sweet's house, following the "S" icon on the map. Now that the Grove Street Families have started to get a grip on the neighborhood again, they're going to need some firepower. Smoke suggests a visit to Emmet, an old friend who sells stolen firearms.

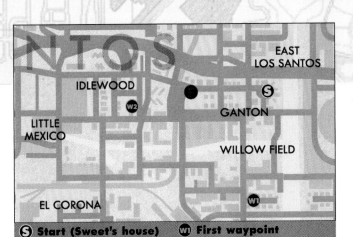

EAST LOS SANTOS

IDLEWOOD

W2

LITTLE MEXICO

GANTON

WILLOW FIELD

EL CORONA

W1

S Start (Sweet's house)
● Finish (Binco clothes)
W1 First waypoint (Emmet's guns)
W2 Second waypoint (Smoke's house)

Directions

Go with Smoke to Emmet's House

Enter the car outside of Sweet's house and follow the yellow blip on the map to drive Smoke (already in the vehicle) south to Willowfield. Pull into the red marker at Emmet's house and the boys head into the back yard where Emmet is playing with his guns.

The boys startle Emmet and almost get their heads blown off. He seems to know your family quite well; he knows your mom and thinks you are Brian. Once the formalities are out of the way, Emmet lets you take a 9mm from his cache. This initiates a training sequence.

Free Heat

Try shooting the bottles while crouching.

This mission officially opens Emmet's gun store, which is open for business 24 hours a day. Stop by whenever you need a free 9mm.

Target Practice

Follow the onscreen tips as they instruct you how to use target locking, target cycling, manual aiming, and the advantages of shooting while crouching (your accuracy increases). For details on this skill, refer to the **Game Basics** chapter.

Gun Skill

Your Weapon skill increases with every accurate shot you land. Reaching a high weapon skill level increases your proficiency with weapons. Press the view stats button while on foot to view your Weapon skill.

Each weapon also has its own skill level; the more you use a particular weapon, the more effective it becomes. Other interesting features are unlocked, as well (see the **Weapons** section of this guide for more details).

Drive Smoke Home

Once you have completed targeting training, you are instructed to take Smoke back home. Remember where Emmet lives; you can return to this location whenever you need a free 9mm. A gun icon appears over Emmet's place to help you find it later.

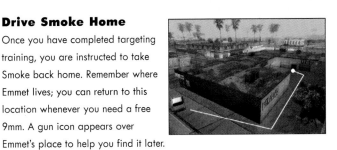

During the drive back to Smoke's house, he starts talking about choices people are forced to make and other stuff that seems very strange. Is this the old Smoke you used to know or has he changed? Take him to his Idlewood home and drive into the red marker.

Cell Phone Call: Sweet

If you haven't purchased any new duds yet, Sweet will call to remind you that neglecting to fly the Grove Street Families colors will earn you no respect!

Buy Some Grove Street Colors at Binco Clothes

Hop back in the car and follow the yellow blip to Binco, a local clothier, and do something about your image. For more information on clothes and the Respect earned, check out the **Game Basics** and **Odd Jobs** chapters. Remember that the Grove Street Families color is green. You want Respect? Fly your colors to gain the most Respect. But remember that almost all clothes will help CJ gain Respect. Exit Binco to complete the mission.

Gettin' Strapped

While you're out and about, pick up an Uzi (Tec-9 or Micro-SMG) using our **Security Services** map at the beginning of this chapter for free weapon locations. Having a Drive-by weapon is helpful in the next mission.

NEW MISSION STRAND OPEN!

Completing Nines and AKs opens up the Big Smoke mission strand. Its first mission is **OG Loc**. You can continue the Sweet strand by returning to Sweet's house, or else head for the new "BS" icon on the map and enter Big Smoke's house to begin the new strand.

Running Out the Dealers

Dealers are often seen walking the neighborhoods of Los Santos; many have actually been seen on Grove Street. These bums ask you if you would like to buy some drugs. No matter if you answer positively or negatively, it ends up being a negative answer... "No, get out of here" or something similar. When you shoot them, they drop $2000 in cash. Dealers often travel in small groups. If you see one, look for more in the area. This is a great way to make big bucks early on!

SWEET mission 5

Drive-By

- **Gameplay Element Introduced:**
  Pay 'n' Spray Shop
- **Cash Gained:**
  $500
- **Respect Gained:**
  6

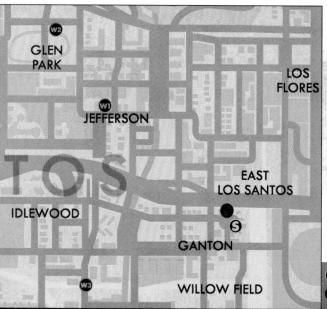

Back at Sweet's (the "S" icon on the map), Ryder lays some disrespect on CJ's driving, but Sweet puts you behind the wheel anyway. Turns out, he wants a little payback for the Ballas attack at the Cluckin' Bell drive-thru.

S Start (Sweet's house) **W1** First waypoint (Begin drive-bys) **W3** Third waypoint (Pay n' Spray)
F Finish (Sweet's house) **W2** Second waypoint (Finish drive-bys)

Directions

Drive Your Homies into Ballas Territory

Get in the car with Sweet, Ryder, and Smoke. As you drive off, Sweet orders you to head for Ballas country. Follow the yellow blip on the map to enter the Jefferson neighborhood where the Ballas hang. When you pull into the red marker, Sweet tells CJ to concentrate on driving while the others handle the shooting. Start cruising around the neighborhood, looking for Ballas.

Remember that threats show up as red blips on the map. Drive close by each one, letting your homies lean out the car windows and cap the Ballas fools. Note the new onscreen indicator bar labeled "Car Health." When it drops to zero, you and your boys are dead.

Drive-by

If you pack an Uzi, you can join the boys in some Drive-by shooting. Participating reduces the amount of time needed for your gang to take out all the Ballas.

Get a Spray Job

When you've iced enough Ballas, your Wanted Level (indicated by the stars in the screen's upper-right corner) goes up and the cops start chasing you down. Your car is now hot, so you need to visit a Pay 'n' Spray or pass through nearby Police Bribes (see our **Security Services** map at beginning of this chapter).

Start driving the Greenwood vehicle toward the nearest Pay 'n' Spray icon (a spray can) on the map. As you approach, you see its red marker in the street. Pull into the marker to enter and have your Wanted Level suspended. The shop also repairs and repaints your vehicle. Normally, this service costs you $100, but this first time it's free.

Probation

A Pay 'n' Spray merely suspends your Wanted Level at first. The wanted stars flash for a short while after you exit the shop. If you commit another crime during this period, the police fully reinstate your Wanted Level. But if you can stay clean for a while, the stars soon disappear.

Take Your Homies Back to the Hood

After you leave the shop, drive back to your Ganton neighborhood, marked by the yellow blip on the map. Grove is back, man. Grove is back! Drive into the red marker to automatically exit the car as a happy Sweet slips you $500 beer money for a job well done.

NEW MISSION STRAND OPEN!

Completing the **Drive-By** mission opens up the Ryder mission strand. Its first mission is **Home Invasion**. You can continue the Sweet strand of missions by returning to Sweet's house, or else head to Ryder's house (marked "R" on the map) to start the new strand.

SWEET mission 6
Sweet's Girl

- **Gameplay Element Introduced:**
  Solo Drive-by
- **Weapon Obtained:**
  Micro-SMG
- **Respect Gained:**
  7

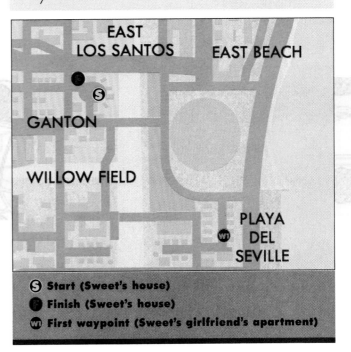

EAST LOS SANTOS

EAST BEACH

GANTON

WILLOW FIELD

PLAYA DEL SEVILLE

- Ⓢ **Start (Sweet's house)**
- Ⓕ **Finish (Sweet's house)**
- W1 **First waypoint (Sweet's girlfriend's apartment)**

Walk into the red marker in front of Sweet's house. CJ explores the premises, calling for his boys, but nobody answers. As he exits, his cell phone rings. It's Sweet, who's holed up at a girlfriend's house on Seville Families turf. He's pinned down by angry Seville boys and needs a ride out.

Heat Up

Before hanging up, Sweet tells you to "drive by Emmet's and get heated." If you don't have a firearm yet, you'd best find Emmet and get one now or use our **Security Services** map at the beginning of this chapter to find free weapons around town.

Directions

Cap the Seville Boulevard Families Pinning Down Sweet

Go to the garage and choose a car. (If you don't have a car stowed, head into the streets and jack one.) Try to recruit a few Grove Street homies to join you. (For details on Gang Recruitment, see the first page of this guide.) Drive toward the red "threat" blip on the map. The trek takes you south through Willowfield, then east to Playa del Seville.

When you see the five Seville bangers under the red overhead cone markers, make a Drive-by pass to open fire, then speed quickly out of range. Their firepower is so great that your car can be annihilated in seconds, so hop out to finish them off on foot. Note that you're trying to kill the green gang members.

Pop and Drop

If your health gets low, keep solid matter between the angry bullets and your soft man-flesh. Use the low walls on either side of the street where the Seville boys lurk, and crouch for cover. Pop up to fire, then duck down to avoid return volleys.

Fetch a Four-door to Pick up Sweet and His Girl

When the last punk drops (and the last red blip disappears from the radar map), Sweet calls and tells you to meet him with a car out front. Find the pristine Greenwood tucked in the covered alley just up the street from the motel (or any 4-door vehicle) and drive it into the red marker. Sweet and his lady hop aboard. Your brother tells you to hustle out because the Seville ain't givin' up.

Get Back to Your Hood

Time to head home. Drive toward the yellow blip on the map, avoiding the Seville cars in aggressive pursuit. On the way, Sweet says the Seville gang is trying to start a war. CJ replies that it's time to bring the families back together. When you get back to the hood and drive into the red marker, Sweet gives you some Respect and heads inside with his lady.

Cesar Vialpando

- **Gameplay Elements Introduced:** Lowriders, how to modify vehicles.
- **New Vehicle Introduced:** Lowrider
- **Cash Gained:** Depends on wager, up to $2,000.

Back at Sweet's house (the "S" icon on the map), sibling rivalry sizzles between sister Kendl and brother Sweet. Sweet doesn't want Kendl to see her "south side" (Hispanic) boyfriend, but Kendl isn't about to listen to a "no-good, narrow-minded, hypocrite gangbanger." Sweet sends CJ to keep an eye on their sister at the lowrider meeting where Kendl is getting together with her man.

IDLEWOOD • GANTON Ⓢ • LITTLE MEXICO • WILLOW FIELD • EL CORONA • Ⓦ¹

Ⓢ Start (Sweet's house) Ⓦ¹ First waypoint (Loco Low Co garage)
● Finish (Unity station)

Directions

Go to the Garage in Willowfield

Hop into a car and follow the yellow blip on the map to the Willowfield neighborhood. Drive into the red marker to enter the garage and meet the lowrider mod mechanic. He invites you to try out a lowrider with custom springs and hydraulics that lets you raise and lower the body—in other words, a lowrider. He then tells you about the lowrider competitions at Unity Station in El Corona.

Back Up Lowrider Into Mod Garage

Do what the screen says—back it into the garage. You are now inside a car mod shop called Loco Low Co. The Upgrades window opens, offering several types of lowrider modification services. (For details on this, refer to the **Mod Garages** section in our **Odd Jobs** chapter.) For now, your cash flow is probably low, so just select Quit to exit the garage. There is no need to modify the appearance of your vehicle in order to pass this mission.

Open Garage

Return to the Loco Low Co. garage anytime you want some lowrider modification. Note that it's marked on the map by a wrench icon.

Go to the Lowrider Meeting

Drive toward the new yellow blip on the map in El Corona. Find the Unity Station building with the red trim and enter its parking lot to find the red marker. Drive into the marker to begin the lowrider competition.

Wager and Compete

A young man in a blue face scarf asks for your wager as the Wager window appears. The minimum wager is $50, so check your wallet before you take a chance. This is a fairly easy challenge, so if you're confident in your ability, make a large wager. As the mission unfolds, an interesting lady asks to join you and slips into the seat beside you.

Follow the directions. See the circle at the bottom of the screen? A series of arrow icons passes through this circle in random order. You must push the appropriate button in the direction indicated by each arrow as it passes through the circle.

When your lowrider bounces to the rhythm, you score points. Bad bounces add points to the Opposition. For the full scoop on this contest, check out the **Lowrider Challenge** section in our **Odd Jobs** chapter.

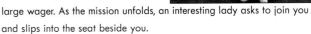

NEW ODD JOBS AVAILABLE!

*Completing the **Cesar Vialpando** mission opens the Lowrider Challenge odd jobs. Between missions, return to the location just outside Unity Station (marked by the lowrider icon on the map) and find the man by the red marker on the sidewalk. Step into the marker to trigger the competition at the station, then enter to wager and earn extra cash.*

Meet Cesar

When you win, a thrilled Kendl congratulates you and tries to introduce you to her boyfriend, Cesar Vialpando. The initial meeting doesn't go well, with Cesar's homies looking for trouble. But Cesar calls off his dogs and tells you he loves and honors Kendl—"she's my girl for life." You sense he's trustworthy, so you're cool with it—for now, anyway. And hey, he likes your ride, man. In any case, it's time to leave El Corona.

 Cell Phone Call: Cesar

A short time later, Cesar Vialpando calls you. He compliments your driving and offers a way to make some cash: lowrider racing. He suggests you drop by his place in El Corona so he can take you to the meet. This puts a "CV" on your map to mark your contact point with Cesar; it also opens up yet another mission strand.

At this point, you've got several options with multiple mission strands open. We'll continue on to Cesar's mission, but note that you can head to several different locations.

NEW MISSION STRAND OPEN!

*Completing the **Cesar Vialpando** mission triggers a phone call from Cesar that opens up the Cesar mission, **High Stakes, Low Rider**. You can continue to Ryder, or else head to Cesar's Garage (marked "CV" on the map) to start the mission.*

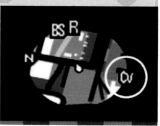

CESAR mission 1
High Stakes, Low-Rider

⊛ **New Contact Point:**
Cesar Vialpando's house and garage in El Corona (Los Aztecas turf)

⊛ **Gameplay Element Introduced:**
Lowrider racing

Ⓢ **Cash Gained:**
$1000

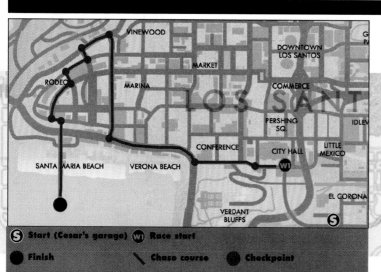

Ⓢ Start (Cesar's garage) ⓦ Race start

⬤ Finish ╲ Chase course ⬤ Checkpoint

Cesar is dating your sister, Kendl. He also likes hot, jacked-up cars that go fast, so the man can't be all bad. Are you still driving your lowrider? If not, find one, because you can't trigger this mission without one. (See the Tip on the next page for a convenient lowrider location.) Drive it into the red marker by Cesar's garage. Cesar tells CJ about some great lowrider racing, and offers to take him there.

Directions

Follow Cesar to the Races, Drive Onto the Starting Grid

Simply drive behind Cesar. His car (identified by a blue marker overhead) leads you west out of El Corona, then north to the race start location in Verdant Bluffs. Drive into the red marker to trigger the racing sequence.

Race Through the Red Markers

You begin in sixth place out of six racers—that's right, dead last. But your impeccable driving skills should make up that handicap easily. Well, maybe not easily. Handling a lowrider is a challenge. Follow the series of red checkpoints to race through the course. Each checkpoint has an arrow that indicates the way to the net one. Keep an eye on your radar map—the location of the next checkpoint appears as a red radar blip—or just follow the cars ahead of you, if you see any.

The course winds through many Los Santos neighborhoods (Verona Beach, Marina, Vinewood, Richman, Rodeo) and finishes in spectacular fashion at the Brown Starfish Bar and Grill at the end of the Santa Maria Beach pier. You must come in first place to win the race.

MISSION PASS (1 OF 6)

Completing *High Stakes, Low-Rider* gives you one of the six prerequisites needed to open the big *Reuniting the Families* mission later in the Los Santos Finale mission strand.

new mission strand
THE RYDER STRAND

✅ **Prerequisite:**
Completion of **Drive-By** mission in the Sweet mission strand

✴ **Contact Point:**
Ryder's house on Grove Street in Ganton

⊕ **Total Respect Gained Throughout Strand:**
17

Ryder wants guns, lots of guns, and the three missions in this strand are all about getting them. You're introduced to burglary for fun and profit, and you also get to throw stuff out of the back of vehicles at friend and foe alike. Man!

Home Invasion

Gameplay Elements Introduced:
Performing burglaries
Accomplice:
Ryder
Respect Gained:
5

PREREQUISITE NEEDED!

*This mission is available only after you complete the **Drive-By** mission in the Sweet mission strand.*

the story

Follow the "R" icon on the radar map to find the red marker outside Ryder's house. The mission triggers only between 12:00 and 20:00—it's a night mission. When CJ finds him in the back yard, Ryder's pretty fried. He tells CJ about a retired vet with a stash of military weapons. The two of you decide to pay him a little visit that night, although Ryder seems too wired for a job like this.

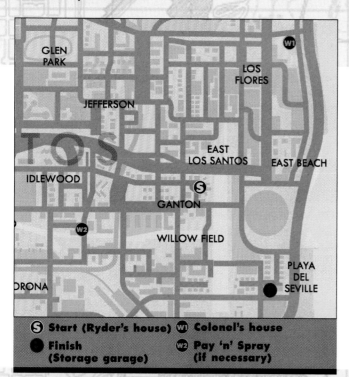

S Start (Ryder's house) **W1** Colonel's house

● Finish
(Storage garage)

W2 Pay 'n' Spray
(if necessary)

Directions

Park Truck Near the House, Get the Guns Before Daylight

You start out behind the wheel of a Boxville delivery truck with Ryder as your passenger. Note the onscreen Daylight timer counting down in the upper-right—you have eight minutes to break, enter, burgle, and escape this heist. Drive fast and follow the yellow radar blip to the target house in East Beach. When you arrive, Ryder sends you in while he stays outside to keep watch.

Enter the House

Enter the marked door. Inside, you see you're violating the abode of the venerable Colonel Fuhrberger. Note the onscreen Noise bar; don't let it fill up or the Colonel will awaken. Crouch to move quietly, and sneak. A green marker hovers over each crate. The first one is just across the room to the right.

Steal At Least Three Crates of Guns

Creep toward the crate and pick it up, then carry the crate slowly to the front door. (If you try to crouch while carrying the crate, you'll drop it, so just walk slowly.) Outside, hustle with the crate to the back of the truck and load it in. Then go back into the house for another.

Cop Favorite

Colonel Fuhrberger is clearly well-liked by the local police, because you immediately earn a two-star Wanted Level if you kill the former military man! Alerting the police makes getting to the lockup much tougher..

Continue your stealthy movement. Go through the door opposite the stairs, then spot the green marker in the back-left corner of the next room, between the two rows of cabinets. Nab it and move slowly back outside. Load the second crate onto the truck.

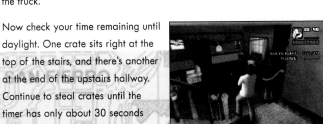

Now check your time remaining until daylight. One crate sits right at the top of the stairs, and there's another at the end of the upstairs hallway. Continue to steal crates until the timer has only about 30 seconds remaining. If you're feeling lucky, grab the weapons crate in the colonel's bedroom, but be extra quiet.

Don't Wake the Colonel!

If your noise awakens the colonel and he calls the cops, you get a two-star Wanted Level and your truck will be too hot to take to the lockup. If he actually sees you, the colonel will whip out his Shotgun! Hurry outside to the truck as the police arrive and drive to the Pay 'n' Spray in Willowfield to lose the heat.

Drive Truck to the Lockup, Park it Inside

When the daylight timer gets below 10 seconds, you hear warning music. Make sure you're out of the house and have collected at least three crates before the timer expires.

When it reaches zero, Ryder and CJ will get back into the truck. Follow the yellow radar blip south to the safety of the lockup building in Playa del Seville. (On the way, CJ tries to talk Ryder out of indulging himself so often, but Ryder doesn't want to hear it.) Drive into the red marker outside the lockup to open the garage door, then pull the truck in.

Watch the short tutorial on burglary odd jobs. Jack a car and head back to the hood, following the "R" on the radar map to return to Ryder's crib.

NEW ODD JOBS AVAILABLE!

Completing the *Home Invasion* mission opens the Burglary odd jobs. For more details, refer to the *Burglary* section in our *Odd Jobs* chapter.

Ryder mission 2

Catalyst

Gameplay Elements Introduced:
Toss and catch boxes from a train.

Accomplice:
Ryder

Respect Gained:
7

Ryder's house is open only between 8:00pm and 6:00am for this mission (20:00 and 06:00 military time). CJ walks in on his homey cooking up a pot of foul-smelling "water." Unfortunately, Officers Tenpenny, Pulaski, and Hernandez are close behind. Tenpenny casually mentions that a train is making an unscheduled stop nearby with a little "somethin' somethin'" on board of interest to you. What might that be?

Directions

Shoot Vagos Robbing the Ammo Train

Hop in Ryder's truck and follow the yellow radar blip north to the train halted up in Las Colinas. Unfortunately, a posse of Northside Vagos got in ahead of you. First things first—secure the area. Exit the truck with guns blazing. Red markers indicate the three Vagos soldiers, so they're easy to spot.

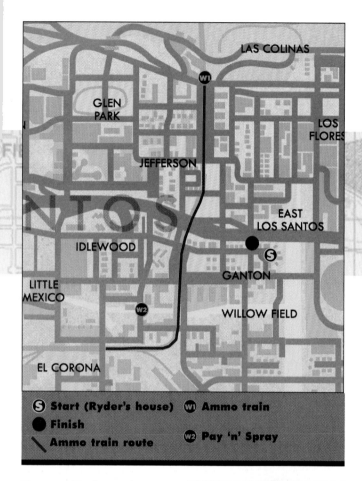

LAS COLINAS

GLEN PARK

LOS FLORES

JEFFERSON

EAST LOS SANTOS

IDLEWOOD

GANTON

LITTLE MEXICO

WILLOW FIELD

EL CORONA

Ⓢ **Start (Ryder's house)** Ⓦ¹ **Ammo train**
● **Finish**
╲ **Ammo train route** Ⓦ² **Pay 'n' Spray**

Toss Boxes of Ammo to Ryder

Now your view switches to first-person perspective as you look backward from the moving train. Your Grove boys speed along the tracks behind the train in Ryder's Picador. You now have about 90 seconds to toss 10 ammo crates to Ryder, who stands in the pickup bed.

Move the targeting reticle over Ryder. Hold down the throw button to power up, then release to throw; you can toss with varying degrees of power this way. There are plenty of crates on the train, so throw fast, experimenting with the power of your throws to get a better feel.

Watch the Clock!

The ammo crate toss is a timed challenge, so watch the onscreen timer, and throw fast!

When Ryder finally catches the last explosive crate, for a total of 10 ammo crates in the truck, you hop off the train and jump back into the Picador.

Protect Train from the Ballas!

When you gun down the last Vago, another cutscene plays. Now a carload of Ballas crash the party. Looks like Tenpenny told every gang in South Central. Just his style—as he said, he likes to let the gangs do his work for him. Fight off the four Ballas raiders, hitting them hard before they can disperse from their car.

Climb Onto the Back of the Train

Once you wipe out the Ballas, Ryder suggests you check out the train. Pick up the dropped weapons and money from the fallen gangbangers, then run into the red marker at the back of the train. CJ hops aboard the flat car and discovers a big shipment of military-style weapons. Suddenly, the engine jolts forward and the train starts rolling! Ryder calls to chill out, he'll be right behind you.

Take the Crates Back to Grove Street

Now it's time to head home. As you might expect, hijacking a trainload of military armaments tends to attract the attention of the authorities. In fact, you now have a three-star Wanted Level! You can try to outrun the police cruisers, but your vehicle is hotter than hot, so it might be a better idea to cool off at the nearest Pay 'n' Spray.

When you finally get back to Grove Street, Ryder drops you off—mission accomplished. This is a good time to enter your nearest safehouse (in this case, The Johnson Family house) and save your progress before beginning a new strand of missions.

MISSION PASS (1 OF 6)

Completing *Robbing Uncle Sam* gives you one of the six prerequisites needed to open the big *Reuniting the Families* mission later in the Los Santos Finale mission strand.

Robbing Uncle Sam

Gameplay Element Introduced:
Using a forklift
New Vehicle:
Forklift
Respect Gained:
5

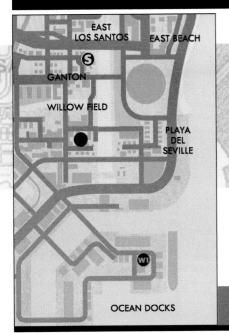

EAST LOS SANTOS · EAST BEACH
GANTON
WILLOW FIELD
PLAYA DEL SEVILLE
OCEAN DOCKS

Back at his place (the "R" icon on the map), Ryder has another big idea. He asks, "Who has more straps than anybody?" The answer, of course, is the military. And there's a National Guard warehouse across town that our man Ryder knows about.

Getting Strapped

Use our **Security Services** map to locate Armor and an accessible AK47 (or at least an MP5) for this mission. Having Grenades or Molotovs is also helpful. The military men wear armor and are a little tougher to take down than the average gangbanger.

 Start (Ryder's house) **Nation Guard depot**
Finish (Storage garage)

Directions

Drive Van to Compound at Ocean Docks

Get in the delivery van out front and follow the yellow radar blip south to the Ocean Docks area. Pull into the red marker outside the National Guard depot and watch the military jeep enter the compound. Ryder seems a little cocky, but hey, you're a Grove Street OG.

This is the spot - National Guard Depot.

Open the Front Gate

Climb over the wall with the gate, gun down the guard, and shoot the switch on the wall behind him. When the gate opens, Ryder automatically drives your van through to the first warehouse door. Follow him and take out the squad of guards that investigates, then approach the

Shoot switch to open warehouse door.

warehouse (the one where your truck is parked) and shoot out the keypad switch to the right of the entry door. When the door opens, nail the pair of guards waiting just inside.

ALTERNATIVE STRATEGY: Explosive Entry

Instead of climbing the wall and allowing the guard to get the first shot, try tossing a Grenade or Molotov over the wall on the right side of the gate. This not only annihilates the guard, but also destroys the gate switch!

Box Management

After killing the first soldier at the front gate, do NOT open the gate. Instead, go to the warehouse in the back, shoot the lock off the warehouse door, kill the soldiers inside, then use the forklift to start stacking boxes toward the front of the warehouse door (not in the middle or Ryder's truck will run them over). Once about six are stacked toward the front, shoot the lock on the front gate to let Ryder in. It's a lot easier to load the boxes into the truck this way since they're closer to the truck.

Use Forklift to Load Boxes Into Your Van

You need six boxes of ammo to be successful. Four are stacked inside the warehouse. Hop aboard the forklift truck and drive up to one of the four boxes on the floor directly ahead. Use the appropriate buttons to con-

trol the forks. After you lift a box, drive to the back of your van to load it in. Make sure that the forks are raised enough to get the load into the van. Repeat this until you've loaded all four boxes from the warehouse floor.

Box Drop

Drive the forklift carefully after you load a box on the fork. If you run into something, the box can fall off!

As you work, Ryder fends off National Guardsmen. If he dies, you fail the mission. Help him out when attackers come. Hop out of the forklift to fight instead of attempting Drive-bys, then return to work when each threat passes. A guard appears after each crate is loaded into the truck.

Get in the forklift truck.

Load Two More Boxes Outside the Warehouse

There are several more boxes of guns outside, around the corner of the warehouse and out in front. You can load a total of six boxes into the van, so go fork up a couple more. When the van is full, exit the forklift and hop in the van.

Head for the Lockup in Willowfield

Now speed over to the storage garage in Willowfield, marked by the yellow blip on the radar map. Ryder rides in back with the goods. Unfortunately, the part-time soldiers of the National Guard refuse to give up, and pursue your van in two Patriots. You tell Ryder to ditch some crates because you're running heavy. Each time you press the throw button, Ryder tosses an explosive crate out the back. Wait until a Patriot is right on your tail, then toss a crate.

Keep driving hard until you reach the lockup down Emmet's alley in Willowfield.

THE BIG SMOKE STRAND
new mission strand

✅ **Prerequisite:**
Completion of **Nines and AKs** in the Sweet mission strand
🏠 **Contact Point:**
Big Smoke's house in Idlewood
\# **Total Respect Gained Throughout Strand:**
23

Big Smoke is Sweet's best friend and a Grove Street homey, but he lives outside of the hood now in Idlewood. His business dealings require muscle and backup at times, and that's what CJ provides in this strand of missions.

BIG SMOKE mission 1

OG Loc

🎮 **Gameplay Element Introduced:**
Bike chase
👥 **Accomplices:**
Big Smoke, Sweet, OG Loc
\# **Respect Gained:**
5

✔ PREREQUISITE NEEDED!

*This mission is available only after you complete **Nines and AKs** in the Sweet mission strand.*

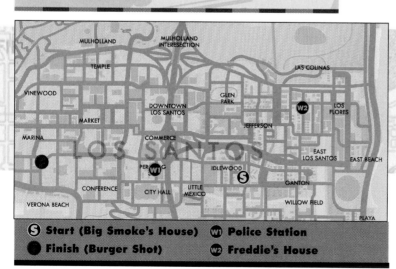

- ⑤ **Start (Big Smoke's House)**
- ⬤ **Finish (Burger Shot)**
- ⑥ **Police Station**
- ⑦ **Freddie's House**

Grab a car and head for Big Smoke's house in Idlewood by following the "BS" icon on the radar map. Sweet and Smoke are both there. One of your homies named Jeffrey, now calling himself OG Loc, is "touching down" (getting released) from prison today. The boys want you to come along to pick him up.

Directions

Pick up OG Loc from the Police Station

Follow the yellow radar blip, heading east to the police station in Pershing Square. On the way, Sweet and Big Smoke joke about Jeffrey's name change to "OG Loc," suggesting he got himself thrown in prison to enhance his music career image. After you drive into the red marker outside the station, you see OG Loc come strutting out with his suitcase and wild attitude. He claims he needs to kill some Brazilian dude named Freddy who dissed him inside.

Drive to Freddy's House

Follow the yellow blip on the radar, driving through Little Mexico and Idlewood to Freddy's house in East Los Santos. On the way, OG Loc tells you about the "hygiene technician" job his parole officer lined up for him. Drive into the red marker when you arrive. Sweet and Big Smoke back out and head home, leaving only you to watch OG Loc's back.

Ring the Doorbell

Follow OG Loc up the stairs to the front door and walk into the red marker to trigger the next scene. Loc starts howling at Freddy from the front yard, and Freddy calls back, alluding to something terrible that happened in prison. Suddenly, Freddy hops on a motorbike and makes a break for it. You and OG Loc hop on a second bike and give chase.

Catch and Kill Freddy

Follow Freddy, the red blip on the radar map. Don't let him get away, or you fail the mission. Stay right on Freddy's tail as he darts from alleyway to alleyway, up stairs and down railroad tracks, all the while taunting OG Loc, who fires away from the back of your bike.

Tire Tracks

Freddy's bike leaves a convenient line of tire tracks. Follow them through twisting turns when you lose sight of him.

Focus on the Chase

You can't kill Freddy until he stops. So focus all of your attention on staying on his tail. His route is the same every time, so if you fail a few times, you'll eventually get to know the path well enough to catch him.

It's a wild and wooly chase, but don't give up. Use the handbrake (bike rear brake) in the tight turns, and add the regular brake (bike front brake) when you need to come to a quick and complete stop. This prevents you from performing unwanted stoppies and possibly tumbling off the bike. Stay with him and Freddy finally hops off his bike and fights with the help of a few yellow-clad Vagos. Dismount and gun down Freddy to trigger the next part of the mission.

Afterwards, you tease OG Loc a bit, then offer him a ride to his new job at the Burger Shot in Verona Beach.

Take OG Loc to the Burger Shot

Hop on the bike and follow the yellow radar blip through the Commerce, Market, and Marina districts to the Burger Shot in Verona Beach. When you pull into the red marker, OG Loc thanks you for the ride and heads inside. While you're here, you might as well step inside and grab a bite to eat!

NEW MISSION STRAND OPEN!

Completing **OG Loc** opens up the OG Loc strand and its first mission, *Life's a Beach*. This provides a new contact point, indicated by "OG" on your radar map.

Running Dog

Gameplay Elements Introduced:
Chasing on foot and superior sprinting

Accomplice:
Big Smoke

Weapons Obtained:
9mm

Respect Gained:
3

the story

Return to Big Smoke's house in Idlewood (the "BS" map icon). As CJ approaches the front door, Officers Tenpenny and Pulaski exit the house. An agitated Smoke says they won't leave him alone, adding that "they think I'm Mr. Big, or something." Then Big Smoke asks CJ to represent the gang with him at a meeting with Smoke's "cousin from Mexico."

Big Smoke explains that his "cousin Mary" is inside, and his description of her finally hits home with CJ—he's talking about a marijuana deal. Then Smoke yells at the Vagos, introducing himself and saying he wants "that grass." The response is not nice. Smoke loses his cool and attacks the guard with a baseball bat. The other Vagos contact runs from you and Smoke on foot.

Chase Down the Gang Member

Big Smoke runs out of gas fast, so now it's just you and the Vagos runner. Chase him, tracking him via the red marker over his head. If you lose visual contact, find the red blip to locate him on the radar map.

Super Sprint

Remember that you can tap the sprint button quickly to activate CJ's Super Sprint for distances determined by the amount of Stamina you currently have. Use it!

The Vagos contact slows down to hop fences, so close in fast and get in your gunshots before he clears the obstacle. If he gets too far ahead, he'll enter a vehicle and make a quicker getaway. So make sure to take him out before this happens.

Use a drive-by weapon so you can move and shoot at the same time. After the target goes down, we suggest you jack a car and drive to your nearest save house for a game save before heading back to Big Smoke's crib.

GLEN PARK

LO FLOR

JEFFERSON

TOS

EAST LOS SANTOS

IDLEWOOD

GANTON

Ⓢ **Start (Big Smoke's house)**

Ⓦ **The meet**

Ⓕ **Approximate finish (depends on where you catch the gang member)**

Directions

Drive Big Smoke's Car to the Meet

Hop in Big Smoke's automobile; Smoke is sitting in the passenger seat. The onscreen message mentions that a trip to Emmet's is in order if you need a weapon—just skip that trip if you're already armed. Follow the yellow radar blip east through Ganton, and then north up into the Vagos turf of East Los Santos. Pull into the red marker to trigger the meet.

BIG SMOKE mission 3

Wrong Side of the Tracks

() **Accomplice:**
Big Smoke

 # Respect Gained:
5

What are Officers Tenpenny and Pulaski doing in Big Smoke's garage? Talking to Big Smoke, that's what. Their abiding interest in Smoke seems to be getting more intense. After Big Smoke rails on Tenpenny, he asks CJ to take a ride with him. Smoke wants to check out a tip that he says "might put us deep in the game."

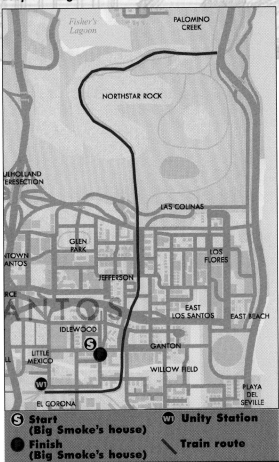

S Start
(Big Smoke's house)

● Finish
(Big Smoke's house)

W Unity Station

\ Train route

Chase Vagos Gang Members on the Motorbike and Take Them Out!

Hop onto the motorbike next to Big Smoke's car and wait for Smoke to jump onboard behind you, then speed onto the tracks and turn left to follow the train. When you catch it, pull up to the train's right side until you see the Vagos atop the engine, marked by red markers overhead. Big Smoke opens fire when you pull alongside.

Stay just right of the rails to get a better shot at the Vagos, but remember that Smoke's Tec-9 doesn't have great range. It's also a good position to avoid hitting any sudden oncoming trains of the Brown Streak Railroad.

Careful! There's a stalled car down the track. The train engine knocks it spinning into your path. Veer around the bodies and debris, and keep up with the Vagos.

Directions

Drive to Unity Station

Big Smoke tells you to drive to Unity Station, the train station across town in Vagos territory. Follow the yellow blip from Idlewood south to El Corona. Drive into the red marker at the station. Smoke tells you he's

looking for some Vagos who are meeting with the Rifa, a San Fierro Mexican gang, to cut some kind of deal. You see the meeting up ahead on a rooftop. Unfortunately for Smoke, the Mexicans spot you and hop onto a moving train.

Take the High Road

As the train tracks bend left at Fisher's Lagoon, far north of Las Colinas, you reach a raised road on the right. Big Smoke suggests you take it, and we concur. You get a better angle on your targets, plus you avoid oncoming trains and a trackside barricade.

Drive Big Smoke Back to His House

Once Big Smoke finally caps the last Vagos gangbanger, make the long trek back to his house. The train battle has most likely taken you far out into the Red County countryside, a good distance north of the Las Colinas area.

Fortunately, your motorbike is a great off-road vehicle, so by all means go cross-country on the first part of your trek back to Big Smoke's house.

On the way back, CJ asks if drugs are to blame for all the violence, or if it was always this way in the hoods. But Big Smoke has no answers. Keep following the yellow map blip. An easy wasy to get back is to follow the train tracks back to Los Santos. When you enter the red marker outside Smoke's house, the mission-ending scene plays. Big Smoke tells you to clear out and stay away from the C.R.A.S.H. fools.

BIG SMOKE mission 4

Just Business

Gameplay Element Introduced:
First-person perspective gunfight as motorbike passenger
Accomplice:
Big Smoke
Weapon Obtained:
MP5
Respect Gained:
10

the story

Big Smoke is messing around in his garage again, and he invites CJ to go for a ride downtown. Big Smoke's "rides" have a way of ending up in gunplay, so get ready for some banging.

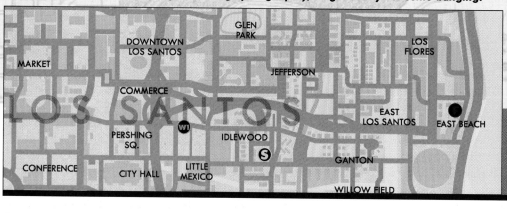

S Start
(Big Smoke's house)

● Finish

W Downtown meeting

Directions

Take Big Smoke Downtown

Start driving west, following the yellow radar blip from Idlewood through Little Mexico. On the way, Smoke promises this isn't a cop errand, but "strictly for the homies." Then he admits the going might be dangerous. Shocker! With the Families making a comeback, the Ballas pushing base, and now Russians moving into the scene, Big Smoke expects that a lot of heavy action is about to go down. When you arrive at the red marker downtown, CJ and Smoke exit the car and cross an upscale plaza. CJ promises Smoke his full support... and within seconds, the fur starts flying.

Keep Smoke Alive and Clear the Area

Big Smoke is under siege from a well-armed security detachment of scary guys in black suits. A message window pops up to remind you that crouching improves your weapon accuracy. Big Smoke also reminds you to use cover. So crouch, use cover, and blast away! Keep Smoke alive until you clear the area. (Smoke's health bar appears onscreen.)

Another info box suggests that if enemies use cover, you can pick them off patiently by precision-targeting with the appropriate button instead of just firing with auto-aim. Personally, we prefer to rush and attack aggressively while targeting the closest enemy and sweeping through the rest using the switch target buttons. Choose whatever approach suits your style. Grab the armor behind the short wall before meeting Smoke.

Get The MP5s!

Having a "drive-by" weapon in your possession before you begin the first person shooting segment of this mission is vital to your success—the Tec9 just won't cut it! Make sure to pick up all the loads of money dropped by the enemies inside, as well as their MP5s.

After you clear out the interior, run to where Smoke crouches by the exit door. You both move outside into the plaza where more security goons open fire. Let Smoke move forward as you lay down cover fire. Use an AK47 for long-range firing and to

avoid running out of MP5 ammo before the next challenge (if you run out of ammo, the gun leaves your inventory). When the area is clear, Big Smoke hops on a nearby motorcycle and CJ automatically slides onto the back.

Just Shoot, Baby

You can't steer the motorbike in this chase sequence; Big Smoke has complete control of the vehicle. Your objective now is to keep the Bike health bar from emptying. Focus your full attention on gunning down pursuers. The sooner you take out the pursing gunmen, the more Bike health you retain.

Fight Off the Pursuers

Two things happen: Security guards start tailing you in vehicles, and your perspective shifts. Move the targeting reticle and shoot. Blast the enemy motorbikes, ignoring the mas-sive car-carrier truck that falls in

next. (It soon hits a bus and veers down a side street.) Try to aim for armed riders, gas tanks, and tires (in that order of importance). Next, clear out the three-car roadblock to continue on your way. Aim for the gas tank on the center car to take them all out quickly. Pivot your aim to the front of the bike and destroy the car with the two gunmen standing nearby just before the flood control trench.

Ignore the Car-Carrier

You can't hurt the big car-carrier transport that dogs you in this mis-sion, so don't waste any fire on it. Concentrate on the motorbikes and automobiles.

Big Smoke knows a way out—the Los Santos flood control trench. He claims it leads up past Grove Street. You have no choice but to believe him, so focus on picking off the mul-tiple motorbikes and cars pursuing you as Smoke makes his run through the city storm drains. Hey, who are these guys anyway?

Keep Clear of Cars

Enemy cars can cause serious damage when they explode, so don't blast them if they're right next to you.

Suddenly the car-carrier transport returns by taking an awesome flyer from the street above down into the trench. More enemy cars roar down a spill-way into the trench, too. Eventually, the truck maneuvers in front of you and starts dropping its cars in your path. If you survive all this, you come to another enemy roadblock at the far end of the trench. This time, Big Smoke executes a breathtaking ramp jump over the blockade.

Your view now faces front. Smoke draws your attention to the old sewer up ahead. First shoot the vehi-cle up ahead to blow up the gun-men nearby, then shoot out the sewer gate on the right side of the trench so Smoke can veer into the sewer tunnel. Pick off the last fleet of motorbikes. Note several clusters of explosive barrels behind you as Smoke speeds down the tunnel. If you nail barrels just as the pursuing bikes pass them, you can wipe out multiple bikes with one shot.

When the coast is finally clear, Big Smoke drops you off on a street near the ocean in East Beach and heads off to dump the stolen motorbike. This completes the Big Smoke mission strand. Find a vehicle and drive to an icon representing another mission strand.

MISSION PASS (1 OF 6)

*Completing **Just Business** gives you one of the six prerequisites needed to open the big **Reuniting the Families** mission later in the Los Santos Finale mission strand.*

✅ **Prerequisite:**
Completion of the **OG Loc** mission in the Big Smoke mission strand
🏠 **Contact Point:**
Burger Shot restaurant in Verona Beach
Total Respect Gained Throughout Strand:
22

OG Loc may seem a little goofy, but he's a Grove Street homeboy, and so he's family—sort of. His passion is for rapping, and most of these missions revolve around that endeavor.

OG LOC mission 1

Life's a Beach

🎮 **Gameplay Elements Introduced:**
Conversation system, dancing
🔒 **Odd Job Introduced:**
Dancing
Respect Gained:
3

✔ PREREQUISITE NEEDED!

*This mission is available only after you complete the **OG Loc** mission in the Big Smoke mission strand.*

the story

As you learned earlier, OG Loc works at a Burger Shot restaurant as a condition of his parole. This first mission of the strand is night-based, so step into the red marker between 22:00 and 06:00 at the "OG" icon location on the radar.

Loc is found mopping up outside after hours. OG Loc tells CJ he's planning a party, but he needs a sound system. Loc heard a good mobile system in a van at the restaurant's drive-thru window; the vehicle was heading for a beach party. He wants you to look into "borrowing" the system.

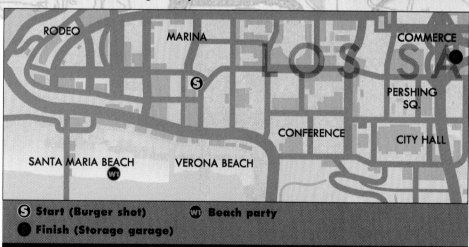

RODEO
MARINA
COMMERCE
LOS SA
PERSHING SQ.
CONFERENCE
CITY HALL
SANTA MARIA BEACH
VERONA BEACH

Ⓢ **Start (Burger shot)** ⓦ **Beach party**
● **Finish (Storage garage)**

💡 Night Moves

This is a night mission. You can enter the red marker outside the Burger Shot only between 10pm and 6am (22:00 and 06:00). If you arrive at any other time, a message tells you when to come back.

💡 Buy a Save House

If you've accumulated enough cash from Odd Job missions, consider buying some property for another save house near the Burger Shot in Verona Beach where OG Loc works. This saves you a lot of driving time.

Directions

Go to Beach Party and Talk to the DJ

Drive to the party at Santa Maria Beach, following the yellow blip on the radar. Drive right across the sand to the water's edge to find the party. Make sure you don't run over any

partygoers or you'll fail the mission—party pooper! Get out of the car and walk into the red marker to trigger your conversation with the female DJ.

A text window explains the conversation system—Left triggers a negative reply, and Right triggers a positive reply. Be positive with the DJ and she'll invite you to dance. Your goal is to impress her with your dancing and earn an invitation into the van. Then you can make your move.

Win the Dance Contest

When the dancing begins, a circle appears at the bottom of the screen and a series of button icons starts scrolling through the circle. Press the corresponding button at the precise moment each icon hits the circle. Pressing buttons to the beat of the music helps you more than trying to exactly target the button icons. Every well-timed button press triggers a good dance move, whereas an incorrect button press triggers a pathetic failure. If you score 4000 points or higher, the DJ will invite you into the van.

Steal Sound Van and Get it Back to the Garage

Follow the DJ to the sound van (with the blue marker above it) and get in on the driver's side. Drive away and start following the yellow blip on the radar map. The DJ falls out of the van and angry partygoers will open fire and give chase, so get out fast.

Drive to the location in Commerce, a "Cheap Parking" storage garage. The mission ends when you drive into the red marker outside the garage. You can then jack a car and follow the "OG" icon on the radar map back to the Burger Shot restaurant for the next mission.

NEW ODD JOBS AVAILABLE!

Completing the Life's a Beach mission opens access to the Dancing odd jobs. For more on this, check out the section on Dancing in the Odd Jobs chapter.

OG LOC mission 2
Madd Dogg's Rhymes

Gameplay Element Introduced:
Stealth
Weapons Obtained:
Knife, silenced pistol
Respect Gained:
4

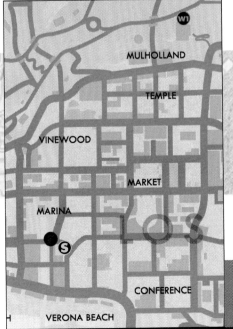

the story

OG Loc is one of the worst rappers in the history of American music. Among other things, his rhymes are lame. CJ suggests hiring a writer (what a shocking notion), but OG Loc has a better idea. If he can acquire the rhyme book of famous rapper Madd Dogg, he'd never have to inflict his noxious rap on the gang ever again. The benefits of this are not lost on CJ, and he agrees to the scheme.

S Start (Burger shot)
● Finish (Burger shot)
W Madd Dogg's mansion

Go to Madd Dogg's Mansion

Get in your car and follow the yellow radar blip north through Marina, Vinewood, and Temple to Madd Dogg's mansion in the hills of the Mulholland neighborhood.

When you arrive, you learn that the main door is around back. Get out, find the marked door, and enter.

Learn About Stealth

This triggers a tutorial about stealth. The rhyme book is in Madd Dogg's recording studio, and his personal security guards are patrolling the building. The radar screen shows each guard as a red blip, which points in the direction the guard is facing. Moving while crouched makes less noise.

Your first "stealth kill" is set up for you. While wielding a knife, crouch, sneak right up behind the first guard, and target the enemy. Notice how CJ raises his arm slightly with the knife. Target the subject and press the shoot button to perform the stealth kill, cutting the guard's throat.

White to Blue

If the white blip that represents you on the radar map turns blue, it means you are hidden in the shadows. Patrolling guards can't see you!

Eliminate the Second Guard

Sneak down the hallway beyond the first guard. A second guard patrols around the swimming pool area in the next room. Observe him to determine his patrol route; don't enter the room until he's facing away from you. Then crouch, step through the doorway, and turn left to get into the dark corner before the guard rounds the pool and patrols toward you. Wait until he passes, then creep up behind him to make another stealth kill.

Eliminate the Third Guard

Move across the pool area and through the next door. A third guard is coming down the hall. Find a suitable place to hide before he spots you, preferably an area with shadows. We know just the place. Take the first doorway on the left, ducking into the side room. Move to the far end of the room, which is bathed in darkness, then turn around and watch for the guard to pass by in the hallway. Crouching, sneak up behind him when he pauses in the next doorway, and then perform another stealth kill.

Sneak Past the Fourth Guard

Continue along the hallway as it bears left. Look for a nice Health power-up in the next room on the right, and then continue down the hallway. The next room features a very long burnished wood bar with a fourth guard standing (and drinking) behind it. Crouch and walk the length of the bar to stay out of his sight. Before you proceed, you see a quick cutscene of a fifth guard sitting on a sofa in the TV room, the next room just past the bar.

Sneak Past Guard in the TV Room

Stay crouched after you get past the bar, and continue creeping along the long sofas in the TV room past the guard. (You can also reach over the sofa and slit his throat if you're feeling particularly cruel.)

Eliminate Final Guard and Grab the Rhyme Book

Proceed down the corridor beyond, following the hall around two corners. Veer left through the next doorway into another darkened room where you can nab some Body Armor. (If you had continued straight down the hall instead, you'd come face to face with the last guard.) Crouch and move to the next doorway. You should see a colorful painting on the wall just across the hall.

Note the guard icon on your radar. He's very close, just around the corner to the right—fortunately, he's facing away from you. Creep around the corner and perform a stealth kill. You can now grab the rhyme book, which floats near some recording equipment.

Find a Silenced Pistol for the Escape

Time to retrace your route back out. You learn that Madd Dogg's guards are using silenced guns. Such a weapon would be most handy to have in a stealth mission, so let's find

one. Exit the recording studio and, crouching, enter the darkened room ahead. A guard stands with his back to you in the next doorway. Perform a stealth kill and nab his Silenced Pistol.

Crouch down the hall, carefully turn the corner, and snipe the next guard with your new silent gun. Continue out of the mansion, silencing guards in the TV room, bar, and swimming pool room on your way back to the front door.

Take Rhyme Book Back to OG Loc at the Burger Shot

Outside, avoid shooting any cops who might be lurking (if you tripped the alarm, for example) to keep your Wanted Level down and grab the BMX bike near the mansion's door. Ride downhill, then jack a car and follow the yellow radar blip to reach OG Loc back at the Burger Shot. Your homey is pleased with this ice cold delivery.

Cell Phone Call: Tenpenny's

Soon CJ gets an ominous cell call from Officer Tenpenny. The corrupt cop accuses CJ of avoiding him, and wants to meet in the donut place in the middle of the Market district: "We need to talk." This adds the "C" (for C.R.A.S.H.) icon to your map, marking the location of the Donut Shop.

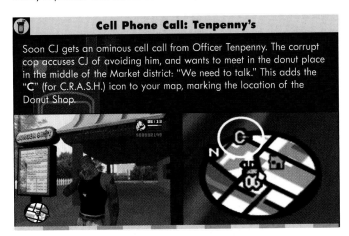

NEW MISSION STRAND OPEN!

*Completing the **Madd Dogg's Rhymes** mission brings a cell phone call from Officer Tenpenny that opens up the C.R.A.S.H. mission strand and its first mission, **Burning Desire**. You can continue the OG Loc strand of missions by returning to the Burger Shot, or else follow the "C" on the map to the Donut Shop to start the new strand.*

OG LOC mission 3

Management Issues

Gameplay Element Introduced: Ejecting from moving vehicles

Respect Gained: 5

Visit OG Loc's Burger Shot ("OG" on the radar map) between noon and 5:00pm (12:00 and 17:00) for this mission. Loc is in a frenzy about Madd Dogg's manager. He claims the man is trying to blackball Loc from the music business. OG Loc wants CJ to cap the dude. But how?

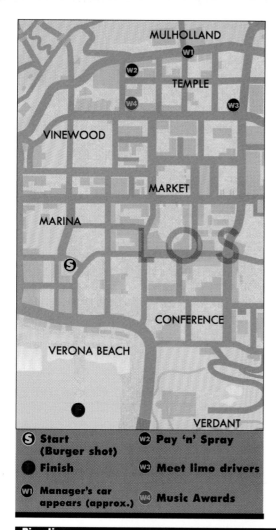

- **S** Start (Burger shot)
- **●** Finish
- **W1** Manager's car appears (approx.)
- **W2** Pay 'n' Spray
- **W3** Meet limo drivers
- **W4** Music Awards

Directions

Find Manager's Chauffer

Get a car and drive. Soon OG Loc calls to report that Madd Dogg's manager has a limo driver who just left a Burger Shot across town in the Market district. The driver's planning to pick up the manager at the Music Awards later. Follow the red radar blip through Market until you find the manager's car. (It has a red marker over it.)

Damage Car to Force the Driver Out

Ram the manager's car so the driver stops and gets out. Careful! He's packing heat, and he opens fire on you. Gun him down and take his car. If the manager's car is badly damaged from when you rammed it, you must get it repaired. Look for the nearest spray paint icon on the map and take the car to the Pay 'n' Spray there for repair. Or to avoid causing too much damage, take two or three drive-by shots at him.

Time Limit

You must get the manager's car *without damage* to the drivers' rendezvous no later than 10pm (22:00).

Meet Up With Other Drivers Before 10pm... and Don't Damage Your Car!

Drive very carefully as you follow the yellow radar blip to the rendezvous spot with the other drivers. If you damage the car on the way to the rendezvous, you must get it repaired again. Once you find the red marker at the rendezvous point, park carefully in that spot. Important: Make sure your car faces the same way the other VIP cars are facing! Don't hit either of the other two cars while parking.

If your vehicle is in good repair, you take off in a caravan to the Music Awards. Be ready to go! Keep your car between the other two cars all the way to the awards ceremony. Tilt the Left Analog Stick up while driving to get an overhead view. This provides a better view of the distance between the two cars you are sandwiched between.

Drive to the Pier and Bail Out

At the theater, cameras flash and the celebrity music crowd files out to its limo fleet. Madd Dogg's manager gets in his car and asks you to drive back to Dogg's mansion. But you have other plans, of course. Follow the yellow radar blip to the pier at Verona Beach.

The security team in the manager's other two cars dog you at first, trying to rescue "The Principle." You can outrun them fairly easily, however. On the way, the manager tries to bribe you into letting him out, even offering a record contract. Ignore him, and when you finally reach the Verona Beach pier, floor it. Then punch your Bailout button just before the pier's end. Note that if one of the security vehicles spots you, you'll have to take care of them too.

Find the nearby BMX bike and ride to your Verona Beach save house (if you have one) to save your game. Next, head directly back to OG Loc's Burger Shot. It's not far from the pier—again, just follow the "**OG**" icon on the radar map.

OG LOC mission 3

House Party

Accomplice: Sweet

Respect Gained: 10

OG Loc's days as a "technician" are over. Yes, he's a parole violator now. And if he's going back to a cell, he'd like one last party first—a big one. All CJ has to do is show up, although it might be nice if he was lookin' good.

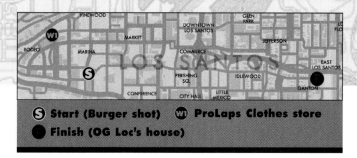

⑤ Start (Burger shot)   ⓦ ProLaps Clothes store

● Finish (OG Loc's house)

Directions

Get Some New Threads and a Haircut

The house party starts at 8pm (20:00) and ends at 6am (6:00) at OG Loc's house, with its location indicated by the "**OG**" on the radar map. Before you go, pick up some

new clothes and get a haircut, jack. You'll find a barbershop right across the street from the Burger Shot, so get a 'do first.

You have to go a little farther, to the Rodeo district, to find some clothes stores. Try our favorite clothier, SubUrban. Or drop into Pro-Laps, the sports clothing store.

Head to OG's

After getting the 'do and buying new clothes, OG Loc calls and says the party is jumping, but he had a "disaster"—he can't rap because his microphone is broken. You promise to come right over, and so you should.

Follow the "**OG**" icon on the radar map to OG Loc's house party. When you arrive, the joint is jumping and your dogs are all there, including Ryder and your brother, Sweet.

But suddenly, a Grove boy brings news of an impending Ballas hit on the party. Sweet organizes a welcoming committee, blocking the street with cars and rounding up as many Grove homies as possible.

Defend Your Hood From the Attackers

Start fighting! This is a wild turf battle. The Ballas come in big numbers, and they attack in staggered waves. Identify Ballas targets by the red markers over their heads. The first wave of eight Ballas hits you head-on in the street. Use your cars for cover.

Hit the Enemies on the Bridge Above

The second Ballas wave features just four attackers, but they fire down from a strong position high on the nearby overpass bridge. Use auto targeting or precision aiming to pick them off one by one.

Help Sweet Defend Against the Last of the Enemies

A final wave of 12 Ballas attacks up some neighborhood alleyways. This is the wildest fight yet, with rival gangbangers coming from multiple directions. Keep moving, rushing from pocket to pocket of enemy attackers. Crouch and roll to avoid gunfire. When the battle is finally over, your boys regroup and return to the party. CJ is amazed, saying he's never seen Ballas roll with that much strength before.

MISSION PASS (1 OF 6)

*Completing **House Party** gives you one of the six prerequisites needed to open the big **Reuniting the Families** mission later in the Los Santos Finale mission strand. Note that if Sweet dies during this mission, it ends in failure.*

✓ **Prerequisite:**
Completion of **Madd Dogg's Rhymes** mission in OG Loc strand
✸ **Contact Point:**
Donut Shop in the Market district of Los Santos

The C.R.A.S.H. mission strand is a quick pair of missions for the corrupt Officer Frank Tenpenny.

C.R.A.S.H. mission 1

Burning Desire

🎮 **Gameplay Elements Introduced:**
Setting fires with Molotovs, quelling fires with a fire extinguisher, girlfriends

🔫 **Weapons Obtained:**
Molotovs, Fire Extinguisher

✓ PREREQUISITE NEEDED!

This mission is available only after you complete the Madd Dogg's Rhymes mission in the OG Loc mission strand.

the story

CJ finally heads to the Donut Shop to meet with his friendly, upstanding C.R.A.S.H. buddies, Officers Frank Tenpenny and Eddie Pulaski. Tenpenny makes it clear that he "owns" you and expects your full cooperation if you want to earn your freedom. He gives you an address where a Vagos thug is holed up. It's clear what the job is—ice the gangbanger for the fine officers.

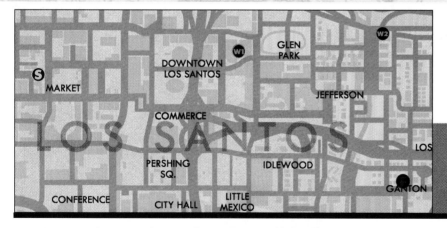

RING DONUTS
BUY 2 Get 1 FREE

Ⓢ **Start (Donut Shop)**
W1 **Molotov stash**
W2 **Gang house**
 Finish (Denise Robinson's house)

Directions

Get Molotovs Hidden by the C.R.A.S.H. in a Downtown Alleyway

Hop in your car and head toward the green weapon blip on the map to the east. You end up on an alley staircase amongst Downtown Los Santos high-rises. Get out of the car and run up the stairs to the green marker, which hovers over the Molotovs. Pick them up, then hop back in your car.

Visit Gang House and Torch It

Now drive through Glen Park and Jefferson toward the yellow blip on the map in East Los Santos. When you arrive at the gang house, you get some onscreen instructions.

Toss Molotovs Into the Five Downstairs Windows

When you arrive at the apartment building, you find the area protected by several Vagos gangmembers. Run 'em over and jump out of your car before their gunfire destroys your vehicle. Gun down the survivors. There are more Vagos scattered around the apartment complex, so keep your eyes open as you begin torching the place.

The five target windows are marked by small, glowing red markers. Just wield a Molotov, line up CJ in front of each marked window, and throw. Remember, you don't want to suffer splash damage, so toss the Molotovs from a good distance. After each good throw, you get a message that says, "Burn, baby, burn. Now hit the next room."

When enemy bangers open fire on you as you move around the house, switch to your favorite weapon and gun them down. Shoot out windows, too, as you circle the house. When the area is secure, firebomb the remaining red-marked windows.

Once you've nailed all five, a cinematic plays. You see a girl trapped inside the flaming house!

Save the Girl Upstairs

Time is tight. You can see the girl's health bar in white onscreen. Follow the yellow map blip! It leads you to the front door (marked in yellow) of the gang house. Enter the house, then run up the stairs in the back of the house. Continue along the upstairs hallway to the last doorway on the left, where a fiery passage blocks your route to the girl. CJ tells her to hold on.

Find Fire Extinguisher in the Kitchen

Run back downstairs and veer left into the kitchen. Nab the fire extinguisher there and quickly review the onscreen instructions for its use.

Take Fire Extinguisher Upstairs and Rescue the Girl

Hustle back upstairs to the flaming doorway at the end of the hall. Use the Fire Extinguisher to douse the flames in the doorway, then approach the girl. (She's indicated by a blue marker.)

The building starts to collapse. The hallway you just traveled through is blocked. Extinguish the fire in the room across the hallway, then enter the original hallway on the other side of the blockage. Douse the flames before the stairs, then head

downstairs. Extinguish the kitchen fire and work your way toward the front door. Make sure the girl keeps following you, then exit the house. Whew!

Outside, the girl (Denise Robinson) thanks you and hops in the car. Turns out, she lives just off Grove Street, and she knows who you are. Follow the yellow blip across the map to Ganton and drop Denise off at her place. She suggests you give her a call sometime.

An info box lets you know that Denise now is your girlfriend and gives you some good, solid relationship advice: "Keep her happy and she'll love you." Her house now appears on your map marked by a red heart, the Girlfriend icon.

Cell Phone Call: Sweet

The next time you exit your car, Sweet calls. He's angry because some "base-head fool" has been buying drugs from the Ballas in Glen Park and supplying them to his Grove brothers. Sweet wants you to hit the Ballas hard, take over one of their neighborhoods, and flush out your traitorous homeboy. Sweet's "S" icon appears on the map at that location.

Dating Denise

This might be a good time to go on a date with Denise Robinson, the girl you saved from the burning house. She's only available at certain times of the day and her entertainment preference is random. For more information on girlfriends and dating, see the **Odd Jobs** section of this guide.

MISSION STRAND RE-OPENED!

Completing **Burning Desire** re-opens the Sweet mission strand (putting the "S" icon back on the map) and its next mission, **Doberman**.

C.R.A.S.H. mission 2

Gray Imports

Gameplay Elements Introduced:
New AI used in shootout, with enemies ducking, side-stepping, rolling, etc.

the story

Head back to your contact point at the Donut Shop in the Market area, marked by the "C" on your radar map. CJ's officer buddies collar him outside the shop. Tenpenny explains how he likes the "status quo"—he likes an even balance of power in the ghetto, with no tribe getting too powerful. But word on the street is the Ballas are cutting a deal for some serious firepower from Russian arms dealers. Officer Tenpenny suggests you check out a freight warehouse down in the Ocean Docks area. You might not like what you see...

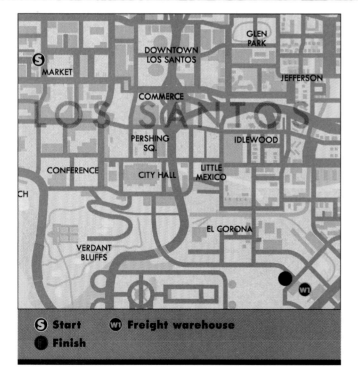

S Start **W1** Freight warehouse
F Finish

Recruit Some Homies

This is a great mission to bring along some help. Before heading to the Donut Shop, recruit as many (green clothed) homies from your territory, and drive them to the Donut Shop to pick up the mission. Refer to the first page of this guide for details on gang recruitment.

Directions

Visit Docks Where the Ballas and Russians are Dealing

Hop in your vehicle and follow the yellow radar blip on the long drive from Market to the Ocean Docks area. When you arrive at the red marker, you see a lot of grim look-

You will have to find some way inside.

ing guards outside a warehouse where you're told the Russians and Ballas are having a meeting. You also get a glimpse of a well-guarded warehouse door opened by a nearby keypad. No doubt that's the way to the meeting.

This will be a new kind of fight, as you face more agile attackers and hostile forklifts, among other things. Here's a good approach: Facing the entrance gate, turn right. Drive completely around the perimeter of the warehouse complex, taking left turns

until you find a warehouse entrance on the left side of the road where railroad tracks lead into a large interior loading area.

Big Forking Bang!

Careful! Two of the forklifts in the yard is moving explosive barrels. You can suffer lethal damage if you shoot them when you're too close.

Hop out and run along the empty freight cars to the far door, exiting into the warehouse complex's inner yard. Hop out of the rail trench to the right and work your way toward the stacks of shipping containers. There are several stacks of shipping

containers around the area and any will serve the purpose. Climb to the top of a stack and hold this position to take on all the forklifts and armed guards. This high post keeps the forklifts from ramming you with their explosive cargo and gives you a great bird's-eye view of all the exterior enemies. Mow 'em down using the AK-47 or MP5. Target the forklifts and watch them explode, taking out multiple enemies!

Body Armor

As you approach the warehouse door, note the Body Armor on the fire escape ladder to the right. Climb to the top of the shipping containers and run toward the balcony. Leap from the edge of the shipping container to the balcony and press the climb button to latch onto it. No matter if you land on the upper or lower balcony, you will still run into the Armor and collect it.

Approach the warehouse door. Note the keypad to the door's left. By all means, blast it with your weapon—the keypad falls off and the door slides open—but be ready for the pair of well-armed guards waiting just inside. Slay them and enter the warehouse. Watch out, though! Another guard lurks just around the corner, up on a distant catwalk.

The Meeting is in the Office in the Back

Now start working your way carefully through the warehouse's crate stacks, crouching as you move, and side-rolling or strafing around corners. Shoot through gaps in the stacks whenever possible. Watch out for a guard on a high scaffold, and keep an eye out for goodies like Body Armor and Health. Target the various explosive barrels scattered along the route to take out multiple enemies more quickly.

Eventually, you get through the crates and see a raised walkway. There's a door on the upper level. This is the room where the Russians are meeting the Ballas. But one last squad of goons guards the area. Pick them off one by one. You can eliminate one

guard easily by shooting the large pallet of crates suspended from the ceiling so it drops on him. This suspended pallet and the explosive barrels can be auto-target by pressing the target button when facing these objects.

Take Out Russian Arms Dealer Inside the Office!

When the area is cleared, pick up the enemies' weapons and find the AK-47 behind the crates in the back of the room under the upper walk-

way. Select the AK-47 and climb the stairs to the upper level. Three more enemies meet in the room upstairs, two Ballas and one Russian arms dealer.

Take out the first gang member in the room from the stairs. Crouch and head to the left side of the door without entering the room. If you enter the room, the Russian will take off running through the back door and a long chase will ensue—he'll eventually enter a car and possibly escape. To prevent this from happening, take aim into the room from the outside edge of the doorway and defeat the remaining gang member, then shoot any part of the Russian's body you can see. Keep shooting the black-suited arms dealer until he's dead—it'll take a lot of bullets.

If you nail the Russian arms dealer in the office, the mission is complete. Take the Body Armor from inside the office, then make your way back through the warehouse and out to your car. Head back to Ganton and the Johnson House to save your game.

If you **miss** him in the office, however, the dealer runs out a back door. Follow him! If he stays alive, he'll run to a car and try to escape. The exterior warehouse is now well guarded with armed gunmen. If you take time to eliminate them, the Russian gets even farther away. Try to avoid the battle and just hop on the BF-400 motorcycle near the warehouse entrance and chase him down. If the arms dealer gets away, you fail the mission.

He has got in a ! Chase him down and take him out!

MISSION PASS (1 OF 6)

Completing Gray Imports gives you one of the six prerequisites needed to open the big **Reuniting the Families** mission later in the Los Santos Finale mission strand.

THE SWEET STRAND (PART 2)
new mission strand

✅ **Prerequisite:**
Completion of Part 1 of Sweet strand, plus the **Burning Desire** mission in the C.R.A.S.H. strand

✳ **Contact Points:**
Ammu-Nation, Sweet's house on Grove Street

Completing the **Burning Desire** mission re-opens the Sweet strand for two last missions. Sweet's getting serious about re-establishing Grove dominance over the local area. He's ready to take the fight to the enemy.

SWEET part 2, mission 1

Doberman

🐾 **Gameplay Elements Introduced:**
Gang warfare, buying weapons at Ammu-Nation

\# **Respect Gained:**
40

✔ **PREREQUISITES NEEDED!**
*This mission is available only after you complete all previous Sweet strand missions, as well as the **Burning Desire** mission from the C.R.A.S.H. strand.*

★ **AMMU-NATION** ★
FOR ALL YOUR DAILY FIREARM NEEDS

SAGA APPROVED
SAY YES TO GUNS

the story

*Catch the mission name? That's right—you the dog, baby. A cell phone call from Sweet after you complete **Burning Desire** triggers this mission. The "S" icon representing the Sweet mission appears at the local Ammu-Nation. Your job here is to single-handedly wipe out all Ballas in the designated Glen Park neighborhood, and gun down the Grove Street homey chilling there, too.*

*This mission introduces the element of gang warfare to San Andreas. After you complete **Doberman**, neighborhoods you control (green areas on the map) begin to suffer random incursions from rival gangs. You can launch your own raids into enemy territory, as well, seeking to acquire turf, gain respect and followers, and expand Grove Family influence. For more information on taking over territories, refer to the Odd Jobs chapter in this guide.*

doberman

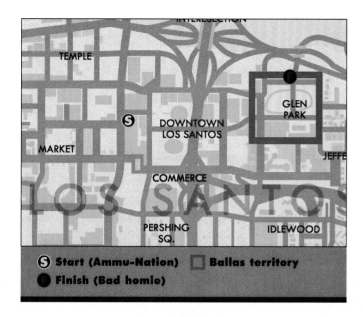

Start (Ammu-Nation) ☐ **Ballas territory**
Finish (Bad homie)

Directions

Drop in Ammu-Nation

Follow Sweet's "**S**" icon on the radar to find the Ammu-Nation weapons store in the commercial Market area of west-central Los Santos. Enter and beef up your arsenal a bit if necessary. If you don't have some

sort of handheld automatic weapon, like the Micro-SMG or Tec-9, we recommend you pick one up now for the ability to perform Drive-bys. A Shotgun is a nice weapon in a close-range turf war, too.

Eliminate Enemy Ballas in Glen Park to Claim the Turf

Hop in your vehicle and follow the Families icon (a little man) on the radar map. As you approach Glen Park, you get notification that Ballas

territory is marked in purple on the radar. Most of the designated area is a grassy park studded with palm trees surrounding a pond. Ride into the purple area and start hunting down Ballas.

Territory Icon

The Families icon on the radar marks the territory to attack. The icon remains on the radar until you clear the area to gain ownership.

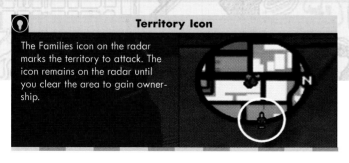

Ballas, Come Out and Play!

Performing Drive-bys or running over rival gang members will not provoke a gang war; you must exit the vehicle and take them out while on foot.

Wipe Out All Three Ballas Waves

Run around the park, picking off every purple-clad Ballas gangster in sight to provoke a gang war. (Once three or four gang members are killed, the purple area glows an angry red, a text message appears onscreen, and the war starts.) The Ballas gang members start appearing as purple blips on the radar, and they come at you in three waves. Keep moving and rolling, and look for Health and Body Armor power-ups that appear scattered in streets and alleys throughout the area during territorial wars.

Choosing Battleground

Try to find a fortified area, one that makes it hard for the Ballas to surround you. Backyards make excellent battlegrounds. The enemy funnels up the driveway, which makes them easier to pick off. Backyard fences can be used to duck behind for cover, and remain excellent cover when you stand up and shoot at the enemy.

Watch for Cops!

Police officers patrol the park, sometimes mingling with the Ballas. If you gun down a cop, you are given a single wanted star. Look for the Police Bribe tucked in the tunnel walkway below the bridge.

Once you survive the third wave of attacks, the territory belongs to the Grove Street families and turns green on the radar. You can find green-clad homies in this area now. The game warns you that your territory will come under constant

attack, so be ready to defend it. For details on this, see **Gang Warfare** in our **Odd Jobs** chapter.

You Found the Grass, Now Kill Him!

Your victory exposes the bad homey, and you see him rush out of a house just north of the park. Note that he's wearing black. Follow the red radar blip to track him. Some of his boys

run right at you and open fire. Waste them, then scoop up any items dropped by fallen foes and hop in a vehicle.

Sweet's "**S**" icon reappears on your map after you pass the mission, marking the location of his house on Grove Street. Follow the "**S**" back to the hood. When you arrive, be sure to pick up the money you earned by taking over turf. A "**$**" icon now appears in front of The Johnson Family's garage. The more territory you take over, the more money that is generated daily.

Watch the Hood!

Rival gangs will start encroaching on Grove turf now, so keep an eye out for attack warnings and flashing red areas on the radar.

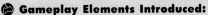

SWEET part 2, mission 2

Los Sepulcros

⦿ **Gameplay Elements Introduced:**
Picking up fellow gang members for mission help

⧈ **Respect Gained:**
10

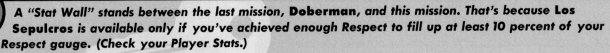

THE STAT WALL: PREREQUISITE NEEDED!

✔ A "Stat Wall" stands between the last mission, **Doberman**, and this mission. That's because **Los Sepulcros** is available only if you've achieved enough Respect to fill up at least 10 percent of your Respect gauge. (Check your Player Stats.)

If you're not quite there yet, try passing any other missions available in alternative strands first, then invade another gang's turf. Gaining territory gives CJ a good boost of Respect. You can also gain Respect by tagging, and by killing rival gang members (a by-product of invading enemy territories).

the story

This is a daytime-only mission, triggered between 9:00 and 17:00 at Sweet's house. Sweet has heard from Officer Tenpenny that all the Ballas OGs will be at a funeral for one of their boys you gunned down in **Drive-By**. Big brother wants to hit them all at once, getting revenge for the Ballas hit at their Mom's burial.

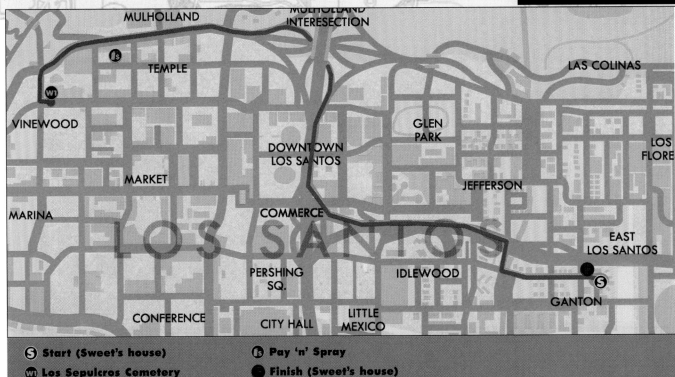

MULHOLLAND

MULHOLLAND INTERESECTION

TEMPLE

LAS COLINAS

VINEWOOD

GLEN PARK

LOS FLORE

DOWNTOWN LOS SANTOS

MARKET

JEFFERSON

MARINA

COMMERCE

LOS SANTOS

EAST LOS SANTOS

PERSHING SQ.

IDLEWOOD

GANTON

CONFERENCE

CITY HALL

LITTLE MEXICO

Ⓢ **Start (Sweet's house)**

Ⓟ **Pay 'n' Spray**

Ⓦ **Los Sepulcros Cemetery**

Ⓕ **Finish (Sweet's house)**

Directions

Get Nearby Gang Members to Join You

You should have plenty of Respect now—enough to gather at least two green-clad gang members. Blue markers indicate available gang members. Target each gang member with the target button, then press Up to recruit him. Recruit two for a full car for Drive-by purposes.

Four Minutes to Los Sepulcros

A timer starts counting down from four minutes the moment you re-enter the car after recruiting your gang members for the job. You now have four minutes to drive to the red marker by the back wall of Los Sepulcros Cemetery. For details on recruiting a gang, refer to the first page of this guide.

Get in the Car with Your Gang and Go to the Ballas Funeral

Hop in the car; the two homies will join you. Follow the yellow radar blip to Los Sepulcros Cemetery. It's a long haul all the way through Idlewood, Commerce, and Market, so drive fast. On the way, Sweet lays out his plan. He wants to go around back of the cemetery and sneak in over the wall. CJ mentions that Kane, a Ballas leader, will be there. Sweet says Kane will bug out at any hint of trouble, so the plan is to enter the cemetery quietly.

Drive to the Back of the Cemetery Before Ballas OG Kane Arrives

When you find the red marker at the cemetery fence, climb over and approach Sweet. He tells you to take up positions and wait for Kane. When Kane arrives, he's wearing Body Armor.

Kill Kane! Don't Let Him Escape!

Sweet heads straight for Kane, but the other Grove boys will follow you if you press the Up directional button. Lead them across the cemetery toward the gunfire and start icing Ballas. Fight your way toward the sedan that Kane arrived in. Kane is the red blip on radar, and he has a red marker over him. Nail him! The armor makes him tough to bring down, so use tombs for cover.

When Kane finally goes down, Sweet leaves to acquire a getaway car and orders you to take out the rest of the Ballas. Once you clear the area, hop in the nearby car with the blue marker overhead where Sweet sits waiting. Then follow the yellow radar blip to drive your brother safely back toward the hood. Note that you have a two-star Wanted Level now, so duck into the Pay 'n' Spray just a couple of blocks east of the cemetery to get the heat off your back.

MISSION PASS (1 OF 6)

Completing Los Sepulcros gives you one of the six prerequisites needed to open the big Reuniting the Families mission later in the Los Santos Finale mission strand.

✅ **Prerequisites:**
Completion of **Gray Imports, Los Sepulcros, Robbing Uncle Sam, Just Business,** and **House Party** missions
\# **Total Respect Gained Throughout Strand:** 15

The Grove Families have been feuding long enough. Sweet Johnson wants the bad blood to end and unity to prevail amongst the brothers, but it won't be easy. Nothing is easy when there's a rat in the hood...

LOS SANTOS FINALE mission 1
Reuniting the Families

🎧 **Accomplice:**
Sweet
\# **Respect Gained:**
15

PREREQUISITE NEEDED!

✔ *This mission is available only after you complete the final mission in each of the following mission strands: Sweet, Ryder, Big Smoke, Cesar, C.R.A.S.H., and OG Loc. That means you must complete* ***Gray Imports, Los Sepulcros, Robbing Uncle Sam, Just Business, High Stakes, Low-Rider,*** *and* ***House Party*** *before you can try to reunite the families.*

The "S" Icon

When you finish the Sweet mission strand by completing Los Sepulcros, the "S" icon disappears from the maps if you haven't passed all four of the other strand-ending missions (**Gray Imports, Robbing Uncle Sam, Just Business, High Stakes, Low-Rider,** and **House Party**). Once you pass all of those missions, the "S" icon returns to the map and becomes your contact point for the Los Santos Finale strand.

the story

Follow the "S" icon on the radar map to get to Sweet's house, where CJ finds Sweet, Big Smoke, and Ryder talking about cleaning up the hood. Sweet says: "The Ballas been pumping our guys full of base for too long, while we argue amongst ourselves." He's set up a meeting with all of the other Family leaders at the Jefferson Motel.

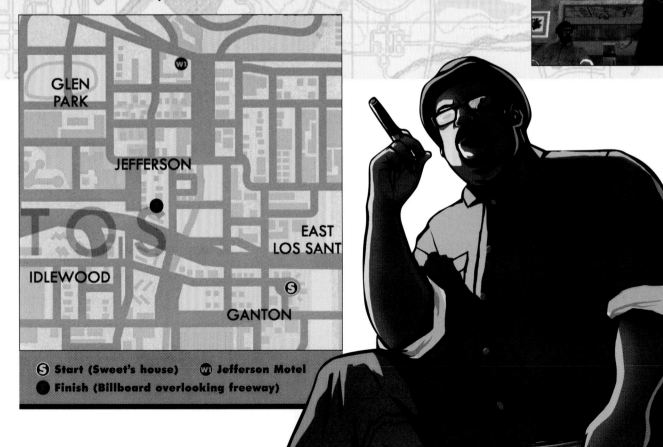

GLEN PARK

JEFFERSON

EAST LOS SANT

IDLEWOOD

GANTON

Ⓢ **Start (Sweet's house)**   🚩 **Jefferson Motel**
● **Finish (Billboard overlooking freeway)**

Directions

Drive Crew to the Motel

Sweet, Smoke, and Ryder hop in a car—and you know who they want to drive. Get behind the wheel and head north to the motel, following the yellow blip on the radar map. On the way, Sweet orders everyone (and especially Ryder) to stay cool during the meeting. When you arrive, Sweet says it's strictly one rep per family, so he's going in alone. You, Smoke, and Ryder wait in the car.

Tension is high as soldiers from the other Families mill about the motel. Suddenly, police helicopters swoop in and drop SWAT teams in the lot while other police units come crashing down on the scene from all directions, cordoning off the area. Chaos ensues, with gang members firing at the cops and each other. CJ refuses to leave Sweet behind, so Big Smoke gets behind the wheel and drives away.

Get Sweet Safely Out of the Motel

Fire at cops in the immediate area of the parking lot if you want, but a better tactic might be to simply sprint for the nearby door (indicated by the yellow marker) on the lower level of the motel.

Inside, the war continues. If you're low on health, you can purchase drinks at the vending machine in the lobby for a quick boost. Then climb the stairs and proceed down the upper hallway, gunning down SWAT members as you go. When you reach the central atrium, more SWAT troops will descend from the helicopter through the skylight! Before heading down the next hallway, find the Body Armor up the stairs in this first area.

🔑 The Lady's Got Protection!

Did you see that lady run across the first hallway into the room on the left? Follow her into the room and CJ will take a short time-out to smooch with the scantily clad woman. After the two lip lock, CJ receives full Health!

🔑 Nab a M4

If you don't already have a good Assault Rifle, like the M4, be sure to pick one off fallen SWAT team members along the route. This fight will go much better with that weapon.

Sweet's location is marked by the blue blip on your radar. Fight your way down the next hallway, marked "Rooms 5-8." Take out the SWAT guys on and around the stairs in the next atrium, then continue around the next corner and down the hallway, marked "Rooms 9-12." Watch out for SWAT cops hanging down from ceiling ducts and rolling out of rooms into the hallway. Craziness!

Find Sweet (with a blue marker over his head) in the second room on the right side of the hall. The two of you try an escape via the roof, but another police helicopter hovers overhead.

Protect Sweet and Destroy the SWAT Helicopter

The helicopter finds Sweet in its searchlight, and Sweet's health bar appears onscreen. Open fire on the copter, using the rooftop air conditioner units for cover. You must destroy the threat from above before the four SWAT sharpshooters aboard can kill Sweet. Pick off the sharpshooters first, then pour your fire into the bird until it explodes.

Follow Sweet

Run after Sweet, down the stairs and into the street. Smoke and Ryder pull up in the car; you and Sweet automatically jump in. Off you go!

Pick Off Your LSPD Pursuers

Someone hands you an AK-47 for this final chase and your perspective shifts to first person. Police helicopters, cruisers, and motorcycles are soon in hot pursuit. Big Smoke drives, leaving you free to pick off pursuers in this classic "rail-shooter" sequence. Rotate your view and press the shoot button to fire.

Cars pull up on either side of you from time to time. Swivel and shoot! The first segment is cruisers only, but then motorcycles join the chase. Some cycle cops actually jump onto your car! Pick them off quickly, or they'll do damage to the overall Car Health, now measured by an onscreen bar.

Sweet Advice

Listen to Sweet for clues on to where you should focus your attention from moment to moment. If he says, "Eyes front, CJ!" you'd better swivel around to face the direction you're traveling.

The ride is wild, but stay calm and try to relax as you shoot. Smoke drives through a car wash at one point to try to shake the heat. Then your AK-47 jams as Smoke smashes through a roadblock and a helicopter drops in to attack, cleaning the remains of the roadblock crew off your hood. Finally, the brakes give out and you enjoy a flying, flaming finale. That Sprunk billboard is just ruined, isn't it?

LOS SANTOS FINALE mission 2

The Green Sabre

 # Respect Gained:
15

---

the story

Follow the "S" on the radar map back to Sweet's crib. Sweet gives an emotional speech, calling on the boys to "show the Ballas what bangin' is all about." Grove Street is king! He then sends everyone out for weapons and calls for a rendezvous downtown under the Mulholland Intersection.

But the moment CJ steps outside, he gets a phone call from Cesar Vialpando. Cesar wants CJ to come and see something—a sight he insists is very important. He says, "You won't believe it, I swear."

Directions

Meet Cesar Under the Freeway

Follow the yellow radar blip southeast to meet Cesar in Verdant Bluffs. Pull into the red marker when you arrive, then walk over to Cesar's car (blue marker overhead) just down the alley, parked not far from City Hall. Get in the car to trigger a scene.

MULHOLLAND
INTERESECTION

LAS COLINAS

GLEN
PARK

DOWNTOWN
LOS SANTOS

LO
FLO

JEFFERSON

COMMERCE

SANTOS

EAST
LOS SANTOS

PERSHING
SQ.

IDLEWOOD

GANTON

CITY HALL

LITTLE
MEXICO

WILLOW FIELD

Ⓢ **Start (Sweet's house)**   🅦 **Meet Cesar**
⬤ **Finish (Ballas ambush)**

Cesar points out a very disturbing sight. First, a couple of Ballas OGs slink out of a nearby doorway, then Big Smoke and Ryder follow! They push open a garage door to reveal Officer Tenpenny and a Green Sabre—yes, that Green Sabre, the very vehicle used in the drive-by that gunned down CJ's mother.

It's clear that Big Smoke, Ryder, Tenpenny, and the Ballas gang have some kind of mutual deal, and it doesn't look good. Clearly, Smoke has sold out his Grove brothers. Then it suddenly becomes clear to CJ that his brother, Sweet, and the homies are walking into a trap.

Get to the Ambush Before Sweet is Killed

Drive like mad to the Mulholland Intersection by following the yellow blip on radar. Sweet's health bar appears onscreen, and it starts to dwindle as you travel. You don't have much time, so cut loose and use all the driving skills you've acquired thus far. On the way, CJ tries to call Sweet, but gets the voice-mail message instead.

SAN FIERRO

When you finally reach the meeting spot, you see the ambush in progress. Whip right into the red marker to trigger a quick scene in which Sweet takes a hit and drops. CJ explains Smoke's betrayal to Sweet, who tells him to run before the cops arrive. But CJ ain't a buster no more!

Hold Off the Ballas Until the Cops Arrive

You need to keep the Ballas at bay until the police arrive. Defend your position from the waves of attackers, including some carloads that arrive in a drive-by attack. Use your circle of cars as cover from the hail of bullets. Shoot Ballas and their vehicles, too. Exploding cars can take out multiple attackers.

The police finally arrive, triggering a scene with your good friends, Officers Tenpenny and Pulaski. CJ awakens with a hood over his head, which Tenpenny pulls off. The good news: Tenpenny tells you that Sweet is alive in a prison hospital. The bad news: Tenpenny has a little job for you.

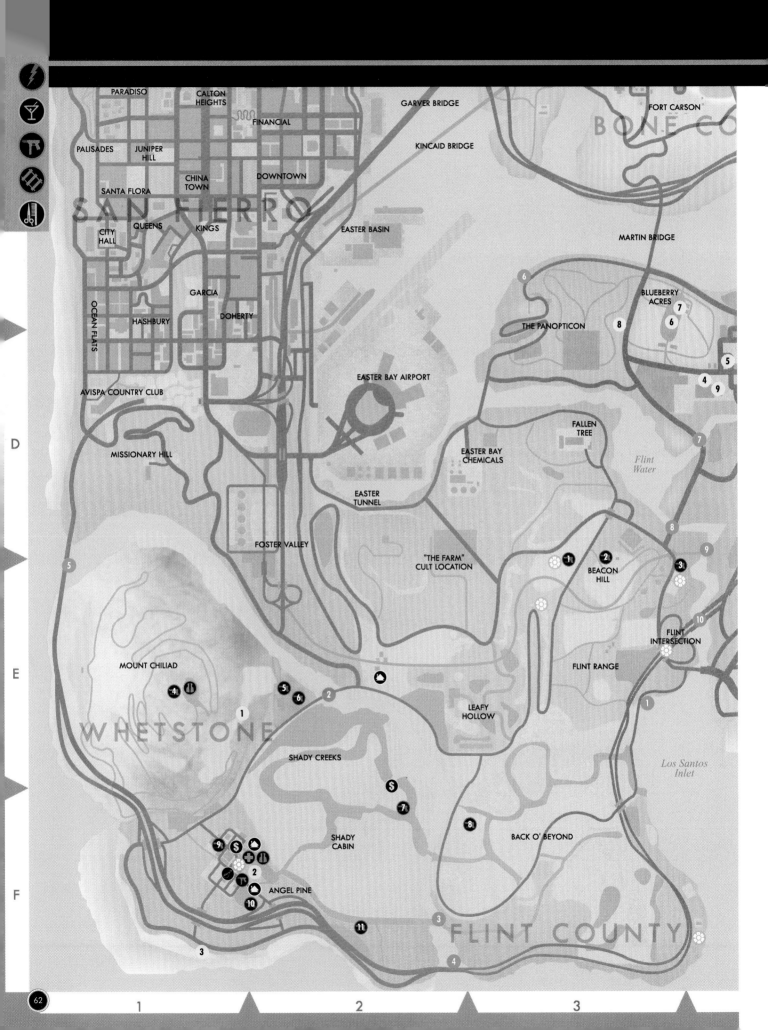

PARADISO

CALTON HEIGHTS

GARVER BRIDGE

FORT CARSON

FINANCIAL

KINCAID BRIDGE

BONE CO

PALISADES

JUNIPER HILL

DOWNTOWN

SANTA FLORA

CHINA TOWN

MARTIN BRIDGE

SAN FIERRO

QUEENS

KINGS

EASTER BASIN

6

BLUEBERRY ACRES

CITY HALL

7

THE PANOPTICON

8

7

6

GARCIA

DOHERTY

5

OCEAN FLATS

HASHBURY

4

9

AVISPA COUNTRY CLUB

EASTER BAY AIRPORT

5

D

MISSIONARY HILL

FALLEN TREE

7

EASTER BAY CHEMICALS

Flint Water

EASTER TUNNEL

8

FOSTER VALLEY

"THE FARM" CULT LOCATION

1

2

3

9

5

BEACON HILL

10

MOUNT CHILIAD

FLINT INTERSECTION

4

5

6

2

FLINT RANGE

1

E

1

LEAFY HOLLOW

WHETSTONE

Los Santos Inlet

SHADY CREEKS

S

7

8

9

S

SHADY CABIN

BACK O' BEYOND

2

10

ANGEL PINE

3

10

F

11

3

FLINT COUNTY

3

4

1   2   3

chapter 2
Badlands

Welcome to the bucolic countryside! Officer Pulaski informs CJ that Big Smoke "does exactly what he's told." Tenpenny warns him to stay away from Smoke, or Sweet will suffer a rough time in prison. As for their little job, it seems an ex-police officer has turned State's evidence that threatens to bring down Tenpenny's gig. The ex-cop is hiding in the witness protection program, ready to be debriefed by Internal Affairs investigators in a lodge up on Mount Chiliad. CJ's job: Take out the snitch.

However, Tenpenny also wants proof—a photograph of the corpse. Pulaski gives CJ a camera, then the cops drive away, leaving CJ stranded in Angel Pine, a trailer park community in the Whetstone County countryside west of Los Santos. Some call this country The Badlands. Maybe there's a good reason why.

RESTAURANTS

 Cluckin' Bell . . . . .Angel Pine F1

POINTS OF INTEREST

Ammu-Nation
Angel Pine • F1

Hospital
Angel Pine • F1

Safehouses
Angel Pine • $20,000 • F2
Angel Pine • N/A • F2
Whetstone • $100,000 • E2

Security Services

WEAPONS
1. **Flamethrower** • Flint County. • In front of cabins. • E3
2. **Cane** • Beacon Hill. • Inside fenced-in area near windmill. • E3
3. **Cane** • Flint County. • Inside walls of RS Haul. • E3
4. **Parachute** • MountChiliad • Top of Mount Chiliad. • E1
5. **Desert Eagle** • Whetstone • Scrap yard warehouse. • E2
6. **Shovel** • Whetstone/Chiliad • Scrap yard, beside a mound of scrap. • E2
7. **Flamethrower** • Shady Creeks • In a copse of trees. • F2
8. **Country Rifle** • Back O' Beyond • On top of mound in middle of nowhere. • F2
9. **Golf Club** • Angel Pine • Angel Pine residential garage. • F1
10. **Micro-SMG** • Angel Pine • Trailer park behind trailer. • F2
11. **Fire Extinguisher** • Whetstone • Outside Whetstone Xoomer station. • F2

POLICE BRIBES
• **Shady Creeks** • Over the forded river. • E2
• **Angel Pine** • In alleyway behind sheriff station. • F1

BODY ARMOR
• **Mount Chiliad** • Top of the peak. • E1
• **Angel Pine** • Behind restaurant wall. • F1

Unique Attractions

UNIQUE STUNT JUMPS
1. **Mount Chiliad** • Jump off this wooden ramp at a decent speed. This ramp is used in Cobra Run in the Chiliad Challenge (race 3). • E1
2. **Angel Pine** • Jump northwest on this ramp out of the trailer park and land on the orange tiled roof over the road. • F1
3. **Whetstone** • Jump east off this sand dune. • F1
4. **Blueberry** • Run up the smashed pallet ramp at FleischBerg, then jump over the truck trailers. Must land safely on the other side. • D4
5. **Blueberry** • Drive east up the wooden set of stairs behind the building with the Sprunk billboard. Must clear the building that you're jumping over. • D4
6. **Blueberry Acres** • Race through the previous barn and jump north/northeast over the barn. • C3
7. **Blueberry Acres** • Race through this barn heading north/northeast. It's best in a car, because the landing usually involves a crash through a wooden fence. • C3
8. **The Panopticon** • Make the short jump over this narrow ravine. • C3
9. **Blueberry** • Jump northwest over trailers from pallet ramp. Clear truck and land on other side. • D4

OYSTERS
1. **Flint County** • Where the beach meets the cliffs, just North of Los Santos Inlet. • E3
2. **Whetstone** • Under a large bridge, to the East of Mount Chiliad. • E2
3. **Flint County** • Under this rickety wooden bridge, situated to the East of Angel Pine. • F2
4. **Flint County** • Under bridge beside open sea, situated to the East of Angel Pine. • F2
5. **Mount Chiliad** • Under bridge leading from Mount Chiliad to San Fierro. • E1
6. **The Panopticon** • Just off the beach in the north west corner of the Panopticon. • C3
7. **Red County** • Under the bridge to the South of Blueberry. • D4
8. **Flint Water** • Under this bridge, that spans the southern river of Flint Water. • D3
9. **Los Santos** • Under this rail bridge, to the West of Los Santos. • D4
10. **Los Santos** • Between the motorway bridges, just West of Los Santos leading to Flint County. • E4

FLOWERS (6 of 40)
• **Flint County** • Behind 69 building. • F4
• **Flint Intersection** • In grassy median. • E3
• **Flint County** • Front of gas station. • E3
• **Flint County** • Middle of the big trees. • D3
• **Flint County** • Next to road at the hairpin turn. • E3
• **Angel Pine** • By trash dumpster next to Lovin' A Loan. • F1

Badlands

◉ Item Introduced:
Camera

So here you are, stranded by Tenpenny in the middle of west redneck hell—and worse yet, you're forced to do a dirty job for him. You start off facing the lovely trailer homes of Angel Pine, a small Whetstone County community. Note the "C" icon on your map. This is your first contact point. Cross the road and follow the "C" icon into a trailer park, where you find both a red marker and a save-game disk. Walk into the disk to save your game, then step into the red marker to trigger the mission.

Directions

Kill Witness and Bring Back Proof

A yellow blip now appears on your radar map. That's where the witness is holed up. Before you begin the hunt, take a moment to review the instructions for camera use. Snap a few photos for practice, if you want.

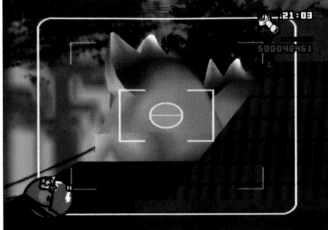

◉ Get a Mini

Your cop pals stripped you of all your weapons, but don't fret—you can find a Tec-9 floating behind the easternmost home in the trailer park. You'll need this weapon to shoot from your vehicle.

You can also find some free Body Armor in the alley beside the local restaurant. Visit the local Ammu-Nation for your weapons-shopping convenience.

MOUNT CHILIAD

WHETSTONE

SHADY

ANGEL PINE

Ⓢ **Start (Trailer park)**
◐ **Body Armor**
W2 **Mountain road marker**
W3 **Road fork (go left)**
W4 **Cabin**
● **Finish (Trailer porch)**

Use the Sanchez dirt bike parked up against the trailer next to the save disc, then follow the yellow radar blip. It takes you down a highway to another red marker at the entrance to a mountain road that winds up Mount Chiliad.

Ascend the Mountain to Find That Snitch!

Head uphill and veer right to follow the mountain road. The road makes a switchback around one precarious hairpin curve, and then comes to a fork. The left fork is clear, but the path to the right is barricaded. Guess which fork leads to a well-visited cabin? Yes, veer left. (The right fork just switchbacks all the way up Mount Chiliad.)

Follow the road all the way to the cabin. As you approach, the scene cuts to a quick view of FBI guards pacing. Drive toward the cabin to attract their attention. The moment they engage you, the snitch hops into a car and makes a run for it!

Immediately turn and give chase. You don't have to kill the FBI guards to trigger the snitch's run or to chase him down. In fact, killing feds raises your wanted level and brings a police reprisal, so avoid that. Why make things harder than they have to be?

 Surprise the Snitch

Go around the back of the cabin and kill the snitch before he gets in the car!

Chase and Kill the Snitch, Photograph the Evidence!

Follow the snitch down the hill. Perform a Drive-by to stop the escaping vehicle. Sometimes he loses it on the rough terrain and wipes out without your assistance. Rub him out, then equip the camera and snap a photo of the corpse.

Take Camera to the Drop

Get back on your vehicle and ride back down the mountain to Angel Pine. Follow the new yellow radar blip to the drop location at the same trailer home where you started the mission. Walk into the red marker on the porch to drop off the camera.

Cell Phone Call: Cesar

Shortly after you drop off the camera, you get a cell phone call from Cesar Vialpando. He's checking up on you and says Kendl, your sister, is worried. You explain how you're stuck out in Whetstone. Cesar says he's got some backup coming out to protect you; he wants you to meet at the diner in Dillimore, over in Red County. When you hang up, a question mark icon appears on your radar map. Grab a vehicle and follow the "?" on the long haul to Dillimore.

Save Yourself a Trip

Save as soon as possible so that you don't have to make the trip back to Angel Pine again (if you mess up and want to reload an old save).

First Date

the story

When you finally arrive in Dillimore and enter the red marker outside The Welcome Pump, CJ meets Cesar's cousin—she's holding off two men at knifepoint and threatening emasculating acts. Catalina is a fiery woman, to say the very least. Her passion is armed robbery, and her tactics aren't very ladylike.

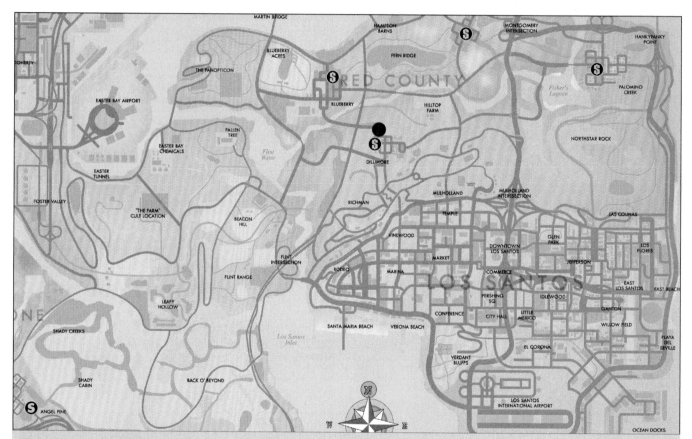

⑤ Cut-scene at Trailer

● The Welcome Pump (Meet Catalina and unlock missions)

⑤ Catalina's Robbery Targets

Familiar Face

Grand Theft Auto fans may remember Catalina as a central character in **GTA III**.

When you regain control outside, grab one of the nice Freeway hog cycles in the parking lot. Catalina hops aboard with a plan to "take this county for every stinking cent."

She explains she's cased four soft targets, all of which now appear on the map, marked by dollar sign icons. You can pursue the four jobs in any order. We'll start with the gas station just down the street.

BADLANDS mission 3

Tanker Commander

🚗 **Vehicle Introduced:**
Tanker
💲 **Cash Gained:**
$5000
🔒 **Odd Job Opened:**
Trucking

Head a short distance down the street in Dillimore to the nearest "$" icon on the radar map, a Gasso gas station. ("We Have Gas!") After Catalina's charming opening statement, you learn that a locked door and bulletproof glass keep you from getting at the takings. Cat spots a big truck and tanker, which then calls for a change of plans.

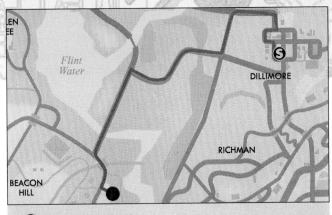

$ Gasso Gas Station
● RS Haul

The angry gas station attendants refuse to give up, and start pursuing in a car. As you drive away, Cat says she knows a guy who will pay for your rig and cargo. A new yellow blip appears on your radar map.

Directions

Enter Truck Cab and Attach it to the Tanker

Note the big gasoline tanker trailer near the truck cab. Hop into the driver's seat and pull forward until you're in front of the tanker trailer, then switch to your rear view and slowly back the cab under the front of the trailer to hook up.

Drive Rig to Catalina's Buyer, Don't Allow Pursuers to Disconnect Trailer!

Start driving toward the yellow blip. (Check mission map on the previous page for the best route.) Note the Health bar now onscreen. Your pursuers open fire whenever they manage to pull up alongside of you, but don't get rattled. Keep a steady

pace and make easy, controlled turns. Don't let your rig jackknife out of control or the trailer may disconnect, causing mission failure.

When you finally reach Catalina's contact across the water in Flint County, drive into the red marker at the RS Haul trucking facility. Your pursuers will meet a fiery end here if they're still chasing you. Catalina makes her deal with Mr. Whittaker

for a wad of cash, and Whittaker offers CJ the opportunity to run freight for him. This opens up the Trucking Odd Jobs for future fun and profit. Catalina then takes off on a motorcycle, leaving CJ stranded.

NEW ODD JOBS AVAILABLE!

Completing the Tanker Commander mission opens access to the Trucking Odd Jobs. Come back to RS Haul between missions to attempt one of the game's truck-driving jobs. For details on this, see the Trucking section of our Odd Jobs chapter.

Keep on Truckin'

This is a good time to take a break from the missions and do some trucking; it not only helps you learn the countryside, but it's also a nice source of income if you're low on cash—especially since all of your weapons are taken after Los Santos.

Cell Phone Call: The Truth

CJ gets a cell phone call from a mysterious voice who calls himself The Truth. He claims you have a mutual friend and business partner, insinuating that it might be Tenpenny. He has a room at a motel in Angel Pine. The location is now marked on your map with a "TT" icon. You must complete this mission next before you can return to the Catalina robbery missions.

Body Harvest

🚗 **Vehicle Introduced:**
Combine Harvester
⊕ **Respect Gained:**
5

the story

Follow the "TT" icon on the map to the Budget Inn Motel (the sign is missing a few letters) back in Angel Pine. Inside the room, Officer Tenpenny is high as a hang-glider and introduces CJ to a man he calls The Truth—a big-time marijuana farmer up in Flint County. Tenpenny says Truth will be supplying you with "the finest weed" for delivery, but you must pay him in cash. As a test of trust, The Truth wants CJ to steal a combine harvester from a compound of survivalist right-wingers across the ridge from Truth's farm.

Directions

Visit Farm Where Combine Harvester is Located

Take your vehicle and exit town to the north, then follow the yellow blip northeast from Angel Pine. Your route skirts Mount Chiliad and crosses the river into Flint County to the entrance of The Farm, home of a survivalist cult. When you reach the spot, you see a red marker right off the highway.

Drive into the marker to get a quick cinematic of the harvester, located in the field toward the back of the farm. You also see that several groups of survivalists are working, and you can bet they'll be hostile to a Los Santos gangster ripping off their machinery.

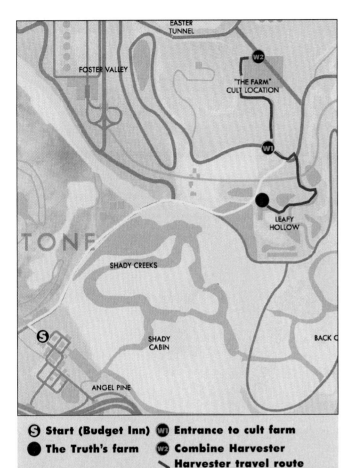

S Start (Budget Inn) **W1** Entrance to cult farm
● The Truth's farm **W2** Combine Harvester
⟍ Harvester travel route

Enter Farm and Steal the Combine Harvester

The harvester is now indicated on radar by the blue blip. The direct strategy is to gun your vehicle around the right perimeter fence of the farm. This way, you avoid debilitating combat and get to the target quickly. You will be spotted almost immediately, however, so make a quick beeline to the harvester in the back field.

An alternate approach is to enter on foot. Take the same woodsy route to the back field, but move with stealth to avoid detection. When you reach the field, wait until the harvester takes its pass closest to you and make a wild sprint. Get up beside the cab to draw out the driver, who opens fire. Hop in and drive away!

Take Combine Harvester Back to The Truth's Farm

Here's where you come to understand this mission's title. The angry cultists give chase, but you now control a four-ton vehicle with sharp rotating blades in front. Turn it on your pursuers! Chew them up in front and spit them out the back!

Grind your way out to the road, then start back to The Truth's farm in Leafy Hollow on the other side of the ridge to the south. Follow the country roads, using the yellow radar blip for general guidance. (Check our map for the best route.)

Some cultists follow in a pickup truck; try to ram them, catching their vehicle in the Combine blades.

When you finally drive the Combine Harvester into the red marker inside The Truth's barn, you'll trigger his appearance. The Truth sincerely thanks you and says he'll be in touch when the weed shipment is ready. In the meantime, you must get that cash payment together.

Cell Phone Call: Cesar

Cesar calls first. He says his gang, the Aztecas, have fallen apart and there's a price on his head, maybe Kendl's, too. CJ tells him to get a place with Kendl in Angel Pine and they can meet up. When you hang up, the "CV" icon appears on your radar. Enter the BF Injection on the nearby dirt drive and follow the "CV" back to a familiar trailer in Angel Pine.

the story

King in Exile

You get a short break from action in the next couple of brief missions as you reconnect with your sister, her boyfriend, and your sort-of girlfriend. When you follow the "CV" to the red marker outside the trailer home in Angel Pine, CJ walks in on Cesar and Kendl.

Directions

Meet Cesar and Kendl

Cesar is hot and says he wants to "cap me some dope dealers." He knows the bad guys: Tenpenny, Pulaski, and former brother, Big Smoke. CJ can't believe Smoke is a pusher, but Kendl convinces him it's true. Cesar explains that Smoke sends a car up to San Fierro twice a week to pick up trunk-loads of "white" (cocaine). CJ decides to keep an eye on the highway to San Fierro, and tells Cesar to lay low.

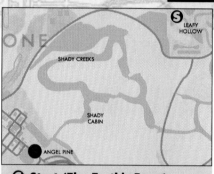

S Start (The Truth's Farm)
● Cesar and Kendl

 Cell Phone Call: Catalina

Soon you get an angry call from Catalina wondering where you've been. This puts a pink "C" (for Catalina) icon on the map, far away up in Fern Ridge. Head for that location! You don't want to make her angrier than she already is.

First Base

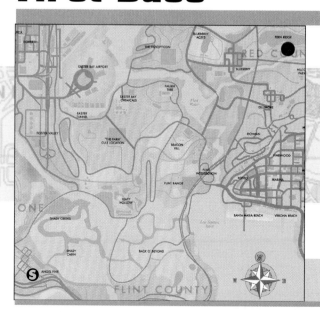

It's a long haul from Angel Pine up to Fern Ridge. When you finally arrive at Catalina's cabin, she won't answer when CJ knocks or calls at the front door. What's going on?

S Start (Trailer)
● Catalina's hideout

Directions

Meet Catalina

Suddenly, Catalina jumps CJ from behind and holds a gun to his head. After some strange foreplay, Catalina admits she loves him. Now all three of her remaining planned robberies reappear on the map as dollar sign icons.

Hop into Cat's Buffalo in her driveway with Catalina and head for the northernmost "**$**" icon—the Off Track Betting parlor in Montgomery. On the way, listen to some scary stuff from Catalina about what happens to the men in her life.

BADLANDS mission 7

Against All Odds

Weapon Gained:
Remote Explosives

Cash Gained:
$2,000

The OTB (off-track betting) parlor in Montgomery is called the Inside Track. CJ isn't keen on the idea of robbing the place, but Catalina hands him some satchels of explosives and goads him into it. When you enter the place, Catalina takes charge of crowd control in her inimitable way, gunning down innocent bystanders who annoy her.

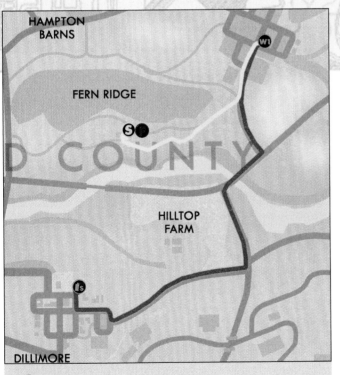

HAMPTON BARNS

FERN RIDGE

HILLTOP FARM

DILLIMORE

- **$** Start (Catalina's hideout)
- **W1** Off Track Betting
- **Ps** Pay 'n' Spray
- ● Finish (Catalina's hideout)

Directions

Use Satchel Charges to Blast Open Security Door and Safe

Press the shoot button to toss the Satchel at the red security door, holding down the button longer before you release it to increase the throwing distance. Try to get one to stick directly to the door, then switch to the detonator that appears in

your weapon slot. Get a safe distance away and press the shoot button again to detonate the charge and blast open the door.

Throw Carefully
You have a limited number of Satchel Charges, so don't waste them by tossing wildly.

Enter the safe room and use another Satchel on the safe. After you destroy it, CJ automatically cleans out the money and you end up outside the OTB with Catalina. Unfortunately, you emerge with a one-star Wanted Level that can eventually grow to three, and every cop in Red County is bearing down on you.

OTB Odd Job

The OTB machines inside the "Inside Track" can actually be played when not in a mission. See the **Off-Track Betting** section in our **Odd Jobs** chapter for more details.

Get to a Pay 'n' Spray!

This is a no-brainer. The county police are relentless, so peel out and head south. Check our map on the previous page to find the nearest Pay 'n' Spray, located back in Dillimore, then run!

Squad cars and helicopters bear down on you from all directions—attempting road blocks, ramming your car, and so on. Meanwhile, Catalina shoots at them and howls things like, "I've killed hundreds of pigs like you! I hope it takes you long to die!" When you finally reach the Pay 'n' Spray, pull in to remove the Wanted Level.

Return to Catalina's Place

Drive toward the yellow radar blip on the map, which marks the location of Catalina's cabin up in the Fern Ridge area. On the way, CJ and Cat have a deep, sensitive discussion about their relationship. Upon arrival, Catalina graciously hands over $2000 of the OTB parlor take, and you get the Mission Passed message.

A red marker appears in front of Catalina's cabin. Get out of the vehicle to save your game at the nearby disc icon. Then, if you've completed two robbery missions with Catalina (and you have, if you're following this walkthrough), you'll get a call on your cell phone.

Cell Phone Call: Cesar

Cesar says he's found some good street racing, mostly cars from San Fierro. If CJ wants to make some money, says Cesar, get a fast car and meet him and Kendl just south of Montgomery. This puts a "**CV**" icon on the map. Now you have a choice of two locations to visit. Let's continue our felonious rampage with Catalina first.

Triggering Cesar's Call

Cesar will call CJ about the street racing south of Montgomery only after you complete any two of the four Catalina robbery missions. It can be **any** combination of two, because you can commit the four robberies (the ones marked by a dollar sign on the map) in any order.

Gone Courting

Step into the red marker. CJ approaches Catalina's cabin again and, after yet another tender exchange of abiding love, our east-side Bonnie and Clyde hit the road again. The last two robbery missions reappear as "$" icons on the map.

FERN RIDGE

ED COUNTY

HILLTOP
FARM

S Start (Catalina's hideout)

● Finish (Catalina's hideout)

Local Liquor Store

- 🚗 **Vehicle Introduced:**
  Quad
- 🧍 **Accomplice:**
  Catalina
- 💲 **Money Gained:**
  $1000

This time, drive west toward the liquor store in the sleepy town of Blueberry. When you drive into the red marker, CJ and Catalina prepare to hit the liquor store. Suddenly, a quartet of cowboys on Quads moves in first! They grab the cash and three escape on the Quads, but Cat guns down the fourth fellow and commandeers his vehicle.

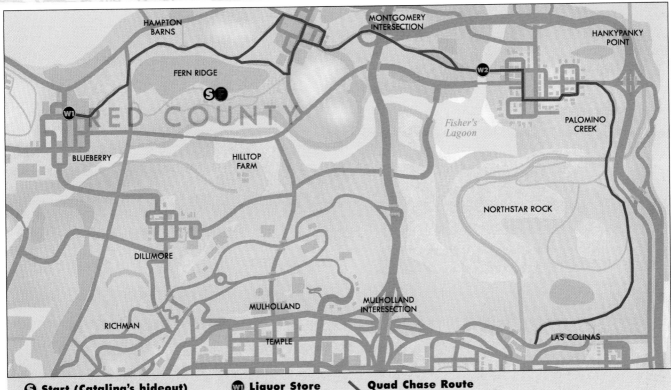

- **Ⓢ Start (Catalina's hideout)**
- **● Finish (Catalina's hideout)**
- **W1 Liquor Store**
- **W2 Bridge Jump**
- **╲ Quad Chase Route**

Directions

Catch Quad-bikers and Get the Money

As you might expect, you drive and Cat shoots. However, if CJ has a mini-submachine gun (preferably the MP5), he can shoot straight ahead and to either side, adding his fire-power to Catalina's. Follow the red blip on the radar map to tail the other three cowboy hoods. Your Quad is an all-terrain vehicle, so cut corners when you can to gain on your foes. (See the chase route on our map.)

🕐 Get an MP5!

Purchase or find an MP5 before taking this mission or before you enter the red marker outside the Liquor Store. Adding to the Quad Drive-by with Catalina will make short work of the escaping thieves.

🔑 Get the Cash Last

When you gun down each quad-biker, he drops a briefcase full of cash. You can just leave it behind and keep chasing the remaining bikers. The game marks the location of each dropped briefcase with a green blip on your map, so you can return and pick up the cash later after you hunt down the last quad-biker.

Early on, you reach a fork in the path, and the cowboys split up— two go left, one goes right. We suggest you follow the duo that splits left. However, you can follow either direction, because their paths will converge again. This happens several times during the chase. Note that the fleeing bandits always re-converge after splitting up.

It's a long chase that runs through the towns of Montgomery and Palomino Creek, so don't give up if you spin out of control. Just recover and go back after your prey. In most cases, you overtake the fleeing bikers quickly after a mishap. Once you finally take out the third and final quad-biker, gather up all the dropped briefcases of cash.

Take Catalina Back to the Hideout

Once you've nabbed the third briefcase of cash, return to Catalina's cabin. You're probably very far from the hideout, maybe as far as Las Colinas, so use the map to reach a nearby inhabited area and jack a car. Then drive the streets and highways as you follow the yellow radar blip back to the cabin. After you drop off your woman, you'll get your $1000 reward and pass the mission. Dismount your vehicle and you'll receive another cell phone call.

	Make the Leap

Get ready for this awesome stunt jump over a shattered wooden bridge midway through the quad-bike chase. You can earn a Unique Stunt Bonus of $500 if you hit it cleanly.

	Cell Phone Call: Cesar

Cesar reports he's got the low-down on Big Smoke's crack deliveries! Every Monday and Friday, Smoke's cash leaves Los Santos for San Fierro. Then, every Wednesday and Saturday a courier delivers the "yay" back to Big Smoke. CJ promises to keep an eye out for these deliveries, and the "CV" icon reappears on the map. We'll check it out shortly.

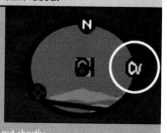

BADLANDS mission 8
Made in Heaven

the story

After Cesar hangs up, Catalina calls. She's her usual cheery self, and sweetly asks CJ to drop by. Since you're already standing in front of her cabin, this seems like the best destination to visit right now. Particularly since Catalina's threat of making kabobs out of certain body parts if you don't show up soon seems like something this woman would actually consider.

FERN RIDGE

Ⓢ ●

ED COUNTY

Ⓢ **Start (Catalina's hideout)**
● **Finish (Catalina's hideout)**

Directions

Follow the "C" icon and walk into the red marker in front of Catalina's cabin hideout. She bursts through the front door, scaring the hell out of CJ (and you, too, probably). She's fed up with love, she's in a really bad mood, and she wants to be just business partners from now on. Okay, baby, whatever! Hop in the Buffalo.

Small Town Bank

Accomplice:
Catalina

Cash Gained:
$10,000

Follow the last "$" icon east to Palomino Creek, then enter the red marker. Catalina puts CJ on crowd control—a really good idea, considering how she handled that job in the OTB heist. CJ gets the drop on the bank guard, and Catalina goes to empty the safe.

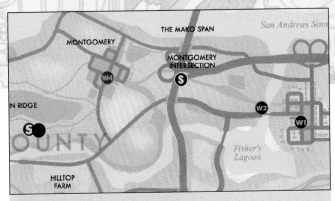

- **$ Start (Catalina's hideout)**
- **W1 Bank**
- **W2 Bridge Jump**
- **$ Police Bribe**
- **W4 Cop Ambush**
- **● Finish (Catalina's hideout)**

Directions

Keep Your Gun Trained on the Staff

All four bank staffers, including the guard, start with their hands up, then each employee slowly tries to lower their hands. When you point your gun at anyone, their hands shoot right back up. The guard wants to shoot you, and the others want to trigger the bank alarm. Keep your gun pointed and moving, keeping everyone's hands up as high as possible.

Eventually, however, someone manages to lower enough to sound the alarm. This triggers a bulletin to the local cops, tipping them off to the bank robbery. Now you have a three-star Wanted Level!

Catalina tells you to smash the ATMs. Blast all three ATMs with your weapon or bust them open with a melee weapon to nab the cash. Catalina leads you to the back door and blasts it open with her Shotgun.

Fight Your Way Down the Alley

Police are crawling all over the neighborhood. Fight your way down the back alley, looking for snipers on rooftops, as well as cops on foot. It's like running a gauntlet, with shooters lining the walls on either side! Once you nail a target on one side, swivel your sights quickly to the other side of the alley.

As you approach the red dumpster near the exit from the alley, you hear the unpleasant drone of a police helicopter, and then a pair of motorcycle cops suddenly wheel into the alley. Their presence is actually welcome, because once you gun them down, Catalina tells you to grab one of the HPV1000 bikes and follow her.

Follow Catalina on the Motorcycle

Two more motorcycle cops decide to mix it up with you, but stay on Catalina's tail (she's the blue blip on your radar) as she exits town and rides up a broken wooden bridge with a gap in the center. Line yourself up on the center of the bridge and make a flying leap over the gap.

One pursuer is lost on this stunt jump, while another gets thrown off in the chase under the roads. Consider getting close enough to unload your Submachine Guns in their direction. The consequence of your actions, however, will raise your Wanted Level, so keep an eye out for a Police Bribe along the way (indicated on our mission map).

 Police Bribe

Look for the spinning Police Bribe under the Montgomery Intersection.

Eventually, Catalina gets knocked off her bike and is surrounded by three Police Rangers at an intersection in Red County. Zoom in close, pause to pick up Catalina, and accelerate quickly to make your escape back to her hideout at Fern Ridge. You get a sweet cash payout for this mission.

Since this is your fourth and final Catalina robbery mission, no more "**$**" icons remain on the map. However, the "**CV**" icon reappears. Time for some racing!

BADLANDS mission 10

Wu Zi Mu

 **Cash Gained:**
$5000

the story

Racing fast cars! There's just nothing better. Cesar and CJ share this love. Find a good, redneck muscle car, like the Phoenix, (or just grab the Buffalo next to Catalina's shack) and head for the "CV" icon just south of the Montgomery Intersection in Red County. Pull into the red marker to meet Cesar at the street racing site.

A slick, very formal gentleman in black approaches with his entourage. He welcomes CJ to the meet, and introduces himself as Wu Zi Mu—"my friends call me Woozie." He explains how the races are run for cash or pink slips.

PREREQUISITES NEEDED!

This mission is available only after you complete any two of the four Catalina-planned robbery missions. *Tanker Commander* and *Against All Odds* are the two robberies we completed first in this walkthrough. But again, it could be any combination of two robberies (including the *Local Liquor Store* and *Small Town Bank* missions) because you can select Catalina's jobs in any order.

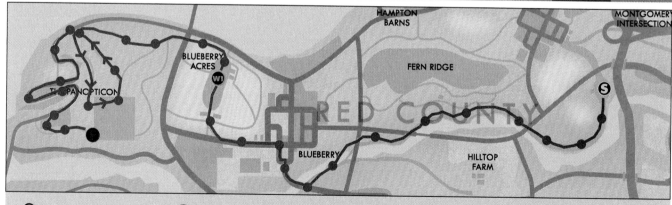

Ⓢ **Race Start**   Ⓦ **Barn Jump**   ╲ **Race Course**
● **Race Finish**   ● **Race Checkpoints**

Directions

Win the Race!

It doesn't get any more straightforward than this. Just run fast, run hard, and beat the other three racers. As in the lowrider race in Los Santos, look for and drive through the glowing red checkpoints that mark the race course.

Keep in mind that this is gritty street racing, so the course crisscrosses well-traveled highways, runs down miles of country roads, winds along Red County's riverfront, and veers through backcountry and beach paths. At one point, you even roar through a barn

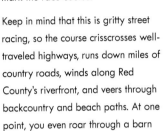

and make a totally insane stunt jump over farm buildings onto a slanted roof. (This earns you a Unique Stunt Bonus, of course.) Therefore, you must not only drive fast, but also with extreme awareness and control. You can also skirt the farm entirely by going wide around the fence, then back in for the checkpoint on the other side of the farm.

Street Racing Tip

This isn't an oval race track! Keep looking ahead on your Pause Menu, planning for the next crazy stretch and watching out for traffic on the roads. Expect the unexpected. Don't get sucked into a tunnel vision of the road.

The race winds west and then weaves through The Panopticon area to the finish line. You must finish in first place to pass the mission. When you finally win the race, Wu Zi Mu admits you drive with style. He suggests you give him a call if you're ever in San Fierro. Now why would you ever be in San Fierro?

Police sirens cut the conversation short, and it's time to jet. CJ automatically hops in his car. A red marker appears just up the road; its location is marked by the "CV" icon on your map.

Farewell, My Love...

◯ Property Gained:
Garage in San Fierro

Drive into the red marker in the street racing site at The Panopticon. Hey, it's Catalina... and she's angry. (What a surprise.) She's also wielding a Crowbar. After abusing CJ and his car a bit, she drops a bombshell—she's in love with another fellow, a non-talkative guy. Surely you recognize him from Grand Theft Auto III. Ahhh... memories. Okay, time to race!

PREREQUISITES NEEDED!

✔ **This mission is available only after you complete all four of the Catalina robbery missions, plus both the Wu Zi Mu and Body Harvest missions.**

Directions

Win the Race!

This is the same course as in the Wu Zi Mu mission, but in reverse. By now, you should be a decent driver, so use your instincts and run hard. As before, you must win the race to pass the mission. For more tips on this race, see "Badlands A Race" in the Los Santos Race Tournament.

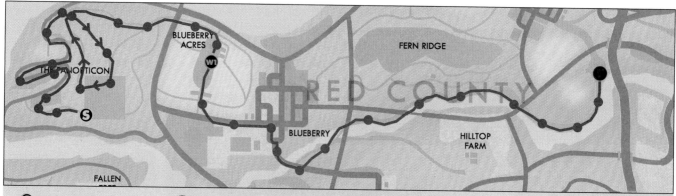

S Race Start   **W1** Barn Jump   \\ Race Course

● Race Finish   **●** Race Checkpoints

After finishing victorious, Catalina tells CJ he won unfairly. But she and Claude have to pay up anyway, so Cat hands over the deed to a garage in San Fierro. After the Mission Passed! screen, you get another phone call.

Cell Phone Call: The Truth

The Truth says he's got the goods for you, but warns that "people are listening to us." After a paranoid digression, he hangs up and the "TT" icon reappears on your map.

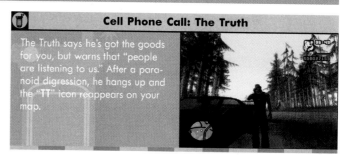

BADLANDS mission 12

Are You Going to San Fierro?

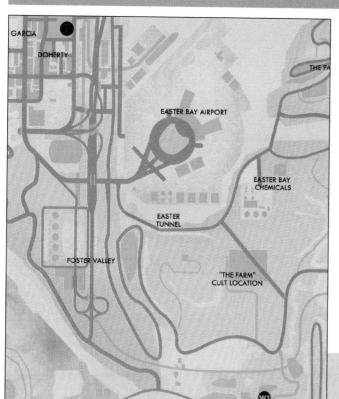

S Start

W1 Weed Fields

● Finish (CJ's house)

🚗 Vehicle Introduced:
Mothership

🔫 Weapons Obtained:
Flamethrower, RPG

 # Respect Gained:
15

PREREQUISITES NEEDED!

✔ This mission is available only after you complete all four of the Catalina robbery missions, plus both the **Body Harvest** and **Farewell, My Love...** missions.

Drive up to The Truth's weed farm in Leafy Hollow by following the "TT" radar icon. When you arrive, you pay The Truth and, as he puts it, "the karmic circle closes." But not in the way anyone could foresee, because suddenly, the sound of a distant police chopper fills the air. The Truth tosses CJ a flamethrower to torch the fields. Hurry!

Directions

Help The Truth Destroy the Weed

You have just five-and-a-half minutes until the cops arrive via chopper. (Note the onscreen timer labeled, "Cops Arrival" that counts down from 5:30 in the upper-right.) To burn a weed field, shoot flames over it until you hear the beep tone, then quickly move on to the next field. Listen for that tone! Don't waste any more time on a field once you hear it, even if the field isn't fully destroyed yet. The beep means you've shot enough flames, and now that weed patch can burn out by itself. You can also just run up and down the field, burning with abandon, for a less careful and often more efficient tactic.

> ### Strafing Burn
>
> A good technique is to set up at one end of the field, hold down the target button and the Fire button, then strafe along the entire length of the field. Work you way methodically from side to side, row by row.

When a good portion of the fields are smokin', The Truth hustles away to fire up a mini-bus he calls the Mothership. Finish burning the fields on your own. When you finally set fire to the last field, the onscreen message says, "Go and speak to The Truth." By all means, do so.

Speak to The Truth

Sprint to The Truth's Mothership, indicated by the blue blip on the radar map. When you enter the red marker next to the mini-bus, CJ points out the police copter now closing in for the kill. But The Truth gives CJ a rocket-propelled grenade (RPG) launcher.

Take Out the Chopper

The RPG works in first-person view. Move the targeting box over the helicopter above and fire. One or two well-placed shots should do the trick. Aim carefully, though. You have only 10 rockets, and time is running out!

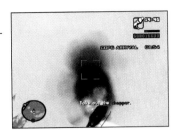

Get Inside the Mothership

After the chopper drops, find the Mothership mini-bus (under the blue marker) and hop inside. The Truth pulls over and asks you to take the wheel; he hasn't driven in 15 years. Follow the yellow blip on the map to drive the Mothership to the garage in San Fierro (which you won in the **Farewell, My Love...** mission).

On the way, CJ automatically calls Cesar and tells him to bring Kendl and meet in the garage. Continue the journey north and enjoy the illuminating conversation with The Truth. Learn about spy satellites, religious relics at the Pentagon, the insidious number 23, the uses of aluminum foil, and other critical survival skills.

To find the garage, head north through Foster Valley to the Doherty district on the east side of San Fierro. Follow the yellow radar blip to the garage location in Doherty. This mission finally ends when you drive into the red marker outside the garage.

Congratulations! You're finally out of the Badlands.

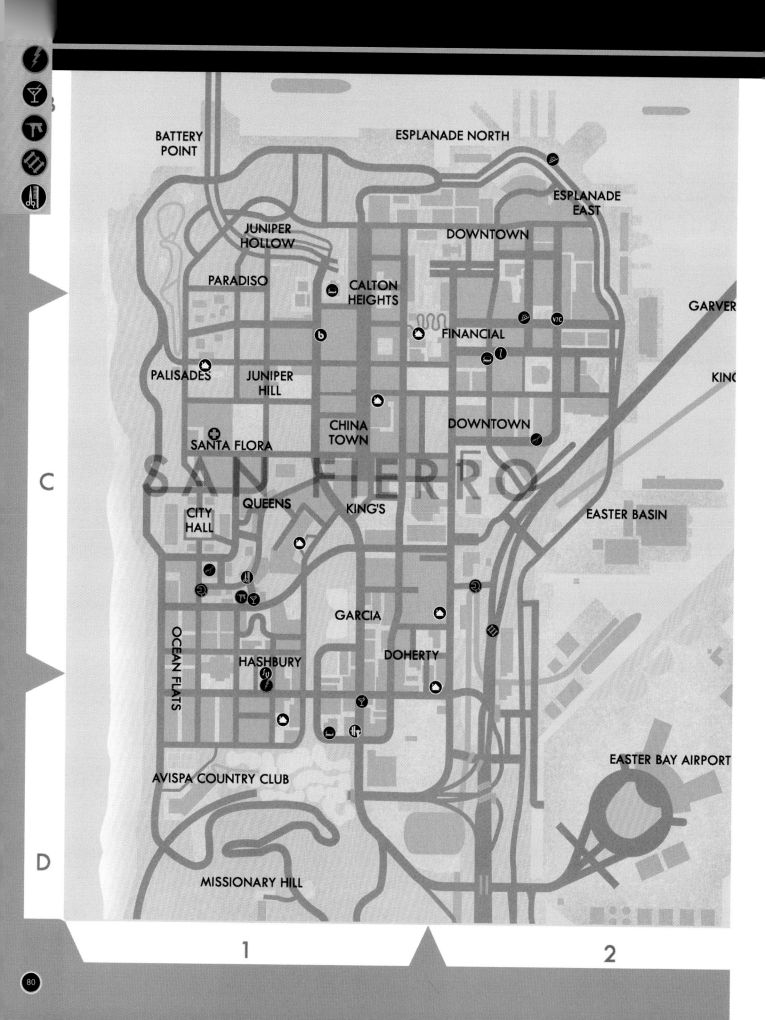

BATTERY
POINT

ESPLANADE NORTH

ESPLANADE
EAST

JUNIPER
HOLLOW

DOWNTOWN

GARVER

PARADISO

CALTON
HEIGHTS

FINANCIAL

KIN

PALISADES

JUNIPER
HILL

DOWNTOWN

SANTA FLORA

CHINA
TOWN

C

SAN FIERRO

EASTER BASIN

QUEENS

KING'S

CITY
HALL

GARCIA

OCEAN FLATS

DOHERTY

HASHBURY

EASTER BAY AIRPORT

AVISPA COUNTRY CLUB

D

MISSIONARY HILL

chapter 3
San Fierro

The steep hills of San Fierro rise in splendor above the chilly, choppy waters of San Fierro Bay. It's a bright cosmopolitan town with just enough seamy underbelly to keep things interesting. Here, far from the Grove Street hood, CJ settles into his newly-won garage—and along with The Truth, Cesar, and sister Kendl, he seeks a new start in a city by the bay.

RESTAURANTS

Burger Shot	Garcia	D1
Burger Shot	Downtown	C2
Burger Shot	Doherty	D1
Cluckin' Bell	Queens	C1
Cluckin' Bell	Downtown	C2
Well Stacked	Esplanade	B2
Well Stacked	Financial	C2

CLOTHING

binco	Calton Heights	C1
SubUrban	Hashbury	D1
Victim	Financial	C2
Zip	Financial	C2

POINTS OF INTEREST

Ammu-Nation	Queens	C1
Barbershop	Queens	C1
Gym	Garcia	D1
Hospital	Santa Flora	C1
Car Modification	Ocean Flats	C1
Car Modification	Easter Basin	C2
Tattoo Parlor	Hashbury	D1
Train Station	Easter Basin	C2
Bars/Strips		
Safehouses		

As in Los Santos, San Fierro features several overlapping mission strands that you can complete in a variety of ways. We'll organize the missions according to these strands, but you may (and in some cases must) move through the chapter by hopping between strands.

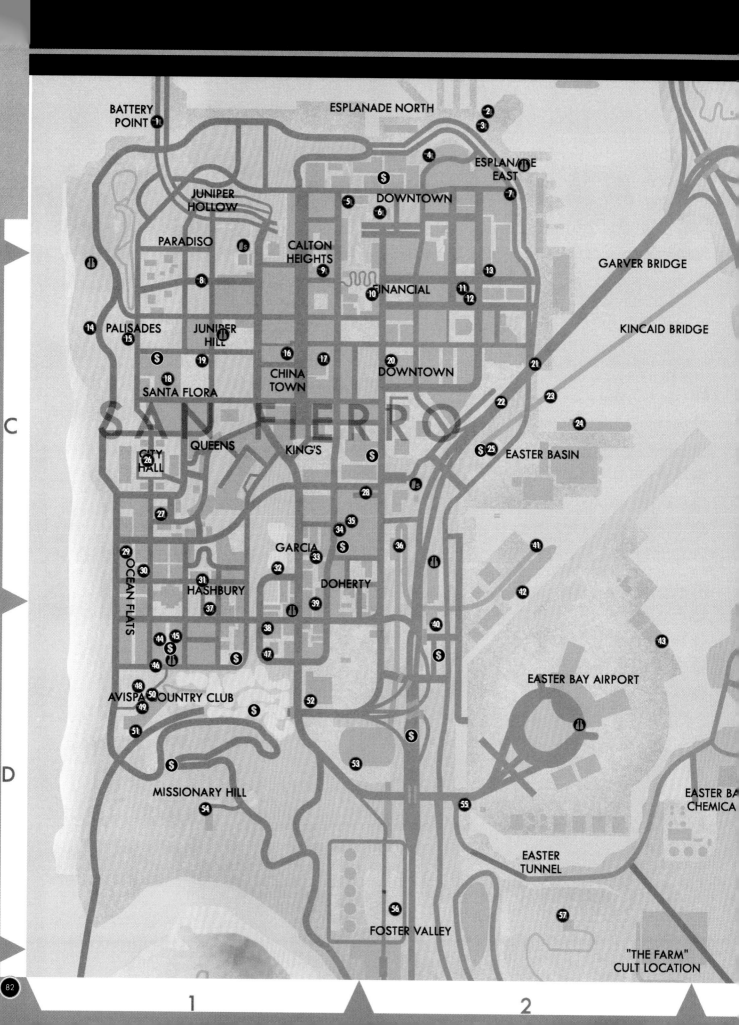

BATTERY POINT

ESPLANADE NORTH

JUNIPER HOLLOW

PARADISO

CALTON HEIGHTS

DOWNTOWN

ESPLANADE EAST

FINANCIAL

PALISADES

JUNIPER HILL

SANTA FLORA

CHINA TOWN

DOWNTOWN

GARVER BRIDGE

KINCAID BRIDGE

SAN FIERRO

QUEENS

KING'S

CITY HALL

EASTER BASIN

GARCIA

DOHERTY

OCEAN FLATS

HASHBURY

AVISPA COUNTRY CLUB

EASTER BAY AIRPORT

EASTER BAY CHEMICA

MISSIONARY HILL

EASTER TUNNEL

FOSTER VALLEY

"THE FARM" CULT LOCATION

Security Services

WEAPONS

1. **Tec-9** • Battery Point • Behind Jizzy's • **B1**
2. **Micro SMG** • Esplanade North • Next to the area where "Follow the Ped" mission occurred • **B2**
3. **Camera** • Esplanade East • **B2**
4. **Camera** • Esplanade East • On top of car carpark • **B2**
5. **Tec-9** • Calton Heights • In grassy area behind building • **B1**
6. **Camera** • Calton Heights • Behind church • **B2**
7. **Sniper Rifle** • Downtown • On roof of building across from Otto's Autos • **B2**
8. **Satchel** • Paradiso • Corner house, on concrete steps • **C1**
9. **Brass Knuckles** • Calton Heights • Parking lot behind apartments • **C1**
10. **Camera** • Calton Heights • **C2**
11. **Camera** • Financial • **C2**
12. **Parachute** • Financial • On top of Big Pointy Building (go inside) • **C2**
13. **Cane** • Financial • Outside Victim clothes store • **C2**
14. **M4** • Palisades • Back yard of home • **C1**
15. **Camera** • Palisades • Behind Tuff Nut Donuts • **C1**
16. **Camera** • Juniper Hill • In alleyway • **C1**
17. **Katana** • Chinatown • In back alleyway • **C1**
18. **Cane** • Santa Flora • Front doors of hospital • **C1**
19. **Camera** • Santa Flora • Parking lot next to hospital • **C1**
20. **Camera** • Downtown • Inside building • **C2**
21. **Parachute** • Garver Bridge • As the bridge approaches the water • **C2**
22. **Camera** • Garver Bridge • As the bridge leads into the city • **C2**
23. **Minigun** • Kincaid Bridge • On the bridge that leads to Las Venturas • **C2**
24. **Tear Gas** • Easter Basin • Cargo hold of aircraft carrier • **C2**
25. **Fire Extinguisher** • Easter Basin • Outside of the Xoomer gas station • **C2**
26. **Camera** • City Hall • Next to the steps • **C1**
27. **Camera** • Ocean Flats • Behind Cluckin' Bell • **C1**
28. **Chainsaw** • King's • On top of dilapadated building • **C1**
29. **Shovel** • Ocean Flats • Front yard of house • **C1**
30. **Cane** • Ocean Flats • Back yard of house • **C1**
31. **Katana** • Hashbury • Bottom of stairs near pedestrian walkway • **C1**
32. **Baseball Bat** • Garcia • On baseball diamond • **C1**
33. **Desert Eagle** • Garcia • In back lot • **C1**
34. **Pool Cue** • Doherty • Hidden behind fallen piece of concrete in construction yard • **C1**
35. **Flamethrower** • Doherty • Underneath fallen concrete slab in construction yard • **C1**
36. **Camera** • Cranberry Station • Inside train station • **C2**
37. **Cane** • Hashbury • In open part of concrete walkway • **D1**
38. **Chainsaw** • Doherty • Inside Final Build Contruction area • **D1**
39. **9mm** • Garcia • In alleyway • **D1**
40. **Shotgun** • Doherty • On top of corner building • **D2**
41. **Camera** • Easter Basin • On peninsula at water's edge, just north of airport • **C2**
42. **Flamethrower** • Easter Basin • On the freight liner next to the docks • **C2**
43. **RPG** • Easter Bay Airport • At water's edge, east of terminal • **C2**
44. **MP5** • Ocean Flats • Front yard of house near corner by fence • **D1**
45. **Cane** • Ocean Flats • On steps near front door of house • **D1**
46. **Cane** • Ocean Flats • In front yard of house • **D1**
47. **Camera** • Garcia • Next to Burger Shot • **D1**
48. **Chainsaw** • Avispa • On tennis court • **D1**
49. **Camera** • Avispa • Near the entrance to the Country Club • **D1**
50. **Golf Club** • Avispa • At the entrance to the Country Club • **D1**
51. **Stachel** • Avispa • Behind the Country Club • **D1**
52. **Nitestick** • Doherty • On crosswalk steps • **D1**
53. **Country Shotgun** • Foster Valley • ??? • **D1**
54. **Camera** • Missionary Hill • Rear of parking lot • **D1**
55. **Camera** • Easter Bay Airport • In grassy area of intersection • **D2**
56. **AK-47** • Foster Valley • Behind rocks at Foster Valley complex • **D2**
57. **Sniper Rifle** • "The Farm" • Inside small wooden shed • **D2**

POLICE BRIBES

- **Ocean Flats** • In alleyway behind houses • **D1**
- **Hashbury** • In an alleyway • **C1**
- **Calton Heights** • In a steep walkway • **B2**
- **Doherty** • In Shady Industries lot • **C2**
- **Avispa Country Club** • In the tunnel underpass • **D1**
- **Easter Basin** • On train tracks next to Xoomer station • **C2**
- **King's** • Near building under construction, behind fence • **C2**
- **Santa Flora** • In alleyway behind apartments • **C1**
- **Missionary Hill** • Along the windy road • **D1**
- **Doherty** • Back alleyway behind R.S. Haul • **D2**

BODY ARMOR

- **Ocean Flats** • Back yard of house • **D1**
- **Garcia** • In an alleyway behind Dom's • **D1**
- **Doherty** • Concealed from view9 behind Solarian Industries' building • **C2**
- **Esplanade East** • On concrete pier • **B2**
- **Palisades** • At the botom of a cliff • near the beach behind row of houses • **??**
- **Juniper Hill** • In Supa Save parking lot • **C1**
- **Easter Bay Airport** • Outside parking garage • **D2**

PAY 'N' SPRAY

- **Juniper Hollow** • **C1**
- **Downtown** • **C2**

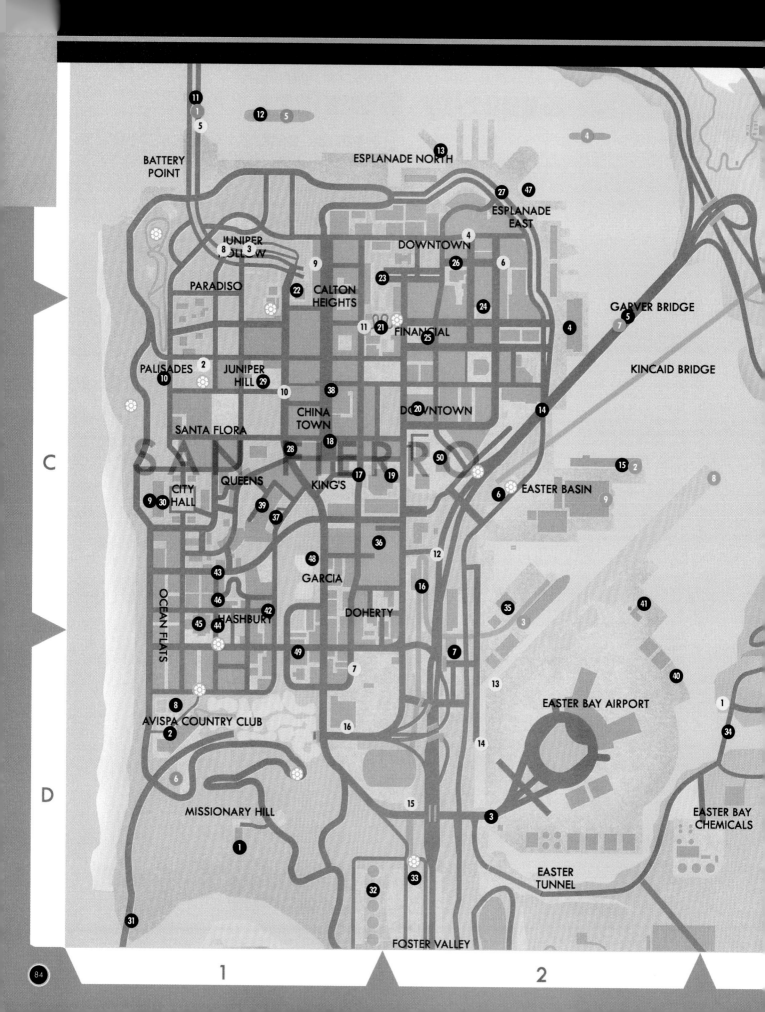

BATTERY
POINT

JUNIPER
HOLLOW

PARADISO

CALTON
HEIGHTS

ESPLANADE NORTH

ESPLANADE
EAST

DOWNTOWN

FINANCIAL

GARVER BRIDGE

KINCAID BRIDGE

PALISADES

JUNIPER
HILL

SANTA FLORA

CHINA
TOWN

DOWNTOWN

SAN FIERRO

EASTER BASIN

QUEENS

KING'S

CITY
HALL

GARCIA

DOHERTY

EASTER BAY AIRPORT

OCEAN FLATS

HASHBURY

AVISPA COUNTRY CLUB

EASTER BAY
CHEMICALS

MISSIONARY HILL

EASTER
TUNNEL

FOSTER VALLEY

Unique Attractions

▲ UNIQUE STUNT JUMPS

1. **The Panopticon** • Hit this banked mound of earth just to the west/northwest to land on the San Fierro Airport runway. • **D3**
2. **Santa Flora** • Jump off the backyard hillside to clear the buildings to the south. • **C1**
3. **San Fierro** • Use the large road/hill south of this walkway between the houses. Speed off the hill behind the houses, jumping over the border and landing safely. • **B1**
4. **Downtown** • Drive up Michelle's steps heading north and land on the building opposite the multi-story parking garage. • **B2**
5. **Battery Point** • Drive up the scaffolding over Jizzy's club and fly off the scaffolding next to the Gant Bridge north into the water (there's a beach nearby to exit the water). • **B1**
6. **Esplanade East** • Head east over these steps inbetween buildings and land at least on the rooftop beyond. • **B2**
7. **Doherty** • Drive through the dilapidated building and out of the Los Cabras compound and land in street. • **D1**
8. **Juniper Hollow** • Jump northeast over the large cement ramp. Use the hilly street prior to it to build up speed. Avoid the wall just before it and go up the ramp as straight as possible to land in the street below. • **B1**
9. **Calton Heights** • Use the street to the east of ramp between the homes (over tunnel) and jump into the street below. Since distance is the key, use the NRG-500. • **B1**
10. **Juniper Hill** • Utilize the supermarket parking lot ramp. Jump east across the road and land in the crowded alley. • **C1**
11. **Financial** • Jump the wooden stairs at the top of the winding street. • **C1**
12. **Easter Basin** • Jump the rusty ramp near Transfenders and land on the highway. • **C2**
13. **Airport** • Jump out of the San Fierro Airport using this ramp and land on the Easter Basin docks. • **D2**
14. **Airport** • Use this ramp to jump out of the San Fierro Airport heading west. • **D2**
15. **Foster Valley** • Use this ramp to jump east from the stadium parking lot and land on the freeway. • **D2**
16. **Doherty** • Jump the freeway using the pedestrian steps. You must clear the freeway. • **D1**

⬤ OYSTERS

1. Gant Bridge • Landing point for a USJ under the Gant bridge. • **B1**
2. Easter Basin • At the bow of the aircraft carrier in Easter Bay. • **C2**
3. Easter Basin • Under the stern of the large freighter in dock. • **C2**
4. San Fierro Bay • At the bow of freighter in the middle of the bay. • **B2**
5. San Fierro Bay • Under the west side of the ship that features in the Da Nang Thang. • **B1**
6. Missionary Hill • In a pool behind Avispa Country Club. • **D1**
7. Garver Bridge • Under the water support of the Garver Bridge. • **C2**
8. Easter Bay • End of the Easter Bay Airport Runway. • **B1**
9. Easter Bay • In an Easter Bay Dock. • **C1**

✿ FLOWERS

- **Easter Basin** • In between gas pumps in gas station • **C2**
- **Easter Basin** • Next to collapsed road, Downtown • **C2**
- **Foster Valley** • In plant bed on pedestrian walkway above road • **D2**
- **Calton Heights** • In grassy area of windy road • **C2**
- **Missionary Hill** • On hairpin turn • **D1**
- **Juniper Hollow** • Next to soda machine in Xoomer gas station • **C1**
- **Santa Flora** • In back yard of home • **C1**
- **Ocean Flats** • Next to dumpster • **D1**
- **Palisades** • Next to fountain in grassy area • **B1**
- **Palisades** • In front of houses • **??**
- **Hashbury** • On grassy area near war monumnet • **D1**

📷 PHOTO OPS

1. Next to tower on top of Missionary Hill. • **D1**
2. Domed Tower in Avispa Country Club. • **D1**
3. Airplane sign at the entrance to Easter Bay Airport. • **D2**
4. Clock face on Clock Tower next to Garver Bridge. • **C2**
5. East on Garver Bridge between supporting structure. • **C2**
6. On top of rotating X at the Xoomer gas station in Easter Basin. • **C2**
7. Between tanks at Shady Industries in Doherty. • **D2**
8. Above tennis court nets in Avispa Country Club. • **D1**
9. West of the domed building in City Hall. • **C1**
10. In the middle of the Donut at Tuff Nut in Palisades. • **C1**
11. Before the first support tower of the Gant Bridge when leaving San Fierro. • **B1**
12. Mast on the Da Nang Boat north of San Fierro. • **B1**
13. Conning tower on submarine in Esplanade North. • **B2**
14. One of the Kincaid Bridge girders on the San Fierro side. • **C2**
15. Aircraft carrier bridge in Easter Basin. • **C2**
16. Cranberry Station above and between the train tracks. • **C2**
17. Highest point in tower of building in Kings. • **C1**
18. Above the ground and next to building in China Town, across from the Trolley Station. • **C1**
19. Top of skyscraper in Kings, between the two middle flag poles. • **C1**
20. Sculpture inside Zombotech building Downtown. • **C2**
21. In the middle of the curviest road in Calton Heights. • **C1**
22. Next to rotating burger at Burger Shot in Juniper Hollow. • **B1**
23. Lamppost in the middle of the road at tunnel entrance in Calton Heights. • **B1**
24. Aerial on top of skyscraper in the Financial District. • **C2**
25. Baseball player statue in the park downtown. • **C2**
26. The side of tall building in the Financial area. • **B2**
27. The sign at the entrance to Pier 69 in Esplanade North. • **B2**
28. At the top of the chimney of a building in Queens. • **C1**
29. Above the entrance to the Supa Save in Juniper Hill. • **C1**
30. The middle two columns on the front of City Hall. • **C1**
31. Above the bridge leaving San Fierro through the southwest. • **D1**
32. The second northernmost, round tower in Foster Valley. • **D1**
33. High above the plants in the middle of a Foster Valley roof garden. • **D2**
34. The bridge connecting Red County and the Panopticon. • **D3**
35. High above the curved lip of the dry dock in Easter Basin. • **C2**
36. At the top of the tall crane at Doherty Construction Site. • **C1**
37. Entrance to the Vank Hoff Park Hotel in Queens. • **C1**
38. Middle roof in China Town Gateway. • **C1**
39. The back of the Vank Hoff Park Hotel in Queens. • **C1**
40. The gas storage tanks on the eastern edge of the Easter Bay Airport. • **D2**
41. The Air Traffic Control Tower Antenna at the Easter Bay Airport. • **C2**
42. The Hashbury & Garcia Joint Festival Banner. • **C1**
43. The movie theater in Queens. • **C1**
44. High above one of the center gravestones in Hashbury. • **C1**
45. The Ocean Flats Church spire. • **C1**
46. The Hippy Shopper store in Hashbury. • **C1**
47. The rock formation in the bay of Esplanade East. • **B2**
48. Above home plate in the park in Garcia. • **C1**
49. The Final Build Construction sign in Garcia. • **D1**
50. High up between the two tall buildings Downtown. • **C2**

THE COURIER MISSIONS

Cesar's boys have a sharp eye out for couriers who handle the drug transactions between Big Smoke's gang back in Los Santos and a shady crime syndicate based in San Fierro. There are two types of courier missions.

COURIER mission 1

Big Smoke's Cash (Monday and Friday)

Twice a week, on Mondays and Fridays, CJ gets a call from Cesar informing him that Big Smoke's courier is leaving Los Santos with six packages of money. The courier drives a big Patriot SUV marked by a red blip on the map. He starts out

at Big Smoke's house in the Idlewood area of Los Santos and drives the long route up to the Pier 69 district in San Fierro.

Respond positively, then intercept the courier before he reaches his destination. The courier carries six packages of cash. Each time you ram the Patriot, he drops a package of $300, so you can nab all $1800 if you ram him six times. If the Patriot is destroyed, the mission ends with no more cash packages available.

COURIER mission 2

Yay Courier (Wednesdays and Saturdays)

Twice a week, on Wednesdays and Saturdays, CJ gets a call from Cesar informing him that a motorbike courier is leaving the desolate Back O' Beyond region south of San Fierro. This is the second half of the drug transaction. The courier has a backpack filled with "yay", destined for Big Smoke in the Idlewood area of Los Santos. The courier's motorbike is marked by a red blip on the map.

Respond positively, then intercept the motorbike courier before he reaches his destination. Your best bet is to find a motorbike, quad bike, or some other good off-road vehicle, as the courier's route cuts cross-country. Catch him quickly, because if you hit him with gunfire, you can puncture the courier's backpack and a steady stream of white leaks out behind him. This reduces the amount of cash you earn by scoring the backpack when you finally gun down the courier.

THE GARAGE STRAND

This strand is comprised of three missions, the second of which is a C.R.A.S.H. errand. CJ and Cesar, with a guiding hand from Kendl, try to establish a legitimate business and expand their base of operations.

Wear Flowers in Your Hair

● Gameplay Element Introduced:
The city of San Fierro

When CJ enters the old Xoomer garage, Cesar and Kendl are waiting to share in the joy of garage ownership. Yes, the place is a wretched disaster, but Kendl challenges CJ to do something constructive for once. The Truth knows some good mechanics and offers to take CJ to meet a couple of guys.

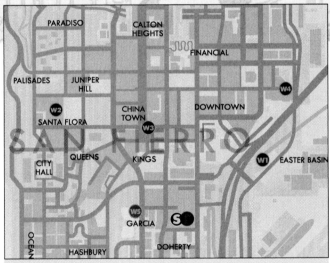

- **S** Start (CJ's garage)
- **W1** Jethro
- **W2** San Fierro Medical Center
- **W3** Dwaine
- **W4** Police Station
- **W5** Zero
- **●** Finish (CJ's garage)

Directions

Get in Car and Drive to Jethro's Job

Jethro works at a garage in the Easter Basin area, just northeast of your location in Doherty. Drive to the blue blip on the map and listen to The Truth's running commentary. When you enter Easter Basin, he explains that it's Vietnamese gang territory, very dangerous. When you arrive at Jethro's garage, it's a Xoomer too!

Jethro should fit in quite nicely at your new place. Drive into the red marker and obey the onscreen message. Jethro crawls out from under a tow truck and is happy to join you. CJ explains his plan to do car mods, lowriders, and all that stuff.

Drive to the Hospital

Next, The Truth directs you to the hospital in the Santa Flora district, west of here. Follow the red-cross icon on the map to the hospital. When you arrive, The Truth makes you wait until a slow-moving van drives past. What's that all about? He won't say. Then he's ready to look for Dwaine, who's working a Hotdog van at the tram terminal in the Kings district to the east.

Find Dwaine's Hotdog Stand

Follow the blue radar blip and listen to The Truth's odd explanation for his hospital visit—something about a sub-dermal neurophone. When you reach the Hotdog stand in Kings, honk the horn again and bring Dwaine on board. He wants in, but he has some business to take care of first, and drives off in his Hotdog van. Next stop: the Downtown police station.

Visit the Police Station

Follow the blue police icon to the Downtown station. When you arrive, the Truth starts talking weird again, and we see the same slow-moving van pass by. Very strange. Your next destination is an electronics shop run by a guy named Zero. The Truth thinks he can help you.

Visit Zero's Shop

Follow the blue radar blip southwest through Kings into the Garcia district to find the shop named Zero RC. Drive into the red marker and honk the horn. Zero sits out front, and hops in your car. The Truth introduces you and says Zero's the man you should talk to about any electronics needs.

Back to the Garage

Now follow the yellow radar blip back to your garage in Doherty, where Dwaine's hotdog van is now parked. CJ talks to his new crew and introduces them to Cesar, then Kendl lays out her theory of property development—buy a dump, fix it up, sell it, get rich. Sounds good!

Note that CJ's garage is your contact point for the rest of this strand. Its location is marked on the map by the "CJ" icon.

Cell Phone Call: Zero

After the scene, CJ ends up outside, and he gets a phone call from Zero. Zero's landlord is selling the building where he has his electronics shop. CJ tells Zero he might be interested in investing in the property. When the call ends, a Property icon (a green house) appears on your map, representing Zero's building. You can go there at any time and purchase it, which opens a new strand of missions.

NEW MISSION STRAND OPEN!

*Completing the **Wear Flowers in Your Hair** mission and then purchasing the property where Zero's shop is located opens up the Zero mission strand and its first mission, **Air Raid**. (See The Zero Strand section later in this chapter for details on purchasing Zero's building.)*

BETWEEN MISSIONS

Beef Up!

Use time between missions to explore San Fierro and build up your skills. Check the map for Cobra Martial Arts, the workout gym down in the Garcia district; check out the dance action at the clubs in town; drive wild in the Corvin Stadium or down south to Flint County; and consider an upgrade to your clothes and hair. If you have cash to spare, shop at the local Ammu-Nation, too. And don't forget to eat! CJ needs to maintain his energy.

555 WE TIP

This mission brings back CJ's C.R.A.S.H. connection, but uses the garage as a base of operations. Walk into the red marker outside CJ's garage. This triggers a phone call from Officer Tenpenny. He wants you to frame the San Fierro D.A. who's trying to nail him and Pulaski. The scam: Plant some weed in the D.A.'s car, then make an anonymous call to the "555 WE TIP" crime-fighters hotline. Despite his hatred for Tenpenny, CJ is more than happy to take down a D.A., and agrees to the plan.

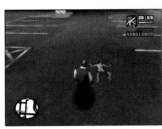

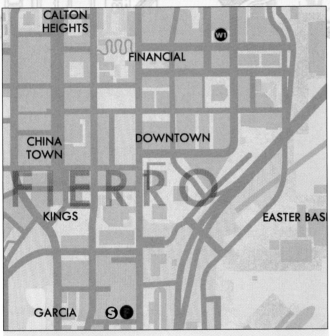

S Start (CJ's garage)

W1 Vank Hoff Hotel

● Finish (CJ's garage)

Follow the Valet to the Underground Parking Lot

The valet-driven car has a red marker overhead and is indicated by a red blip on radar. Follow the car around the corner to the underground garage, staying tight on its tail.

Take Out the Valet and Grab His Uniform

Inside the garage, wait for the valet to exit the car. Chase him down quickly and terminate his pitiful life. Pick up the valet's uniform.

Kill Unseen

Don't let anyone see you murder the valet. Otherwise, you'll pick up a one-star Wanted Level, which foils your plan.

Go to Valet Car Port and Wait

Run back to the valet port, the spot where the valets wait outside the hotel. When you approach, one of them says: "you must be the new guy" and tells you to get in line.

Walk into the nearby red marker to learn that the D.A. is driving a blue Merit. Your goal: Be the first valet to reach his car!

Identify and Enter the D.A.'s Car When it Arrives

Watch the street carefully. One of the other valets helps by pointing out the D.A.'s car as it approaches. When you see the dark blue car, hustle over to it. If another valet gets inside the Merit first, yank him out!

Directions

Head Downtown to the Vank Hoff Hotel

Get a car and follow the yellow radar blip to the Vank Hoff Hotel in the Financial district near the heart of Downtown. Drive into the red marker to learn that the hotel oper-

This hotel operates a valet service. The D.A. will be dropping his car off here shortly.

ates a valet service. The D.A. will be dropping off his car here shortly. As you watch, a valet picks up a car to park.

Hurry to the Garage to Plant the Drugs!

Once you've got control of the D.A.'s car, a four-minute timer starts counting down. Hurry! Head back to your garage in Doherty. Just follow the yellow blip on the map. Avoid running over pedestrians or running into police vehicles. If you get a Wanted Level, the mission will be failed—your cover will be blown. When you arrive, park the car in the garage. The drugs are automatically planted inside the car. Now you must return it to the valet's underground parking lot.

Park in the Marked Parking Space

You have to beat the clock, but don't be too reckless because the D.A. will notice if his car is anything but spotless. Avoid damage at all costs! Keep under control, accelerating hard only when you see a long, clear stretch ahead. If you ding up the car, you must take it back to your garage for repair. Follow the yellow blip to the garage and drive carefully down the underground ramp. Park in the space with the red marker, then exit the car.

Leave Car Port and Call 555 WE TIP

Follow the yellow radar blip up the ramp and out of the car port to another red marker across the street. CJ calls the 555 WE TIP hotline and the cops make the bust on the D.A.

Officer Tenpenny will be so pleased. Now jack a car and follow the "CJ" icon to head back to your garage in Doherty.

> **NEW ODD JOBS AVAILABLE!**
> *Completing the 555 WE TIP mission opens up the Valet Parking odd job. Return to the marker at the valet car port between missions to trigger valet missions. For details on this, see Valet Parking in our Odd Jobs chapter.*

GARAGE mission 2

Deconstruction

- **Gameplay Element Introduced:** Demolition
- **New Vehicles Introduced:** Cement truck, Bulldozer

the story

Back at CJ's garage, the new crew is working hard, and the cars are looking fine. But some construction workers up the hill have been disrespecting Kendl. Big mistake on their part—now CJ plans to "discuss" the situation with them. As a side benefit, you might just get extra room to expand your business, too.

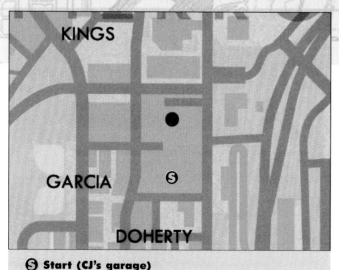

KINGS

GARCIA

Ⓢ

DOHERTY

Ⓢ **Start (CJ's garage)**
● **Finish (Construction site)**

Directions

Destroy All Six Portables Before the Police Arrive!

Sometimes a man's work is fun, and this is a good example. Your job here is to really mess things up. Use construction machinery to "deconstruct" all six of the site's portable buildings (each one marked with a green overhead marker and shown as a green blip on radar) and kill the foreman. Your ultimate goal is to scare off the construction firm.

This mission gives you three destruction options: a crane, a bulldozer, and some explosive barrels. If you're feeling really creative, you can try all three.

Don't Bulldoze Barrels!

Don't run your bulldozer into the explosive barrels sitting near some of the portables. The resulting explosion will cripple the bulldozer and kill you. A good tactic: before you bulldoze, run around the site and shoot all the barrels to blow them up, just to be safe.

Option 1: Use Bulldozer to Destroy Portables

Walk into the construction area and climb aboard one of the site's bulldozers. Next, simply drive it headlong into marked portables, splintering them into smithereens.

What Counts in a Crunch

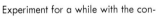

Once you destroy the first portable, a timer starts counting down from three minutes, which is how long you have until the police arrive. Every time you smash a portable, the game helpfully notes how many portables are left to destroy.

Option 2: Use Crane to Destroy Portables

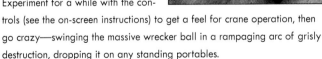

To use the crane, find and enter the red marker on the ground near the tall, yellow structure. CJ takes control of the huge piece of equipment.

Experiment for a while with the controls (see the on-screen instructions) to get a feel for crane operation, then go crazy—swinging the massive wrecker ball in a rampaging arc of grisly destruction, dropping it on any standing portables.

Option 3: Use Explosive Barrels to Destroy Portables

Look around the site. Notice the red barrels sitting next to some of the portables? Yes, those are **explosive** barrels. Shoot to detonate each one, damaging any nearby portable.

Bury the Foreman and His Toilet

After the last portable falls, the site foreman emerges from one of the mobile toilets. When he sees the destruction, he slinks back into the john to hide. Using a bulldozer, find his mobile toilet (the one with the red marker overhead) and push it into the nearby ditch.

Finally, hop in a cement truck and back it up to the ditch, ending up in the spot with the red marker. The truck automatically fills the ditch with cement. Ha! No more disparaging comments about passing women from **this** crew.

Cell Phone Call: Jethro

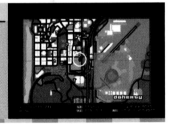

Soon after his rampage ends, CJ gets a call from Jethro, who tells you about the Advanced Driving School just up the road from the garage in Doherty, south of CJ's garage. As Jethro so eloquently puts it: "**Dude!** Like, **whooaaah!**"

NEW MISSION STRAND AVAILABLE!

*Completing the **Deconstruction** mission and answering the first phone call from Jethro opens up the Driving/Racing strand, marked by a red "S" icon on your map, and its first mission, Driving School. For more information on Driving School and Tournament Races, refer to our **Odd Jobs** chapter.*

THE SYNDICATE MISSIONS

$ Cash Available in Strand:
$94,000

 # Respect Gained in Strand:
285

This long strand of missions takes you into that seamy underbelly of San Fierro we mentioned earlier. It also introduces you to the San Fierro source of all the junk flowing south into Los Santos.

SYNDICATE mission 1
Photo Opportunity

⊙ Item Obtained:
Camera

 # Respect Gained:
15

the story

Return to CJ's garage to trigger a call from Cesar, who's got a tip about a Ballas car coming into town for a big drug deal. He's tracking the vehicle at the Mulholland intersection. CJ realizes this is their chance to ID the supplier and rushes off to meet Cesar.

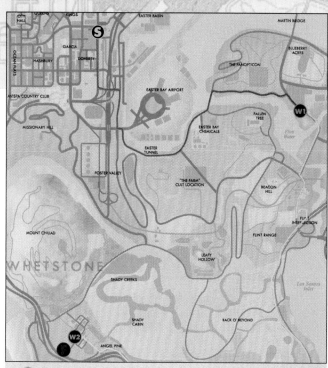

- **Ⓢ Start (CJ's garage)**
- **W1 Meet Cesar**
- **W2 Lovin' A Loan (roof)**
- **F Finish (Gas station)**

Directions

Pick up Cesar

Jack a car and follow the blue blip on your radar south out of San Fierro, then east toward Blueberry in Red County. You finally hook up with Cesar under a FleichBerg billboard, just southwest of Blueberry.

Hop in Cesar's car and drive. Cesar says the Ballas were headed toward Angel Pine. Ah, your favorite town.

Head Down to Angel Pine

Here's another long trip. Tracking the yellow blip on your maps, set a course for Angel Pine, clear down in Whetstone County to the southwest. When you finally arrive, drive into

the red marker next to the "Lovin' A Loan" building.

Get Up on the Roof

Get out of the car and climb the stairs to the roof of the building. IMPORTANT: Read the next section **before** you walk into the red marker on the rooftop!

Photograph All Four Targets

A meeting of the drug-running Loco Syndicate is about to take place. You must take four close-up photos of the Syndicate's attendees, but they appear only briefly as they arrive. If you miss just one of the photo opportunities, you fail the mission! So pay attention to where you must aim the camera, zoom in, and shoot.

Walk into the red marker on the roof to trigger the photography sequence:

First Shot: Leave the camera in its starting position and zoom in straight down the parking alley ahead with the green trash can. When Cesar says, "There it is, holmes!" Ryder's pickup truck appears and parks in the alley.

Zoom in on Ryder a bit, and wait until he gets out of the truck and the red marker appears over his head. As he walks away from the truck, he pauses several times, so zoom in tight until the onscreen message reads "Take the photograph," then shoot a close-up photograph of Ryder.

Camera Clues

Pay attention to the onscreen messages. The game prompts you to zoom in further if your shot isn't tight enough. When the zoom and aim are sufficient, the message reads, "Take the photograph."

Second Shot: Keep the camera view focused on the alley with the green trash can where Ryder just parked. A second car pulls in and parks. Repeat the photography procedure to get a good close-up of this mustachioed gentleman in a striped shirt. Cesar says his name is T-Bone Mendez.

Third Shot: As T-Bone Mendez steps out to the street, a brown sedan pulls up from the right and the driver, a man in a suit, steps out. Take his picture! He moves toward T-Bone and the parking alley.

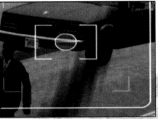

Fourth Shot: Next, a Broadway vehicle moves down the street from the left. This is the trickiest shot. Another unfamiliar man gets out on the passenger side. Zoom in and snap that picture, quickly, while he's facing you! But you'd better hurry, as he turns away within seconds. If you fail to get a face shot, you fail the mission.

After you get all four photos, CJ and Cesar automatically climb down from the roof and drive away to a gas station to discuss what they just saw. Cesar says you should split up and meet back at the garage, and then he drops you off. Mission passed! Before you return to San Fierro, make sure to save your game. Step out onto the highway, jack any kind of vehicle, and make the long trek back to your garage in San Fierro.

SYNDICATE mission 2

Mission: Jizzy

 # Respect Gained:
20
$ Cash Gained:
$3000

the story

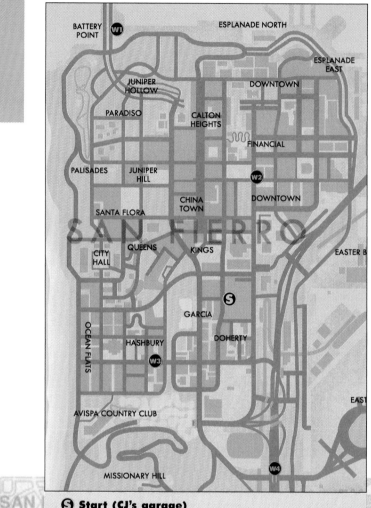

- **S** Start (CJ's garage)
- **W1** The Pleasure Domes
- **W2** Hotel
- **W3** Rival pimp
- **W4** Van beneath overpass

Directions

Go to Jizzy's Club

Drive north to The Pleasure Domes Club. Its location is marked with the "L" icon (for Loco) on the map. The club is **beneath** the Gant Bridge in the Battery Point district, so turn right onto the last side street before you get onto the actual span of the bridge.

Pull into the red marker to trigger a scene in which CJ offers his services to Jizzy, trying to win his confidence. Jizzy has several tasks for CJ to perform.

Drive Jizzy's Girl Downtown

Get in the Broadway and follow the yellow radar blip through Juniper Hollow and Calton Heights to the Downtown district. Enjoy the intellectual conversation between CJ and the nice girl on the way. When you drive into the red marker Downtown, the girl hops out and Jizzy gives you another errand via his car phone—ice a rival pimp who's been messing with Jizzy's girls.

Waste the Pimp in Hashbury

Follow the yellow blip south to the Hashbury district to the location in front of a restaurant. The rival pimp has a red marker overhead when you arrive, and he's hassling one of Jizzy's girls. Run over the pimp with your car if you can, or just hop out and gun him down. Do not perform a drive-by or you risk killing the girl. If she dies, it's mission over!

Easy enough! But when you call Jizzy, he has another job. Some violent psycho in Foster Valley has been killing Jizzy's girls. Go check it out.

Save Jizzy's Girl

Head east through Garcia and Doherty to the freeway, then follow the yellow blip south toward Foster Valley. When you arrive on the scene, the two "punters" are abusing one of Jizzy's girls outside their van under the freeway overpass. A Health bar for the girl appears onscreen—get there as quickly as possible before her health dwindles too far.

Hop out of the car and rush to her rescue, gunning down both punks. Get back in Jizzy's pimp-mobile to report your success. He has one last job for you. A customer wants to take one of Jizzy's girls (the one you dropped off Downtown) out of the business. The fool wants to give her a life of legitimacy. Kill him!

Get to the Downtown Hotel

Drive all the way back north to the Downtown district and follow the yellow blip to the hotel. When you arrive, pull into the red marker to see the target escort Jizzy's girl from the hotel entrance to a white limo with a backup SUV carrying a bodyguard.

Eliminate the Target and His Protection

The limo and Huntley SUV take off. Follow and pull alongside the SUV first to open fire. Or, drive ahead of the convoy and shoot them with rockets as they approach. Keep firing until you destroy the bodyguard's car, then pull up next to the limo. Chase and spray it with gunfire until it, too, is ablaze. The heavy limo has a hard time climbing hills. This gives you more time to put a lot of holes in it as it slowly ascends steep inclines. Note that you can blow up either car first; the order doesn't matter. CJ calls Jizzy with the report, and the pimpmeister is pleased. Now head back to the The Pleasure Domes Club, the "L" icon on the map.

The next time you get out of the car, Woozie calls. He'd like you to drop by his "little betting shop" in Chinatown sometime to talk. This puts a new "W" icon on the map, representing Woozie's place. We'll cover the Woozie strand of missions later in this chapter. For now, head back to The Pleasure Domes, following the "L" icon on the map.

NEW MISSION STRAND OPEN!

Completing Jizzy opens up the Woozie mission strand and its first mission, Mountain Cloud Boy.

SYNDICATE mission 3

T-Bone Mendez

 # Respect Gained:
20

$ Cash Gained:
$5000

When CJ returns to The Pleasure Domes, Jizzy is having a lively discussion with T-Bone Mendez about percentages. He introduces CJ to T-Bone, who suddenly gets an urgent phone call about a Syndicate cash run that's been ambushed. CJ gets roped into the rescue mission.

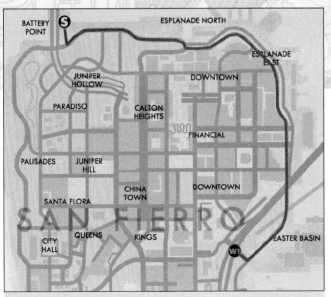

S The Pleasure Domes Club
W Ambushed van

Directions

Get to the Ambushed Van

Get a vehicle and rush south to the Downtown ambush site, marked by the blue blip on the map. As you arrive, the thieves try to escape by splitting up on four motorbikes, each carrying a package of stolen cash. CJ automatically hops on a nearby motorcycle.

Chase Down Bikers and Collect All Packages

Follow the red radar blips! The thieves split up almost immediately after you give chase, so you must do some backtracking around San Fierro to retrieve all four packages. Pull up closely to each biker and either gun him down (drive-by style) or just snatch the package from his hands.

Nab the Packages Before the Bikes Reach Rendezvous Destination

After exactly five minutes on the game clock, any remaining thieves start gunning their bikes toward a rendezvous point. You must collect all four packages before they reach it.

Return Packages to The Pleasure Domes Club

When the final package is recovered, return to Jizzy's place under the Gant Bridge, now indicated by the yellow blip on your radar.

Mike Toreno

 # Respect Gained:
25
$ Cash Gained:
$7000

the story

Back at the The Pleasure Domes Club, an upset T-Bone is sure that someone with knowledge of the operation is hitting the Syndicate's runners. Then his fear is confirmed. Mike Toreno, the Loco Syndicate leader, calls from a van making a yay run. The van's been hijacked, and Toreno's trapped in the back! CJ joins Jizzy and T-Bone as they exit to find the boss.

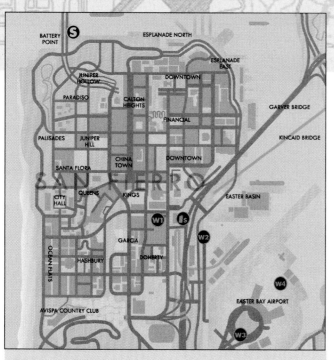

S The Pleasure Domes
W1 Construction site
W2 Easter Basin docks
W3 Airport security entrance
W4 Stolen van halts
Js Pay 'n' Spray

Directions

Follow Toreno's Clues

The first part of this mission is a pure timed driving test. Mike Toreno will try to talk you to his location by giving clues based on what he hears. But his cell phone battery has only five minutes of juice left. As the mission begins, an onscreen timer starts counting down from 5:00.

Get in the blue-marked car with T-Bone and start heading south. T-Bone reports that Toreno can hear seagulls and heavy machinery. The first guess is the construction site in Doherty right next door to CJ's garage, and a yellow blip appears on the map there. Drive to that location as fast as you can!

Go to Docks in Easter Basin

When you arrive at the first landmark in Doherty, Toreno says he can hear a truck reversing. He reports busy truck traffic, a freight depot perhaps. CJ suggests the van is in the dock area. Next stop: The docks in Easter Basin. Step on it!

To the Airport, Quickly!

When you reach the Easter Basin area, Toreno hears gunfire, and theorizes that the hijackers just shot their way through a security gate. CJ knows there's no heavy security at the docks, but there is at the air-

port's freight depot. Accelerate to the new yellow blip on the map at Easter Bay Airport—and hurry, Toreno's cell phone battery is almost dead.

When you reach the airport security entrance, which leads to the runways, you find dead security guards and a breached gate. Drive inside. T-Bone says the "tag" should work now, and a Signal bar appears onscreen. He tells you that Toreno hid a transponder in the coke shipment.

Use Toreno's Signal Bar to Find the Van

The transponder signal intensifies as you get closer, so watch the signal bar. When it rises, you're getting warmer, but if it lowers, you're moving away from the van. Head left or

right after you pass through the gate and climb the ramp up onto the tarmac. Hurry! When Toreno's phone battery dies, so does he.

Kill Those Goons

Once you finally spot the van, you face another dilemma. It has a two-motorcycle escort. Pull up beside the small convoy and help T-Bone ice the bikers. When the enemy group stops, more goons pile out of the

van and open fire. Circle the group and fire away, or hop out and fight on foot until you wipe them out. When the last thug drops, T-Bone lets Mike Toreno out of the van.

Easy on the Van

Remember, Toreno's trapped inside the van. If you direct too much gunfire at the vehicle and it explodes, Toreno dies and you fail the mission.

Destroy Van and Escape

Toreno's a bit on edge, and wants to torch the van and split. Step back and open fire on the van with your heaviest weapon. When it blows, it's time to run. Your Wanted Level is up to three stars! Get in the nearby

Stretch limo and wait for Toreno and T-Bone to get inside. You cannot use any of the aircraft nearby, as they will not accommodate all three of you.

Drive-up Service

If Toreno and T-Bone don't follow you to the car after you destroy the yay-filled van, you might be too far away to trigger their "following" instinct. Just get in and drive over to them. They'll hop right in.

Escape the Airport

The airport police are now in hot pursuit. Burn rubber across the tarmac and follow the yellow radar blip to flee the airport. Drive around the terminal to find the ramp leading down, then follow that road back

through the security gate and out of the airport.

Find a Pay 'n' Spray to Lose the Heat

Unfortunately, you're not home free yet—you still have a three-star Wanted Level. Follow the green spray paint can icon on the map to the nearest Pay 'n' Spray up north

on the border between the Doherty and Downtown districts (also indicated on our mission map on the previous page). It's a wild ride, with both Toreno and T-Bone hanging out of the car, spraying gunfire at pursuing police cruisers. When you reach the Pay 'n' Spray, drive inside for a new engine and paint job.

Return to the Pleasure Domes

Now take a leisurely drive back to Jizzy's sex club up at Battery Point under the Gant Bridge. On the way, Toreno interrogates CJ about his past and checks his wallet. When you get to the The Pleasure Domes Club and drive into the red marker, Toreno compliments you on a good job, then tells you to scram—mission passed.

Drive back to your garage in Doherty. Save your progress when you get there!

Cell Phone Call: Jizzy

When you step into the red marker outside your garage, Jizzy calls and says his business associates need a little assistance. He tells you to meet T-Bone at the gas station next to the docks in the Easter Basin; he's waiting for you in a four-door sedan. When you hang up, a blue blip appears on the map at the Easter Basin destination.

Outrider

Weapons Obtained:
Sniper Rifle, RPG
Respect Gained:
25
Cash Gained:
$9000

the story

Head northeast to Easter Basin, following the blue radar blip. Find the Xoomer service station where the designated four-door sedan sits with a blue marker overhead. When CJ approaches, nobody's inside, and the place seems deserted. But when he gets in the car, T-Bone pops up and nearly strangles him, asking who he works for. Then Mike Toreno appears and says there's a shipment to pick up. What kind of shipment do you suppose it is?

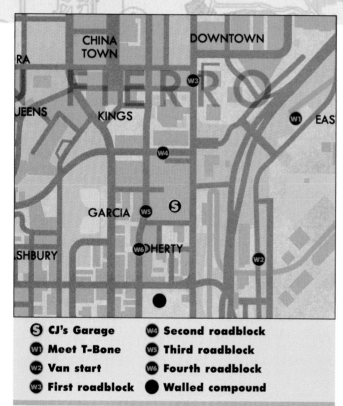

- **S** CJ's Garage
- **W1** Meet T-Bone
- **W2** Van start
- **W3** First roadblock
- **W4** Second roadblock
- **W5** Third roadblock
- **W6** Fourth roadblock
- **●** Walled compound

Pick up Escort Bike

It's important to acquire the Sniper Rifle and Rocket Launcher near the van, then hop onto the motorbike under the blue marker. Your job is to destroy several roadblocks before the van reaches them. Take a shortcut around the back of Shady Industries, across Cranberry Station, and head for the first roadblock. This lets you gain time to destroy the other roadblocks.

Rocketeer Tip

Although the Rocket Launcher's rate of fire is fast for its type, keep in mind that you have only 20 rockets of ammo. So don't get crazy with your trigger finger!

Use the Rocket Launcher to Destroy First Roadblock Before Van Arrives

Turn north and speed ahead of the van toward the first roadblock, marked as the red blip on the map. Stop a fair distance away from the police units blocking the street, then produce your Rocket Launcher and sling a few rockets into their midst. After eliminating the roadblock, hop on your bike and proceed to the next one.

Clear Second Roadblock

Zip south through the destroyed roadblock, then continue in this direction down the road toward the next roadblock. This one's tougher to clear. You can launch rockets into the cruisers and take out cops on the ground, but two snipers shoot at you from high up on the freeway overpass to the left. Fight fire with fire by whipping out your Sniper Rifle to eliminate the distant shooters.

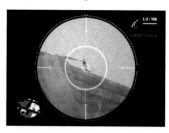

Directions

Drive to Van's Location

Follow the yellow blip south to the van, which is also in the Easter Basin district. Drive into the red marker. Toreno tells you to get out and grab a bike. He's flying in a yay shipment and he wants to make sure it gets to the crack factory, so he's assigning "outriders" to escort the van.

Clear Third Roadblock

Toreno's van is probably right on your tail by now, so hustle around the corner toward the third roadblock. Again, sling rockets to clear the cruisers and ground troops, then use the Sniper Rifle to pick off cops stationed high on the walls to the left.

Destroy Final Roadblock

The final roadblock lies directly ahead, a short distance down the street from the third roadblock. After destroying it with rockets and cleaning up with Sniper Fire, hop back on the motorbike (or take off on foot)

and escort the van into the high-walled compound marked by the yellow blip on the map—near the border of the Garcia and Doherty districts.

Once the van is inside, CJ tells the driver he plans to draw the cops away from the crack factory. You pass the mission, but you now have a three-star Wanted Level, so the pursuit will be intense and relentless. Fortunately, the safety of your garage in Doherty is not far away. Note also that a "C" icon suddenly appears on your radar, right on top of your garage location. Guess who's in town? Drive out of the compound and make the run to your garage.

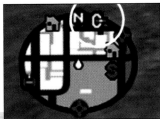

Snail Trail

🔫 **Weapon Obtained:**
Sniper Rifle

When you walk into the red marker outside your garage, C.R.A.S.H. Officers, Tenpenny and Pulaski, wait in the office. It seems a journalist is poking into their lucrative little side business and plans to meet with an informant today. Tenpenny wants both the reporter and his contact silenced—permanently, of course.

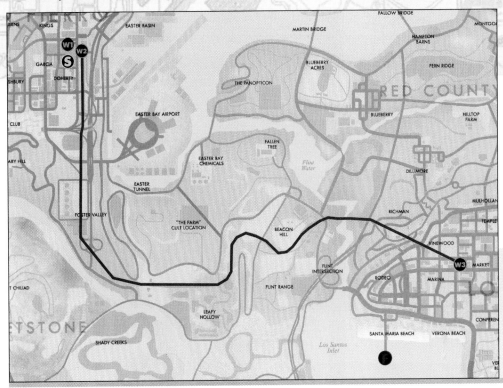

- **S** CJ's garage
- **W1** Sniper Rifle (in pipe)
- **W2** Cranberry Station
- **W3** Market Station
- ● Reporter meets informant
- ＼ Train route

Find the Sniper Rifle at the Construction Site

The C.R.A.S.H. guys thoughtfully leave a weapon to make your job easier. Find the Sniper Rifle marked by the green blip on your radar. It's right next door, hidden in the now-abandoned construction site—the same one you terrorized back in the **Deconstruction** mission. Look for it tucked inside a section of sewer pipe. Pick up the weapon and you get a message that the reporter is at Cranberry Station.

Find Reporter at Cranberry Station, Follow Him to the Informants Meeting

Get a vehicle and drive southeast toward the yellow blip on your radar. It's not far to Cranberry Station, but soon you get another message.

The Train is Arriving—Hurry!

You don't have much time before the reporter leaves on the train. But don't worry—you can't make it, no matter what you do. As you approach, the train pulls away, heading for Market Station in Los Santos. Drive onto the tracks and follow it!

Stay on Track

Avoid swerving side to side across the rails as much as possible. Some of the parallel tracks have oncoming trains or just end at barriers. Bumping over the rails reduces your control.

Follow That Train!

Stay on the train's caboose all the way to Market Station. It's a long haul south through Foster Valley, then east through Flint County. Just stay on the tracks! You can't get lost. When the train finally arrives at its destination, the reporter prepares to exit.

Follow Reporter Out of Station

Hop out of your vehicle and climb up onto the station platform. If the reporter suspects he's being tailed, he'll get spooked and abandon the interview. In fact, a "Spook-o-Meter" appears onscreen. Keep an eye on it as you follow him; if the meter gets too high, you get a warning message, and need to back off a bit. Remember that your target has a red marker overhead, so it's fairly easy to keep him in sight, even from a distance. Don't get too far away either, or you'll lose the reporter and fail the mission.

Follow Reporter's Cab

The reporter climbs the station stairs and heads toward the sidewalk to hail a cab. You need a car to follow him from this point. Jack one quickly, then park and wait. When the reporter gets into a cab, follow it.

If you lose direct sight of it, just check your radar, where the reporter's cab appears as a red blip. He takes some evasive turns around the Market Station area—he's paranoid, no doubt—so stay sharp.

Eventually, the cab heads west through Vinewood and Rodeo, then zig-zags southwest to Santa Maria Beach before driving out onto the pier.

Assassinate the Reporter and His Contact

The reporter is ready to meet his contact. Hop out of your vehicle and wield the Sniper Rifle. Both targets stand and chat in front of the Brown Starfish Bar and Grill. Zoom in and nail one of them with the first shot. The other target will start running, making him difficult to hit via the scope of the Sniper Rifle. Better to switch to another weapon, run him down, and finish him. Mission passed.

After you finish the job, make the long trek from Santa Maria Beach north to Doherty. Depending on the day of the week, you might get a phone call from Cesar reporting a courier mission to hit.

SYNDICATE mission 7

Ice Cold Killa

 # Respect Gained:
30
$ Cash Gained:
$12,000

Step into the red marker outside CJ's garage between 20:00 and 6:00 for this night mission. CJ runs inside and frantically searches his trunk. When Cesar asks if he's okay, CJ explains that Woozie left him a message. If CJ can get Jizzy's phone after the pimp's made the call to learn the location of a meeting, CJ can call the number, too. He can then ambush the Ballas pushers from Los Santos. Cesar gives CJ a pistol with a silencer for the hit.

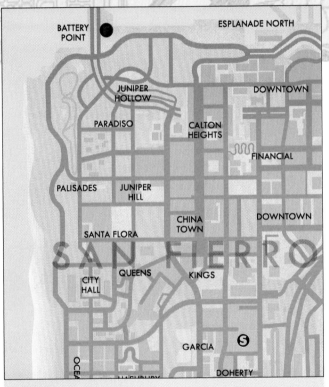

$ CJ's garage
● The Pleasure Domes

Directions

Visit Jizzy at The Pleasure Domes Club

Hop in a vehicle and follow the yellow radar blip north to the Pleasure Domes in Battery Point under the Gant Bridge. When you step into the red marker outside the club, a door guard won't let CJ through the doors. You'll have to find another way inside. Do not target the guards and try to enter forcefully. If you do so, the guards will open fire.

Enter the Club Via Skylight

Note that the club is directly beneath the bridge. Go around the left side of the building. See the scaffolding that runs up the bridge support? Climb its wooden ramp until you're directly over the Pleasure Domes building, then jump down onto the roof and enter through the open skylight.

Sneak Down to Jizzy

Inside, follow the catwalk down to a platform, then find the stairs and continue down to the next level. Keep working your way downward from one level to the next until you find and enter the red marker.

This triggers a sequence where Jizzy announces he is "about to make that special call." He then dials the number of the answering machine that gives the location of the Syndicate meeting with the Ballas.

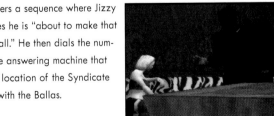

CJ needs that phone so he can hit redial and listen to the meeting location message. He approaches Jizzy and puts a gun in the pimp's face, but Jizzy's boys start a gunfight and Jizzy makes a run for it. A gunfight erupts inside the club. Try

to take out the gunmen without taking damage, or run directly to the exit. Take your time; Jizzy won't leave the club until CJ exits the club, too.

Hunt Down Jizzy and Retrieve the Phone

Cap the gunmen and exit via the front door of the club. Jizzy and his man hop into a car and speed off. Take the nearby Stretch limo and follow. Pull up beside Jizzy's car and open fire until the car crashes or explodes and both targets drop dead. Run to Jizzy's body and grab his phone. CJ automatically calls Cesar and asks him to meet at Pier 69.

Pier 69

⊘ **Accomplice:**
Cesar
⊕ **Respect Gained:**
40
⑤ **Cash Gained:**
$15,000

the story

Drive to the red icon on the map marking Pier 69 in the Esplanade North district along San Fierro's northern waterfront. Cesar calls down from the roof of a building, telling CJ to come up and join him.

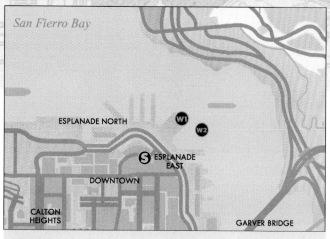

San Fierro Bay

ESPLANADE NORTH

Ⓦ W1
Ⓦ W2

Ⓢ ESPLANADE EAST

DOWNTOWN

CALTON HEIGHTS

GARVER BRIDGE

Ⓢ **Meet Cesar**

Ⓦ **T-Bone**

Ⓦ **Speedboats (chase Ryder)**

Directions

Go Upstairs and Meet Cesar

Go around the right side of the building and climb the stairs at the back to meet Cesar. He shows CJ how T-Bone's security is already in place on rooftops all around the pier.

Painless Descent

A jump from the rooftop hurts a bit, but it takes a while for Cesar to catch up. Better to take the stairs down.

Woozie's Triad gang members are deployed down at Pier 69's side entrance, ready to help. But they start moving toward the roof too soon! T-Bone's rooftop sentries will have them outmanned! If the Triad leader is killed, you fail the mission.

Clear Roof So Triads Can Proceed

Use the Sniper Rifle to pick off all six Syndicate guards on the Pier 69 rooftop across the road—three on the right, three more on the left. Do it quickly! As Cesar points out, the Triads are getting cut to pieces.

When the final rooftop guard drops and T-Bone arrives with reinforcements. Then Ryder shows up. Toreno is nowhere to be seen at first, but then his inbound helicopter appears. Unfortunately, Toreno's aerial approach blows the ambush; Toreno

can see the bodies on the roofs! After dropping tear gas canisters, he bugs out and the meeting blows apart as everybody runs.

Find and Kill T-Bone!

Descend the stairs from your rooftop, making sure Cesar follows you. Sprint across the road to Pier 69; switch from the Sniper Rifle to a more suitable weapon, like the AK-47, as you go. The quickest way to reach T-Bone is to run along the outer edges of the pier to reach him at the end while avoiding several of the enemies who are located in the center of the pier area.

Use Speedboat to Chase Down Ryder

Ryder takes the lead boat, so crawl into the second craft (the one with the blue marker) and give chase. Use the red radar blip to track Ryder if he gets too far ahead. When you catch his boat, pull alongside and waste him, drive-by style.

When you finally reach the waterfront, T-Bone tries to rush behind a planter on the dock. Nail him! Watch as CJ and Cesar combine to finish him off, blasting him into the water. Ryder then makes his escape by diving over the railing into the bay.

Kill Ryder

Time for some payback for betrayal. Cesar can't swim, so this one's up to you. Run straight for the railing and climb over it to drop into the cold bay below. Swim after Ryder, following the red marker over his head. Ryder swims toward a pair of speedboats moored near a tiny island.

When you finally ice Ryder, Cesar calls and says he'll see you back at the garage. Your speedboat is fast and the waterways are light on traffic, so steer the craft all the way back west and look for a dock in Easter Basin. Then jack a car and drive back to Doherty.

SYNDICATE mission 9

Toreno's Last Flight

- **Weapon Obtained:**
  RPG
- **Respect Gained:**
  50
- **Cash Gained:**
  $18,000

When you return to CJ's garage, Woozie calls with hot information. Toreno is about to move his merchandise via helicopter. In fact, the drug kingpin is at a Downtown helipad right now. Let's go!

Directions

Rush the Helipad and Stop Toreno

Get into a vehicle and drive north-ward to the Downtown helipad, following the yellow blip on the radar. When you arrive, Toreno's goons open fire from the ground and up on the helipad. Use your vehicle to run down attackers in the street, then hop out and return fire.

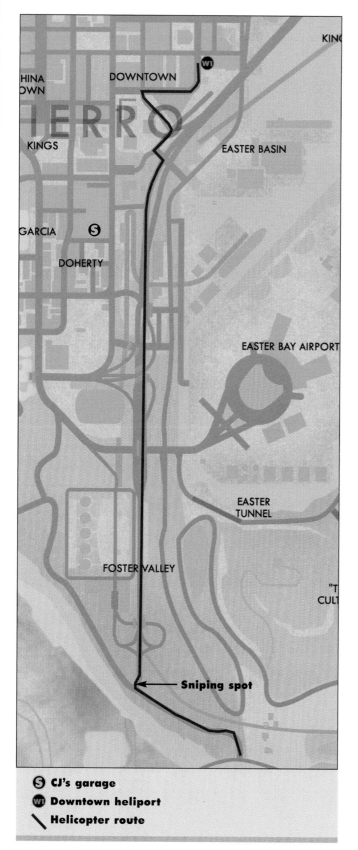

S CJ's garage

W Downtown heliport

**** Helicopter route

Run around the right side of the structure and fight your way down the hill to the stairway leading up to the helipad. (You see Toreno's van, its back door hanging open, just past the stairs.) As you approach the first landing, a cutscene shows Toreno's helicopter taking off. Too late! The chopper's airborne!

Get Rocket Launcher to Bring Down the Helicopter

Continue upstairs onto the helipad, wipe out the guards, and grab the Rocket Launcher spinning on the near-left corner of the pad, then hustle back downstairs and jack a good, fast vehicle. There's a motorcycle near the entrance to the area. Note that a "Heli Health" bar now appears on screen. Your goal is to lower that bar to zero somehow.

Sniping From Afar

If you have difficulty staying alive as you run and gun your way to the helipad, then snipe the majority of the baddies around the helipad, on the helipad, and those that rush toward you when the shots ring out from the road across the street to the west of the helipad.

Shoot Helicopter Down From Freeway

Head south down the street that runs in front of the helipad. Follow as it curves west, then take the first left. Veer downhill, jog left and then right, and zoom up the entrance ramp onto the freeway. (Follow the red blip on your radar if you get disoriented.)

Once you're heading south on the freeway, you should see the helicopter up ahead. It will follow the freeway down past Foster Valley. Accelerate well past the chopper, then quickly dismount your vehicle and wield the Rocket Launcher.

Gauge the helicopter's flight path and position the targeting box slightly ahead of where the craft will fly, then pop the Fire button just as the bird flies into box. Try to get four or five well-targeted shots as the chopper flies past you and down the freeway.

If you continue to miss the helicopter, hop back in (or on) your vehicle and speed down the freeway ahead of the chopper again. One of the best places to snipe the copter is at the T-intersection at the end of Foster Valley. Drive ahead of the

copter, get out of your vehicle, and wait for the copter to arrive. When it does, open fire! Note that the copter will hover in place at this location for quite a few seconds. When it goes down, CJ says, "Excellent. Toreno can't have survived that fireball."

Pick an Icon, Any Icon

Your next move depends on which missions you've passed so far. There's one more mission in this Syndicate mission strand, **Yay Ka-Boom-Boom**, but you cannot attempt it unless you've also completed all five of the Woozie-related missions, too.

If you haven't done so yet, then head for the "W" icon on your radar and complete the Woozie mission strand. However, if you've got $30,000 to spare (and you should by now), you can visit Zero's shop in the Garcia district and buy the building, thus becoming Zero's landlord and opening up the optional (but very fun) Zero strand of missions (see our **Odd Jobs** chapter for details).

MISSION PASS (1 OF 2)

*Completing **Toreno's Last Flight** gives you one of the two prerequisites needed to open the Yay Ka-Boom-Boom mission later.*

Yay Ka-Boom-Boom

Gameplay Element Introduced:
Car Bombs
Respect Gained:
60
Cash Gained:
$25,000

Back at the garage, Cesar congratulates CJ on a job well done, but CJ isn't celebrating. It seems his Los Santos hood is splintering apart over the yay, and now he's got the murder of a homey on his hands. Cesar insists CJ has done something good, but Woozie points out the dealing isn't over until you take out the crack factory.

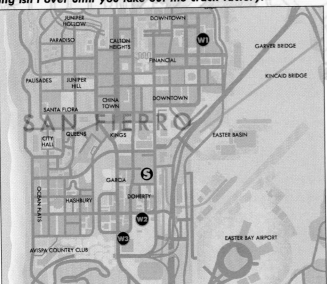

- **S** CJ's garage
- **W1** Bomb Shop
- **W2** Entrance to compound
- **W3** Ramp into crack factory

PREREQUISITE NEEDED!

*This mission is available only after you complete **Toreno's Last Flight** from the Syndicate mission strand, plus the final mission of the Woozie mission strand, **The Da Nang Thang**. In other words, you can't play this mission until you've completed the entire Woozie mission strand and all of the previous Syndicate strand missions.*

WHERE'S MY ARSENAL?

Note that you'll enter this mission with only those weapons that were acquired during the Da Nang Thang mission. Go to a local Ammu-Nation and stock up beforehand.

Pick Up the Wired Car From Bomb Shop

After the cutscene, CJ gets a call from one of Woozie's workers. He's rigging up a car with explosives to destroy the crack factory. Grab a car and follow the yellow blip north to the Downtown bomb shop.

AK Job

If you don't have an AK-47 yet, drop into your local Ammu-Nation and pick one up for this job.

Drive into the red marker outside the shop. Inside, CJ takes the wheel of the wired car and learns it has a delayed timer, giving him time to get out after triggering the detonation sequence.

Eliminate the Guards at the Crack Lab

Drive south, following the yellow blip to the entrance of the Syndicate crack factory, a walled compound just south of CJ's garage.

The front gate is closed, but if you do a Drive-by (or just get out of the car) and gun down the two gate guards, the gate opens so more guards can pour out in support. Take advantage of the moment and rush your attackers, clearing the area, then wheel the wired car into the compound yard.

Use Ramp to Enter the Crack Lab

Drive around to the back of the yard. As you approach a pair of white fuel tanks, turn right and steer the car straight up a short ramp and into the warehouse interior.

Park Car Near Chemical Containers

Once inside, turn left and stop. Get out and move through the warehouse, gunning down any guards you can find to clear the area. Return to the wired car and drive through to the red marker near the tall chemical tanks on the crack factory's back wall. Walk up to the bomb and activate it.

Evacuate Building Before Bomb Explodes

Time to jet! You have exactly 40 seconds to fight your way out of the warehouse. Watch out for the shooter on the catwalk high on the right side. Shoot him first, then take aim at other targets on the run. Don't be distracted by anything, no matter how "interesting." Run out of the warehouse through the nearest doorway. If you make it out in time, the factory goes up in a fireball.

Escape Via Main Gate

But it ain't over yet... You still need to escape the walled compound. More angry guards rush you or take potshots from atop containers and crates. There's no timer, so don't be hasty. Move carefully through the

yard, using cover and side-rolling around corners. A good Assault Rifle is worth its weight in gold right about now.

One last obstacle remains, however. As you approach the main gate, it slowly slides shut. You're trapped!

Use Car to Ramp Over Wall

Fortunately, a car enters just as the gate closes. Jack a vehicle (the one with the blue marker overhead) and run the gauntlet to the back of the yard again, then turn around and drive as quickly as possible into the decrepit building with the collapsed ceiling.

The fallen ceiling forms a perfect ramp that allows you to shoot onto a stack of crates and bounce over the compound wall into the city street. Drive back to CJ's garage in Doherty to complete the mission.

After CJ hangs up, a new "**?**" icon appears on your radar, indicating the location in Tierra Robada. You are free to go there now, but proceed to the next section if you haven't completed the Zero strand of missions yet.

 Cell Phone Call: Mystery Man

Soon CJ gets a phone call from a mysterious man who claims to be a friend with information about Sweet. He invites CJ to visit his ranch in Tierra Robada—across the Garver Bridge, head south, he says. The "friend" gets a tad demanding by the end of the conversation.

---

new mission strand

THE ZERO STRAND

(S) **Cash Available in Strand:**
$15,000

Once Zero calls CJ to say his shop's landlord is selling the building, you can purchase the property for $30,000. If you have the funds, go to the building's location (marked as a green house icon) in the Garcia district of San Fierro. Walk into the spinning green house marker just outside the front door of Zero's shop and buy the property.

The shop now appears as a "**Z**" icon on the radar. You get a cell phone call from Zero to confirm the purchase. (He wasn't around for the deed signing because he was "on a reconnaissance mission deep within enemy territory.") This officially opens up the Zero strand of missions.

ZERO mission 1

Air Raid

(car) **New Vehicle Introduced:**
RC Baron
(S) **Cash Gained:**
$3000

Go to the "Z" icon on the map and walk into the red marker outside Zero's shop. CJ enters and greets Zero, who is not exactly cheery today. Berkley is back! A mortal enemy ever since Zero beat him in the Science Fair, Berkley now seeks cruel revenge. When Zero's radar alarm goes off, Zero vows to fight to the end, and drags CJ up to the roof.

the story

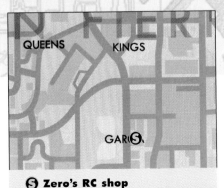

(S) **Zero's RC shop**

Use the Minigun to Eliminate Enemy Threats

The game perspective switches to first-person shooter. Berkley has launched a full-scale attack on Zero's three rooftop transmitters. CJ calls the attacking mini-biplanes "just toys," but they drop very real bombs. Start firing the minigun, and start nailing the incoming bogies. Meanwhile, Zero runs around with a fire extinguisher, trying to save his transmitters.

Use the minigun to eliminate the enemy threat.

A Time counter (counting down from 3:10) and a Signal bar appear onscreen. You must defend Zero's transmitters and keep their signal alive for three minutes to avoid failing the mission. The mini-biplanes go down easily, but they're hard to hit. Watch for them passing directly overhead as they make bombing runs. If they approach in squadrons of four or five, strafe back and forth across their formation. Do not shoot Zero! If he dies, you fail the mission.

Victory!

If even one transmitter survives the three-minute attack, you win the mission and Zero shouts out one of our favorite lines in the game: "As long as we have opposable thumbs, **we will fight you!**" After the victory, walk into the red marker outside Zero's shop for the next mission.

ZERO mission 2

Supply Lines

$ Cash Gained:
$5000

---

the story

Berkley has humiliated Zero by hanging him on a closet hook... by his underwear. CJ helps Zero down, and then helps him plot revenge. The plan: Use a prototype mini-bomber called the RC Baron to knock out couriers (both vans and bikes) delivering goods for Berkley's mail order business.

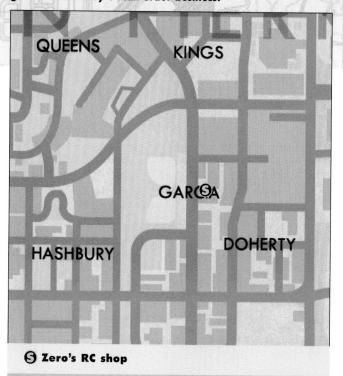

QUEENS
KINGS
GARC$A
HASHBURY
DOHERTY

$ Zero's RC shop

Directions

Destroy the Couriers!

Five couriers make deliveries around San Fierro for Berkley's business. Red blips indicate their locations on your map. Your RC Baron starts with only five and a half minutes of fuel, indicated by the onscreen Fuel gauge, so you must work quickly.

Fly to the nearest red blip—preferably the one to the west of your starting location (the courier on the bike). Dispose of him, then go for the van nearby and to the east around the corner. The courier has a red marker overhead, making it easy to spot him below. Drop the RC Baron behind the courier and open fire, following close if the target manages some evasive maneuvers. If you nail a van, the driver bails out. Shoot him, too! As the onscreen message says, "Punish him for his war crimes!" Death to courier drivers!

Courier Worrier

Berkley's couriers are armed and will return fire if you don't take them out in your first pass. Watch out for the crisscrossing power lines above San Fierro streets, as well.

Continue the hunt. All in all, you target three vans and two bike couriers. After the fifth Berkley courier suffers the blazing vengeance of Zero, you have one last task.

Fly Back to Zero's Roof

Hurry! If the Baron runs out of fuel before reaching Zero's roof, you fail the mission. Speed your RC Baron back to its base, which is marked now by the yellow blip on the map. When you get close, you can see

the red marker on Zero's roof. Fly the Baron into the marker to complete the mission. You end up back on the street outside the Zero RC shop. Walk into the red marker to trigger the last Zero mission.

New Model Army

🚗 **New Vehicle Introduced:**
RC Goblin

💲 **Cash Gained:**
$7000

Zero girds his loins for battle—a final, apocalyptic showdown with Berkley and his robotic minions. Zero will drive a remote-controlled car called the Bandit across No Man's Land to Berkley's HQ. Your job is to fly a Goblin mini-helicopter in support, helping the Bandit reach its destination.

💲 **Zero's RC shop**

Directions

Support Zero's Bandit

Your Goblin has a magnet that can pick up metal objects. You have exactly eight minutes to complete this mission, with an onscreen timer counting down from 8:00. Zero has three Bandit mini-cars, but he can

drive only one at a time. The current Bandit has a blue marker overhead, and a blue blip indicates its location on your radar map.

Remove Bridge Barrel

When the mission starts, Zero's first Bandit starts moving down the road toward Berkley's base. The first impediment is a barrel blocking the bridge. Lower the Goblin down over the barrel and pick it up so the Bandit can proceed.

Remove Road Barrel

Unfortunately, Berkley has a Goblin, too. He uses his mini-copter to block the path of your Bandit. First, he drops another barrel on the road. Go pick it up to free the Bandit again. You can destroy Berkeley's helicopter with a bomb. Hit him near his base as he's hovering to collect a can.

Destroy Berkley's Tanks

The next obstruction is a gap in the road that must be bridged. Here's where it behooves you to ignore Zero's whining demands. If you bridge the gap as he insists, his Bandit continues moving up the road right into the gun sites of Berkley's Tiger mini-tanks.

Three Tigers lurk along the route leading to Berkley's base. When Zero's Bandit gets into range, they open fire and inflict serious damage. Our advice is to leave the Bandit stuck at the impassable river for a while. Instead, hustle back to the base to pick up a bomb, then return and drop it on the first enemy tank lurking along the road that leads to Berkley's base. Repeat for the other two Tigers along the road.

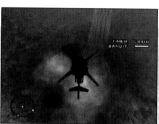

Bridge River with Plank From Base

With the Tigers eliminated, you can relax a bit knowing that Zero's Bandit won't be destroyed while you're rushing back and forth from your base. Now pick up one of the five long planks on the ground in your base. Carry it back to the gap, and drop it over the river to bridge the chasm.

Clear Final Obstacles

Now you're essentially home free. Pick up another plank from your base and bridge the second gap up ahead on the road. Then fly along the route and clear any other barrels dropped by Berkley's Goblin. Watch as Zero's Bandit rolls into Berkley's base, and listen to Zero gloat.

Asset Acquired!

Completing the **New Model Army** mission solidifies the Zero RC store as a solid, rent-paying tenant. This property will now generate revenue up to a maximum of $5000. Make sure you collect it regularly by returning to the location and moving through the "$" icon in front of the store.

Bombs Away

Bombs give you a one-drop tank knockout. You can drop other objects, like barrels, onto Tigers to damage them, as well, but bombs give you the best bang for the buck.

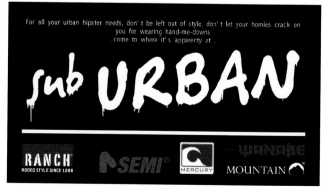

THE WOOZIE STRAND

⑤ **Cash Available in Strand:**
$45,000

Respect Gained in Strand:
100

Wu Zi Mu, or Woozie to his friends, heads a San Fierro-based gang known as the Mountain Cloud Boys, a branch of the Chinese Triad family. Their home is in China Town, and some eccentric characters populate the group. You must complete this strand in order to advance from San Fierro into the next area of the game.

WOOZIE mission 1

Mountain Cloud Boys

👤 **Accomplice:**
Woozie

Respect Gained:
10

⑤ **Cash Gained:**
$5000

Follow the "W" icon on the map to Chinatown and walk into the red marker outside Woozie's place. As CJ heads upstairs to meet Woozie, a guard tells him about "the boss's curse"—he's blind! CJ wonders how that can be, given the car racing last week.

When CJ enters the office, Woozie greets CJ as a friend and explains how things work in his organization. (Here CJ makes an amusing attempt to test Woozie's blindness.) He reintroduces himself as the boss of the Mountain Cloud Boys, and says his job is to mediate disputes between local Triads without bloodshed. For example, Woozie plans to meet with a Triad who failed to "show face" at the last Tong meeting, gathering of all the local families. He asks CJ to join him.

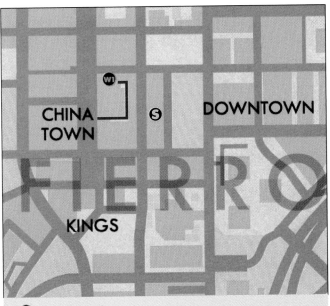

⑤ **Woozie's place**

Ⓦ **Storehouse**

╲ **Alley to Blood Feather storehouse**

Directions

Take Woozie to the Tong Meeting

Get a car, make sure Woozie gets inside too, and drive around the block to the storehouse owned by the Blood Feather Triad. (Follow the yellow radar blip if you get lost.) On the way, Woozie says some small-time Vietnamese gangs have been making trouble recently, and their newfound courage makes him nervous. When you arrive and drive into the red marker, Woozie looks for a loose cobble on the sidewalk.

As Woozie leads the way in, a group of men suddenly sprint out of the nearby alley. Woozie senses that something is not right. As the blind man proceeds around the alley corner, hand out in front of him, CJ is a bit confused. Follow him as he leads you through an open security gate—one that Woozie says in usually locked.

Noodle Up

Grab a bite to eat at one of the food stands in the alley. CJ can always use an energy boost.

You soon find the reason for all the confusion: a brutal ambush! The Blood Feathers lie slaughtered, wiped out. A Triad reports it was a Vietnamese ambush, then a carload of Da Nang boys, one of the local Vietnamese gangs, smashes through the gate behind you and hops out, ready for battle.

Escape Alley Trap and Protect Woozie

Woozie's health bar now appears onscreen. If he dies, the mission ends in failure. Open fire on the attackers up the alley. Woozie helps, inflicting decent damage for a blind guy. Keep moving forward, trying to lead Woozie out of the alley as you fight through Da Nang attackers.

A sniper opens fire at the bend, and another squad of Da Nang attackers rush down the alley. Woozie stays low and tells you to take out the sniper. Gun down the attackers first, then target the sniper who is posted up high on the left side of the alley near the J-shaped steam pipe that protrudes from the wall.

When you finally get near the alley entrance, CJ and Woozie automatically hop into the car parked there. More Da Nang boys drive up and block the alley, but CJ backs into them, smashing his way out.

Let Woozie Destroy the Attacking Da Nang Cars

Time for a little car-to-car shootout fun; Woozie provides drive-by firepower while you drive. Two red Da Nang Thang cars chase you. Spin around and let the enemy pull up beside you so Woozie can blast them with remarkably accurate gunfire, uh, for a blind guy. Add your own drive-by skills, too, of course. Say, did we mention that Woozie is blind?

Drive Woozie Back to His Place

After you dust both Da Nang boys' cars, follow the yellow radar blip back to Woozie's headquarters. When you drive into the red marker outside, Woozie gives you $5000 worth of appreciation for your help. Watch that blind guy **sprint** into his building—with one hand held out, of course.

WOOZIE mission 2

Ran Fa Li

 # Respect Gained:
15
$ Cash Gained:
$6000

Back at Woozie's place, CJ meets Shuk Foo Ran Fa Li, an eloquent gentleman who runs the Red Gecko Tong on the West Coast. Someone has sent word that a Vietnamese crime family, the Da Nang boys, is moving to the United States. Woozie thinks this may explain the bold attack by the local Vietnamese on the Blood Feather Triad. The shuk foo wants a package retrieved from an airport drop—a package he considers "most important to the matter at hand." CJ offers to make the pickup.

Directions

Pick Up Car From Airport Car Park

Grab a vehicle and head south, following the yellow radar blip to the Easter Bay Airport. Find the red marker at the top of a ramp leading down into the airport's parking garage. If CJ needs some armor, there is some located just outside the entrance to the airport's parking garage.

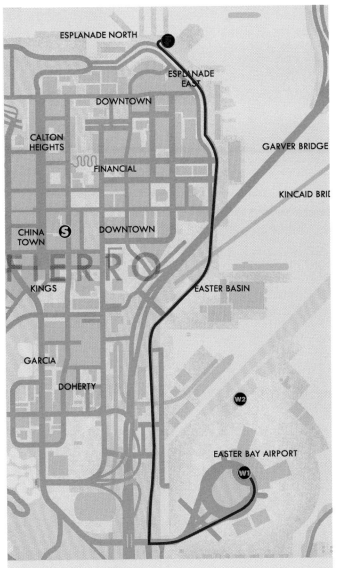

S Woozie's place
W1 Airport parking entrance
W2 Sabre (underground parking)
● Lockup garage
＼ Path

Get the Sabre!

Drive straight down the ramp and past the intersection until you see the striped "No Entry" sign, then take a left into parking area "D." The target car is a red Sabre with a blue marker overhead. Abandon your car and get into the Sabre. Guess what? It's an ambush.

It's an ambush, the Da Nang Boys are covering the exits!

Drive the Sabre Back to Triad Garage

Your next goal is to take the Sabre back to the designated garage, next to Woozie's HQ in China Town. However, the Da Nang boys block some of the obvious exits with delivery trucks. Keep following the exit signs to the ramp, but drive down the entry ramp, going against the direction of the road arrows.

A few Da Nang boys attack on foot. (As you pass, they shout, "That's our property!") Simply blow past them, proceeding through the parking garage gates and out into the airport circle. Follow the circle around to the ramp leading up to the freeway, dodging around Da Nang roadblocks.

○ Damage Meter

A Sabre Damage meter appears onscreen; if it drops to zero, you lose the mission. Duck into a Pay 'n' Spray if the damage gets bad. This will totally restore the damage meter!

As you approach the freeway ramp (just past the overhead airport sign), Da Nang motorcycle pairs fall in behind you. Take out the shooters on the bikes if you want, outrun your pursuers to the lockup garage on the Esplanade North waterfront, then head back to the red marker outside Woozie's place in China Town.

PAY N' SPRAY

NEED A FRESH PAINT JOB FOR THAT OLD RIDE? BODYWORK DONE TOO, FOR ROCK BOTTOM PRICES!

Lure

 # Respect Gained:
50
$ Cash Gained:
$8000

the story

The Da Nang Boys have tracked Foo Ran Fa Li to Woozie's place, and will attempt an assassination if he tries to leave. Woozie wants to "lure these lizards out into the baking sun." CJ agrees, and suggests a diversion for "Mr. Farlie." He'll drive Fa Li's car and lead the Da Nang killers into the countryside. Then Fa Li can leave safely.

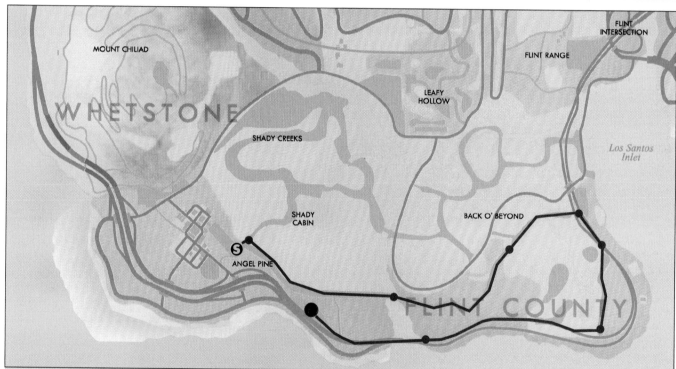

- Ⓢ **Location after Trip Skip**
- \ **Chase course**
- ● **Checkpoint**
- ● **Finish**

Directions

Get Into Decoy Car

The key to this mission is to avoid getting your rear door blown off by Da Nang gunfire. If they see that Fa Li isn't in the back, you fail the mission. Hop into the SUV and start driving. If you fail this mission and return

Drive out to the countryside.

to try again, then a "Trip Skip" appears onscreen; when you use it, you jump ahead to later that day. You end up just outside of remote Angel Pine.

Stay Put

Do not get out of the decoy car at any time! If the Da Nang Boys see you, the mission ends in failure.

Drive into the nearby red marker to trigger the chase. Two motorcycles, each with two Da Nang Boys aboard, fall in behind you and open fire. Don't fight back. Run!

Follow Checkpoints Through Countryside

Your goal is to make it through eight checkpoints (the red glowing columns). The next checkpoint is always marked as the red blip on your radar. Keep moving!

Note that a Damage meter appears for the vehicle. If it drops to zero, the damage is so severe that the Da Nang Boys can see inside and discover your deception. If the damage gets bad, stay far out in front of your pursuers so they can't get a peek at you. If a motorbike manages to pull up beside you, veer into it to slow it down and return fire to kill the shooter.

When you reach the tunnel, hang on—you're almost home free. Drive into the eighth and final checkpoint at the roadside service station to trigger a phone call. As the Da Nang cycles roar past, CJ reports his success and learns that Mr. Ran Fa Li has been delivered to safety.

Make the long drive from Whetstone County all the way back to Woozie's Triad headquarters in San Fierro—again, it's the "W" icon on the map.

WOOZIE mission 4

Amphibious Assault

- **Gamplay Element Introduced:**
  Swimming
- **Respect Gained:**
  25
- **Cash Gained:**
  $11,000

Walk into the red marker outside Woozie's China Town place between 20:00 at night and 6:00 in the morning for this night mission. Woozie suspects that a Triad informer is supplying info to the Vietnamese crime family. He wants CJ to bug the Da Nang gang's meeting place, located in a boat in the Vietnamese area of the harbor. Note that it's important to get CJ's lung capacity up from its starting value to trigger this. If it's not high enough at the start of the mission, you cannot take part. If this occurs, simply head for the ocean and practice some underwater swimming until the skill increases high enough.

Directions

Go to the Docks

Grab a car and head northeast to the foggy waterfront in the Esplanade North district, indicated by the yellow blip on your radar. When you arrive at the red marker, you get an overview of the situation. The boat is anchored offshore; at night, you can see its spotlights sweeping the water. You also learn that Da Nang Boys in boats patrol the route you must swim. CJ wastes no time, diving right into the water.

Next, you get a brief swimming tutorial. Just follow the onscreen instructions to practice your strokes. Swim through the two checkpoints, then dive and swim through the underwater tunnel. Surface when prompted, then swim down the narrow cave.

The boat that you have to plant the bug on is anchored out at sea.

Basic Swim Controls

The blue bar onscreen is your breath meter. As you swim underwater, the meter drops. Once the meter hits zero, your health will decline steadily until you can surface and breathe again. Your breath meter then slowly fills back up.

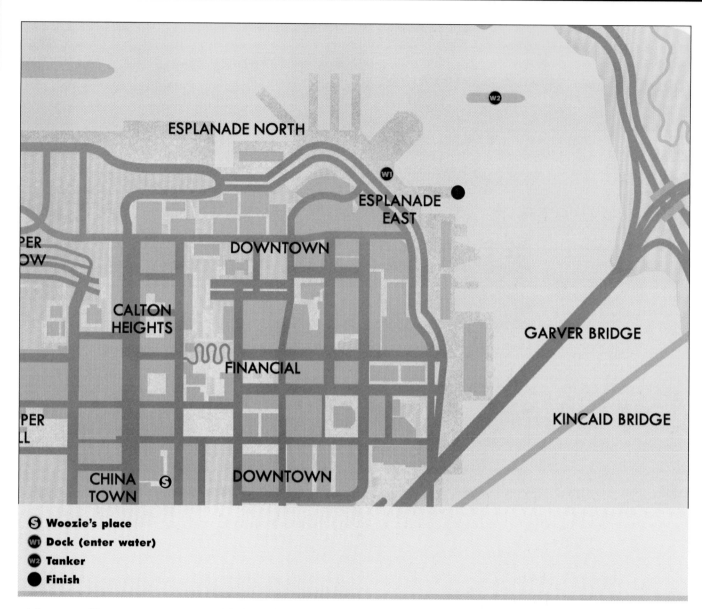

ESPLANADE NORTH

W2

W1

ESPLANADE EAST

PER OW

DOWNTOWN

CALTON HEIGHTS

GARVER BRIDGE

FINANCIAL

PER LL

KINCAID BRIDGE

CHINA TOWN

S

DOWNTOWN

S **Woozie's place**
W1 **Dock (enter water)**
W2 **Tanker**
● **Finish**

Pick Up Knife at Cave's Bottom

When you come to another underwater tunnel, dive down and look for the knife under a green marker. Swim through the knife to nab it. Continue forward until you see the red column marker where you can surface again. Let your breath meter fill up, then dive down again and swim through the red circle that leads to the last underwater tunnel. Swim through and surface in the bay.

You get another assessment of the situation. Two patrol boats guard the main route to the Da Nang Boys' ship. If they spot you, dive underwater to lose their attention. Don't swim on the surface or you'll be spotted for sure.

Swim to Tanker

Your destination is the tanker marked as a yellow blip on the radar. The red radar blips indicate the Da Nang Boys' patrol boats. Swim toward the tanker. If one of the searchlights spots you on the surface, the guards open fire.

Swim underwater as often as possible to avoid detection by patrol boats or tanker searchlights. If a patrol boat spots you on the surface, dive underwater and wait until it passes, then resurface to replenish your breath meter.

Read Your Radar

Note that your radar map shows you the detection circles of the searchlights and the patrol boat locations (the red blips) around the tanker.

Board the Tanker

Swim under the tanker and emerge on its far (northeast) side, where you find a small boarding dock with stairs leading up to the deck. Climb out of the water and ascend the stairs to the deck.

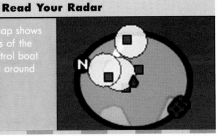

Sneak to Back of Tanker

The boarding stairs put you near the bow of the tanker. The meeting room is near the stern, so you must sneak the length of the ship to get there. On deck, crouch and move with stealth down the "alley" of container stacks to avoid detection by the guards onboard.

Arm yourself with the knife; using a gun will alert others to your presence. As you move down the length of the ship, you encounter several guards with their backs to you. Sneak up behind each one in a crouch and perform a stealth kill. When you reach the back of the ship, climb the stairs and enter the aft compartment.

Plant the Bug

Proceed below deck, moving quietly down the stairs for stealth kills, until you reach the red marker. Step into the marker and plant the bug.

Escape Tanker and Return to Docks

Retrace your route back upstairs to the top deck and take a running leap over the side into the water. Dive and swim underwater as far as you can toward the docks. The patrol boats will hound you if you surface too soon; dive back underwater to lose them.

Check your radar. The yellow blip is at the tip of a long pier. Swim to the pier and climb the low platform to the red marker to end the mission. Then follow the "W" icon back to the red marker outside Woozie's place.

The Da Nang Thang

⊕ Respect Gained:
30
⑤ Cash Gained:
$15,000

the story

Woozie's excited and ready to finish up this business with the Da Nang Boys crime family, thus sealing his place in the Red Gecko Tong. He's learned that the core components of the Da Nang Boys' transfer to the United States—the family, their trusted bodyguards, and a massive shipment of heroin—are being smuggled into San Fierro from a container ship moored offshore.

Woozie sends his man, Little Lion, in a helicopter for some fly-bys of the ship. CJ offers his help, but Woozie declines. Yet CJ feels tied to Woozie and his fortunes now. After Woozie leaves, CJ talks his way onto Little Lion's helicopter.

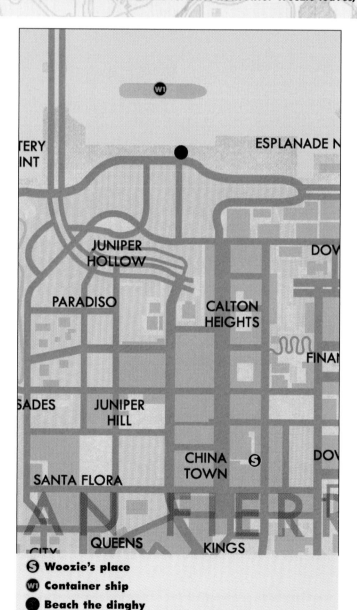

⑤ Woozie's place
W1 Container ship
● Beach the dinghy

Directions

Shoot Ship Guards from Helicopter

The perspective switches to first-person, with CJ firing a gun from the helicopter. The copter starts circling the container ship. Open fire! Unfortunately, the helicopter takes RPG fire from the ship and goes down into the bay after just one pass. (You can't avoid this.) CJ survives, and you take control of him as he floats in the water near the wreckage.

Swim to Freighter

This is easy enough. Swim to the red marker beside the ship. CJ automatically climbs the ladder onto the ship. The crew assumes no one survived the fiery helicopter crash, so you have the element of surprise on your side. But you lost all weapons except your knife in the crash, so nab some firepower from the enemies.

Move Stealthily Into Ship's Hull

The first few guards are facing away from you, so you can make several stealth kills if you crouch and approach quietly. This is a good tactic for CJ because he incurs no risk of damage. Again, be sure to nab any weapons dropped by the slain guards. After you round the container stack, find the low wooden box and start your climb there. As you climb to each new level of the stacks, look carefully for posted guards. Again, try for stealth kills.

Chances are good you'll eventually be spotted, especially when you reach the top of the container stack. After clearing out the first area of containers, you reach a gap. Drop down to the deck and cross to another huge stack of containers. Use the small cardboard box to start your climb up this second stack.

Hidden Heart

Don't miss this Health power-up tucked in a dark alcove!

Beware of guards posted at checkpoints and just around corners as you work your way through the stacks toward the back of the ship. You reach a hole in the deck that leads below into the hold where you can see a red marker.

Run around the hole to the far side, then hop down the containers that are stacked like steps. Walk into the red marker to trigger a scene. A man approaches a container and demands quiet from a container full of smuggled refugees. A trio of guards then spots you.

Take out Refugees' Guard Unit

Eliminate the first guard and climb up the crates on the right side of the hold. An enclosed area holds a weapon and some Body Armor. Nab them both, hop back over the boxes, and fight your way along the crate corridor—it curves back and forth in a series of U-turns through the hold. Also, be aware of the grenade-tossing guard near the end of this area. To avoid this guard, quickly peer around the corner to make him throw his grenade. After this explosion, sprint toward him and take him out!

Shoot Padlock on Front of Refugees' Container

Upon reaching the solitary red container, you hear voices calling for help. Target the padlock on the container and blast it apart. The door opens and people stagger out claiming that "the Snakehead tricked us." A scene shows this Snakehead fellow up on the ship's bridge, and he's got a really big sword.

Proceed to Cabin to Kill Snakehead and His Bodyguard

Retrace your route back to the hole and climb out of the hold onto the main deck. Scale the nearby stack of containers (following the yellow radar blip) to reach the entry corridor to the bridge. Careful! Two guards are posted atop the staircase to the left.

Climb the staircase to face the Snakehead, who tosses CJ a sword. Fight and kill him. Make sure to target select the enemy before you start swinging.

Go Back to Meet Refugees

Follow the blue blip back to the deck hole, where the grateful refugees wait. After they shove off in a dinghy, guide your own boat back to shore. Steer straight south to the shore and just beach it, then climb out onto the docks. Jack a car on the nearby road and follow the red icon to return to your garage in Doherty. Ahhh! Isn't it great to be back home?

MISSION PASS (1 OF 2)

*Completing **The Da Nang Thang** gives you one of the two prerequisites needed to open **Yay Ka-Boom-Boom**, the final mission of the Syndicate mission strand.*

THE STEAL CARS STRAND

$ **Cash Available in Strand:**
$20,000

After you complete all of the **Back to School** driving tests plus the **Yay Ka-Boom-Boom** mission from the Syndicate strand, Jethro calls with news that he and Cesar have used their contacts to get a customer "wishlist" of cars, but they have to turn them around fast—that is, unload them soon after "acquiring" them. (Hence, the name of this strand.) A showroom just around the block called Wang Cars has just come up for sale, and Jethro thinks it would make a nice, legit-looking front for their acquisitions.

Start the strand by heading over to Wang Cars (green house icon on the map) just up the street north of CJ's garage and plunking down $50,000 for the showroom. Wang Cars becomes a car icon on the radar, and the cars you steal for the garage business now show up in the showroom. The contact point for these missions is your garage property in Doherty, now marked by a "CV" icon. Head home after making the showroom purchase to start the new strand of missions.

STEAL CARS mission 1

Zeroing In

\# **Respect Gained:**
5

$ **Cash Gained:**
$5000

PREREQUISITES NEEDED!

This mission is available only after you complete Back to School and Yay Ka-Boom-Boom.

the story

Kendl interrupts a poker game to question the direction of the business enterprise, then Zero enters. He's constructed a tracking device that can hack into the satellite cellular system. This new gadget lets you pick up cell phone signals and plot their location. CJ can use it to "zero in" on a car on your customer wish list. The car's owner makes frequent cell phone calls. Every time she places a call, her current location appears as a red blip on the map that slowly fades.

Directions

Don't Let Her Trail Go Cold!

Track your way toward the red blip on the radar. Note that the target's signal blip starts out red, slowly turns yellow, fades away completely, and then starts the cycle all over again when she makes a new call. Stay close to keep her position updated. If you don't reach each new signal before it fades away completely, you've let her car get too far away and you fail the mission.

Don't let her trail go cold.

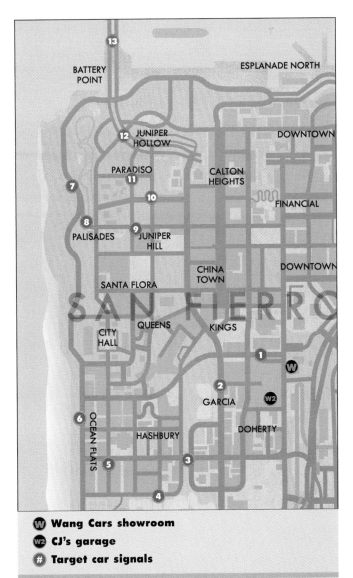

-  **Wang Cars showroom**
- **CJ's garage**
- **#** **Target car signals**

 **Chase Route**

The chase leads from Doherty north into Kings, veers sharply south-west to zigzag through Garcia and Hashbury, and then west into the Ocean Flats district. From there, it curves north along the coast through City Hall toward the Pallisades and Paradiso, and then doubles back south and east into the Juniper Hill district.

Next, the target car turns and speeds north from Juniper Hill into Juniper Hollow, back west into Paradiso, then doubles back into Juniper Hollow and north to Battery Point. Whew!

Clip Her Back End to Spin Her Out of Control

When you get close enough to see the target car, note that it has a red marker overhead. Note also the onscreen prompt to use the P.I.T. technique you learned in the **Back to School** driving mission to spin the target car with minimal damage. Just pull up beside the car on either side and nudge your front fender into its rear fender. You can also just ram the rear bumper.

Steal the Car

Once you've clipped the car, the scared driver hops out and the marker overhead turns blue. Steal the car and follow the yellow radar blip back to your garage in the Doherty district.

 **Mod Shop Open for Business!**

Once you complete **Zeroing In**, a street racer mod shop called Wheel Arch Angels opens for business in the Ocean Flats district. For more on mod shops, see our **Odd Jobs** chapter.

Test Drive

 # Respect Gained:
5
$ Cash Gained:
$5000

Follow the "CV" icon to your garage in Doherty and walk into the red marker. Cesar has found two more cars on the wishlist, both parked in the showroom of Otto's Autos across town. Go get 'em!

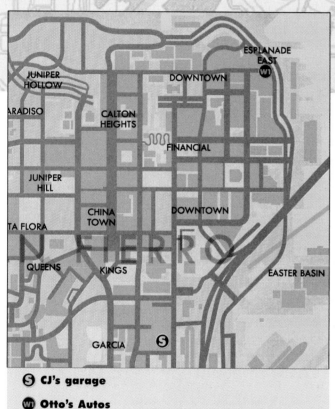

$ CJ's garage

W1 Otto's Autos

Directions

Visit Car Showroom

Follow the yellow radar blip to Otto's Autos in the northern part of the Downtown district. On the way, Cesar talks about his growing love for San Fierro, and the boys discuss Kendl's interest in building a business. They also talk about Truth and

his odd views. When you arrive and drive into the red marker, Cesar explains that the cars are in the second floor showroom, and leads CJ upstairs. CJ and Cesar each get into one of the cars.

Stay Close to Cesar As You Return to Garage

Cesar drives right through the second-story glass window, with CJ right behind. Follow Cesar (the blue blip on your radar map as he speeds through San Fierro on a wild

ride that tests many of your Driving School skills. First, he zigzags back and forth across the path of a streetcar climbing a hill. This stunt attracts the attention of the San Fierro police, giving you a two-star Wanted Level!

Trigger a Nitro!

Soon Cesar triggers a nitro burn for a short burst of acceleration. Follow suit by your vehicle's own nitro burn. Afterwards, tail Cesar down a hill and past some more pursuing police units. He leads you off-road through

a city park to avoid a roadblock. Cesar knows lots of shortcuts.

Follow Cesar Into the Alleyway

Next, Cesar veers down a narrow alleyway that turns into a trap. Quickly back up! Then follow Cesar as he races around the block and zigzags through an obstacle course of various objects.

When you get through that, you're finally clear to drive at your own pace back to the garage just ahead in Doherty.

Customs Fast Track

Accomplice:
Cesar

Respect Gained:
5

Cash Gained:
$10,000 (minus damage)

CJ and Kendl talk about Sweet and the situation back on Grove Street. Meanwhile, Cesar gets a tip that a crated vehicle matching another car on their customer's wishlist is being loaded onto a container ship at the docks. Cesar's contact marked the container with a spray can.

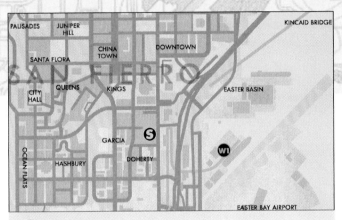

S CJ's garage

W Dockside crane

Directions

Get in Car with Cesar and Drive to the Docks

Hop in the car and follow the yellow radar blip eastward to the docks at Easter Basin. On the way, CJ explains how to get a crated car off a container ship—with a dockside crane. They agree to divide the tasks, with CJ running the crane and Cesar cracking the container.

Get in the Crane

When you arrive at the base of the crane, get out of the car and walk into the red marker. After getting inside the crane, CJ discovers that three containers sit on the deck, but none of them is marked with paint. Cesar suggests you try one at a time.

Pick Up a Container with Crane and Move it Ashore

Lower the crane magnet onto a container, then raise the container and move it over the red marker on the dock. Remember, you can change the camera view if necessary. Use the shadow to determine where the container will drop.

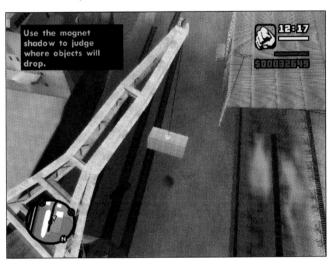

Use the magnet shadow to judge where objects will drop.

When the shadow is directly on the red marker, lower the container carefully into the marker. If you drop it from too great a height, the container (and car within) will be destroyed and you'll fail the mission.

Cesar says you got the wrong car. Swing the crane back and pick up another container. Keep trying until you get the correct container. (It's always the third one you lower.) Cesar drives the car out of the container and waits for CJ. Suddenly, a car pulls up and three thugs hop out with guns blazing.

NEW ODD JOBS AVAILABLE!

Completing the *Customs Fast Track* mission unlocks the Export/Import odd jobs. Travel back to the Easter Basin in San Fierro between missions to check the board listing cars wanted for export, then find them and deliver them to the big container ship moored at the dock. For details on this, see the *Export/Import* section of our *Odd Jobs* chapter. You can make big bucks by exporting vehicles, so try this soon if you need cash.

Help Cesar!

Cesar's health bar appears onscreen. Exit the crane and wipe out the three thugs before they wipe out Cesar. Soon a second carload of thugs pulls up to attack. Eliminate them, too, then prepare for a final wave of two attackers who approach on foot from down the dock. When they fall, hop in the hot car and head west, back to the garage in Doherty.

Puncture Wounds

 # Respect Gained:
5
$ Cash Gained:
$5000

the story

Cesar pulls up, ranting with lunatic anger. He's found another car on the customer's wishlist and tried to tail it, but the vehicle is too fast and its driver is too crazy. You cannot ram a target car because the damage would reduce or even negate its value to your customer. But CJ gets a brilliant idea—mod a car with Stinger traps and use them to puncture the target car's tires.

Directions

Use Modified Car to Chase Target Car

Hop into the vehicle. You learn that it's been modified to drop Stingers behind it. A Stinger is a spiked trap designed to puncture tires. When dropped, it spreads across one entire lane of the road. You get a total of three Stingers for the mission. Drive south toward Foster Valley, tracking the target indicated by the red blip on the radar. The target car works its way south across the bridge into Whetstone County, then heads toward Angel Pine.

Drop Stinger to Puncture Target's Tires

When you finally reach the target, follow until you get on a stretch of road with no turns coming up in the near distance. Pass the vehicle and get directly in front of it, then quickly drop a Stinger. If you time it right, the target runs over the Stinger and pops its tires.

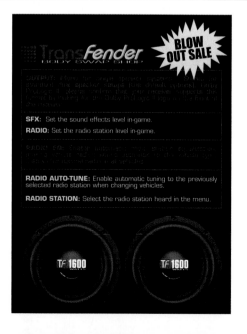

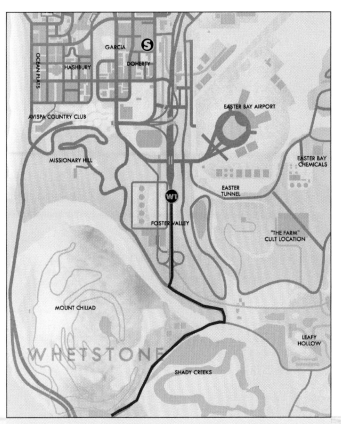

- **S** CJ's garage
- **W1** Target car starts here
- **/** Target car route

Return Car to the Garage

Get out and run toward the target car. As you approach it, Cesar calls; CJ reports his success. Then he automatically repairs the tires and takes the wheel of the car. Drive it back to your garage in Doherty.

Asset Acquired!

Once you complete the last mission of the Steal Cars strand, you earn the deed to the Wang Cars building. Now a money-making property for you, the business generates revenue up to a total of $8000. Be sure to come back regularly and walk through the "$" icon to pick up the cash.

Odd Jobs
& Other Pastimes

This chapter contains complete coverage of all the Odd Jobs in the game. It mentions where to find them, how to activate them, how to defeat them, and what is gained by completing them. The Odd Jobs are arranged into two basic categories: those that are a prerequisite to 100% completion of the game and those that are not.

REQUIRED ODD JOBS

The required Odd Jobs are arranged into two categories: collection and miscellaneous. We've organized them this way to keep Tagging, Photos, Horseshoes, and Oysters in an easy-to-find section. We'll cover those first. The other required Odd Jobs are listed later in this chapter.

Collection Odd Jobs

LOS SANTOS TAGS

Reward
When all tags are sprayed you earn a lot of respect and four weapons appear inside the Johnson Family's Home. The AK-47, Tec-9, Sawn-Off Shotgun, and Molotov Cocktails spawn in the kitchen.

Details
The Gang Tags are spread across the Los Santos area of San Andreas. You must spray these tags with a spray can. Spray are found in various locations around San Andreas, but the easiest one to get is in your bedroom of the Johnson Family house on Grove Street. This can continuously spawns here after completing **Tagging Up Turf**. To spray a tag, you must equip the spray can, target the rival gang tag and "fire" the spray can while within range. See our Los Santos map, screen shots, and descriptions to precisely locate each tag.

SAN FIERRO PHOTO OPS

Reward
When all the Photos are taken, these four weapons spawn outside your Xoomer Garage in Doherty, San Fierro: Micro-SMG, Grenades, Shotgun, and Sniper Rifle.

Details
The Photo Ops are spread around San Fierro's many picturesque tourist sights. To acquire a Photo Op, you must take a picture of it with a camera. Cameras are located in many places, the most obvious being inside your bedroom at the Johnson Family home on Grove Street. If you'd rather not use our maps to locate the Photo Ops, you can find them on your own by searching the city at night; Photo Ops glow just after midnight (00:01).

When you look through the camera lens at these glowing areas, you can spot a small floating camera icon. This is what you must include in your shot. Keep in mind that these camera icons also appear through the camera lens during the daytime; they're just harder to find. You do not need to save the pictures if you don't want to. (Refer to the Weapons section of this guide for details.) See our San Fierro map, screen shots, and descriptions to precisely locate each Photo Op.

LAS VENTURAS HORSESHOES

Reward
When all the Horseshoes are collected, your Gambling Luck increases dramatically and these four weapons spawn outside The Four Dragons Casino in Las Venturas: M4, MP5, Combat Shotgun, and Satchel Charges.

Details
Horseshoes are spread across Las Venturas. Collecting each one increases your luck at the gambling odd jobs in the various casinos around Las Venturas. See the Las Venturas map, screen shots, and descriptions to precisely locate each Horseshoe. Tip: Get the Jetpack from the Verdant Meadows Airstrip after completing Green Goo. It makes collecting the high ones much easier.

SAN ANDREAS OYSTERS

Reward
Lung Capacity and Sex Appeal stats are boosted.

Details
Oysters can be found all around San Andreas, except for on dry land. Oysters live underwater and can only be found in the water. See the following maps, screen shots, and descriptions to precisely locate all the Oysters.

UNIQUE STUNT JUMPS

Insane jumps is one thing, Unique Stunt Jumps are another. Hidden throughout San Andreas are 70 Unique Stunt Jumps. Finding these on your own is no easy task; there aren't any clues except a mound, ramp, or cliff that looks like it would be fun to hit at high speed. All of these jumps can be performed easily in a fast motorcycle, such as the NRG-500. However, many of these jumps can also be performed in a PCJ-600 or other motorcycles, and even with some cars. You may win stunt bonuses when hitting these jumps, but you don't truly complete a jump until you are awarded the Unique Stunt Jump Bonus ($500). This means going a little further or landing in a specific area or rooftop. Unique Stunt Jumps are not required for 100% completion.

FLOWERS

Flowers are not a Collection item, per se, as they do not contribute to achieving 100% completion. However, they do help you earn points with your girlfriends (see the **Girlfriends** section of our **Odd Jobs** chapter for details). There are 40 Flowers growing around San Andreas and each one brings you a step closer to relationship bliss with your love interests. Refer to our **Unique Attractions** maps at the beginning of each chapter of the walkthrough to locate each Flower.

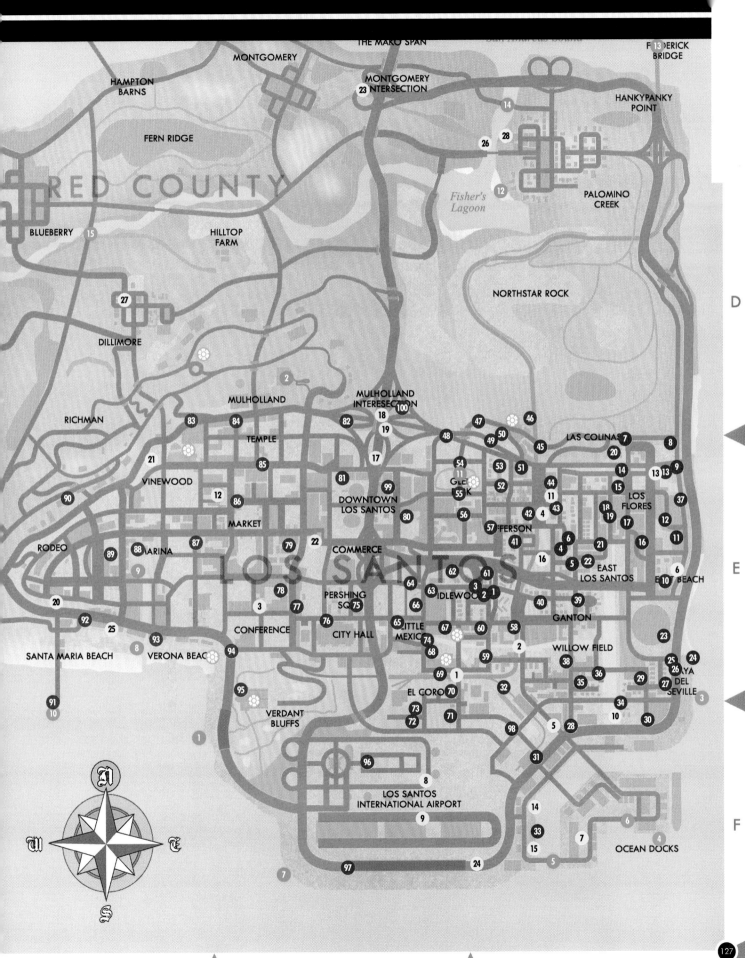

THE MAKO SPAN

San Andreas Sound

MONTGOMERY

F**13**DERICK BRIDGE

MONTGOMERY
23 NTERSECTION

HANKYPANKY
POINT

14

HAMPTON
BARNS

28

26

FERN RIDGE

12
Fisher's
Lagoon

PALOMINO
CREEK

RED COUNTY

NORTHSTAR ROCK

BLUEBERRY **15**

HILLTOP
FARM

27

DILLIMORE

2

MULHOLLAND
INTERESECTION
100

MULHOLLAND

47 **46**
LAS COLINAS **7**

RICHMAN

82
18
19

48

49 **50**

20
8

83 **84**

45

14
13 **13**
9

TEMPLE

17

54
53 **51**
52

15

LOS
FLORES

37

21

85

55RK

44
11

18
19
17

VINEWOOD

81

42 **4**
43

12

90

12
86

99

DOWNTOWN
LOS SANTOS

56

57FFERSON

6

16

11

MARKET

80

41

4

21

87

16

5 **22**

6

RODEO

22

EAST
LOS SANTOS

E**10** BEACH

89
88ARINA

79

COMMERCE

LOS SANTOS

9

62
61

40 **39**

20

78

64
63 IDLEWOO**3**

2 **1**

GANTON

23

92

3

77

PERSHING
SQ **75**

66

2

WILLOW FIELD

25 **24**

25

76

58

38

26

93

CONFERENCE

CITY HALL

65LITTLE
MEXIC**74**

67 **60**

2

36

27AYA
DEL
SEVILLE

8

94

68

59

35

29

3

69 **1**

34

30

95

EL CORO**70**

32

10

91
10

SANTA MARIA BEACH

VERONA BEAC

73
72

71

98

5 **28**

VERDANT
BLUFFS

31

1

96

14

8

33

7

9
LOS SANTOS
INTERNATIONAL AIRPORT

15

OCEAN DOCKS

9

5

6

4

7

97

24

D

E

F

4

5

6

LOS SANTOS GANG TAGS

IDLEWOOD
On the side of a large bridge. Part of Tagging up Turf mission.

IDLEWOOD
On the front of a house. Part of Tagging up Turf mission.

IDLEWOOD
On a brick wall in this back alleyway. Part of Tagging up Turf mission.

EAST LOS SANTOS
On the corner wall of a Mexican food restaurant. Part of Tagging up Turf mission.

EAST LOS SANTOS
Climb to the roof opposite of the Cluckin' Bell; it's on the wall. Part of Tagging up Turf mission.

EAST LOS SANTOS
On the wall behind the Cluckin' Bell restaurant. Part of Tagging up Turf mission.

LAS COLINAS
South side of southern yellow house.

LAS COLINAS
On the wall of the large apartment that overlooks the sea.

EAST BEACH
On the wall of the building opposite of Colonel Fuhrburger's house.

EAST BEACH
On the wall of the car park located behind the pedestrian overpass on the beach.

EAST BEACH
On the bottom floor of the multi-story car park.

EAST BEACH
On the wall of a building just off the main road leading to the Los Santos Forum.

EAST BEACH
Behind the Body Armor in the back alleyway.

LOS FLORES
Back garden opposite the vacant billboard.

EAST LOS SANTOS
On the wall by the crossroads.

EAST BEACH
On the "S"-shaped road in the central East Beach area.

LOS FLORES
On the back alleyway wall in central Los Flores.

EAST LOS SANTOS
On a wall in the dark, crooked back alleyway.

EAST LOS SANTOS
In a crooked, narrow back alleyway.

EAST LOS SANTOS
On the side of some large brown steps.

EAST LOS SANTOS
Inside the tunnel on the wall of the car wash exit.

EAST LOS SANTOS
Behind the railings near the desolate shop's backyard.

EAST BEACH
On the wall of the Los Santos Forum.

PLAYA DEL SEVILLE
On the wall that faces the beach; southeast of the Los Santos Forum.

PLAYA DEL SEVILLE
On the wall of the house just opposite the Los Santos Forum.

PLAYA DEL SEVILLE
On the short wall in front of apartments.

PLAYA DEL SEVILLE
On the wall of the basketball courts.

OCEAN DOCKS
On one of the bridge's support beams.

PLAYA DEL SEVILLE
On a wall in front of some generators.

OCEAN DOCKS
On a street corner wall.

OCEAN DOCKS
Outside of the warehouse on a wall.

WILLOWFIELD
On the side of a bridge in the flood control area.

OCEAN DOCKS
On the wooden wall near the docks.

OCEAN DOCKS
On the side of the flood control wall.

WILLOWFIELD
On the side of the 98 cent store.

WILLOWFIELD
On the side of the Sushi Man store.

37

EAST BEACH
Climb onto the roof of the eastern pacific house; it's on the wall.

38

WILLOWFIELD
On the wall of the drive-thru restaurant.

39

GANTON
On the side of the foundation of the overpass.

40

GANTON
Behind the car park railings, on a wall.

41

JEFFERSON
Inside the garage, on a wall.

42

JEFFERSON
End of large church.

43

EAST LOS SANTOS
In the back alley of the desolate liquor store.

44

EAST LOS SANTOS
In an underground car park in the residential area, on a wall.

45

LAS COLINAS
Inside of the train tunnel (used in "Catalyst").

46

LAS COLINAS
On the back of this house.

47

LAS COLINAS
In-between these houses, on one of the walls.

48

GLEN PARK
On a wall in this building's courtyard.

49

LAS COLINAS
In the narrow alleyway.

50

LAS COLINAS
On the wall on the bottom side of the zig-zag slope.

51

JEFFERSON
On the side of the hotel in Jefferson featured in Reuniting the Families.

52

JEFFERSON
On the fence in this back alleyway with garages.

53

JEFFERSON
In narrow alleyway across from the park, on the brick wall.

54

GLEN PARK
Under the bridge by the pond.

55

GLEN PARK
On a wall in this narrow alleyway.

56

GLEN PARK
On a fence in the corner of the skate park.

57

JEFFERSON
On a wall in the hospital's garden.

58

IDLEWOOD
On the side of the 24-hour motel car park.

59

WILLOWFIELD
On the side of the supermarket car park.

60

IDLEWOOD
In the alcove with the wire window.

61

IDLEWOOD
In the residential courtyard, on a wall.

62

IDLEWOOD
Side of the apartments in the residential area.

63

IDLEWOOD
On the wall in the shallow alcove of this building.

64

LITTLE MEXICO
On the side of the building on the street corner.

65

LITTLE MEXICO
On the side of the corner building.

66

LITTLE MEXICO
On the wall down the side of this building.

67

IDLEWOOD
Climb to the roof of the car wash; it's on the back of the sign.

68

EL CORONA
On the wall with lots of other graffiti.

69

EL CORONA
On the side of this home, near the top level.

70

EL CORONA
On the wall of a bar near the street corner.

71

EL CORONA
On the side of the supermarket.

72

EL CORONA
On the green fence.

 **73 EL CORONA**
On the side of this house.

 **74 IDLEWOOD**
At the bottom of the flood control wall.

 **75 PERSHING SQUARE**
On the building opposite the large, town hall-like building.

 **76 PERSHING SQUARE**
On the side of the large, town hall-like building.

 **77 COMMERCE**
On the side of the building called "Regal".

 **78 VERONA BEACH**
On the balcony just past the top of the stairs.

 **79 MARKET**
At the base of the space-like building.

 **80 DOWNTOWN LOS SANTOS**
Just past the food court, near the two trees.

 **81 DOWNTOWN LOS SANTOS**
At the top of the long, crooked steps.

 **82 MULHOLLAND**
On the northwest wall of the car park under the Mulholland Intersection.

 **83 VINEWOOD**
On the side of the small building on the street corner.

 **84 TEMPLE**
On the wall of the building on the street corner.

 **85 MARKET**
At the base of the building on the street corner.

 **86 MARKET**
At the end of the first floor ledge of this building.

 **87 MARKET**
Climb to the top of the first floor roof of this building; it's on the back wall.

 **88 MARINA**
On the wall near the wooden pier, at the bottom of the stairs.

 **89 RODEO**
On the brick wall behind the large billboard.

 **90 RODEO**
On the back wall of the Vinyl Countdown store.

 **91 SANTA MARIA BEACH**
At the end of pier by the big wheel, on a back wall.

 **92 SANTA MARIA BEACH**
At the base of the shop fronts on the beach.

 **93 MARINA**
At the corner of the building leading to the beach.

 **94 VERONA BEACH**
At the base of the wall on the corner shop.

 **95 VERDANT BLUFFS**
Climb to the rooftop of the observatory; it's on a wall.

 **96 LOS SANTOS INTERNATIONAL**
On the southern wall of the control tower building.

 **97 LOS SANTOS INTERNATIONAL**
On a wall facing the top of the roof of the entrance to the tunnel.

 **98 WILLOWFIELD**
On the front of this house.

 **99 DOWNTOWN LOS SANTOS**
At the base of the skyscraper.

 **100 MULHOLLAND**
On the support beam of the spaghetti junction.

◤ LOS SANTOS/RED CO. UNIQUE STUNT JUMPS

1 El Corona, jump going east onto the railway platform rooftop (it's possible to make the jump in a PCJ).

2 Idlewood, jump south on the bridge structure. Drive fast between the railroad and trees to miss the tree near the jump.

3 Verona Beach, head north using the building's steps as a ramp; try to land on the next building to avoid a spill.

4 Jefferson, drive north up the pedestrian walkway steps. This jump is possible on a bike or in a car.

5 Ocean Docks, drive approximately south by southeast over the mound of dirt behind the metal wall. Stop short of running into the next freeway wall.

6 East Beach, drive to the west up the pedestrian steps (it's an easy jump on an NRG). Clear the parking lot wall behind the steps.

7 Ocean Docks, drive south up the wooden ramp and land on the corrugated roof. This jump is possible in a variety of vehicles.

8 LS International, use the boarding ramp to get over the airport fence.

9 LS International, use the small sign/ramp here and drive east. Clear the concrete and the red 06L-2 sign.

10 Ocean Docks, drive west up these steps and make it onto the adjacent building.

11 East Los Santos, head west up and over these steps; you must make it to the railway tracks.

12 Market, jump east over the steps, over the roof, and land on the road.

13 East Beach, drive through the brick patio and through the hole in the stone wall, then jump far down to the street below without landing in the ocean

14 Ocean Docks, drive north up the stairs and land in the street.

15 Ocean Docks, just south of the previous jump. Go south up the dock stairs. Again, avoid landing in the ocean.

16 East Los Santos, head to the west up the steps at basketball courts.

17 Mulholland Intersection, go north up the cement ramp on the freeway walkway.

18 Mulholland Intersection, drive south up the cement ramp on the freeway walkway.

19 Mulholland Intersection, jump the cement ramp underneath the freeway heading southeast and land in the parking lot.

20 Rodeo, go south up the small grassy knoll and land on the Yacht Harbor pier.

21 Vinewood, to the west of the parking lot slope. Jump over the next rooftop and land on Sunset Road.

22 Commerce, drive north up the ramp out of the flood control trench.

23 Montgomery Intersection, jump off the dirt mound at the end of freeway heading west at the Montgomery Intersection

24 LS International, go west up the cement ramp between the airport and the ocean on the freeway prior to the underpass.

25 Santa Maria Beach, from the beach, drive east up the steps underneath the promenade.

26 Red County, jump over this bridge heading east into town. This jump is suitable with any vehicle.

27 Dillimore, jump this ramp heading south and land at least in front of the Gasso gas station or past the sheriff's office.

28 Palomino Creek, drive west over the broken bridge, as was the case with Catalina in the "Rob Bank" chase.

LOS SANTOS/RED CO. OYSTERS

1. Verdant Bluffs, near the entrance to the Bluffs Tunnel.

2. Mulholland, inside Doc G's pool.

3. Playa del Seville, at end of the beach pier.

4. Ocean Docks, beside the most Southern Ocean Docks pier.

5. Ocean Docks, under the bridge, just East of Los Santos Airport.

6. Ocean Docks, under bridge, situated on the small "island" part of the Docks.

7. Los Santos, just off the beach, West of Los Santos Airport.

8. Verona Beach, under the Pedestrian Bridge.

9. Marina, under flood control bridge in the Marina area.

10. Santa Maria Beach, south of the lighthouse.

11. Glen Park, under park bridge in pond.

12. Fisher's Lagoon, at the end of the pier, South West of Palomino Creek.

13. Frederick Bridge, underneath the middle that connects Las Venturas to Los Santos.

14. Red County, under the bridge, North West of Palomino Creek.

15. Red County, under these 2 bridges, just East of Blueberry.

San Fierro & Badlands Collection

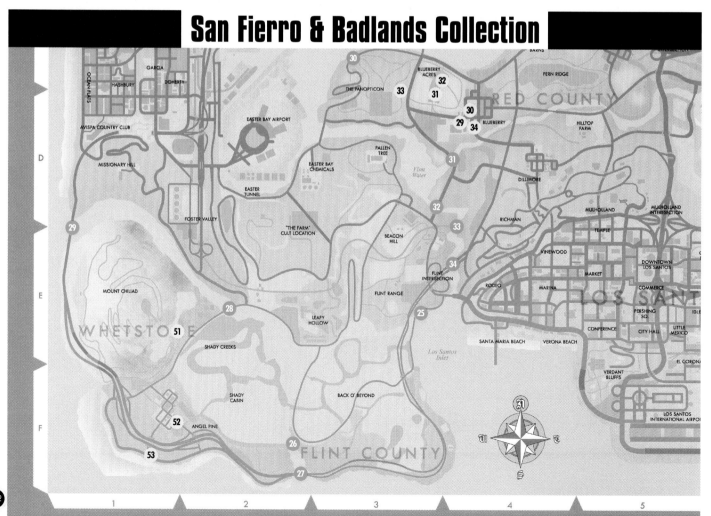

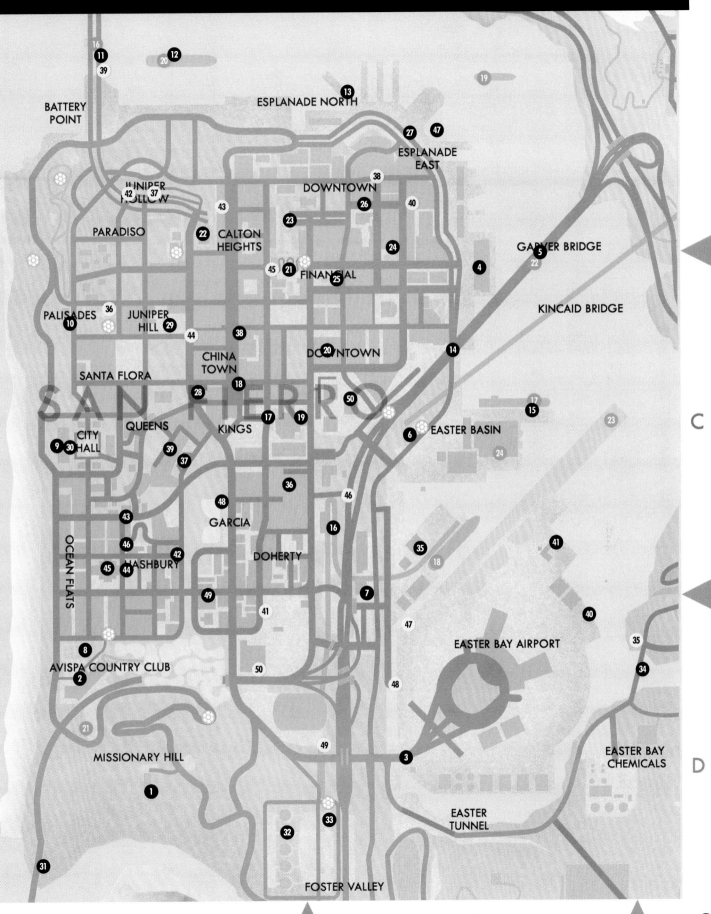

BATTERY
POINT

JUNIPER
HOLLOW

PARADISO

CALTON
HEIGHTS

ESPLANADE NORTH

DOWNTOWN

ESPLANADE
EAST

GARVER BRIDGE

KINCAID BRIDGE

FINANCIAL

PALISADES

JUNIPER
HILL

SANTA FLORA

CHINA
TOWN

DOWNTOWN

QUEENS

KINGS

EASTER BASIN

CITY
HALL

GARCIA

DOHERTY

OCEAN
FLATS

HASHBURY

EASTER BAY AIRPORT

AVISPA COUNTRY CLUB

EASTER BAY
CHEMICALS

MISSIONARY HILL

EASTER
TUNNEL

FOSTER VALLEY

SAN FIERRO

C

D

1

2

Next to tower on top of Missionary Hill.

Domed Tower in Avispa Country Club.

Airplane sign at the entrance to Easter Bay Airport.

Clock face on Clock Tower next to Garver Bridge.

East on Garver Bridge between supporting structure.

On top of rotating X at the Xoomer gas station in Easter Basin.

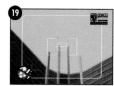
Between tanks at Shady Industries in Doherty.

Above tennis court nets in Avispa Country Club.

West of the domed building in City Hall.

In the middle of the Donut at Tuff Nut in Palisades.

Before the first support tower of the Gant Bridge when leaving San Fierro.

Mast on the Da Nang Boat north of San Fierro.

Conning tower on submarine in Esplanade North.

One of the Kincaid Bridge girders on the San Fierro side.

Aircraft carrier bridge in Easter Basin.

Cranberry Station above and between the train tracks.

Highest point in tower of building in Kings.

Above the ground and next to building in China Town, across from the Trolley Station.

Top of skyscraper in Kings, between the two middle flag poles.

Sculpture inside Zombotech building Downtown.

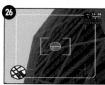
In the middle of the curviest road in Calton Heights.

Next to rotating burger at Burger Shot in Juniper Hollow.

Lamppost in the middle of the road at tunnel entrance in Calton Heights.

Aerial on top of skyscraper in the Financial District.

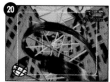
Baseball player statue in the park downtown.

The side of this tall building in the Financial area.

The sign at the entrance to Pier 69 in Esplanade North.

At the top of the chimney of a building in Queens.

Above the entrance to the Supa Save in Juniper Hill.

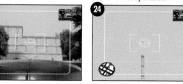
The middle two columns on the front of City Hall.

Above the bridge leaving San Fierro through the southwest.

The second northernmost, round tower in Foster Valley.

High above the plants in the middle of a Foster Valley roof garden.

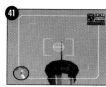
The bridge connecting Red County and the Panopticon.

High above the curved lip of the dry dock in Easter Basin.

At the top of the tall crane at Doherty Construction Site.

Entrance to the Vank Hoff Park Hotel in Queens.

Middle roof in China Town Gateway.

The back of the Vank Hoff Park Hotel in Queens.

The gas storage tanks on eastern edge of Easter Bay Airport.

The Air Traffic Control Tower Antenna at Easter Bay Airport.

The Hashbury & Garcia Joint Festival Banner.

The movie theater in Queens.

High above one of the center gravestones in Hashbury.

The Ocean Flats Church spire.

The Hippy Shopper store in Hashbury.

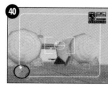
The rock formation in the bay of Esplanade East.

Above home plate in the park in Garcia.

The Final Build Construction sign in Garcia.

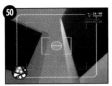
High up between the two tall buildings Downtown.

SAN FIERRO/BADLANDS UNIQUE STUNT JUMPS

Blueberry, run up the smashed pallet ramp at FleischBerg, then jump over the truck trailers. Must land safely on the other side.

Blueberry, drive east up the wooden set of stairs behind the building with the Sprunk billboard. Must clear the building that you're jumping over.

Blueberry Acres, race through the previous barn and jump north/northeast over the barn.

Blueberry Acres, race through this barn heading north/northeast. It's best in a car, because the landing usually involves a crash through a wooden fence.

The Panopticon, make the short jump over this narrow ravine.

Blueberry, jump northwest over the trailers from the pallet ramp. Clear the truck and land on other side.

RED COUNTY
Hit this banked mound of earth just to the west/northwest to land on the San Fierro Airport runway.

SANTA FLORA
Jump off the backyard hillside to clear the buildings to the south.

SAN FIERRO
Use the large road/hill south of this walkway between the houses. Speed off the hill behind the houses, jumping over the border and landing safely.

SAN FIERRO
Drive up Michelle's steps heading north and land on the building opposite the multi-story parking garage.

SAN FIERRO
Drive up the scaffolding over Jizzy's club and fly off the scaffolding next to the Gant Bridge north into the water (there's a beach nearby to exit the water).

SAN FIERRO
Head east over these steps inbetween buildings and land at least on the rooftop beyond.

SAN FIERRO
Drive through the dilapidated building and out of the Los Cabras compound.

SAN FIERRO
Jump northeast over the large cement ramp. Use the hilly street prior to it to build up speed. Avoid the wall just before it and go up the ramp as straight as possible to land in the street below in the distance.

SAN FIERRO
Use the street to the east of ramp between the homes (over tunnel) and jump into the street below. Since distance is the key, use the NRG-500.

SAN FIERRO
Utilize the supermarket parking lot ramp. Jump east across the road and land in the crowded alley.

SAN FIERRO
Jump the wooden stairs at the top of the winding street.

SAN FIERRO
Jump the rusty ramp near Transfenders and land on the highway.

SAN FIERRO
Jump out of the San Fierro Airport using this ramp and land on the Easter Basin docks.

SAN FIERRO
Use this ramp to jump out of the San Fierro Airport heading west.

SAN FIERRO
Use this ramp to jump east from the stadium parking lot and land on the freeway.

SAN FIERRO
Jump the freeway using the pedestrian steps. You must clear the freeway.

MOUNT CHILIAD
Jump off this wooden ramp at a decent speed. This ramp is used in Cobra Run in the Mount Chiliad Challenge (race 3).

ANGEL PINE
Jump northwest on this ramp out of the trailer park and land on the orange tiled roof over the road.

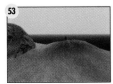
WHETSTONE
Jump east off this sand dune.

SAN FIERRO/BADLANDS OYSTERS

16 — Landing point for a USJ under the Gant bridge.

17 — At the bow of the aircraft carrier in Easter Bay.

18 — Under the stern of the large freighter in dock.

19 — At the bow of freighter in the middle of the bay.

20 — Under the West side of the ship that features in the Da Nang Thang.

21 — In a pool behind Avispa Country Club.

22 — Under the water support of the Garver Bridge.

23 — End of the Easter Bay Airport Runway.

24 — In an Easter Bay Dock. . .

25 — Where the beach meets the cliffs, just North of Los Santos Inlet.

26 — Under a large bridge, to the East of Mount Chiliad.

27 — Under this rickety wooden bridge, situated to the East of Angel Pine.

28 — Under bridge beside open sea, situated to the East of Angel Pine.

29 — Under bridge leading from Mount Chiliad to San Fierro.

30 — Just off the beach in the north-west corner of the Panoptican.

31 — Under the bridge to the south of Blueberry.

32 — Under this bridge that spans the southern river of Flint Water.

33 — Under this rail bridge, to the West of Los Santos.

34 — Between the motorway bridges, just west of Los Santos leading to Flint County.

Desert & Las Venturas Collection

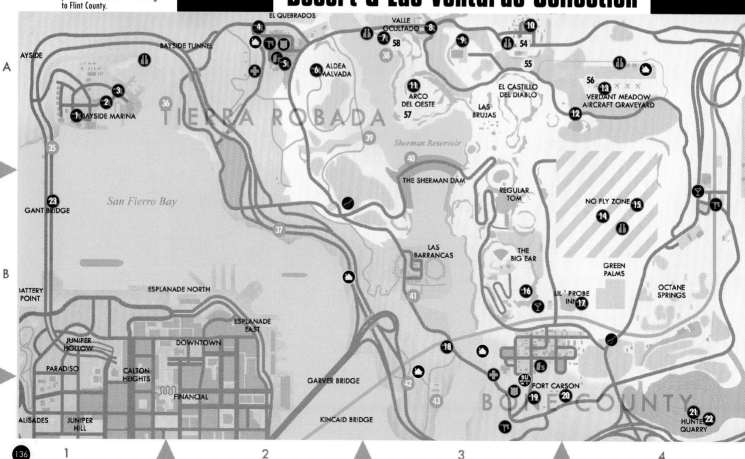

EL QUEBRADOS · VALLE OCULTADO · AYSIDE · BAYSIDE TUNNEL · ALDEA MALVADA · ARCO DEL OESTE · TIERRA ROBADA · BAYSIDE MARINA · Sherman Reservoir · EL CASTILLO DEL DIABLO · LAS BRUJAS · VERDANT MEADOW AIRCRAFT GRAVEYARD · THE SHERMAN DAM · REGULAR TOM · NO FLY ZONE · GANT BRIDGE · San Fierro Bay · THE BIG EAR · GREEN PALMS · OCTANE SPRINGS · LAS BARRANCAS · BATTERY POINT · ESPLANADE NORTH · LIL' PROBE INN · JUNIPER HOLLOW · ESPLANADE EAST · PARADISO · DOWNTOWN · CALTON HEIGHTS · GARVER BRIDGE · FORT CARSON · FINANCIAL · BONE COUNTY · PALISADES · JUNIPER HILL · KINCAID BRIDGE · HUNTER QUARRY

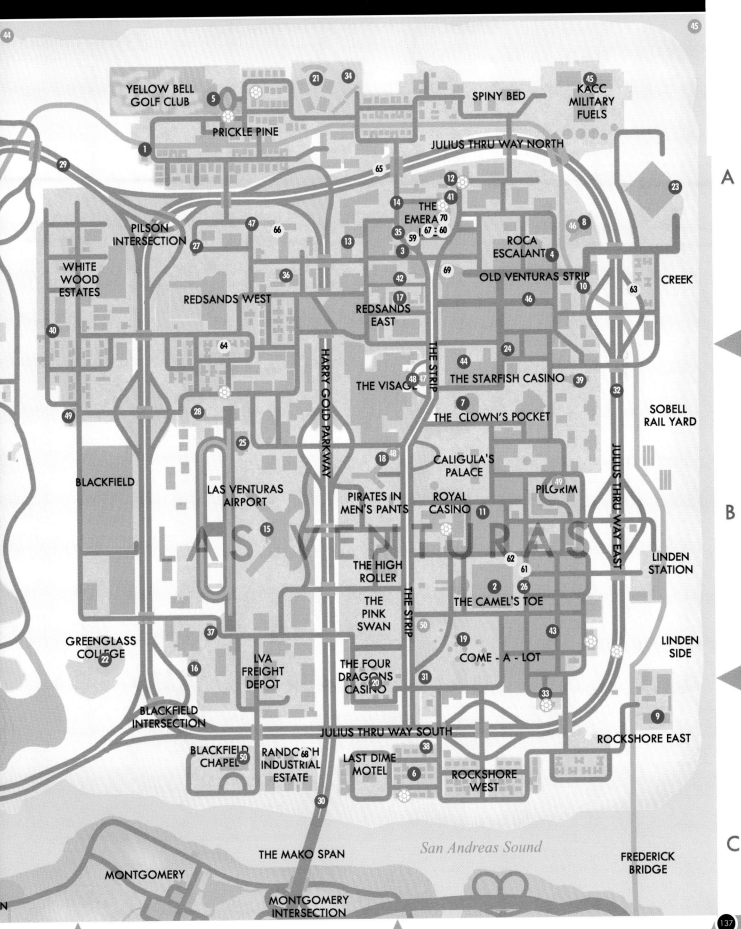

44

45

YELLOW BELL
GOLF CLUB
5

21   34

SPINY BED

KACC
MILITARY
FUELS
45

PRICKLE PINE

1

JULIUS THRU WAY NORTH

29

65

12

23
A

47   66

14

41

THE
EMERA 70
67 : 60

46   8

PILSON
INTERSECTION
27

13

35
59

ROCA
ESCALANT
4

CREEK

WHITE
WOOD
ESTATES

3

69

OLD VENTURAS STRIP
10

63

36

42

46

40

REDSANDS WEST

17

REDSANDS
EAST

24

32

SOBELL
RAIL YARD

49

64

THE STRIP

44

THE STARFISH CASINO
39

BLACKFIELD

48 47

THE VISAGE

7

THE CLOWN'S POCKET
B

28

LINDEN
STATION

25

18 48

CALIGULA'S
PALACE

PILGRIM
49

LAS VENTURAS
AIRPORT

PIRATES IN
MEN'S PANTS

ROYAL
CASINO

11

15

62
61

THE HIGH
ROLLER

2
26

THE CAMEL'S TOE

LINDEN
SIDE

37

THE
PINK
SWAN

THE STRIP

50

19

43

GREENGLASS
COLLEGE
22

COME - A - LOT

16

LVA
FREIGHT
DEPOT

THE FOUR
DRAGONS
CASINO
20

31

33

9

BLACKFIELD
INTERSECTION

JULIUS THRU WAY SOUTH

ROCKSHORE EAST

BLACKFIELD
CHAPEL
50

RANDO 68 H
INDUSTRIAL
ESTATE

LAST DIME
MOTEL

38

6

ROCKSHORE
WEST

30

THE MAKO SPAN

San Andreas Sound
C

FREDERICK
BRIDGE

MONTGOMERY

MONTGOMERY
INTERSECTION

5

6

137

ⓊLAS VENTURAS HORSESHOES

1 Prickle Pine, in the porch of this house in Las Venturas suburbs.

2 Camel's Toe, at the very top of the pyramid.

3 Emerald Isle, on top of gift shop on corner.

4 Roca Escalante, on top of the Erotic Wedding Chapel.

5 Yellow Bell Golf Course, on the roof of the golf house in front of a rear window.

6 Rockshore West, in one of the back yards.

7 The Clown's Pocket, on top of The Clown's Pocket building.

8 Roca Escalante, in the middle of the guitar-shaped swimming pool at the VRock Hotel.

9 Rockshore East, above a dumpster behind the warehouse.

10 Old Venturas Strip, inside the Railway Tunnel.

11 Royal Casino, in the northwest corner of the parking garage on the third floor.

12 Julius Thruway North, hidden in this small garage enclosure.

13 Redsands East, on top of the roof, across from the 24-Seven.

14 Emerald Isle, at the very top of the Emerald Isle building. Use the Jetpack or parachute to reach it.

15 Las Venturas Airport, behind the main airport building.

16 Blackfield Intersection, hidden in a small gap between the warehouse and a wall.

17 Redsands East, on the back of the Motel on the second floor.

18 The Pirates in Men's Pants, hidden in the bushes.

19 Come-A-Lot, atop one of the towers at Come-A-Lot.

20 The Four Dragons Casino, on the roof of The Four Dragons Casino above the garage.

21 Prickle Pine, in this shallow pool at an apartment complex.

22 Greenglass college, in middle of the courtyard in front of the college.

23 Creek, hidden behind a strip mall on the outskirts of town.

24 Starfish Casino, on top of the Venturas Steaks Drive-thru.

25 Las Venturas Airport, just to the east of the northern section of the runway.

26 The Camel's Toe, on the east side of the Pyramid on a ledge.

27 Pilson Intersection, floating above this wall.

28 Las Venturas Airport, just west of the northern tip of the runway.

29 Las Venturas, under the "Welcome" sign.

30 Randolph Industrial Estate, hidden below a bridge on the way out of town.

31 Come-A-Lot, at the top of the Come-A-Lot sign. Use the Jetpack to reach it.

32 Julius Thruway East, on the east side of the Victim billboard. Use the Jetpack.

33 Las Venturas, on the roof of the Wedding Chapel.

34 Prickle Pine, stashed behind the gate to one of the tennis courts.

35 Emerald Isle, in a small enclosure near the Emerald Isle.

36 Redsands West, on the overhang of a Casino next door to the Steakhouse Restaurant.

LVA Freight Depot, at one of the truck docks.

Rockshore West, in a back yard, next to this trash can.

Starfish Casino, on a ledge above the Arts & Crafts shop.

Whitewood Estates, behind the warehouse.

Emerald Isle, between gas station and carwash.

Emerald Isle, in the southwest corner outside of the parking garage.

Come-A-Lot, in second story window of red apartment building.

Starfish Casino, in the corner of a dark alleyway.

KACC Military Fuels, in a small, secluded alleyway.

Old Venturas Strip, inside the S of CASINO.

Redsands West, on top of some packing crates. Use a vehicle to jump on the fence and then up to the Horseshoe.

The Visage, underneath the waterfall.

Whitewood Estates, in front of this building.

Blackfield Chapel, on the roof of the Chapel.

LAS VENTURAS/DESERT OYSTERS

Between the Gant Bridges northern most support and a cliff.

East of the Bayside lighthouse by a rocky outcrop.

Hidden from view by a small roadside wall. North of the San Fierro Docks.

End of a jetty at this lakeside house.

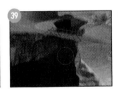
Under wooden bridge to the northwest of the Sherman Dam.

Under the west control tower of the dam.

Under the metal bridge just south of Las Barrancas.

Small tributary leading into San Fierro Bay, west of Toreno's House.

Under the water in this boat shed at Toreno's House.

Bone County beach, North West of Las Venturas.

The northeast corner of the map.

Under the diving board at the VRock pool.

Under a waterfall at The Visage Casino.

In front of skull, at the front of the Pirates in Men's Pants Casino.

In the pool in front of The Pilgrim Hotel.

In the Come-A-Lot Casino moat.

◢ LAS VENTURAS/DESERT UNIQUE STUNT JUMPS

54
Las Payasadas, head east over the tarp-covered dirt pile and jump over the massive chicken.

55
Las Payasadas, hit the steps to the overlook while going south; must successfully land this one.

56
Verdant Meadows, speed up the westernmost plane's wing going northeast. This should enable you to clear the plane to the northeast.

57
Arco Del Oeste, head west along the wooden path and over the canyon river. A motorcycle is the best option here.

58
Valle Ocultado, hit the ramp against the wall of this shack. The jump is a success even if you land in the water; find the nearby beach to exit from the water.

59
Las Venturas, jump south out of the top level of the Emerald Isle multi-story garage and land on the roof of the Souvenir Shop.

60
Las Venturas, drive up the stairs to the rooftop of the multi-story garage and drive to the adjacent roof. Drop down to the south side of building, then jump the ramp to the east off the ledge.

61
Las Venturas, jump east from the northeast corner stairs of The Camel's Toe casino, across the street and parking lot, and land on the Pawn Shop rooftop beyond the parking lot.

62
Las Venturas, adjacent to the steps in the previous jump. Jump north from these steps and land on top of the building directly to the north.

63
Creek, jump to the west off this ramp and land on the northbound section of freeway.

64
Redsands West, jump north from this ramp and land on a ledge on the building to the north.

65
Las Venturas, heading east, use this wooden ramp to make it over the freeway bridge (use one of the faster bikes).

66
Las Venturas, use the wooden ramp between the storage containers to jump north onto the westbound section of freeway.

67
Las Venturas, use the ramp to jump east out of multi-story parking garage.

68
Randolph Industrial Estate, use rickety ramp to jump north out of the warehouse compound.

69
Emerald Isle, speed west through the wooden poles and use the ramp (go through the Police Bribe) and jump over the street.

70
Las Venturas, this jump is the same as jump #60, but this time jump off the ramp on the north side of the building (the lower ledge).

Miscellaneous Required Odd Jobs

This is where you'll find the details surrounding all the miscellaneous Required Odd Jobs. You must complete these to achieve 100% completion of the game. The following missions are listed in alphabetical order, for ease of use. Note, however, that some Odd Jobs are stashed within larger categorical headings, such as "Stadium Events" or "Vehicle Missions."

BMX Challenge

Details

After completing Big Smoke (the first mission), head to the BMX park and get on the BMX bike parked near the large half-pipe on the east side of Glen Park. You can try the BMX challenge at the beginning of the game, if your cycling stat is at least 20%.

Gotta Have Bike Skills

It's best to take part in this challenge when you have a Cycling Skill over 80%. A skill this high allows for a higher bunny hop ability, which enables CJ to easily reach the high coronas. These areas are definitely the toughest ones to reach.

Collect all of the checkpoint coronas peppered throughout the skate park while remaining on the bike. The clock starts with 10 seconds and an additional 10 seconds is earned for each checkpoint that is collected. The mission ends in failure when time runs out. Another way to lose is to fall off the bike and fail to return to the bike within 24 seconds.

✅ **Prerequisite**
You must have a Cycling Skill of 20% to trigger this mission.
🔘 **Location**
BMX Park in Glen Park, Los Santos
🔘 **Reward**
A step toward 100% completion.

It's strongly recommended to collect all the easy coronas first of the 19 red corona checkpoints. Then use this accumulated time to access the more difficult checkpoints, like the half pipe coronas. Replay this mission as often as you like to top your best score.

Chiliad Challenge

Details

Chiliad Challenge consists of three events, all of which involve downhill mountain biking. During any event, you have 25 seconds to get back on the Mountain Bike should CJ fall off; if not, the mission ends in failure. In this downhill checkpoint race, you

must finish in first place to open the next event. This section contains maps and strategies for all three Chiliad Challenge events.

⊖ **WARNING: Don't Drive-by!**

We tried it; you won't like it! Don't try to tip the scales in your favor by blasting away at the other bikers in drive-by fashion. This will result in a disqualification from the race. But, you can stop short of the finish line and pull out your sniper rifle. Then, pick off the other riders after they have crossed the finish line.

Chiliad Challenge Race 1: Scotch Bonnet Yellow Route

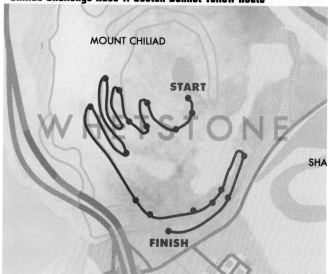

Competitors: 5

It may take a few attempts to get a feel for the downhill checkpoint course. The challenge will be easier, though, if your Cycling Skill is high. Basically, you won't fall off the bike as easily.

Use the back brake in the turns to perform powerslide cornering, and speed pedal in the straightaways to push past the competition. If CJ falls over the edge of the mountain, the game automatically places him back on the path. Winning this race opens the Birdseye Winder challenge, so head back up to the top of the mountain!

Chiliad Challenge Race 2: Birdseye Winder Yellow Route

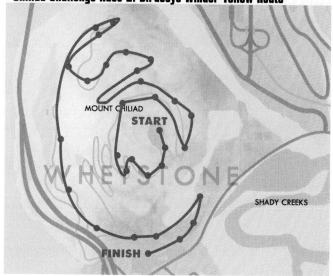

Competitors: 5

Up until the fifth checkpoint, this race is the same as the first race. Things change around checkpoint 6, as the route heads down a new side of the mountain. Checkpoint 9 is a dangerously sharp turn, so slow down early and use powerslide cornering.

Watch out for some sharp turns after checkpoints 14 and 16; each one has a blind corner so proceed cautiously or risk pedaling off the edge of the mountain. Save CJ's sprint energy for speeding through checkpoints 21 to 23. There's a lengthy straightaway here that is perfect for high-speed action. Finish first to unlock the last Chiliad course, Cobra Run.

Chiliad Challenge Race 3: Cobra Run

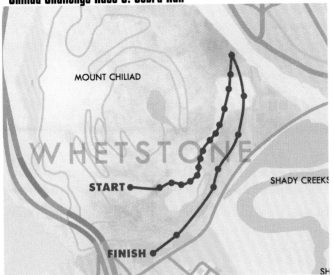

Competitors: 2

Cobra Run starts from the same location on the top of Mount Chiliad as the other two races, but the view shifts to a starting line located elsewhere on the mountain. What makes this race so difficult is the snake-like board-walk at the bottom of the first slope. The good news is that there are only two competitors. The bad news is that they negotiate the boardwalk like it was a four-lane highway!

Use both brakes to hold it together at the bottom of the first slope and get on the snake-like boardwalk as soon as possible. Take it easy on the boardwalk and use the brakes often to navigate the twists and turns. After the walkway, there are plenty of opportunities to pass the competitors.

There's a large cliff jump just beyond the wooden walkway. Build up plenty of speed to clear the large mound at the bottom; if not, you'll come to an abrupt stop if you hit it. Then it's smooth sailing after the first hairpin turn. Stay close to the moun-tainside and always turn towards the mountain when cresting blind turns.

Upon successfully completing all three races, you can replay the chal-lenges again to top your best times.

Courier

There are three courier challenges in San Andreas, one each in Los Santos, San Fierro, and Las Venturas. Each challenge consists of multiple stages, much like the vehicle missions. Each city-specific courier challenge is per-formed using a 2-wheeled vehicle.

Get on the vehicle located at the job pick-up location to start the challenge. Drive around town and throw packages through drop-off coronas before the allotted time runs out. There are more packages than corona drop-off loca-tions, so the better your aim, the more money you'll make. A monetary reward is given for leftover packages, as well as time remaining on the clock.

The drop-off coronas are red glow-ing rings that appear on the radar as yellow blips. Throw the package through the red corona and travel to the next ring as fast as possible. When each corona has received its delivery, return to the job start loca-tion and stop in the red marker to collect a payment.

Do not, however, get off the vehicle as the next stage will start momentari-ly. Each subsequent stage brings more delivery locations at greater dis-tances, thus making the challenge much more difficult. The following sec-tion details all three courier challenges.

Missed Throws

Missed throws are costly, since the end reward is partially based on leftover packages. Each extra package is worth $100! So, if a thrown package misses its mark, run over the missed package before throwing another one to return it to your inventory.

Los Santos Courier

⊛ Location
Roboi's Food Mart in Commerce, Los Santos

⑤ Reward:
Completion of Los Santos Courier turns Roboi's Food Mart into an asset property. Swing by daily to pick up the $2000 it generates.

⊜ Vehicle Used
BMX

Stage 1

The Los Santos Courier mission starts by hopping on the BMX that is outside Roboi's Food Mart in Commerce. You have three minutes, six packages, and only three drop-off locations. All three locations are close to the job pick-up location, as well. Use the in-game map to plot the quickest route, but keep in mind that the final location is always Roboi's Food Mart. The final drop-off does not appear as a blip on the radar until all deliveries have been made.

Stage 2

In this stage, things change as there are six packages to deliver to four coronas within five minutes. The coronas are more widespread then the previous stage. Try delivering the packages in the following order: Market, Temple, Idlewood, then Verdant Bluffs (drag the crosshairs on the in-game map across the drop-off locations to display the area name).

Stage 3

In stage 3, there are seven packages to deliver to five locations within five minutes. Try making the deliveries in the following order (refer to the in-game map): Conference Center, Verdant Bluffs, Idlewood, Pershing Square, then Verona Beach.

Stage 4

In stage 4, there are six deliveries to make within eight minutes with a total of eight packages. During this stage, rely heavily on the large map instead of the in-game radar, as this could cause delays by heading down dead-end roads.

Try collecting the packages in this order: Santa Maria Beach boardwalk, Santa Maria Beach lighthouse (head north across the grassy field to cut the corner), Vinewood, Temple, East Beach, then to the Playa Del Seville fuel tanks.

San Fierro Courier

⊛ Location
Hippy Shopper in Queens, San Fierro

⑤ Reward:
Completion of San Fierro Courier turns Hippy Shopper into an asset property. Swing by daily to pick up the $2000 it generates.

⊜ Vehicle Used
Freeway

Stage 1

The first stage of the San Fierro Courier mission begins after mounting the Freeway motorcycle parked outside the Hippy Shopper in Queens. For stage 1, there are six packages to deliver to three drop-off locations within three minutes.

The three coronas are very close to the Hippy Shopper, so this one isn't tough to accomplish.

Stage 2

Stage 2 consists of four drop-off locations, six packages, and a total of five minutes to complete the task. Try starting with the corona in City Hall to the west followed by China Town, Downtown, and save the Garcia location for last. Zip back to the Hippy Shopper to collect your cut.

Stage 3

Stage 3 has five drop-off locations, seven packages, and a total of five minutes to complete the task. Try going in this order: Ocean Flats, Palisades, Paradiso, China Town, then Doherty. Cut corners when it is safe to do so. By following this route, it's possible to finish the mission with over a minute remaining.

Stage 4

Stage 4 has six drop-off locations, eight packages, and a time limit of six minutes. Try this order: Avispa, northeast to Cranberry Station, take the tunnel Downtown, then go east to the second Downtown corona. Go to Juniper Hollow last.

Las Venturas Courier

◉ **Location**
Burger Shot, Redsands East, Las Venturas

💲 **Reward:**
Completion of Las Venturas Courier turns Burger Shot into an asset property. Swing by daily to pick up the $2000 it generates.

🚗 **Vehicle Used**
Faggio

Stage 1

Jump on the Faggio outside of the Burger Shot in Redsands East to begin the Las Venturas Courier missions. The first stage has three drop-off locations, six packages, and a time limit of three minutes.

Stage 2

Stage 2 has four drop-off locations and six packages that must be delivered within five minutes.

Try this delivery route: start with the northernmost Las Venturas Airport delivery followed by the southern Las Venturas Airport stop. Next, head east to The Camel's Toe Casino corona, then go north up The Strip to the Royal Casino drop-off.

Stage 3

There are five drop-off locations, seven packages, and a five-minute time limit for stage 3. The drop-off locations almost form a nice, oval course, except for the oddball location that's a little too far south to make things easy.

Try this route: start with the Red Sands West corona followed by the Las Venturas Airport drop-off. Head east to the Royal Casino corona (southern Strip location), then drive north up The Strip near the Old Venturas Strip corona. Make the final drop-off the one at the Red Sands East.

Stage 4

Stage 4 consists of six drop-off locations, eight packages, and a seven-minute time limit. This one is tough. Try using the following route to attain the more troublesome drop-off locations.

Drive east to the Roca Escalante corona, followed by the Spinybed neighborhood drop-off. Drive west to the Prickle Pine corona, then southwest to the Redsands West location. A short wall surrounds the Redsands corona, which makes it tough to reach quickly. The entrance to this facility is on the northeastern corner of the property. Find a dirt road exit on the southwest side of the building near a nice billboard.

Finally, rush to the Whitewood Estates corona, then head south to the Blackfield corona. The corona in the Blackfield location is enclosed by another short wall. Approach the arena from the south entrances. Find the corona in the recessed area beside the arena. Now haul it to the

Burger Shot in Redsands East, also using the northern parking lot exit to leave the arena.

Exports & Imports

Details

After completing the main story mission, Customs Fast Track, vehicle Exporting and Importing is unlocked at the car crane on the docks in San Fierro (the same crane that is used in Customs Fast Track). A list of vehicles for exporting is written on the large chalkboard near the car crane. You must acquire a vehicle that is on the export list, drive it to the docks and then, using the crane, place it on the ship. Upon doing so, the vehicle is removed from the export list and a cash reward is given. The export list comprises 10 cars, and 10 more cars appear after the first 10 are delivered. There are three lists of 10 cars each, for a total of 30 cars to export!

Prerequisite
Complete Customs Fast Track mission
Location
The Easter Basin Docks in San Fierro

Great New Alert Feature!

After completing Customs Fast Track, a cool new feature appears. Each time you enter a vehicle that is on the Export list, a text message sends a reminder that the current vehicle you're driving can be exported. When this happens, save the car in one of the many save house garages. By doing so, the vehicle hunt becomes much easier since you can store cars for safe keeping.

Crane Operation

It's possible to operate the car crane much like the one that lifted vehicles for exporting in the previous games. To make moving the car onto the ship quicker and easier, park the stolen vehicle in front of the crane and near the ship.

Drive It Up!

You can actually drive vehicles up the ship ramp and park them in the red marker, but it's a risky process, as you will likely damage the vehicle in the process. However, this method is a bit quicker than moving the vehicles by crane (depending on your proficiency with the crane).

Export Boards

The following table illustrates the three different car export boards. Keep in mind that the next board does not appear until the previous board has been cleared. For a visual reference of each vehicle, refer to the "Vehicle Showroom" section in this guide. Notice that the amount of money to be earned from this Odd Job is much more than any other Odd Job in the game. After collecting all of the vehicles on the list, a bonus reward of $215,000 is given. That's enough to buy a couple of sports cars!

EXPORT BOARD

Board 1	Reward	Board 2	Reward	Board 3	Reward
Patriot	$40,000	Slamvan	$19,000	Blade	$19,000
Sanchez	$10,000	Blista Compact	$35,000	Freeway	$10,000
Stretch	$40,000	Stafford	$35,000	Mesa	$25,000
Feltzer	$35,000	Sabre	$19,000	ZR-350	$45,000
Remington	$30,000	FCR-900	$10,000	Euros	$35,000
Buffalo	$35,000	Cheetah	$105,000	Banshee	$45,000
Sentinel	$35,000	Rancher	$40,000	Super GT	$105,000
Infernus	$95,000	Stallion	$19,000	Journey	$22,000
Camper	$26,000	Tanker	$35,000	Huntley	$40,000
Admiral	$35,000	Comet	$135,000	BF Injection	$15,000

Imports

The very same blackboard that contains the exporting list also has a list of cars available for importing. Walk up to the board until a text message appears asking if you would like to view vehicles for purchase.

The Import menu displays a list of the days of the week. Notice that the Club ($28,000), Perennial ($8,000), and Jester ($28,000) are the only vehicles available from the start. Also note that they are each only available on two days of the week.

When you choose a car for importing, it appears on the deck of the ship. You must drive it off the ship, or use the crane to lower it to the ground. The vehicle's cost is deducted from your cash total. The cars available for importing depend on a couple of factors: 1. The day of the week; 2. Which cars have been unlocked by fulfilling the exporting requirements.

Days of the Week

If you haven't already noticed, the day of the week is abbreviated on the bottom corner of the Performance Stat screen. Check to see what day it is before trying to order a vehicle.

Once the exporting process begins, each vehicle delivered for export also becomes available to import. Bonus cars are also unlocked for importing as the export lists are fulfilled. One bonus rare vehicle available for import is awarded after making five and ten export deliveries on each export list (see the following table below). Each rare vehicle is only available on a certain day of the week. The text message that appears after delivering a vehicle usually indicates that only one vehicle has been added to the import list. During the following delivery intervals, the message states that "Two cars have been added to the import list."

RARE IMPORTS

# of cars collected	Vehicle Unlocked Board 1	Cost	Board 2	Cost	Board 3	Cost
5	Monster	$32,000	Bandito	$12,000	Vortex	$20,800
10	Windsor	$28,000	Turismo	$76,000	Bullet	$84,000

Fix Damaged Vehicles

Do not deliver a damaged vehicle for exporting, as it will reduce the vehicle's export price. Take it to a Pay N' Spray if damage occurs, then head for the crane.

Freight Train

Details

The trains in Los Santos stop at Unity Station or Market Station, while the ones in San Fierro stop at Cranberry Station. In Las Venturas, the trains stop at the following three train stations: Sobell Train Yards, Linden Station, and Yellow Bell

Station. Hijack a train when it stops at any of the stations. Simply run up to the engine, yank the engineer out, and accelerate. After gaining control of a train, begin the Freight Train challenge.

Each train only has two controls: accelerate and stop. Keep in mind that it takes a train a very long time to reach its top speed and it also takes a while to slow it to a complete stop.

When the mission begins, a yellow blip appears at the next closest station. This marks the cargo delivery location. The goal is to stop the engine in the red marker to complete the first stage; stopping any other section of the train in the red marker does not count. The time limit, dis-

tance to the next train station, and the train's speed is displayed on the right side of the screen. The mission will end in failure if you do not reach the checkpoints within the time limits, or you derail the train off its track.

 Free Public Transportation

Once you complete the Freight Train challenge, you can walk up to any train passenger car and take a free ride.

Prerequisite
Complete Yay Ka-Boom-Boom mission
Location
Jack a train when it stops at any train station
Reward
$50,000 (plus free transportation)

Study the tracks using the in-game map (train tracks appear as red lines on the map and radar) and look for sharp turns. The controller begins to shake at speeds nearing 50 mph, which is a high speed warning. Slow down the train to about 45 mph or less when taking really sharp turns.

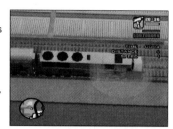

Use the distance meter and the speed meter to judge when to slow down so that the train stops inside the red marker. If the train over-shoots it mark, back up and stop inside the marker for a second chance. After stopping in the marker, the cargo is offloaded and it's time

to move to the next stage of the challenge. Money is earned and bonus time is added to the clock for the next delivery.

To complete a level, make five successful deliveries in a row. Upon completing the first level, exit the train and catch another train to start Level 2. Complete Level 2 (there are only two levels) to earn $50,000!

Gyms

Fat & Muscle Stats

Gyms are for ridding CJ of excess fat and improving his stamina and physique (muscle). A nice physique raises his Sex Appeal and earns him more Respect. Fitness actually plays a 20% role in Sex Appeal and a 4% role in Respect. Muscle plays a 3% role in Respect.

Lose weight by running, swimming, and biking in-game, as well as using the stationary bike, running on the treadmill, and lifting weights. Each of these activities reduces Fat by 2.5% or raises Muscle by 1% per interval (you must lose fat before gaining muscle). One "interval" is equal to about 14 seconds of cycling or running on the treadmill. A weight lifting "interval" is equal to lifting a weight once.

Running, swimming, and biking give you 1.5% Fat and 1% Muscle per interval. This is approximately every 150 seconds for running and 100 seconds for biking and swimming. These activities also add 5% Stamina approximately every 150 seconds for swimming and 300 seconds for biking and running. They also increase CJ's maximum Health 2% approximately every 600 seconds. WARNING: If you don't have any Fat, these activities will actually burn 1% Muscle every interval!

WARNING: Workout Limit!

If you lose 40% Fat or gain 20% Stamina or build 20% Muscle, you will reach the daily allowed limit in the Gym and will not be allowed to workout for another 12 hours.

Treadmill and Stationary Bike

Workout Results

The treadmill is used to increase CJ's Stamina stat, which enables him to sprint longer. The higher the Stamina stat, the longer CJ can sprint during one attempt.

Fat & Stamina Stat

Using the treadmill and the stationary bike allows you to lose Fat faster than any other in-game exercise (swimming, running, biking). For every 14-second interval on these machines, you can lose 8% Fat and gain 4% Stamina.

Bench Press

Workout Results

Using the bench press increases CJ's Body Muscle (after the Fat is worked off), which is exhibited in his outward appearance. An increase in muscle mass also helps increase CJ's Sex Appeal. Melee attacks also inflict more damage.

⊖ WARNING: Muscle Atrophy

Keep in mind that no matter how much you work out, muscle will always be deteriorating very slowly. It could be days until you notice the change. This will keep you coming back to the Gym to maintain your desired figure.

Dumbbells

Workout Results

Using the dumbbells has the same effect as using the bench press; it increases CJ's Body Muscle. As with the Bench Press, CJ exhibits physical signs of increasing muscle mass. Melee attacks also cause more damage.

Boxing Event, Martial Arts, Kick Boxing

Walk into the red marker near the trainer at the punching bags.

Target the trainer and press the attack buttons to punch. When he goes down, attack him with kicks until the targeting reticule turns black. When the trainer falls in defeat, the new moves appear: **Running Attack**, **Ground Attack**, and **Combo Attack**.

Los Santos Gym

⊘ Gym Prerequisite

Gyms open after completing Sweet's mission, Drive-Thru

✷ Location

The Los Santos Gymnasium is located on a corner in Ganton, very close to Grove Street. Find another gym at Verona Beach.

% Reward

The workout equipment improves CJ's Respect, Body Muscle, and Stamina. With enough Body Muscle, it's possible to also unlock the fight trainers in the gyms.

Details

The Gym is open at every hour of every day. All gyms are stocked with a treadmill, dumbbells, a bench press, and a cycle machine. Each Gym also employs a fight instructor who is trained in a particular fighting style. Spar with the instructor to learn new moves.

Los Santos Boxing Trainer

Training Results

Complete the challenge to learn three new fighting moves.

Training Prerequisites

Work out on the bench press or dumbbells and surpass the "buff" stage of the Body Muscle stat until a text message appears indicating that new fighting moves can be learned. A red marker appears in front of the boxer working out on the punching bags in the Los Santos Gym.

San Fierro Gym

⊛ Location

The San Fierro Gymnasium, the Cobra Marital Arts gym, is located in Garcia. Locate the dumbbell icon in San Fierro for the exact location.

San Fierro Martial Arts Trainer

Training Results

Complete the challenge to learn three new fighting moves.

Training Prerequisites

Work out on the bench press or dumbbells and surpass the "buff" stage of the Body Muscle stat until a text message appears, indicating that new fighting moves can be learned. If you already earned this in Los Santos, you do not need to earn it a second time.

Las Venturas Gym

⊛ Location

The Las Venturas Gymnasium, called Below the Belt, is located in Redsands East. Locate the dumbbell icon in Las Venturas for the exact location (there's a Bomb Shop next door to it).

Las Venturas Kick Boxing Trainer

Training Results

Complete the challenge to learn three new fighting moves.

Training Prerequisites

Work out on the bench press or dumbbells and surpass the "buff" stage of the Body Muscle stat until a text message appears, indicating that new fighting moves can be learned. As noted earlier, if you have already earned this once before, you don't need to earn it again.

NRG-500 Challenge

✓ Prerequisite

Gain safe entry into San Fierro.

⊛ Location

Under the covered dry dock at the Easter Basin Docks in San Fierro (near Export/Import car crane).

⊘ Reward

One step closer to 100% completion of San Andreas.

This challenge is very similar to the BMX Challenge in Glen Park, Los Santos, but this time you're on super-fast 2-wheeler in the game! When the challenge begins, several red coronas appear in, around, and above the dry dock. You must col-

lect all the coronas before time runs out. The challenge begins with 10 seconds on the clock. For each corona you pass through, 10 seconds are added to your total time. The check-point coronas appear as red blips on your radar. Remember that triangle blips pointing up are higher than you, and those pointing down are lower.

Details

Find the NRG-500 parked under the dry dock shelter near the Export/Import location in Easter Basin, San Fierro. The bike is in a nook behind a stack of shipping containers. The challenge begins when you mount the bike.

Get all of the coronas inside the bowl first, then go after the one in the middle high above. Once on the outside, drive along the outside edge and get the coronas on the outside. Then return inside the bowl and get the ones up high.

To reach the high coronas, you must first locate them with the camera control and by looking at the blips on the radar. Notice that below the high-floating checkpoints you can find a long, dark shadow on the side of the dock near the top edge. These shadows help you better locate the checkpoint that floats above without using manual camera controls.

Pick a target checkpoint and build up speed inside the dry dock and zip up the slanted wall of the dock. Aim for the shadow cast by the checkpoint above and rocket out of the dock, and through the checkpoint. Repeat until all high-floating checkpoints are collected.

Lowrider Challenge

Prerequisite
Complete the Cesar Vialpando mission.
Location
Outside of the Unity Train Station in El Corona, Los Santos.
Reward
Cash earned during challenge.

A series of arrow icons passes through the circle at the bottom of the screen in random order. Press in the direction indicated by each arrow as it passes through the circle. Concentrate on the beat of the music more than the alignment of the arrows inside the circle. Press firmly in the direction indicated for a higher bounce!

Details

After completing the Cesar Vialpando mission, walk into the red marker on the sidewalk near El Corona's Unity Train Station. The man in the mechanic's jumpsuit points CJ in the direction of the meet, which is just on the other side of the wall in the train station parking lot.

First, purchase some **Hydraulics** from Loco Low Co. if your vehicle doesn't have Hydraulics. Do this before taking part in the job, or the meeting will disperse by the time you return. While in a lowrider vehicle with a Hydraulics system, stop inside the red marker in the train station's parking lot to start this car-bouncing mini-game. Place a wager between $50 and $1000.

To score points, the lowrider must bounce to the rhythm of the music and your button presses must be in sync. Points are awarded to the opposition if you miss, bounce in the wrong direction, or exhibit bad rhythm. Bounce to the rhythm until the song ends and collect your winnings. After completing this challenge, you must wait until the next day to try it again.

Quarry Missions

✅ **Prerequisite**
Complete the Explosive Situation mission.

✴ **Location**
Follow the bulldozer icon on the map and radar to Hunter Quarry in southern Bone County.

💲 **Reward**
Cash awards and completing the missions makes the Hunter Quarry an asset property. Return to the site office to collect $2000 daily.

Details

By completing the Explosive Situation mission, a bulldozer icon appears near the Hunter Quarry in Bone County. Walk up to the site office at the east entrance to the Hunter Quarry, and step into the red marker to begin the first Quarry mission. Each of the seven missions are unique and, once completed, they contribute to the 100% completion of the game. After finishing all seven, you can choose to play them again to beat your best time.

QUARRY MISSION 1
Reward: $500

You are given 3:30 to get into the Dozer and clear the paths before the next delivery arrives. Push all seven rocks (green blips on the radar) over the edge of the quarry trail and into the red markers on the next tier below. The rocks do not have to fall directly into the red markers; just push them over the edge of the trail.

The Dozer has a working loader, but you can leave it down for the duration of this mission. It may take a minute to get used to the Dozer's steering, as the steering revolves around the back wheels. This makes the steering backwards compared to the other vehicles in the game.

QUARRY MISSION 2
Reward: $1000

In this mission, there are several explosive barrels strategically placed around the site that must be disarmed in a set amount of time.

You have 1:29 to get into the Dozer and clear the four bombs. Each bomb cleared adds one minute to your time. The first bomb is behind the site office. Make sure the loader is lowered and roll the barrel into the red marker before the time expires. As soon as the barrel enters the marker, another bomb appears. Continue into the quarry and clear the other three bombs.

QUARRY MISSION 3
Reward: $2000

Some thieves have stolen some equipment and they're escaping in a Dumper. Use the nearby Dumper to destroy their vehicle. To complete this mission, you must remain inside the Dumper. Ultimately, this limits your available choices for destroying the vehicle. The answer is a drive-by!

Enter the Dumper and follow the red blip on the map. The thieves head west on the road closest to the quarry, then eventually head north for Fort Carson. Cut corners to quickly catch up to the truck. Once you catch up to them, perform a P.I.T. maneuver (see "Driving School" section) and blast their Dumper full of lead. When it blows up, the mission ends in success!

QUARRY MISSION 4
Reward: $3000

Although the bombers from the previous mission were caught, their bodies are loaded into a Dumper at the other entrance to the quarry. It's time to dump them before the cops come snooping around, but there's only four minutes to do so.

Jump onto the Sanchez near the site office and head northwest around the outside of the quarry. Look for the checkpoint at the quarry's north entrance. Drive through the checkpoint and enter the Dumper parked in the distance (blue blip).

Drive the Dumper with the dead bodies back to the east entrance near the site office (yellow blip). The Dumper travels over rough terrain with ease, but its large tires cause the vehicle to bounce when driven inappropriately. If a body falls out of the truck, the mission ends in failure. Note that upon entering the quarry, the bodies slide around much more.

Drive down the tiers of the quarry with extreme caution. If the bodies begin to slide out, hit the brakes or slam it into reverse to force them toward the front of the loader. Once you reach the fire, back the truck up and raise the loader to dump the bodies.

QUARRY MISSION 5
Reward: $5000

Drive the Dumper, this time loaded with explosives, to the desert airstrip (Verdant Meadows). The "Deadline" time given for this mission is 3:00.

The most difficult part of this mission is accomplishing it within the time allotted. The drive to Verdant Meadows must be swift, but extreme caution is needed. The mission will end if one of the following occurs: you hit a car, run into a large roadside rock, or drop an explosive barrel.

It's possible to cut through the fields while heading northwest to Verdant Meadows, but a planned route is a necessity. To play it safe, stick to the main roads and make up for lost time on the return trip. If you experience difficulty seeing the traffic ahead of the truck, use first-person view or tilt the camera upward.

Upon reaching the red marker (yellow blip) at the end of the Verdant Meadows runway, use the handbrake and dump the load into the red marker. If the barrels hit outside of the soft soil inside the red marker, the mission is failed. Successfully dump the load to complete the mission.

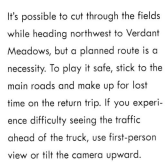

QUARRY MISSION 6
Reward: $7500

A Dumper has spilled its load of explosives all along the train tracks. Use the Dozer to clear the explosives before the next train passes. You have exactly 3:00 to complete this task.

Hop into the Dozer and locate the multiple green blips on the radar covering the nearby railroad (red line on the radar). Quickly head for the tracks and approach the explosives.

There's not enough time to push each barrel off the tracks. Start at the southern end of barrels along the right track and follow the track to the north. As you push through the barrels, they begin to roll off to the side of the tracks as more barrels are pushed into each other. When a barrel is cleared from the tracks, the green blip on the radar disappears.

Sometimes an occasional barrel won't roll far enough away from the track. When this occurs, the green blip remains on the radar. Use the same tactic to remove all of the barrels from the tracks.

QUARRY MISSION 7
Reward: $10,000

In this mission, an officer has been killed. Use the Dozer at the bottom of the quarry to dispose of the body before more authorities arrive. This mission involves a handful of objectives that must be completed in a timely manner. The timer is set at 8:00 minutes to complete this mission.

Jump onto the Sanchez (near the site office) and race into the quarry. With total disregard for the trail, head for the Dozer at the bottom of the quarry (blue blip). Accelerate and jump from tier after tier to reach the Dozer. Note that these jumps will earn an **Insane Stunt Bonus** award.

Two green blips that appear on the radar upon entering the Dozer represent the locations of the HPV-1000 police motorcycle and the officer's body bag. Use the Dozer to push each object into the crane pick-up area (red marker on the quarry floor). It doesn't matter which object is pushed first, just get them both inside the red marker below the crane. The bike is in plain sight, while the body bag is behind a mound of earth.

With both objects in the crane pick-up area, exit the Dozer and ride the Sanchez up the trail to the red marker near the crane. Jump off the bike and enter the red marker next to the crane.

Move the magnet to the left and drop it on top of the body bag or the police bike. Lift and turn the magnet to the right and drop the object into the Dumper's loader (blue blip). Get the object as close to the truck's cab as possible, so there is room for them to slide around. With the bike and the body in the Dumper, exit the crane and enter the Dumper. Carefully drive the Dumper up the trail it was facing and proceed north to the yellow blip. After passing through the site office entrance, dump the body and the bike into the water.

Follow the new yellow blip to the south, across the street and to the water's edge. Back up the truck into the red marker at the edge of the cliff and lift the loader to dump the objects over the cliff into the water below (into the red marker). Once the objects hit the water— and the marker—the mission is complete.

After successfully completing all of the Quarry missions, you can play the missions over again to beat your best time.

Race Tournaments

Los Santos Race Tournament

Prerequisite

Complete the San Fierro mission Deconstruction, then complete the Driving School. A phone call alerts you to the Race Tournaments opportunity.

Locations

After the phone call, four race flag icons appear around San Andreas. There is one in Los Santos, one in San Fierro, and two in Las Venturas. Find these locations on the map and step into the red markers to access that area's Race Tournament menu.

Reward

Cash awards from winning races.

Details

These races are actually illegal street races that involve a variety of vehicles. From the Race Menu, select a race from the multiple races. The Race Menu shows the name of the race, the length of the track, and a map illustrating the course. It also displays the best time and position, if you have attempted it previously. Each race can be replayed an unlimited number of times.

General Rules

The race ends in failure if you destroy your vehicle or an opponent's vehicle. If you leave your vehicle, you have 25 seconds to return to it before the mission is failed.

Each race is a unique checkpoint-style race against computer-controlled opponents through a specific area of San Andreas. Simply pass through the active checkpoint to activate the next checkpoint. A $10,000 cash reward is given to the winner at the end of each race.

 Driving Skill

The higher CJ's Driving and Bike Skills, the better chance he'll have to win the race. For example, the Blade in the Lowrider Race fishtails less often when CJ's Driving Skill is higher. A full Driving Stat bar makes the Lowrider handle much better.

Location

Follow the race flag icon on the Los Santos map to Little Mexico and step into the red marker behind the building.

Details

The nine available races at the Los Santos, Little Mexico Race Tournament are: Lowrider Race, Little Loop, Backroad Wanderer, City Circuit, Vinewood, Freeway, Into the Country, Badlands A, and Badlands B.

Lowrider Race

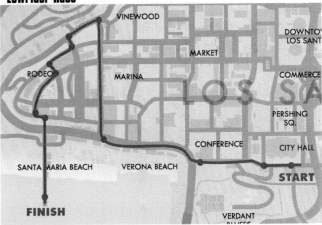

Track Distance: 1.46 miles
Vehicle Used: Blade

A low Driving Skill may lead to difficult handling in the corners with the Blade. The rear of this lowrider feels light, so take it easy in the turns to avoid fishtailing. Use the Blade's surprising top speed to zip past competitors in the straightaways. Watch out for the opposing traffic when entering the Santa Maria Beach boardwalk; turn onto—and stay on—the right side of the road along the boardwalk.

Little Loop

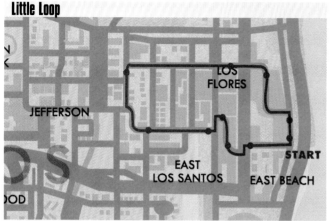

⊕ **Track Distance: 0.82 miles**
🚗 **Vehicle Used: NGR-500**

This motorcycle race begins on East Beach and runs through East Los Santos. From the start, lean forward while accelerating. The NGR-500 is so powerful that you automatically perform a wheelie if you don't push the front end down. Also, hold down the front end as you crest the large hills along this hilly, city course.

Backroad Wanderer

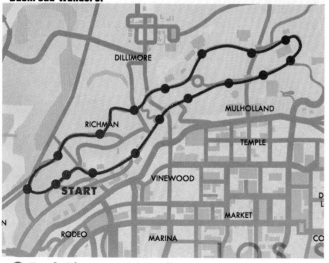

⊕ **Track Distance: 2.05 miles**
🚗 **Vehicle Used: FCR-900 or BF-400**

This motorcycle street race begins in the hills of Richman and loops around in Mulholland, eventually returning to the starting position in Richman. Drive down the middle of the divided roads to avoid traffic.

City Circuit

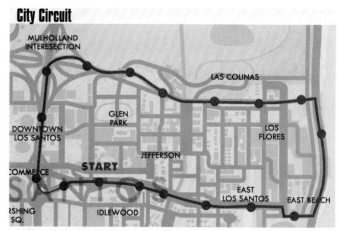

⊕ **Track Distance: 2.26 miles**
🚗 **Vehicle Used: FCR-900**

This motorcycle race starts on the freeway in Idlewood, extends to East Beach, then pays a return visit to Idlewood. Essentially, it's a large, oval-like course with nothing but left turns.

Vinewood

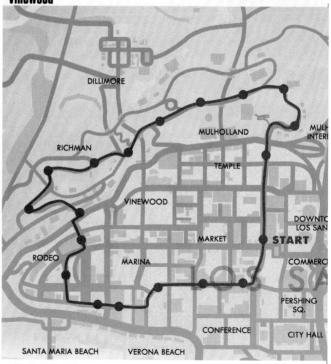

⊕ **Track Distance: 2.41 miles**
🚗 **Vehicle Used: Sunrise**

This sedan and two-door compact car race is one of the tougher challenges in this race circuit. Getting ahead of the competitors early is very beneficial. Notice how all the competitors swerve across the road at the start of the race. To counter this, swerve in the opposite direction.

Freeway

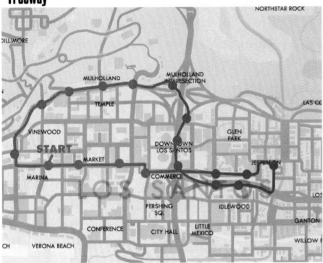

⬡ **Track Distance: 2.62 miles**
🚗 **Vehicle Used: Super GT**

Freeway is a race through the heart of Los Santos against 12 other two-door sports cars. From the start, ride on the left side of the road to pass the pack of competitors to the right. Watch out as everyone swerves to miss slower, non-racing traffic.

Into the Country

⬡ **Track Distance: 5.22 miles**
🚗 **Vehicle Used: Bullet**

Unleash the power of the Bullet in this race, with all of its wide-open roads and straightaways. When this vehicle hits its top speed, the competition will be left in the dust—even before you leave the city! The short drive through northern Red County can be trouble-free once your competitors are out of the picture.

Badlands A

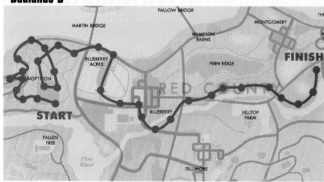

- **Track Distance: 2.99 miles**
- **Vehicle Used: Sabre**

Badlands A and Badlands B are actually one race that has been divided into two parts. You must win both races to earn as much as the other race's pay out. These races may seem very familiar if you completed Catalina's mission, Farewell, My Love.

Make sure you hit the barn-jumping ramp with enough speed to clear the barn. If you don't have enough speed, simply go around it.

Badlands B

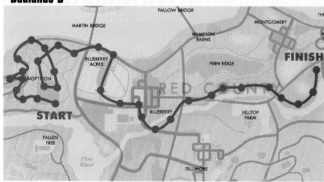

- **Track Distance: 2.99 miles**
- **Vehicle Used: ZR-350**

This race is along the same course as Badlands A, except this time you return back to the Badlands A starting position! Another noticeable difference is the vehicle, which is the ZR-350.

Downtown San Fierro Race Tournament

- **Location**
  Follow the race flag icon on the San Fierro map to the area behind the Wang Car Showroom (an asset property) in Downtown San Fierro. This is just down the block from the Cranberry Train Station and the Garage that you won in the main story missions.

Details

The six races available at the Downtown Race Tournament are: Dirtbike Danger, Bandito County, Go-Go Carting, San Fierro Fastlane, San Fierro Hills, and Country Endurance.

Dirtbike Danger

- **Track Distance: 1.99 miles**
- **Vehicle Used: Sanchez**

The Dirtbike Danger race is an off-road dirt bike race through Back O' Beyond in Flint County. Although it's one of the shorter races, it can be quite trying. The Sanchez is the fastest bike over rough terrain, but it is very light and somewhat difficult to handle. (Get CJ's Bike Skills up to make this race easier.) Pull the front wheel up when exiting bridges that lead to dirt mounds; if not, a face-plant is inevitable.

Bandito County

Track Distance: 2.02 miles

Vehicle Used: Bandito

The Bandito, which has a very low center of gravity, can do amazing jumps at insane angles and still land on all fours. However, there are a couple of places on the course that can be troublesome, so be warned.

Go-Go Carting

Track Distance: 1.18 miles

Vehicle Used: Kart

Since the Kart is so low to the ground, it's capable of insanely sharp turns without turning over. The steering is hypersensitive, though.

One of the toughest challenges is to avoid traffic and pedestrians. Since the Kart is so small and light, hitting a pedestrian can really mess things up.

San Fierro Fastlane

Track Distance: 1.64 miles

Vehicle Used: Alpha

This race goes through the hilly streets of San Fierro, starting in Paradiso and reaching into Juniper Hollow, Calton Heights and the Downtown area. The car of choice is an Alpha, while the competition drives similar 2-door sports cars. When you fly off the crest of a hill, do so in a straight line so that the vehicle doesn't go off-course.

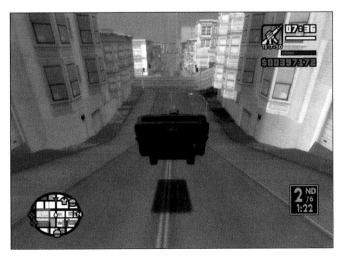

San Fierro Hills

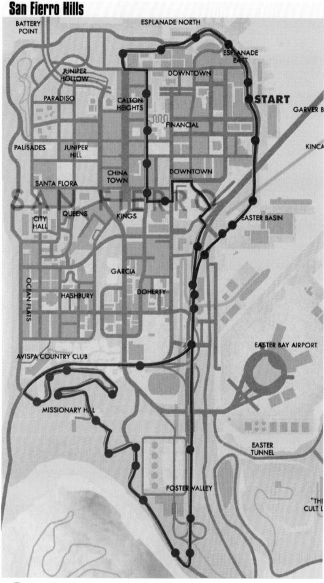

Track Distance: 5.20 miles

Vehicle Used: Phoenix

The San Fierro Hills race begins on the eastern edge of Downtown San Fierro and reaches as far as Mount Chiliad, then snakes back to the starting position. All of the competitors drive vehicles similar to the Phoenix, so it shouldn't be a tough race.

Country Endurance

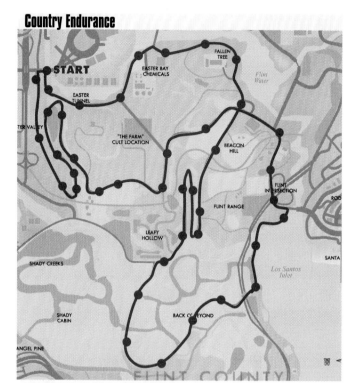

Track Distance: 6.68 miles

Vehicle Used: Bullet

Country Endurance is longer than the San Fierro Hills race. It starts at Easter Bay Airport and tours most of Flint County. Best of all, you get to drive one of the fastest cars in the game—the Bullet!

The toughest competitor is the one driving the Banshee. Try to keep your car in good condition, since this is a long race. Avoid unnecessary collisions with other racers and non-competitors on the road.

Las Venturas Airport Freight Depot Race Tournament

⊗ Location

Follow the race flag icon on the Las Venturas map to the Las Venturas Airport Freight Depot, then enter the red marker on the east side of the building.

Details

The four races available at the Freight Depot Tournament are: San Fierro to Las Venturas, Dam Rider, Desert Tricks, and Las Venturas Ringroad.

San Fierro to Las Venturas

⊗ **Track Distance: 4.85 miles**

🚗 **Vehicle Used: Banshee**

San Fierro to Las Venturas is another fast-paced sports car race. One key is to drive down the right side of the road to avoid slower traffic. Although this is a long race, the Banshee's outstanding speed will prevail in the end.

Dam Rider

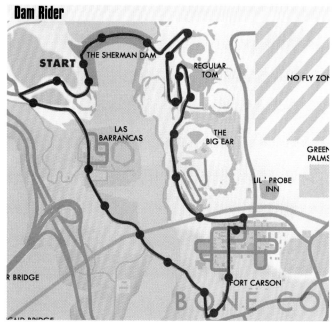

- **Track Distance: 2.67 miles**
- **Vehicle Used: NGR-500**

Dam Rider is much like the last race but this one has some tricky, sharp turns. One of the best features is the fact that the course goes across the Sherman Dam at the end, which is really cool.

Desert Tricks

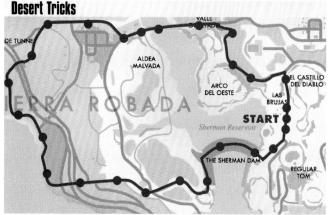

- **Track Distance: 2.91 miles**
- **Vehicle Used: FCR-900**

This is a short race full of tricky turns against some tough competition. Use the straightaways for an aerodynamic speed boost, but back off to make it through a tight turn. Look out for the sharp, right-hand turn into checkpoint 9. There are plenty of opportunities in this race to cut corners.

Las Venturas Ringroad

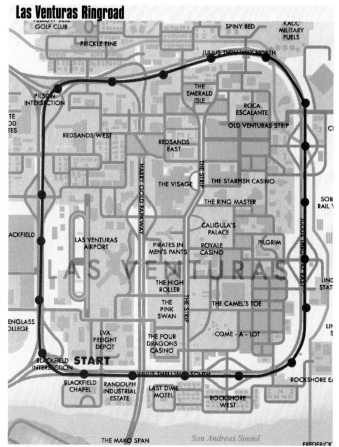

- **Track Distance: 3.70 miles**
- **Vehicle Used: Turismo**

This race begins and ends at the Blackfield Intersection on the Julius Thruway South. Simply hit the gas and let the Turismo burn up the road to leave the competition behind in the first stretch. Use the right shoulder of the road exclusively.

Las Venturas Airport Race Tournament

Location:
Follow the race flag icon on the Las Venturas map to the LVA Airport. Enter the red marker to the right, just inside the entry gate. This gate opens after getting your pilot's license.

Details

It's time to take to the skies in six checkpoint-style challenges. These missions are less of a race and more like a time challenge. To pass these missions, just survive the course and fly through all of the checkpoints. You are not required to land the aircraft after passing through any of the final checkpoints.

The six races available at the Airport Race Tournament are: World War Aces, Barnstorming, Military Service, Chopper Checkpoint, Whirly Bird Waypoint, and Heli Hell.

WARNING: Aircraft Damage

When an aircraft takes damage, it diminishes its ability to fly. If the aircraft is slightly damaged, some fire may become visible but don't bail out since it will usually flame out. Depending on the amount of damage, a second fire may go out as well. If subsequent damage causes a third fire, then parachute out!

Checkpoint Coronas

You don't have to fly directly through the red checkpoint coronas, however, it usually helps to line up the aircraft for the next checkpoint. The rings are slightly thicker on the entry point and taper down to show the direction of the next checkpoint. Use the radar to locate the next checkpoint.

World War Aces

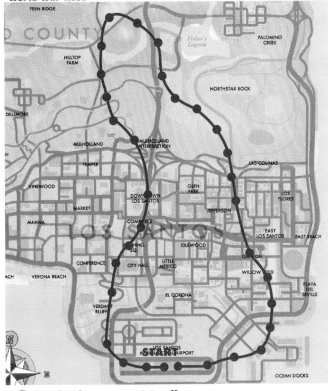

🟊 **Track Distance: 4.24 miles**
🚗 **Vehicle Used: Rustler**

This mission starts from Los Santos International in the Rustler. This is a single prop, WWII combat aircraft with mounted machine guns. This plane has retractable landing gear, so remember to tuck them in after taking off for better handling.

The Rustler is much easier to fly than the Stuntplane. It may not be as maneuverable, but it certainly seems more stable in the air. Remember to do most of your lateral turning by manipulating the tail rudder.

Barnstorming

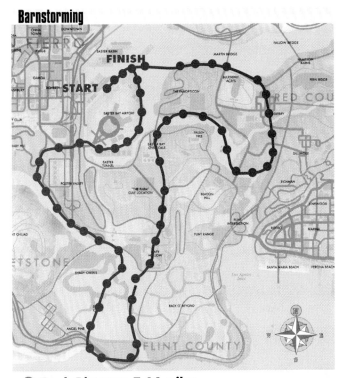

🟊 **Track Distance: 7.64 miles**
🚗 **Vehicle Used: Stuntplane**

The Stuntplane's controls are very sensitive. Make small altitude adjustments by tilting up or down. Do most of your lateral steering (Yaw) using the rudder on the vertical stabilizer.

Military Service

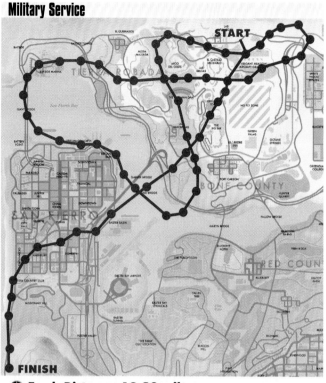

FINISH

Track Distance: 10.80 miles
Vehicle Used: Hydra Jet

This challenge begins in Verdant Meadows Aircraft Graveyard onboard the Hydra Jet, a Harrier-type aircraft.

Fly the Hydra Jet like a helicopter! Keep the jets pointed downward to make the flight controls similar to a helicopter's. Simply hover through the difficult checkpoints early on, then use the aircraft's speed when you become more comfortable with the controls.

Chopper Checkpoint

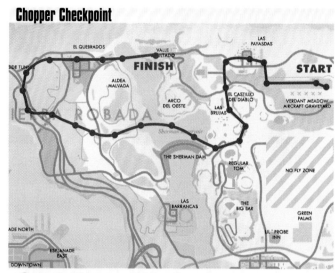

Track Distance: 3.05 miles
Vehicle Used: Maverick

This challenge also begins in Verdant Meadows Aircraft Graveyard.

The Maverick is the craft of choice in this mission, one of the easier choppers to control. There are only 26 checkpoints in this challenge, which pales in comparison to the 60 plus checkpoints in the last two challenges.

Whirly Bird Waypoint

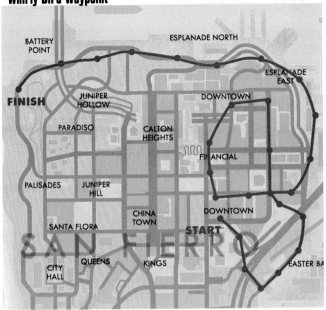

⊕ **Track Distance: 2.73 miles**

🚁 **Vehicle Used: News Chopper**

This challenge begins from a Downtown San Fierro high-rise building. Most of the checkpoints are placed in locations that are dangerous to fly through. Drop down on top of any checkpoints that are wedged between buildings.

Heli Hell

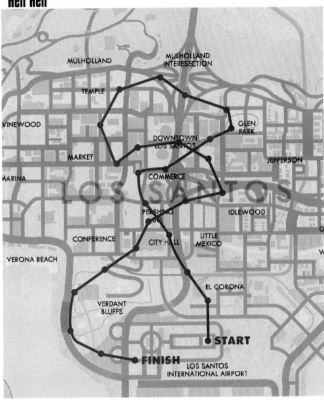

⊕ **Track Distance: 3.08 miles**

🚁 **Vehicle Used: Hunter**

This helicopter mission starts from the Los Santos International airport. Most of the 27 checkpoints are placed in difficult areas for a helicopter to access. Luckily, the Hunter is the most durable of the choppers.

Schools

There are four different vehicle training schools in San Andreas: Driving School, Bike School, Boat School, and Pilot School. They can be played in any order, but only Pilot School is a prerequisite of the main story missions. All schools are marked with a red "S" icon on the radar and map.

If you stop the vehicle at any time once a training course has started that particular training course will end—this applies to all schools. All schools also use the same grading rules. The grading scores are based on a percentage and medals awarded are as follows:

GRADE RANGE	AWARD
70% - 89%	Bronze Medal (a passing grade)
90% - 99%	Silver Medal
100%	Gold Medal

Unless otherwise stated, points are awarded for time taken to complete the given goal(s). There are deductions for damage to the vehicle or cones (if applicable). When you complete the challenges, you can return at any time and use the video machine to replay any of the challenges to shoot for a higher medal. Nice rewards come from your advancement to better medals.

Driving School

 Location:
Doherty, San Fierro
Prerequisite:
Complete the Deconstruction mission.

Reward:

If this is your first time through Driving School, then completing the challenges completes the **Back to School** mission, earns you more Driving Skill, and unlocks the Race Tournaments (also covered in this section of the guide). The table below shows what is earned by receiving medals at Driving School. Once unlocked, these vehicles appear in the westernmost spot of the small lot outside the Driving School.

MEDALS	VEHICLE UNLOCKED
All Bronze (or better)	Super GT
All Silver (or better)	Bullet
All Gold	Hotknife

Details

Enter the red marker in front of the TV monitor in the Driving School facility to begin the challenges. Driving School is an assortment of 12 challenges. Each mission teaches a new skill that can be used to make you a better driver once you leave. Points are awarded on final heading and final position and are deducted for vehicle or cone damage.

	Michelle

The girl with the blue marker over her head who's standing by the water cooler inside the Turning Tricks Driving School can become your girlfriend—if you appeal to her. Refer to the "Girlfriends" section of this chapter for help with Michelle.

The 360

Press and hold the accelerate and brake buttons to begin this challenge. It can only be preformed in rear wheel drive vehicles. The car must perform one complete rotation.

The 180

To do a 180, accelerate to top speed, turn the wheel, and then press the handbrake button around the inside cone at the other end of the course.

Return and stop in the starting position cones, all without hitting a single cone. The faster you complete the challenge, and along with your position in the stopping cones, the higher the medal awarded. Do not touch any cones!

Whip and Terminate

Powerslide around a tight corner and stop in the designated area. This is similar to the last challenge, but the turn is not as tight, making it an easier challenge. Speed as fast as possible through the cones and let your

foot off the gas just before. Quickly perform a fast handbraking turn to the right and stop at the end of the course without hitting any cones.

Pop and Control

In this challenge, you drive a police cruiser through a crooked course of cones. A spiked strip has been placed at the beginning of the course. When you hit the spikes, let off the gas completely and guide the vehicle around the crooked turn in

the cone course, then come to a complete stop at the end without hitting any cones. Amazingly, the only tire that pops is the rear right tire, making the vehicle drag and aim to the left. Compensate by oversteering to the right.

Burn and Lap

The course is a simple oval track made up of cones. You have a choice of clockwise or counterclockwise. You need only complete one direction. You drive a Banshee (one of the best cars in the game), so handling is not an issue. You must complete five laps in as little time as possible. Shoot for less than 40 seconds.

Cone Coil

The cone coil is a training course that combines the powerslide and 180 courses. You must build up speed as you swerve around the first couple of small turns. The more speed you bring into the first turn, the more diffi-cult the second turn will be to negoti-

ate. At the far end of the course, you must perform a 180 around a cone and keep moving back through the course all the way to the starting posi-tion—without hitting a single cone!

The '90'

To do a 90, you must slide the car sideways into the parking space within five seconds. There are two cars parked at the end of the course with a single parking space between them. Burn toward the cars while aiming for the front fender of the car

on the right. Use only the handbrake while jerking the car to the left (when you handbrake and powerslide is half the challenge; do it earlier if you are passing the vehicles and sooner if you aren't reaching them). As soon as your vehicle begins to powerslide and becomes aligned with the parked vehicles, turn the wheel hard to the right to maintain the correct angle. Add in the regular brake to the handbraking to stop the vehicle sooner.

Wheelie Weave

Your objective is to run the left side of the vehicle up the narrow ramp on the left and ride on two wheels until the end of the track (passing through the red marker). The difficult part is not riding that far on two wheels, it's riding that far on two wheels and steering through the red

marker! The car naturally pulls to the left while riding on the right tires. The trick is to turn left as soon as you get on two wheels (turning left makes the car move to the right) and as you feel the car beginning to fall back onto all fours, turn to the right and guide it into the red marker.

Spin and Go

Spin and Go offers a clockwise and a counterclockwise course (you need only complete one direction). You drive a taxi whose rear is facing the course ahead. Use this front-wheel drive vehicle to reverse, then quickly spin around 180 degrees where the course bends. What makes this chal-

lenge difficult is that the controls for steering are backwards until you whip the car around. Once you get over that mental hurdle, the rest is rel-atively simple.

P.I.T. Maneuver

This challenge puts you behind the wheel of a police cruiser. You must perform a PIT maneuver to spin the other cruiser around with minimum damage inflicted to your car. You must also stop as close to the other car as possible. The course is a short one, so act quickly. Burn rubber and

drive up to the left rear fender of the other car and turn right. As soon as the other car begins to spin, apply both of your brakes to stop as close to the car as possible.

Alley Oop

Once again, you drive the Banshee. There's a line of cars parked beyond a ramp near the end of the course. Speed to the ramp and only allow the right side of the vehicle to go up the left side of the ramp. The more you turn into the ramp as you ascend it, the more spin you can

create as the car's tires leave the ramp and you sail through the air over the vehicles. Release the Accelerate button while in the air. Perform one complete turn, clearing the vehicles and landing on all fours at the end of the course, to pass the challenge.

City Slicking

In the final challenge, the instructor trusts you enough to release you to the real streets of San Andreas. Drive to the other side of the city and back without damaging the car too badly. The target time is under 120 seconds.

The time is not so much an issue as the "no damage" part of the challenge. You cannot always predict what will happen in traffic from one end of the city to the other. Here's how to beat this challenge. Burn out of the Driving School parking lot,

veering right and left to enter the main street that runs through the heart of the city. Avoid the curb in the first turn; it could easily cause your car to tip over. Drive as fast as you can while in the middle of the road on the trolley rails to avoid both lanes of traffic. Stay on this road until you must turn right and snake your way down to the red checkpoint Downtown.

Head down the steep hill to the checkpoint with extreme caution. Use your regular brake before and during the descent. Perform a 180 in the checkpoint without stopping the vehicle and head back to the school via the same roads used to reach the checkpoint Downtown. Fly through the finish checkpoint to see how you did in terms of damage and speed. Continue practicing the run until you earn the final Driving School Medal.

Bike School

Prerequisite
Complete Toreno's "Pilot School" (Desert 5) mission to gain entry into Las Venturas.

Location
Blackfield, Las Venturas

Reward
Completing this course raises your Bike (motorbike) Skill percentage. The table below shows what is earned by receiving medals at Bike School. Once unlocked, these vehicles appear at the Bike School on the left side of the entrance (when facing the school).

MEDALS	VEHICLE UNLOCKED
All Bronze (or better)	Freeway
All Silver (or better)	FCR-900
All Gold	NRG-500

Details

Enter the red marker in front of the TV monitor in the Bike School facility to begin these challenges. Bike School is a collection of six small challenges. Points are awarded on final heading and final position, while points are deducted for bike or cone damage.

The 360

You begin on a bike in a circle of cones and must perform a complete 360 degree burnout. Press and hold the brake and the gas at the same time while moving left or right to burn out in a direction of your choice. You are given 15 seconds to complete the challenge. You must complete one full rotation and finish with the proper heading.

The 180

You have 10 seconds to accelerate to top speed, use the handbrake to do a 180-degree turn inside a corner marked by a series of cones, and then return to the starting point. Lean forward for speed (without standing up). Press the handbrake as soon as you reach the first set of

cones. Powerslide through the turn without touching any cones in the process. Burn back to the starting position and come to a complete stop within the cones. Your final stopping position plays a role in the score; try to stop where you started (use both brakes).

The Wheelie

Cones marking the area where a wheelie must be performed are in the middle of the course. Failure to keep a wheelie through the entire coned area results in mission failure. The challenge automatically stops when you enter the middle coned area on two wheels or land on two

wheels while in the coned area. Accelerate hard and pull a wheelie early—before you reach the middle coned area. Make sure to come to a complete stop using both brakes in the stop area without hitting or passing the cones. You have eight seconds to complete this challenge. Don't accelerate thoughout the entire wheelie. Press the gas on and off to make it easier to stop.

Jump & Stop

You're on a Sanchez and must perform a ramp jump. You then need to stop the bike in the designated area—all within an eight-second time period. To do this, simply lean forward and burn down the course toward the ramp. Go up the middle of the ramp and adjust your posi-

tion in midair by leaning forward or backward. Use both brakes to come to a complete stop in the finish area.

The Stoppie

You must drive the bike in a straight line to the stop area. The middle of the course is lined with cones that mark the stoppie area. Failure to keep a stoppie for the duration of the cones will result in failure. If you enter the coned area on two wheels, the challenge automatically ends. It also ends if you land on two wheels while in the center coned area. You have eight seconds to complete the challenge.

The key to winning here is to lean forward to a standing position long before you reach the cones, then tap the front brake just enough to pop the back wheel up. Allow the front wheel to continue rolling. Think of it more as driving—not skidding—on

the front tire. As long as the back wheel does not come down in the center coned area, you've got it made. Once the center cones are cleared, come to a complete stop in the stop area.

Jump & Stoppie

You have eight seconds to reach the stopping area through a straight course with a ramp. You must land the jump, performing a stoppie, and then come to a stop in the finish area.

Lean forward for maximum speed until you go off the end of the ramp. Pull back as you leave the ramp, then lean forward to land on your front tire. Lean too far forward and you'll spill. There's no need to tap the front brake when you land on

the front tire; you're already performing a stoppie roll. Allow the back wheel to lower, then apply both brakes to stop in the stop area.

Boat School

 Prerequisite:
Complete Pier 69 (Syndicate 5) to receive a phone call about Boat School.

Location:
Bayside Marina, Tierra Robada (building at the end of the dock)

Reward:

The chart below shows what is earned by receiving medals at Boat School. Once unlocked, these vehicles appear at a nearby dock, due north of the boat school complex. Notice a Seasparrow (chopper with guns) appears on the nearby helipad and west of the school whether you go to school or not.

MEDALS	VEHICLE UNLOCKED
All Bronze (or better)	Marquis
All Silver (or better)	Squallo
All Gold	Jetmax

Details

The Boat School involves five small challenges. Points are awarded for time taken to complete the given goal(s). There are deductions for boat or buoy damage. Walk up to the red marker in front of the video and monitor inside the Boat School facility to begin the challenges.

Basic Seamanship

You're given a Coastguard boat and must navigate in a straight line into a stopping area. The amount of time you have remaining determines the rating. Go full throttle just before you reach the buoys, then reverse throttle until you stop in the designated area. Release the gas prior to the buoys for best results

Plot a Course

You must guide the Coastguard boat between eight sets of two buoys that form an almost complete oval course. This is a time-based challenge and points are deducted for any damage to the boat. Watch the yellow blips on the radar. The

larger the blips, the closer the buoys are. The key to beating this challenge is to use the first-person view, which allows you to more easily judge distance. You can keep the throttle buried throughout the entire course.

Fresh Slalom

You must guide the Dinghy between 15 pairs of buoys in less than two minutes. Points are deducted for any boat damage. The buoys are at angles to each other. First-person view is strongly recommended. You can go full throttle through the course, but sharp cornering is a must.

Flying Fish

Navigate the Vortex (hovercraft) over the ramp to the left of the start position. The goal is to achieve the furthest landing distance from the ramp while touching down between the two parallel rows of buoys. The greater the distance obtained, the higher the score. You must obtain at least 57 meters to pass. This is also a timed mission; you have only 40 seconds to line up, burn toward the ramp, and execute the jump.

There's a little bit of set up to do in order to jump over 57 meters. Turn to the right out of the harbor, heading for the Gant Bridge. Stay close to the docks, then quickly turn the Vortex around and go full throttle for the yellow blips on the radar.

When the ramp comes into view, line up for a straight shot up the ramp. Try to make the nose of the Vortex enter the water first. This gives you just a little more distance as the front of the boat registers the water re-entry point.

Land, Sea, and Air

You must navigate the Vortex through a course of jumps and rocks, through 23 buoy checkpoints, and finish in less than three minutes to pass.

Navigate through the centre of the each pair of buoys in as quick a time as possible.

Use the first-person view and watch the radar for the most direct route to the next set of buoys. Once you have finished Boat School, you can return to the video setup and replay any of the challenges to try for a better medal. Congratulations, you're a graduate, Skipper!

Pilot School

✓ **Prerequisite:**
Purchase Verdant Meadows Airstrip ($80,000)
✦ **Location:**
Verdant Meadows Airstrip tower

Reward:

Pilot School is first encountered in Learning to Fly, a Toreno mission. Completing this mission earns you $15,000, five Respect points, and you also get a parachute every time you jump out of an airplane. Your Flying Skill is upgraded and you earn a pilot's license, which enables you to access all airports. You also unlock the Casino Strand of missions and the next mission in Toreno's strand. You can always return to Pilot School to gain higher medals. The planes that are unlocked appear in the open hangars to the west of the Pilot School structure. The medals unlock the following aircraft:

MEDALS	VEHICLE UNLOCKED
All Bronze (or better)	Rustler
All Silver (or better)	Stuntplane
All Gold	Hunter

Details

The Pilot School involves 10 challenges. Points are awarded for time taken to complete the given goal(s). Unless stated otherwise, points will be awarded for time taken to complete the given goal(s). There are deductions for damage to the vehicle. Climb the

stairs to enter the structure attached to the save house at the airstrip, then step up to red marker in front of the video and monitor to begin the challenges.

Takeoff

You start the challenge inside a Rustler (a WWII plane with equipped machine guns) waiting for takeoff on the desert airstrip. Start accelerating. As the plane's tail rises, press down to lift the nose of the plane and take off. At this point, you will see a distant corona floating over the end of the runway.

Raise the landing gear for better handling and speed. As the plane climbs and falls, the altimeter to the left of the radar will rise and fall respectively. Fly directly through the first corona, then descend to the next corona. Pull back again and climb toward the last corona.

Land Plane

You begin this mission in the Rustler in mid-flight, during flight and heading for the airstrip runway. Do not hold the Acceleration button; allow the plane to remain at idle speed. Lower the landing gear and tilt forward to descend into the first corona near the runway.

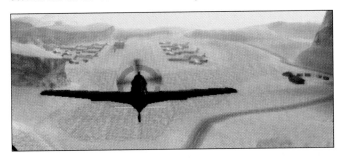

Level the plane as you fly low over the runway and reduce the speed until the plane slowly descends. Keep the nose down, but not so much that you plummet. Bring the plane down gradually and taxi along the runway. Stop in the target zone for extra points. Use the rudder to adjust steering once you're on the runway.

Circle Airstrip

You have a choice of performing this course in a clockwise or counter-clockwise direction. The first part of this challenge is the same as "Takeoff." Take off and head through the first corona at the end of the runway. Note the artificial horizon on the radar displays the plane's altitude.

The challenge suggests using the rudders to adjust your steering in flight. You can also tilt the plane's wings to the left and right to achieve a banking turn. For the sharpest turn possible, use banking with a rudder in the same direction.

As the plane banks and pitches, the artificial horizon changes appropriately.

Bank the plane to the left (depending on the direction you chose in the beginning) to pass through the corona near the dam, then complete the circle of coronas ending with the one near the airstrip.

Circle Airstrip and Land

Again, you have a choice of performing this course in a clockwise or counterclockwise direction. This challenge is exactly the same as the "Circle Airstrip," but combined with "Land Plane." You must take off, circle through the coronas using banking techniques, then land the plane in the marker on the runway.

Helicopter Takeoff

The Hunter is very responsive to the controller commands, especially compared to most helicopters. Much flying time is required to master its controls. In this test, you must lift straight off the runway, rotate and fly forward into the corona at the end of the airstrip.

To reach a higher medal, rotate the helicopter 180 degrees using the tail prop as you lift and reach the goal height. Normally, when you reach the intended height before turning, you are prompted to turn a 180 and face the opposite end of the runway.

Land Helicopter

Again, you pilot the Hunter. You are airborne near the end of the airstrip. Maintain your height as you head to the far end of the runway where a red marker can be spotted. Slow down to hover over the target zone to auto-level the helicopter. Now lower the craft into the red marker.

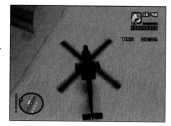

Destroy Targets

You are airborne in the Hunter near the airstrip. There are three vehicles on the far end of the runway that you must destroy. It's a good idea to hold the Gun button for the duration of this first objective, but try to use the rockets to do the most damage. Fly slowly over the vehicles with the nose of the Hunter aimed downward to aim the rockets. Fire like mad; there's no

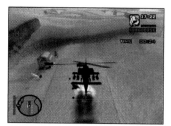

rocket limit. Try to destroy all three vehicles in the first pass. You must try to complete this mission as fast as possible to earn the gold medal. Do not allow the helicopter to get too close to the exploding vehicles or touch down on the ground. One will destroy you and the other will automatically fail the challenge.

Once the vehicles on the runway are destroyed, you receive your next objective: destroy the two moving cars to the southwest of the runway. Turn 180 degrees and head for the vehicles that appear as red blips (downward triangles) on the radar.

Begin shooting far before you reach the vehicles—hoping for a lucky shot.

Your last objective is to land the Hunter in the target zone on the runway for extra points. You can land the Hunter anywhere on the runway to just complete the challenge quickly. But if you're shooting for gold, land in the marker. This concludes the helicopter training courses.

Loop-the-Loop

In this challenge, you pilot a Stuntplane (biplane). The Stuntplane's controls are super sensitive compared to all other airplanes in the game. This means less drastic directional changes are required to keep the plane under control. But this is what allows the Stuntplane to do outrageous tricks and rolls. You cannot retract the landing gear on a Stuntplane.

Maintain your height as you approach the first of two coronas over the airstrip. Keep the plane level so you can see the second corona through the first as you approach. As soon as you pass through the first corona, pull back quickly to do a loop-the-loop. As soon as you see the artificial horizon, flip back over to the

correct position until you spot the second corona. Steer into the second corona to complete the challenge.

Barrel Roll

This challenge has the exact same setup as the last one, but this time you must perform a barrel roll— which is easier since there's not as much disorientation involved. As you pass through the first corona,

press to the LEFT! You must do a counterclockwise roll. Once you perform one complete roll, pass through the second corona to complete the test. The key to a clean roll is to level the plane and press perfectly left—not left-up or left-down.

Parachute onto Target

This is an awesome test and per- haps the most enjoyable, as well. You begin thousands of feet up in the air in a freefall with nothing but a parachute strapped to your back. As you plummet toward the earth,

you are instructed to push forward to dive. The next message says to pull back to put your arms and legs out to slow your descent (this is not neces- sary now).

When you approach the clouds, you are prompted to open the parachute. Do so and guide toward the target on the runway below.

Parachuting

Whenever you exit an aircraft in flight, you will be equipped with a parachute. Your survival depends on how close to the earth you are when you bail out and when you open the 'chute.

Once the 'chute is open, lift your legs up and slow your descent. This allows you to reach targets further off in the distance. If you think you are going to overshoot a target, turn small circles in the air and then realign with the target again.

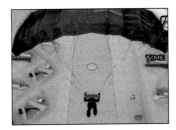

As you approach the target zone, you will see that there are a number of score rings inside the target. The closer you get to the center, the higher your score. Try to land on the small center ring to get the full 35 points! The more quickly you reach

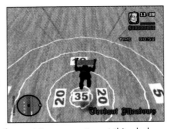

the target, the higher your points. So the next time you attempt this chal- lenge, push forward longer before opening the 'chute, and wait much longer before pulling the ripcord!

Shooting Range Challenge: Ammu-Nation

Prerequisite:
Ammu-Nations are accessible after completion of "Doberman."

Locations:
Find gun icons on the map to locate Ammu-Nations. Not all Ammu-Nations are big enough to accommodate gun ranges, where this challenge takes place. Most "big city" Ammu-Nations have ranges, though.

Reward:
Maxes-out Pistol skill level

Details:

Enter Ammu-Nations (gun icon) that have gun ranges, then step into the red marker in the back room. You compete against two computer- controlled opponents. There are four different weapon competitions, each

consisting of three different rounds. Your targets are always the same, but will move differently through the shooting area. The four weapons stages in order are: Pistol, Micro-SMG, Shotgun, and AK-47. The targets are gangster silhouettes with seven unique targeting points.

Stage 1: Pistol Challenge

Hitman Skill Level

If you wait to compete in this challenge after maxing out your Pistol, Micro-SMG, Shotgun, and AK-47 Weapon Skills, you should have an easier time succeeding. With the Hitman Weapon Skill level comes great advantages (see the "Weapons" section of this guide for more details), the most noticeable being the ability to hold two Pistols or Micro-SMGs.

Round 1

Three targets are dropped in the first round of the Pistol competition. Once you destroy one, the next one drops at a greater distance. Don't squander ammo; reload time is wasted time. Aim and shoot the cen-

ter of the seven different red circles on the target. A hit anywhere outside of the circles doesn't count. To pass this stage, you must destroy your three targets before the competitors destroy theirs.

Round 2

A target drops and moves steadily from the back of the range toward you, then stops until you've shot all seven sections from the target. Once one target is destroyed, another follows the same route, and so on. To pass this stage, you must destroy your three targets before the competitors destroy theirs.

Round 3

In the final round, there's only one target that moves across the targeting range. All competitors shoot the target simultaneously. The first to score 20 points, wins. Points are indicated on the right side of the screen. A point is earned for each piece of the target you remove. Targets continuously drop at varying distances and strafe across the range until someone reaches 20 points.

Stage 2: SMG Challenge

The Micro-SMG challenge is exactly the same as the Pistol challenge, except you'll be using a Micro-SMG. Employ the same strategy used to pass the previous challenge to get through this one. Although the Micro-SMG's rate of fire is significantly greater than that of the Pistol, don't get cocky. You should still use short bursts of fire to hit each red circle on the gangster targets.

This keeps your reload time down to a minimum and allows you to aim with less distraction. Since the bullet spread is less accurate than a Pistol, you can often get away with spraying bullets near the red targeting circles, thereby removing pieces of the target without precise aiming.

Stage 3: Shotgun Challenge

This challenge involves the same rules as the other two, but with a Shotgun. Since the Shotgun's pellet spread is wide, even less precise aiming is required. The higher your Shotgun Skill, the quicker your reload time—and it really helps in this challenge.

Stage 4: AK-47 Challenge

The same rules apply to this challenge, except you'll be using an AK-47. The rate of fire from this weapon makes this challenge a little easier than the other ones. However, the accuracy of this weapon is much greater than the Micro-SMG and Shotgun, forcing you to aim more precisely. Beating this challenge completes the Ammu-Nation challenge. Good job, cowboy.

Stadium Events

Stadium Events include 8-track, Blood Bowl, Dirt Track, and Kickstart challenges. All of these events take place in the three Stadiums found in the three major cities of San Andreas.

8-track

✓ Prerequisite
Opened from the beginning of the game with a high enough driving skill.
◎ Location
Los Santos Forum in East Beach
⑤ Reward
Finish first place to win $10,000, but that's not all! You also unlock the Monster (monster truck) and Hotring racer that spawn in the northwest corner by the red maker.

Tips

This stockcar racing competition is similar to the Hot Ring races in Vice City. The mission is accessed by walking into the red marker outside the Los Santos Forum, where you are then spawned inside the stadium as an 8-track competitor. You must beat 11 other entrants and place first in a 12-lap race. There's no prize for second place.

If you remain cool and drive with extreme caution, you're more likely to win than if you race full throttle and half cocked. This is an exhausting challenge with its share of hazards and dicey turns—one turn in particular causes most opponents to slam head-on into an outside wall!

Your car can't take that much abuse, and if you hit too many walls, you'll never make it to the end of the race. There are no pit stops, so you must treat your car as if it were a fragile egg. Since this is an aggressive sport, you are allowed to take out

opponents. You can try drive-bys to increase the damage to the opponents' vehicles, and use P.I.T. maneuvers to send them to the back of the pack.

Blood Bowl

Prerequisite
Opened when you get to San Fierro.

Location
Foster Valley Stadium in Flint County

Reward
Complete this challenge to win $10,000. Even better, you also unlock the Bloodring Banger, which spawns right in front of the stadium statue near the entry marker.

Details

To begin the Blood Bowl event, enter the red marker outside the Foster Valley Stadium. Inside the stadium, you are then placed in a Bloodring Banger and a computer-controlled passenger rides shotgun. When you approach the competitors, your partner hangs out the window and performs drive-bys on the opposition.

This is a destruction derby style challenge with armed participants. Your opponents may be in cars or motorcycles, or a mixture of both. You have to reach randomly placed checkpoints that appear as red markers in the stadium (yellow blips on the radar).

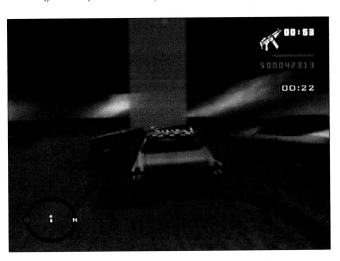

You begin the challenge with 30 seconds on the clock. Each checkpoint reached gives you another 15 seconds. Drive though the checkpoints to increase your overall time. You lose if your overall time reaches zero. You need to get the overall time greater than the target time to win. Target time is one minute.

Damage is inevitable, as you drive through a hail of bullets and unavoidably collide with other vehicles. There are car upgrades that randomly appear around the stadium. Try to get to these upgrades (blue wrench icons) to repair your car. This increases your chances of survival and gets you closer to reaching the overall time challenge.

Just remember it's more about reaching the checkpoints than it is destroying other challengers. Accumulated time is how this challenge is won. Make sure to bring an MP5 to contribute firepower to the drive-bys. Back away from burning

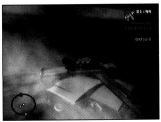

cars to avoid collateral damage, as those vehicles will soon explode. When you complete the challenge, your New Best Time and number of Cars Destroyed is displayed.

Dirt Track

Prerequisite
Opened from the beginning of the game, but you need a Bike Skill of 50% to get in (not Cycling Skill).

Location
Dirtring Stadium in Blackfield, Los Venturas. Dirt Track is only playable on Mondays and Wednesdays; all other days are dedicated to the Kickstart event.

Reward
Obtain first place in the race to win $25,000. The BF Injection is unlocked and spawns near the entrance marker only on the days Dirt Track is open (Mondays and Wednesdays).

Details

Dirt Track is a six-lap stadium motocross race. Your vehicle is a Sanchez and you're up against 11 competitors. The stadium dirt track is a winding course, full of troublesome hills and tight turns. Navigating through the course is only half the challenge; getting ahead of the pack and staying there is the other half.

The lap number and your position in the pack are displayed on the window in the bottom-right corner of the screen. If you fall during the race, you have 25 seconds to remount your bike before you fail.

Stay away from other bikers and slowly work to the head of the pack. Six laps on this course makes for a long race, and you have plenty of time to get to the lead. So take your time and get a feel for the bumps, hills, and hairpin turns.

Kickstart

Prerequisite
Opened from the beginning of the game, but you need a Bike Skill of 50% to get in (not Cycling Skill).

Location
Dirtring Stadium in Blackfield, Los Venturas. Available on every day of the week except Mondays and Wednesdays; these days are dedicated to the Dirt Track event.

Reward
A Dune (a heavy, all-terrain truck) is created outside the stadium near the entry marker on every day of the week, except Mondays and Wednesdays.

Details

Kickstart is a stadium dirt bike challenge consisting of obstacles, ramps, and stunt platforms. Skilled driving and tricks must be performed to reach checkpoint coronas and achieve a high score.

The checkpoint coronas come in three colors, each worth a varying number of points. Green coronas are worth one point, Amber ones are two points, and Red coronas are three points. The high score is 25, so you must earn 26 points to win. You have four minutes to complete the challenge.

A four-minute timer and a counter totaling your points appear on screen below your Wanted Level. If you want to leave the challenge, get off the Sanchez and walk into the red marker near the doorway. If you fall off the Sanchez, you have 30 seconds to get back on before the

mission is failed. Consider attempting this mission after earning a high Motorbike Skill, perhaps after the Race Tournament and the Unique Stunt Jumps—the higher your motorcycle skill, the easier the challenge.

Whether you're just trying to pass the mission or shooting for a stellar score, the process is the same. Just start practicing on the nearest obstacles and, as you ace them, work deeper into the stadium. Master one obstacle after another; you'll make 26 points in a handful of tries.

Valet Parking

✅ **Prerequisite**
Complete San Fierro mission, 555 WE TIP.

🔵 **Location**
Vank Hoff Park Hotel in the Financial district of San Fierro.

💲 **Reward**
Vank Hoff Park Hotel becomes an asset property that accumulates and maxes out at $2000 daily. Pick up your cash daily from the "$" icon created outside of the hotel.

Details

Before taking this job, you must change into the valet uniform you obtained after playing 555 WE TIP. Enter any safehouse and find the uniform stored under "Special" in your wardrobe menu.

Head to the Vank Hoff Park Hotel in Financial, San Fierro, and enter the red marker to begin Valet Parking. Much like the vehicle missions, Valet Parking has multiple levels of increasing difficulty. You are given a set amount of time to park a number of cars. Rush to the vehicle that pulls up to the building and get in as soon as the driver gets out; there are other valets competing to park the cars. You cannot run out into the street and park just any car in the garage; you must only park those cars that pull up to the building to the car port. These vehicles appear as blue blips on the radar and have blue markers hovering over them.

💡 **Driver's Side**

It's best to wait on the small sidewalk island on the opposite side of the car port so that you can quickly enter the driver's side of the vehicle the moment the driver pulls up and exits.

The Parking Garage

Once inside the car, a red marker appears inside the garage below the building. Drive across the sidewalk in front of the vehicle for quick street access. Perform a speedy handbrake right turn in the street to whip the tail end of the car around.

Next, facing the underground garage entrance, speed into the parking garage and quickly park the vehicle in the red marker. The position of the red marker changes each time you enter a new car.

💡 **Camera Control**

As soon as you enter the underground garage, quickly turn the camera to the left to see if the red marker is on the entry side of the garage. This keeps you from turning too early and possibly wasting more time.

Parking Bonus

The position of the vehicle when it comes to a complete stop in the parking space is critical. The better aligned the vehicle is with the parking space lines, the higher your Parking Bonus. For instance, if you were to park the car sideways across the two painted lines, you would receive very little or no Parking Bonus at all. Park it perfectly parallel to the lines and you could earn as many as 15 bonus seconds. However, you must not spend more time aligning the car than the bonus is worth. Parking quickly is the key, while parking perfectly is a secondary objective.

Damage Bonus

Each car begins with a possible 45 Damage Bonus points. If you do not damage the vehicle at all while parking, you receive the full 45-second time bonus. The Damage Bonus is displayed on-screen below the Parking Bonus. Each time you hit something, this number decreases. Receiving bonus time is the key to completing this job.

Taking Out the Valet Competition

If you shoot, beat, or run over a valet opponent until he's dead, you receive a 20-second penalty that is immediately deducted from your time limit. Although you could afford to take out one or two valets when you're on a roll, the possibility of a Wanted Level is definitely not worth it. The arrival of cars is slowed while a Wanted Level is active, and it's even harder to shake the Wanted Level if cops are shooting at you! It's also worth mentioning that you cannot even begin this job if you have a Wanted Level.

If CJ's stamina is high, you'll have no problem mastering the Valet Odd Job. A steady sprint will easily enable him to get to most of the vehicles.

Park & Run

The moment you whip the car into the marked parking space, throw the door open and run as fast as possible back up the parking ramp to the front of the building. You need to catch the next car as the driver is exiting. You cannot take any of the previously parked vehicles in the garage in attempts to avoid the foot race. If the car is stolen or destroyed, you will permanently lose the Valet Uniform! Once you've returned to the front of the building, you may have to wait for more cars to drive up. This is why the parking and damage time bonuses are so important—they help make up for the time wasted while you wait.

Five Levels

The following table illustrates the details of the Five levels of Valet Parking. Complete level 5 to beat the challenge.

VALET PARKING LEVEL DETAILS			
LEVEL	CARS TO PARK	TIME LIMIT	TIP
1	3	2 minutes	100
2	4	2 minutes	200
3	5	2 minutes	300
4	6	2 minutes	400
5	7	2 minutes	Asset acquired

Vehicle Missions

It just wouldn't be Grand Theft Auto be without those beloved vehicle missions! Returning to the series are the Firefighter, Paramedic, Taxi, and Vigilante vehicle missions—but that's not all! Rockstar increased the variety to include Burglar, Pimping, and Trucking missions, too. This section of the guide provides detailed information and tips on all these challenges.

Burglar

✔ Prerequisite
Enter the black Boxville between 20:00 and 06:00 in the following locations:

✪ Location
There are three burglary Boxville locations around San Andreas, one in each major city. Check out our Odd Jobs map (at the beginning of this chapter and on the giant fold-out in the back) for exact locations in Los Santos, San Fierro, and Las Venturas.

$ Mission Completion Level
Reach $10,000 from stolen goods.

$ Reward
The reward from Burglar is the cash made from the burglaries + $3000.

Details

You can make money by stealing items from the residential houses around San Andreas. You can start this mission in a black Boxville at night (between 20:00 and 06:00). When the mission starts, a Daylight

clock appears on-screen. This displays the amount of time you have before morning arrives, which ends the mission automatically. Below the Daylight clock is a cash meter. This calculates cash made from stolen items once the items have been delivered to the lockup.

Casing Houses

You're first objective is to actually find a house to rob. Houses that can be entered have a yellow Triangle marker hovering over their doorways. These usually do not become visible until you are quite close to

the house. That typically means you can't see the yellow markers from the road and, therefore, must actually exit the Boxville and do some footwork.

Parking the Boxville

Once you've found a house to burglarize, park the Boxville as close to the entrance to the house as possible. Many houses have multiple items to steal. A good parking spot speeds up the loading process.

Two Houses are Better Than One

Find two houses together and park the Boxville close to both. Alternate stealing items from the living room of each house. Entering a second house resets the first house.

Burglarizing

A noise meter indicates the amount of sound you're creating, and if you become too loud (i.e. the bar is maxed), you have 10 seconds to leave the home before you are detected by the home owner(s). If you don't leave within 10 seconds, the police are notified and you earn a Wanted Level. If you are seen by any of the people in the house, then a Wanted Level is immediately generated. Some owners may also respond with violence.

Cops Countdown

When you are detected—but not visually—a Cops countdown meter appears below your Cash meter. This displays the amount of time you have to get out of the house before the cops are alerted. This is always 10 seconds. After exiting the home, you can turn right around and re-enter the home to continue burglarizing it again!

Use Your Sprint

You can sprint to an item in the first room and sprint back to the door before the Cops Timer reaches zero. Combine this technique with two houses to maximize your burglaries.

There are various items inside the homes that can be stolen, such as televisions, stereo equipment, and game consoles. Face these items and pick them up. Carry them out of the house and place them in the back of the Boxville.

The Lockups

Each city has its own lockup that appears on your radar as a yellow blip when you get back in the Boxville. You do not receive any money for stealing items until the Boxville has been parked inside the lockup. Each item brings a cash award of $20. Stealing more objects results in a greater bonus. For example, two items gets you $80, three gets you $180, four gets you $320, and so on.

Good Morning!

The mission ends at 06:00 in the morning. Burglarize up to 06:00. You have five minutes after this to get the goods to the lock-up.

Firefighter

 **Prerequisite**
Enter a Fire Truck (anytime).

Location
Anywhere, as long as you're in a Fire Truck. Find Fire Trucks at fire stations or try starting a fire and they will come to you.

Mission Completion Level
12

Reward
You become Fireproof!

Details

Enter a Fire Truck and begin the Firefighter missions. This can be done anywhere at anytime, as long as you are not currently in another mission.

A vehicle fire is reported and a blue blip representing that emergency appears on the map. You are given a set amount of time to reach the fire and extinguish the flames.

Once the fire is extinguished, you receive a cash reward and reach the next Firefighter level, which is displayed on-screen below the time limit. Later emergencies always involve putting out burning victims of the vehicle fires. The higher the mission, the more burning vehicles and people you encounter in a single level.

	Tips

🔥 Pull as close to the burning vehicle as you can. Don't worry; the Fire Truck will not catch fire. Close fires are easier to douse.

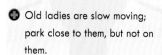

🔥 The Fire Truck is very durable, but this is a long mission, so care for it like fine crystal; Pay 'n' Sprays do not accept Fire Trucks.

🔥 The last thing you want is a Wanted Level, so don't run over anyone. If the cops arrive and try to pull you out of the truck, hose the heat down to keep 'em away!

Paramedic

✓ Prerequisite
Enter an Ambulance (anytime).

⊕ Location
Anywhere, as long as you are in an Ambulance. Ambulances are found at Hospitals. To have one come to you, take out some pedestrians.

Mission Completion Level
12

$ Reward
Boost health to maximum new value of 150.

Details

Also back to the GTA series is the familiar Ambulance mission, Paramedic. A new display now shows how many seats are available in the Ambulance.

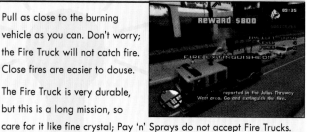

How it Works

Enter an Ambulance and begin the Paramedic missions—as long as you are not currently in a mission. A blue blip, representing a patient, appears on the radar and map. The time limit appears below your Wanted Level. Pull up next to (not on top of) the patient. When the

patient enters the ambulance, a small amount of time is added to the allotted amount to reach the hospital. Try to do these missions outside of the crowded city streets and instead look for less populated areas with local hospitals.

Once the patient is in the Ambulance, the closest hospital becomes the active drop-off location. This appears on the map as a yellow blip. Plot the quickest route to the hospital, stop in the red marker, let the patient out, collect a reward, and then speed off to the next emergency. This completes Level 1.

As levels increase, more patients appear on the map at the same time. Quick planning and smart route plotting is required to balance patient count with seat availability and hospital location. When multiple patients appear on the map, patient drop-offs at the hospital also add 25 seconds to your overall time limit. Use this feature to increase the time limit and to reach more patients.

	Tips

⊕ Ambulances cannot be replaced during a mission; take care of them.

⊕ Old ladies are slow moving; park close to them, but not on them.

⊕ You can burn away from a patient pick-up the moment after they open the Ambulance door; they hang on and enter the vehicle while it's moving!

⊕ Try doing this at a hospital in the country or desert. It is much easier to get around.

Pimping

✓ Prerequisite
Enter a Broadway (anytime).

⊕ Location
Anywhere, as long as you are in a Broadway.

Mission Completion Level
10

$ Reward
When you entertain prostitutes, they give you money.

Details

Before you get started, it's a good idea to arm yourself with some sort of submachine gun, as this could get ugly... and we're not just referring to the girls. In the later Pimping missions, you must force some johns to pay up or wipe them out if they're roughing up your ladies. Enter a Broadway and begin the Pimping mission.

Pimping is very similar to the taxi missions: you pick someone up, you drop 'em off, you go and pick up another, drop them off, and so on. The difference is that you are picking up and dropping off the same two people—your girls.

Activate the mission while in a Broadway and a blue blip appears on the map; this is your girl. When you pick up the girl, a street name appears in yellow at the bottom of the screen, and a yellow blip appears on the map and radar. This is the john location. You have a set amount of time to get there before the john leaves and the mission fails. This time limit is displayed on-screen.

When you reach the customer, your girl gets out and says she'll call you when she needs to be picked up. At the same time, your second girl becomes active. Drive to the blue blip on the radar and stop to pick her up. It's the same drill with her: Find her customer and drop her off safely in the time allotted.

Between Tricks

After dropping off a girl, there's no time limit to reach the next girl who's waiting. In later missions, you can use this free time to repair your vehicle at a Pay 'n' Spray. You need to keep the Broadway in tip-top shape in order to complete the mission.

The Cut

The money and pimping level come into play when you pick up your girl after she finishes with her customer. This money factor begins on your fifth stop, and then every other stop from there on out. You get a cut from the trick ($300), and then the trick amount is multiplied by the current pimping level (level 1 = trick amount x1).

You can keep track of your level by glancing at the Multiplier on the Pimping Payment menu. This only appears when a girl's job is complete. After level 4, the customers start getting rough and you must race to your girls and whack the johns before they harm them.

The john and the girl are usually struggling, so you cannot simply run over the customer without also hurting your girl. You can, however, perform a drive-by or get out of the vehicle momentarily to whack the harassing john. There are also those nonviolent, but cheap, customers who just try to run off without paying.

Taxi Driver

- ✔ **Prerequisite**
  Enter a Taxi or Cabbie (anytime)
- ✪ **Location**
  Anywhere
- # **Mission Completion Level**
  50 fares
- $ **Reward**
  Nitro on all Taxis and Cabbies

Details

Enter a Taxi or Cabbie and begin the Taxi Driver missions. When you find and pick up a customer (blue blip on the radar and map), a Tip meter appears on-screen below the Time Limit, which is a new feature to the Taxi missions. The Tip meter begins full and slowly drains the longer it takes to drop the customer off at his destination (yellow blip). When you get the customer to his destination with any amount of the Tip meter filled, you receive a Speed Bonus. The lower the meter is when you drop off the customer, the lower your tip amount (Speed Bonus).

Taxi Driver has always been a great way to get familiar with the GTA world early on in the game. The places where you drop customers off are usually locations of great interest. In San Andreas, you often drop customers off at bars where video games, pool, gambling, and dancing are available activities.

The time that can be accumulated during Taxi Driver is much more apparent than other vehicle missions (Firefighter, Vigilante, Paramedic). If you shoot for speed bonuses, you'll save time; and the quicker you pick up the next fair, the more their allotted time enhances your overall time limit. Basically, the longer you keep the mission going, the higher your accumulated time becomes—which is very helpful in the later missions when you must drive farther.

Which brings us to "…In-a-Row Bonuses." When you drop off two passengers in a row, you receive a Two-in-a-Row Bonus of $200. Four-in-a-Row is $400, and so on, in multiples of two. Since you must reach 50 fares in a row for the

unlockable, you can imagine the potential money you can make from "…In-a-Row Bonuses! Not a bad way to start San Andreas if you're hurting for cash.

Lastly, cabs can be repaired in Pay 'n' Sprays. This keeps the mission going. Also, people won't get in your cab if it's trashed! You cannot exit the cab or you will immediately cancel the mission.

Trucking

✅ **Prerequisite**
Complete Catalina's Badland Mission "Tanker Commander"

✳️ **Location**
Mr. Whittaker's depot "RS Haul" in Flint County (see the Odd Jobs map fold-out).

#️⃣ **Mission Completion Level**
8

💲 **Reward**
You earn cash during deliveries. Once eight missions have been completed, RS Haul becomes an asset property, generating $2000 a day. Pick it up daily; these asset properties do not accumulate money beyond the daily total.

Details

Return to Mr. Whittaker's depot in Flint County and enter the red marker outside his small office shack. The Trucking mission begins immediately. Once you complete a trucking mission, the next one becomes available when you return to Mr. Whittaker's and step into the red marker again.

The trucking missions will continue non-stop (like most vehicle missions) with new challenges to overcome each time you try. After eight missions, all subsequent missions are similar to the previous ones. You only need to complete eight Trucking missions to contribute to the 100% completion of the game and make RS Haul an asset.

💡 **Lost Your Load?**

Unlike the Catalina mission, Tanker Commander, you won't fail this mission if you lose the trailer. If you lose your load, you have 60 seconds to reattach the cab to the trailer or you fail the mission. The mission is also failed if the load gets destroyed or if you leave the cab beyond the allowed time limit.

Trucking Mission 1
Reward: $1000

The first mission involves a load of goods that must be delivered to a random location. You have two game hours (or two minutes real time) to deliver the load. If you're late, you begin to lose the cash reward. As soon as you receive a mission, pause the game and plot your course using the San Andreas map. Destination locations are random within the same mission.

If you get there in time, you receive the full $2500. Return to the depot to pick up another trucking job.

Trucking Mission 2
Reward: $1500 (possible)

You must deliver a fragile load to Montgomery, East San Andreas (the first of a couple of random locations). You begin with $1500 and a Damage meter. The more damage the load takes, the less money you stand to earn upon delivery. The

cash display reflects the money lost according to the Damage meter below it. Drive carefully! There's no time limit, but the longer you take, the more likely it is that something could happen to the cargo.

Trucking Mission 3
Reward: $2000 (possible)

You must deliver illegal goods to a radom location. The illegal goods attract unwanted police attention, and when you pull out of the depot, you automatically receive a three-star Wanted Level.

There's no Damage meter in this mission, so the goods in the truck are protected and your cash reward is safe as long as you reach the destination.

Trucking Mission 4
Reward: $3000

The fourth trucking mission involves taking a load to Angel Pine (or the 24/7 in Shady Creeks). There's no police attention this time, but you do have to make the delivery in a little over five game hours (or five minutes real time) to get the money. The cash payoff is reduced according to how late the delivery becomes. Get to the red marker in time to walk away with a whopping $10,000! You don't lose money for damage to this load.

Turn left out of the depot and take the second onramp on the left. Head south along the highway and follow it as it bends west toward the small town of Angel Pine (follow the yellow blip).

Trucking Mission 5
Reward: $4000

From here on out, the trucking missions are stepped up a notch in difficulty. The distance you must carry your load makes this mission difficult. The delivery location could be Battery Point, Easter Basin, or Easter Bay Airport—all of which are in San Fierro.

You begin with $4000. Below this cash display is your Damage meter. Try to keep the meter full. Follow only major roads to your destination. Get the goods to the location (yellow blip) in the best condition possible.

Trucking Mission 6
Reward: $5000

This time you're hauling illegal goods to southern San Andreas (random locations around Angel Pines), which means you'll be outrunning a three-star Wanted Level. The load is not susceptible to damage, so your cash reward upon delivery is secure.

A quick way to get on the nearby highway to the south is to take a left turn out of the depot and turn wide across the road to enter the first onramp on your left. Take a right on the freeway and just keep going, while avoiding cops and damage.

Trucking Mission 7
Reward: $7000

You can receive a $7000 cash award for delivering fragile goods to Green Palms or The Sherman Dam or other random locations in northern San Andreas. This is a timed mission. You have a little over six game hours (or six minutes real time) to deliver the load. The key to delivering your cargo safely is to study the map and find the most direct route possible, then drive safely—rushing only makes things more difficult and it costs you money. The goods are legal, so the cops aren't involved.

Trucking Mission 8: Final Mission
Reward: $10,000

This is the final trucking mission that contributes toward 100% completion of the game. It also unlocks RS Haul as an asset property. However, you can continue these trucking missions for fun and money if you wish. You are carrying highly illegal goods to Las Venturas and there are no damage penalties. You will probably deliver to either Whitewood Estates, Redsands West, or Rockshore East. Regardless, it's a long trip with a four-star Wanted Level!

Once you make the eighth delivery, all the Trucking missions will be complete and all future missions will be of variable distance, difficulty, and reward as the previous missions. That's a big 10-4, good buddy!

Vigilante

✓ Prerequisite
Enter a Law Enforcement Vehicle (anytime).

✳ Location
Anywhere

 # Mission Completion Level
12

$ Reward
Boost Armor to new maximum value of 150 plus cash rewards from each threat eliminated.

Details

To returning players, the Vigilante missions are a core element of the ever growing Grand Theft Auto series. And Rockstar does not disappoint... the Vigilante missions are back and have matured, along with the series. And for you newbies out there, a Vigilante mission is something you absolutely must experience for yourself!

How It Works

Enter any law enforcement vehicle and begin the challenge. Mission-related displays appear on-screen: Time Left, Level, and Kills. After taking out criminals, bonus time and your cash reward are temporarily displayed. A call goes out, "Suspect last seen in a vicinity of..." and a red blip appears on the radar and map. Follow the blip on the radar to the perpetrator in the time allotted. If you don't defeat the criminal before time expires, the mission ends.

At first, the suspect is easily dealt with. Gun him down drive-by style. This completes level 1 of the Vigilante missions. Stay in the car to receive your cash reward, a new objective, and bonus time on the clock to reach the next perp. The criminals become increasingly difficult to catch and defeat as you reach higher levels.

If you exit your vehicle to eliminate criminals on foot or just to bail out from a smoking law enforcement vehicle, you have 60 seconds to enter another law enforcement vehicle to continue the challenge.

Criminals appear as red blips on the map; a single red blip if they're all in one vehicle, multiple red blips if they're in more than one vehicle or if they exit their vehicle(s). You must eliminate all red blips (threats) in order to advance to the next level. If

you fail to meet the time objective or if you cancel out of the mission, you will begin from level 1 the next time you participate in the Vigilante mission.

Tips

Multiple Passenger Drive-bys

Making the Vigilante missions more difficult this time around is the new feature that allows multiple passengers in vehicles to perform drive-bys. As you reach higher Vigilante levels, more criminals pack into a vehicle, which means more guys hanging out of the windows shooting at you! To counter this, recruit three gang members of your own before you enter the law

enforcement vehicle and initiate the challenge. Don't worry, your crew is used to being in a squad car. Once you're on the job, your gang will not only open fire on just about anybody they see, they will also assist with catching criminals!

Choose Your Vehicle Wisely

There's even more variety than ever when choosing a Vigilante vehicle in San Andreas. Enforcers are slow, but sturdy. The HVP-1000 (motorcycle) is

fast and easy through traffic but you have the higher probability of bodily injury. There are also Barracks trucks, FBI Ranchers, FBI Trucks, and Rangers! And the ultimate Vigilante vehicle, the Hunter! Oh yeah... it's back!

Try all the Vigilante vehicles and find one that feels right for you. This will help you reach the recommended level requirement that contributes to 100% completion of the game. A Vigilante mission performed while in the Hunter is called Brown Thunder. We find these missions most manageable, so get all gold medals at Pilot School for your very own (see the Pilot School section of this chapter for details). Make sure to try these missions in first-person view for the ultimate experience!

No Repairs. No Problem!

The restrictions placed on these hot vehicles at the Pay 'n' Sprays can make the emergency vehicle missions quite difficult. These vehicles are just too hot to be touched! This is not as big a problem in Vigilante as it is in Paramedic or Firefighter. Why? Because you can always cre-

ate a Wanted Level, which brings an endless supply of law enforcement vehicles right to you! Controlling the Wanted Level is difficult, though, since you have a time restriction to defeat the threat. Use our Security Services maps at the beginning of each section of the walkthrough to locate nearby Police Bribes and bring your Wanted Level down.

Sirens

Using the sirens—as annoying as they may be after a long haul— actually do clear some drivers from your path. If the sound becomes mentally crippling, turn them on only when needed.

P.I.T. Maneuver

Use the P.I.T. Maneuver learned in Driving School to push the target car around, then stop as close to it as possible to perform a drive-by. Shoot the vehicle until it catches fire. Your next move is to get the heck out of there!

OTHER PASTIMES

This section covers a wide variety of jobs, sports, recreation, and—of course—girls! The jobs in this section are listed in alphabetical order, but some Odd Jobs are listed in larger categorical sections (Gambling or Arcade Games).

2-Player Missions

Surprise, surprise! Two-player in a GTA game! It doesn't get any better than this. Obviously, to play a 2-player mission you need two players and two controllers. These missions don't count toward the 100% completion of the game, but they will lead to hours of gaming goodness.

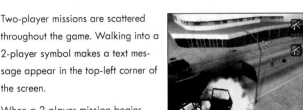

Two-player missions are scattered throughout the game. Walking into a 2-player symbol makes a text message appear in the top-left corner of the screen.

When a 2-player mission begins, two characters appear on-screen. There are two categories of 2-player games: the ones listed in the following section and the 2-Player Run games.

 Kissing Bandit

When both players face each other, a text message indicates that you're able to kiss. The couplings can pretty be hilarious; CJ kissing a priest, or Elvis! Funny stuff.

2-Player Rampage

⊕ **Location**
Pershing Square, Los Santos

Details

This is a classic GTA Rampage mission, but this time it's done with a partner. Since this is a co-op mission, work together to eliminate 15 pedestrians within three minutes. Unlike the 2-player run-around missions, the second player can't choose a character model.

Remember that you can only get so far from the other player's character, as the game limits the distance you can be apart. If you're after a certain target, make sure both characters head in the same distance.

Venture into the street and seek out some pedestrians using Micro-SMGs. When the pedestrians disappear, return to the courtyard to find more. By completing this mission, a "Mission Passed" message appears and the 2-player Skull icon reappears. There's no monetary award except for any money that is picked up from the lifeless bodies.

2-Player Bike

⊕ **Location:**
Montgomery, Red County

Details

At the start of the mission, player one starts in the driver's seat of a motorcycle while player two is the passenger. The objective is to destroy five bikes within 3 minutes. Take off into the nearest street and start shooting motorbikes as they come into view.

Both players have the ability to target and shoot. When multiple bikes appear on-screen, have each player select his own target. Remember that the goal is to destroy the bikes, not the people on the bikes. If things get crazy, try turning on Invert Look in the controller options. The Micro-SMGs will shred the bikes to pieces in no time!

2-Player Cars

⊕ **Location:**
China Town, San Fierro

Details

This mission begins with both players inside a Sentinal. The objective is to destroy five vehicles within three minutes. Vehicles are automatically target locked when they come into view, so unleash some drive-by terror with the Micro-SMGs. The toughest part of this mission is avoiding all of the exploding vehicles and splash damage, so the player who is driving the vehicle needs to be careful.

2-Player Helicopter

⊕ **Location:**
Los Payasadus, Desert

Details

Both players start this mission inside a Police Maverick (helicopter). Although the Maverick isn't equipped with weaponry, both players have access to Tec-9s. In addition to shooting, player one must steer the copter.

Fly along the road and pick off vehicles as they come into view. You can't move the camera around in 2-player missions, so fly forward after making an extreme directional change to get the camera to change view.

2-Player Pedestrians

⊕ **Location:**
The Camel's Toe, Las Venturas

Details

With player one behind the wheel of a Buffalo vehicle, player 2 gets to ride shotgun. With both players equipped with Micro-SMGs, to goal is to kill 15 pedestrians in under three minutes using only drive-by shooting.

2 Player Run-Around

There are five 2-player Run-Around mission icons scattered about San Andreas. The icons resemble two red stickmen standing side-by-side. To trigger one of these missions, step into one of the icons.

When a run-around mission begins, the second player spawns and a text message appears stating that the player has free roam of the city, but the player can't let the cops catch him. The second player can change his character model. The characters available are city dependant. For example, Cowboys are an option in the country and Elvis impersonators are available in Las Venturas.

2-Player Run-around Los Santos

⊕ **Location:**
Idlewood, Los Santos

Details

Player 2 has a choice of six different character models, the funniest being the Cluckin' Bell employee! This game has no rules, so just have fun without getting busted. The mission will end if your character dies or gets arrested.

Don't worry about weaponry, as Knives, Silencers, Tec-9s, M4s, and Shotguns are provided. Note, however, that you cannot pick up dropped weapons but you can do just about everything else. To perform a dual-targeting drive-by, both players must enter the same car; each player cannot drive a different vehicle.

2-Player Run-around Las Venturas

⊕ **Location:**
Royal Casino, Las Venturas

Details

Player 2 can choose from six different character models, including a stripper, an S&M girl, and Elvis! Weapons are plentiful too, with Knifes, Silencers, Shotguns, Tec-9s, and M4s. To replenish any lost health, simply stop at the small food stands.

Girlfriends Run-around

In addition to the five 2-player Run-Around missions, another 2-player Run-Around icon appears at each of CJ's girlfriends' homes (or where you meet them to take them on a date). These icons only appear once they agree to go out on a date and only appear when the girl is available for a date. If you are dating all of the girlfriends, this adds six more 2-player Run-Around icons to the game. Now your buddy can be your girlfriend!

2-Player Run-around San Fierro

Location:
Kings, San Fierro

Details

Player 2 can choose between six characters, including regular pedestrians, a Vagos gang member, and a firefighter. In this Run-Around mission, you have a fire extinguisher, night vision goggles, and the usual array of weapons. With free roam of the city, visit the airport and try to jack an aircraft that seats at least two!

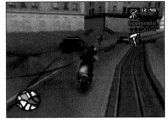

2-Player Run-around Desert

Location:
El Quebrados, Desert

Details

Player 2 can choose from six player models, consisting of mainly country folk, a sheriff, and the gimp! With an arsenal of standard weaponry, head over to Verdant Meadows and see which aircrafts are unlocked there!

2-Player Run-around Red County

Location:
Dillimore, Red County

Details

Most of the same character models are available here, along with the standard 2-player arsenal. Try to hold this small town hostage! The Police Ranger vehicle is abundant when the heat is on, so hop into one and do some real damage!

Arcade Games

The Arcade Games category includes upright arcade machine and console versions of Duality, Go Go Space Monkey, and Let's Get Ready To Bumble.

Duality

Locations:
Bars, homes, restaurants, 24/7s, and clothing stores

Details

The red bar indicates your health status, while the green bar illustrates your energy meter. It empties while accelerating and firing your weapon, but slowly regains energy when you stop both of these actions.

There are big and small asteroids that are either black or white in color. The large black asteroids are worth 10 points; destroy them to avoid taking damage. Do not, however, destroy the large white asteroids; if you do, you'll lose 10 points. Avoid the small black asteroids; running through them costs five points. Collect white asteroids by running through them to earn five points. Each shot fired costs 1 point.

Go Go Space Monkey

Locations:
Bars, homes, restaurants, 24/7s, and clothing stores

Details:

Destroy as many enemies as possible while avoiding enemy fire. You begin the game with three "lives;" after losing them, you can enter your initials on the Hi-Score screen if you performed well.

By destroying an entire string of enemy spaceships, an "S" icon materializes. Continue to destroy strings of enemy ships without getting destroyed to see an "M" icon, and then finally an "A" icon. Pick up these power-ups to increase your firepower.

Let's Get Ready To Bumble
Locations:
Bars, homes, restaurants, 24/7s, and clothing stores

Details
The goal is to collect points by running through flowers. While flying around, avoid the thorny vines or risk a sudden death! The player must collect all 10 flowers in the first stage within two minutes.

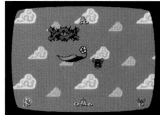

They Came From Uranus
Locations:
Bars, homes, restaurants, 24/7s, and clothing stores

Details
They Came From Uranus resembles the old arcade game "Tempest." You control a ship that circles the outer edges of the screen and fires inward toward enemy ships that appear in the distance (in the center) and work their way closer while flying in a spiraling pattern. See how long you can last with your three lives.

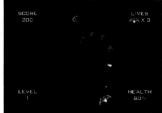

Stores/Businesses

This section of the guide contains information on Barbers, Clothing Stores, Restaurants, and Tattoo Parlors. The most important aspect of this section relates to how these purchases relates to CJ.

Barbers

CJ first visits the barbers as an objective in the second mission, "Rider." After this, the other barber shops open for business. Did you know that CJ's hairstyle affects Ryder's reaction when he catches a glimpse of his head? Did you know that CJ's hairstyle also affects his Sex Appeal and Respect stats? Think about this the next time CJ goes on a date.

There various barbers in San Andreas offer a variety of different cuts. The following is a list of the various haircuts, organized by barbers who offer the same cuts. The list also illustrates how each cut raises CJ's Sex Appeal and Respect percentages.

OLD REECE'S: IDLEWOOD, LOS SANTOS

STYLE	RESPECT % +	SEX APPEAL % +	COST
Cesar	5	15	$50
Cesar & 'Stash	10	10	$50
Cesar & Goatee	10	0	$100
Cesar & Beard	10	10	$80
Afro	15	10	$150
Afro & 'Stash	20	5	$200
Afro & Goatee	20	0	$300
Afro & Beard	20	5	$250
FlatTop	25	25	$500
Jheri Curl	5	25	$350
Cornrow	30	30	$500
High Fade	20	20	$150

BARBER SHOP: PLAYA DEL SEVILLE, LOS SANTOS

STYLE	RESPECT % +	SEX APPEAL % +	COST
Cesar	5	15	$50
Red Hair	10	0	$200
Blue Hair	10	0	$200
Green Hair	20	0	$200
Bald Head	10	20	$10
Bald & 'Stash	15	15	$25
Bald & Goatee	15	10	$25
Bald & Beard	15	15	$50
Slope	20	10	$200
Mowhawk & Beard	10	0	$250
Elvis Hair	0	0	$1000

BARBER SALON: MARINA, LOS SANTOS
THE BARBERS POLE: QUEENS, SAN FIERRO
GAY GORDO'S BOUFON BOUTIQUE: REDSANDS, LAS VENTURAS

STYLE	RESPECT % +	SEX APPEAL % +	COST
Cesar	5	15	$50
Blonde Hair	0	15	$50
Pink Hair	0	0	$200
Blonde Afro	15	15	$300
Blonde Cornrow	30	30	$550
High Afro	15	0	$150
Wedge	20	20	$150
Detail Cut	25	30	$400
Groove Cut	30	30	$500
Mowhawk	20	10	$200
Blonde Mowhawk	10	15	$250
Pink Mowhawk	0	0	$400

Clothiers

The clothing stores in San Andreas fall under six corporate names: binco, Didier Sachs, ProLaps, SubUrban, Victim, and Zip. Binco, ProLaps, and SubUrban open during Sweet's fourth mission, "Nines & AKs." Zip stores open when San Fierro is unlocked, while Victim opens when Las Venturas becomes available.

Walk into the market to try on some new threads.

Wardrobe Closets

Most houses in San Andreas have a wardrobe closet, which is where CJ can change clothes. After purchasing new items from a clothing store, CJ's old outfit is automatically sent to his wardrobe closet.

Purchasing

Note that items available for purchase appear in blue text on the clothing menu screen, while previously purchased items appear in green text. These green items appear in CJ's wardrobe closet.

Clothing Stores & Inventory

There are many stores in San Andreas that fall under six company names: **binco, Didier Sachs, ProLaps, SubUrban, Victim,** and **Zip**. Binco, ProLaps, and SubUrban clothing stores open during Sweet's fourth mission, Nines & AKs. Zip stores open when you enter San Fierro, and Victim opens when you enter Las Venturas. Clothing plays a 4% role in your overall Respect level and 50% of overall Sex Appeal. When entering one of these fine stores, be on your best behavior. If you shoot or even aim your weapon at anyone in the store, the place will go nuts and you are forbidden to continue shopping there until you leave and return.

The following section includes a comprehensive list of every clothing store chain and its inventory. This list also illustrates how purchases affect CJ's Respect and Sex Appeal level.

BINCO	RESPECT % +	SEX APPEAL % +	PRICE
Torso			
White Tank	2	3	$10
Black Tank	2	3	$10
Green Hoody	15	5	$45
White T-Shirt	0	0	$15
L.S. T-Shirt	0	0	$10
Sharps T-Shirt	2	0	$20
Green Shirt	15	3	$40
Checkered Shirt	3	0	$20
Combat Jacket	10	0	$30
Eris T-Shirt	15	7	$35
Eris T-Shirt2	5	7	$35
Track Top	5	9	$70
Legs			
Black Boxers	1	1	$10
Heart Boxers	1	2	$12
Woodland Camo	6	1	$55
Urban Camo	2	1	$55
Gray Pants	0	1	$55
Olive Pants	5	1	$55
Sweat Pants	3	2	$60
Blue Jeans	0	0	$50
Track Pants	5	5	$70
Beige Pants	1	0	$35
Green Jeans	15	5	$60
Green Track Pants	9	2	$40
Shoes			
Sandals	0	0	$15
Sandals & Socks	0	0	$20
Flip-Flops	0	0	$15
Cowboy Boots	1	2	$100
Hi-Top Kicks	2	1	$50
Hi-Top Sneaks	3	2	$100
Green Low-Tops	3	1	$50
Blue Low-Tops	1	1	$50
Black Low-Tops	1	1	$50
Chains			
Dogtags	1	0	$10
Africa Pendant	1	1	$12
Watches			
Pink Watch	0	0	$15
Yellow Watch	0	0	$15
Shades			
Joke Glasses	0	0	$10
Joke Mask	0	0	$20
Eyepatch	0	0	$5
Red Rag	1	0	$50
Blue Rag	1	0	$50
Green Rag	2	0	$50
Black Rag	1	0	$50
Hats			
Red Rag Back	1	1	$25
Blue Rag Back	1	1	$25
Green Rag Back	3	2	$25
Black Rag Back	1	1	$25
Red Rag Front	1	1	$25
Blue Rag Front	1	1	$25
Black Rag Front	1	1	$25
Green Rag Front	3	1	$25
Watch Cap	2	0	$15
Trucker Hat	0	0	$5
Cowboy Hat	0	0	$10
Leopard Cowboy	0	0	$10

SUBURBAN — ITEM	RESPECT % +	SEX APPEAL % +	PRICE
Torso			
White Heat T	5	0	$35
Bobo Ape T	17	13	$115
Red Bobo T	12	12	$80
Base 5 T	15	12	$80
Suburban T	15	10	$60
Mercury Hood	15	10	$70
Base 5 Hood	20	14	$105
Rockstar Hood	17	15	$120
Vest & T-Shirt	0	0	$30
Green Windbreaker	13	5	$30
Black Windbreaker	5	5	$30
Rockstar Sweat	10	10	$60
Legs			
Gray Shorts	0	0	$30
Olive Shorts	5	0	$30
Gray Chonglers	2	1	$50
Green Chonglers	6	0	$50
Red Chonglers	6	2	$50
Blue Chonglers	2	2	$50
Green Shorts	0	5	$30
Red Jeans	0	0	$60
Shoes			
Black Hi-Tops	2	1	$55
Red Hi-Tops	2	1	$55
Orange Hi-Tops	2	1	$50
White Low-Tops	2	2	$70
Gray Low-Tops	2	1	$65
Black Low-Tops	2	2	$65
White Hi-Tops	3	2	$80
Strap Sneakers	3	2	$80
Chains			
Silver Cuban	2	2	$200
L.S. Chain	2	0	$50
Watches			
Face Watch	1	2	$70
Face Black	2	2	$120
Shades			
Red Tint	1	1	$200
Blue Tint	1	1	$220
Hats			
Red Cap	1	0	$40
Red Cap (Back)	1	0	$40
Red Cap (Side)	1	0	$40
Red Cap (Tilt)	1	0	$40
Red Cap (Up)	1	0	$40
Blue Cap	1	0	$40
Blue Cap (Back)	1	0	$40
Blue Cap (Side)	1	0	$40
Blue Cap (Tilt)	1	0	$40
Blue Cap (Up)	1	0	$40
Black Skully	1	0	$60
Green Skully	3	0	$60

PROLAPS

ITEM	RESPECT % +	SEX APPEAL % +	PRICE
Torso			
Rimmers Jacket	10	5	$150
R-Star Jacket	10	5	$200
Dribblers Vest	7	5	$30
Saint's Shirt	7	5	$30
69ers T-Shirt	7	5	$50
ProLaps T-Shirt	7	10	$50
ProLaps Black T	7	10	$50
Bandits Top	7	5	$70
Track Top	10	15	$85
Leisure Top	0	0	$30
Slappers Top	5	2	$150
Baseball T	10	5	$80
Legs			
Track Pants	5	5	$100
Black Track Pants	5	5	$120
Blue Track Pants	5	5	$140
Ball Shorts	5	1	$60
Boxing Shorts	5	1	$60
Dribbler Shorts	5	1	$60
Leisure Pants	0	0	$50
Shoes			
Mid-Top Sneaker	5	3	$115
Black Hi-Tops	3	2	$70
Blue Hi-Tops	2	2	$65
Green Hi-Tops	5	2	$60
Red Sneakers	2	3	$80
Blue Sneakers	2	2	$75
White Sneakers	2	2	$70
White Mid-Tops	4	2	$70
Black Mid-Tops	4	2	$70
Boxing Shoes	0	0	$70
Chains			
Stop Watch	0	0	$20
Saints Chain	1	0	$25
Watches			
Pro-Laps White	0	1	$440
Pro-Laps Black	1	1	$700
Shades			
Aviators	1	1	$150
Sun Glasses	2	1	$150
Hats			
Green Cap	1	0	$40
Green Cap (Back)	1	0	$40
Green Cap (Side)	1	0	$40
Green Cap (Tilt)	1	0	$40
Green Cap (Up)	1	0	$40
Boxing Helmet	0	0	$80
Hockey Mask	2	0	$40
Fullface Helmet	2	1	$150
MotoX Helmet	0	0	$100
Helmut	1	0	$100

ZIP

ITEM	RESPECT % +	SEX APPEAL % +	PRICE
Torso			
Blue Hoody	5	5	$65
Black Hoody	5	5	$65
Striped T-Shirt	5	5	$10
Brown Shirt	5	10	$40
Sky Blue Shirt	7	10	$40
Yellow Shirt	7	10	$40
Gray Shirt	7	10	$40
Plaid Shirt	3	0	$20
Cream Logo T	0	5	$35
Gray Logo T	0	5	$35
Jean Jacket	10	20	$90
Bowling Shirt	7	13	$70
Legs			
Beige Khakis	10	7	$150
Olive Khakis	10	7	$150
Black Khakis	8	8	$150
Blue Khakis	8	7	$150
Beige Shorts	6	3	$80
Blue Shorts	6	3	$80
Shoes			
Gray Boots	5	5	$125
Red Boots	5	5	$135
Brown Boots	2	4	$115
Hiking Boots	4	2	$110
Chains			
Leaf Chain	2	1	$100
Gold Chain	2	2	$350
Watches			
Zip Blue	2	2	$100
Zip Gold	2	22	$220
Shades			
Black Shades	2	2	$100
Brown Shades	2	2	$150
Hats			
Black Sun Hat	2	2	$20
Plaid Sun Hat	2	2	$20
Cap	1	0	$40
Cap (Back)	1	0	$40
Cap (Side)	1	0	$40
Cap Tilted	1	0	$40
Cap Rim Up	1	0	$40

ZIP

clothing to get your teeth into

PROlaps®

The first in sports wear.   Train HARD

VICTIM

ITEM	RESPECT % +	SEX APPEAL % +	PRICE
Torso			
Hooded Jacket	17	15	$75
Gray Jacket	20	25	$1620
Black Jacket	10	20	$300
Biker Jacket	17	15	$320
Chore Coat	15	10	$320
Hawaiian Shirt	7	13	$200
Blue Hawaiian	7	13	$300
Sports Jacket	13	17	$450
Madd Tagg T	5	5	$30
Green Tagg T	5	5	$30
Loc-Down T	5	5	$200
Loc-Down Vest	5	5	$300
Legs			
Leather Pants	8	8	$875
Leather Chaps	0	0	$80
Gray Pants	8	10	$800
Black Pants	8	10	$800
Jean Shorts	9	7	$1000
Shoes			
Cowboy Boots	4	5	$500
Biker Boots	3	3	$145
Snake Skin	5	5	$1000
Chains			
Silver Chain	2	1	$450
Gold Chain	2	2	$550
Watches			
Gold Gnocchi	1	2	$1500
Silver Gnocchi	2	2	$3000
Shades			
Black Shades	2	2	$500
Green Tint	2	2	$400
Hats			
Red Beret	1	3	$900
Black Beret	1	3	$900
Black Cap	2	0	$40
Black Cap (Back)	2	0	$40
Black Cap (Side)	1	0	$40
Black Cap (Tilt)	1	0	$40
Black Cap (Up)	1	0	$40

DIDIER SACHS

ITEM	RESPECT % +	SEX APPEAL % +	PRICE
Torso			
Tweed Jacket	25	25	$5500
Red Jacket	23	25	$4000
Blue Jacket	22	25	$3000
Yellow Jacket	25	25	$6000
Tuxedo	20	25	$7000
Green Jacket	25	15	$5500
Letterman Top	15	5	$1525
Legs			
Red Pants	9	10	$2000
Blue Pants	9	10	$2500
Yellow Pants	10	10	$4000
Tweed Pants	10	10	$3000
Tuxedo Pants	9	10	$3000
Green Pants	10	6	$1500
Shoes			
Black Shoes	5	5	$2500
Brown Shoes	4	5	$1100
Spats	5	5	$350
Chains			
Cross Chain	2	2	$5000
Dollar Chain	2	2	$2000
Watches			
Gold Crowex	3	3	$8000
Silver Crowex	3	3	$5000
Shades			
Black Shades	1	2	$600
Black Rim	2	2	$800
Hats			
Dark Trilby	3	2	$300
Light Trilby	3	2	$300
Black Derby	1	2	$500
Red Derby	2	3	$600
Blue Derby	2	2	$600
Yellow Derby	3	2	$700
Green Derby	3	2	$550
Gray Boater	3	2	$800
Black Boater	3	2	$700

Restaurants

The restaurants in San Andreas open for business during the "Rider" mission (when Rider robs the Well Stacked Pizza place). The three restaurant chains, Burger Shot, Well Stacked Pizza and Cluckin' Bell, have stores all over San Andreas.

There are also a number of other "nicer" restaurants that appear on the map when a girlfriend wants something to eat. Note, however, that is the only time you can eat at these places and the food does nothing for CJ's diet.

Eating Requirements

CJ can eat up to 11 meals within a six-hour period before he will puke! When this occurs, he will lose all of the fat he gained from eating.

Diet meals, like salads, do not add fat to CJ's Fat stat. If you eat a small meal (like a single burger), 1% fat is added, while a medium sized meal (like fried chicken with sides) adds 2% fat to his Fat stat. Lastly, a large meal (like an entire pizza)

adds 3% fat. It takes three trips to a restaurant, eating the full load of large meals each time, to make CJ attain a 100% Fat stat.

OBESITY WARNING!

Becoming obese affects the way CJ moves, like limiting his sprinting ability. Also, his ability to jump and scale walls decreases.

Dieting

There are two ways to lose weight: "dieting" or engaging in aerobic exercise. To "diet," CJ must refrain from eating for 48 game hours, at which time he will begin to lose fat at a rate of 2.5% per hour. After an

additional 26 hours, he will lose Muscle at a rate of 2.5% per hour. After his Fat stat has been completely depleted, he will lose health!

Menus

The following is a list of every restaurant and their menus. Each menu item also has an associated Fat % assigned to it.

WELL STACKED PIZZA CO.

MEAL	PRICE	FAT % +
Buster	$2	1
Double D-Luxe	$5	2
Full Rack	$10	3
Salad Meal	$10	0

CLUCKIN' BELL

MEAL	PRICE	FAT % +
Cluckin' Little Meal	$2	1
Cluckin' Big Meal	$5	2
Cluckin' Huge Meal	$10	3
Salad Meal	$10	0

We pack more calories per square inch than anyone in the world. Guaranteed to keep you full.

CLUCKIN' BELL®

BURGER SHOT

MEAL	PRICE	FAT % +
Moo Kids Meal	$2	1
Beef Tower	$6	2
Meat Stack	$12	3
Salad Meal	$6	0

Tattoo Parlors

Tattoo parlors open during the Ryder mission (there's one next door to the barber in that mission). Tattoos, although they're expensive, can raise CJ's Respect and Sex Appeal levels. The following section contains a list of all four tattoo par-

lors in San Andreas, what they offer, their costs, and how the tattoos affect CJ's Respect and Sex Appeal. It's possible to remove a tattoo, but it costs $400 per tattoo!

IDLEWOOD LOS SANTOS TATTOO PARLOR
WILLOWFIELD LOS SANTOS TATTOO PARLOR
HEMLOCK TATTOO: QUEENS SAN FIERRO TATTOO PARLOR

BODY PART	TATTOO	PRICE	RESPECT % +	SEX APPEAL % +
Upper Left Arm	Nation	$40	2	2
	Grove	$45	2	2
Lower Left Arm	Gun	$50	2	2
Upper Right Arm	Africa	$90	2	2
Lower Right Arm	Cross	$70	2	2
Back	Grove St	$150	3	3
	Westside	$200	3	3
	Los Santos	$150	3	3
	Gun	$450	3	3
Left Chest	Gun	$50	2	2
	Bullet	$90	2	1
Right Chest	Los Santos	$80	2	2
	Los Santos	$45	2	2
	Los Santos	$50	2	2
	Los Santos	$100	2	2
	Los Santos	$65	2	2
Stomach	Grove	$70	2	2
	Grove	$125	2	2
	Grove	$100	2	2
Lower Back	Angel	$450	3	3
	Dagger	$350	3	3

REDSANDS EAST, LAS VENTURAS TATTOO PARLOR

BODY PART	TATTOO	PRICE	RESPECT % +	SEX APPEAL % +
Upper Left Arm	Spider	$72	2	2
Lower Left Arm	Cross	$84	2	2
	Clown	$36	2	2
Upper Right Arm	Web	$60	2	2
Lower Right Arm	Mary	$120	2	2
Back	Card	$240	3	3
Left Chest	Crown	$150	1	2
	Homeboy	$120	2	2
Right Chest	O.G.	$108	2	2
Stomach	Dice	$108	2	2
	Dice	$60	2	2
Lower Back	Masks	$720	3	3
	Cross	$600	3	3

Basketball

✔ **Prerequisite**
Available at the beginning of the game.

✱ **Location**
Random basketball courts

Ⓢ **Reward:**
Bragging Rights

Find one of the many basketball courts scattered around San Andreas that has a basketball near the one of the goals. Note that the appearance of the basketball is random.

The key to putting the rock through the hoop is holding and releasing the button for the appropriate time. You don't need to face the basket before shooting, although it doesn't hurt. CJ automatically faces the basket when he shoots.

Begin the basketball challenge, and make as many baskets as possible before the time expires. Stand inside the red marker on the court and shoot the ball. The game starts with one minute on the clock and 15 seconds is added for each successful basket. After a shot goes in, the red marker moves to a new location.

Beefy Baron

✅ Prerequisite
Finish Zero's mission strand and enter the red marker in the back of the store near the closet Zero was hanging from in a previous mission.

✴ Location
Inside the back room of Zero's RC Shop in Garcia, San Fierro.

💲 Reward
Cash made by destroying Topfun vans.

Details

After completing Zero's mission strand, walk into the back room of Zero's RC shop and enter the red marker near the computer desk in the back corner.

This challenge is very similar to Zero's mission, "Supply Lines" but without the fuel limit. You control an RC Baron that appears on the rooftop of Zero's store. The goal is to destroy as many of Berkley's Topfun vans as possible within three minutes.

Berkley's Topfun vans (red in color) appear all around a few block radius of Zero's shop. The vans do not appear on the radar; you'll have to hunt them down instead. The flight controls are the same as they were in the "Supply Lines" mission.

The machine gun fire from the Baron has a decent spread and is capable of inflicting damage at long-range. Spray bullets as soon as a red van appears.

Dancing

✅ Prerequisite
Complete OG Loc's first mission, "Life's a Beach."

✴ Location
Try Disco Nightclub in Queens, Red County. There are other locations in all of the big cities, as you will soon discover.

Details

Dancing is available in many bars and night clubs around San Andreas. Enter a bar and walk into the red marker on the dance floor. During the challenge, a yellow circle appears near the bottom-center of the screen while button symbols scroll through the circle.

When a symbol appears inside the yellow circle, press the correct button to gain points. The better your timing, the better your score. Various text messages appear to rate your timing skill. These messages include: Bad, Acceptable, Good, Perfect, Great Timing, The Master, and Synchronized!

Gang Warfare

After completing the mission "Doberman," the task of taking over rival gang territories for respect and added income can begin. Note that you don't have to defend these territories, but there are definitely some distinct advantages to doing so.

Taking Over a Territory

Note that each gang has their own color that they wear. This same color is used to designate a particular gang's location on the map. Note that Grove Street, as you should know by now, are green. When the turf wars portion of the game begins, refer to the map and take a look at the territories and their corresponding colors.

First, recruit some fellow gang members to bring along. It's always best to bring along three (in a four-door car), then pick up more as you get close to your intended destination. Before you start a riot, get out of the car and look for other gang members to recruit to maximize your firepower. Note that CJ's level of Running Respect determines how many you can recruit. It's definitely much easier to go into battle with as many "friendlies" as possible. Note, however, that the recruits aren't always the smartest; it's nice, though, to have more bullets flying at the rival gang.

When you're finished recruiting, head to one of the locations highlighted on the map. Drive or walk around until your crew spots one of its rivals; you'll know they've spotted them when your guys start shooting. Then while on foot, take out at least three or four rival gang members. This should start the first phase of the fight. (Note that you cannot start a turf war while inside a vehicle.)

The fight consists of essentially three waves of rival gang members. The first part of the fight is[md]obviously[md]the easiest, as these guys usually pack the least powerful weapons and they always are the smallest in number. Take care during this phase to avoid as much damage as possible, as you'll need plenty of health to make it through the next two phases.

Body Armor & Health

Note that after each phase of the battle, Body Armor and Health (a heart icon) appear randomly in the area in which the fight is taking place. After clearing out the foes, quickly search and area for the power-ups!

The second and third waves have an increase in the number of rival gang members, plus they come with a much more powerful arsenal of weapons. The ultimate goal is to dispatch all three waves without dying. Do so and that portion of the map turns green to represent Grove Street.

Our 'Hood Is Under Attack!

At some point during these turf wars, a Grove Street territory that was previously won will come under attack. This will only happen to territories that border territories ruled by rival gang members. Basically, a territory surrounded by green (Grove Street) will not come under attack; only those next to a rival territory.

When the message "Our 'Hood Is Under Attack" appears on-screen, refer to the map and immediately drive to that location with some recruits. If you fail to respond, the rival gang will take over the territory and you'll be forced to win it back, that is if your goal is to acquire all 54 territories. When CJ and his buddies arrive, just eliminate the rivals as quickly as possible to win back the turf.

Not defending the territory also has an overall effect on CJ's running respect. If you fail to defend the turf, he'll lose respect so do the job right!

Advantages & Disadvantages of Turf Wars

There are many reasons to take part in the gang warfare aspect. First and foremost, it's a great way to increase CJ's running respect. Respect is earned by disposing of rival gang members and taking over territories. Just think how CJ's running respect will rise if you attempt to take over all 54 territories in Los Santos!

Another reason is to make a big-time bankroll. It seems that these gang members carry a lot of extra cash, and it drops when they are killed. Since there are a lot of guys fighting, this is an easy way to bring in the cash. More importantly, the number of territories acquired affects the bankroll that appears outside of CJ's mother's house. The more you take over, the more you can earn per night! It's also an extremely easy way to add additional ammo to some weapons in CJ's arsenal.

Since there's a lot of shooting going on during these turf wars, it's also a great way to increase CJ's weapon skill. Keep it up and you can achieve Hitman status on some of the more powerful weapons!

One of the main disadvantages to taking part is the fact that you're often called to rescue a territory under attack at the most inopportune time. The gang warfare is probably something that should be done during extended game playing periods in which this is what the main focus is on. If not, you'll find yourself switching back and forth between tasks a lot.

Helpful Tactics

As mentioned previously, it's always best to bring only plenty of support. It's never advised to start a turf war with only CJ; bring along as many recruits as possible and use them to draw fire away from CJ while he unloads on the rivals. It's highly unlikely that the recruits will last all three phases, so use other methods to protect CJ.

Look for walls or other objects to hide behind and avoid standing directly in the open where the rival gang members have a clear shot at CJ. If not, his health will definitely suffer. Also, don't wait too long to find and use the Health and Body Armor power-ups that appear in-between phases. It's way too easy to take a lucky shot in the back while running toward the power-up. Try to get onto ledges or rooftops and unload on any unsuspecting thugs, too.

Some of the most effective weapons to use in the second and third stages are Grenades and Molotovs. When a new phase of the battle begins, quickly refer to the on-screen map and look for the red icons representing the other gang members. Avoid getting trapped by two sets of attacks and instead look for a way to bring them all toward CJ at once. Then as they approach, hit them from a distance with a Grenade or Molotov to finish off multiple thugs at a time.

Gambling

Gambling Prerequisite
Complete Toreno's "Pilot School" mission to gain entry into Las Venturas (for casino gambling). Lowrider, Off Track Betting, and Pool can be played in Los Santos

Gambling Rewards:
Cash made while gambling.

Details

There are several opportunities to gamble in San Andreas. There is Off Track Betting in Downtown Los Santos and Montgomery and much larger casinos in Las Venturas. To increase CJ's luck in gambling, find as many Horseshoes as possible.

CJ increases his Gambling skill each time he gambles in a mini-game. The higher his Gambling skill, the more he can borrow against in the casino. And the more he can borrow, the higher the wager he can make when he is down on his luck.

GAMBLING STATS

GAMBLING SKILL %	GAMBLER LEVEL	WAGER & BARROWING MAX
1%	Gambler Level	$1,000
5%	Professional	$10,000
10%	Hi-roller	$100,000
100%	Whale	$1,000,000

WARNING: Don't Leave the Casino a Loser

If you borrow money from the casino and leave owing the casino money (money total in the red), you will soon receive a phone call from the casino owner reminding you that you owe him money. If you do not pay it back and are in the area, you receive a second call where the owner says he's sending his "associates" to pay you a visit. Be on the lookout for the 4-door Vincent; it's full of four, heavily armed roughnecks that shoot on sight. Survive the time limit, and pay the casino back to avoid future confrontations.

Blackjack

Locations
The Four Dragons, Caligula's Palace and Casino in Las Venturas

Maximum Wager
$100 to $1,000,000

Details

As CJ's Gambling skill increases, he can move to tables with higher betting limits. The Blackjack tables in San Andreas follow standard casino-rules.

Making Bets

There are four betting options: increase the wager; decrease the wager; proceed; and quit. Wager information appears in the bottom-left corner of the screen.

After making a bet and choosing "proceed," the dealer's cards appear at the top of the screen and yours appear at the bottom. The total wager, the dealer's score, and your current card total appear in the bottom-left corner of the screen.

Inside Track Betting (ITB)

Location:
Inside Track in Montgomery, Red County; Downtown Los Santos

Maximum Wager:
Amount of money you have.

You will most likely witness the first ITB machine while Downtown in Los Santos or while taking part in the Catalina mission, "Against all Odds."

Enter an ITB facility and approach one of the machines along the walls, then press the appropriate button to play. A list of five horses and their odds, your cash amount, and the betting options appear on-screen. Select a horse and a betting amount.

Easy Money

Stick with the horses with the worst odds. They will win more often than these odds claim—giving a great opportunity for some big winnings. Don't bet all of your money on one race though or you will go broke before you can win big. Make small bets at first. Once you have plenty of money, start making the big bets.

The race begins after selecting the Place Bet option. The game then switches to a screen showing the horse race. To locate your horse, match the horse's color (noted at the top of the screen) with the color of the jockey's jersey.

Pool

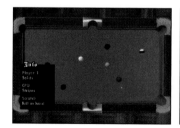

Redsands West

✓ **Locations**
At any of the many pool tables in most bars in San Andreas.
$ **Maximum Wager:**
$1,000 to $100,000 (table dependent)

Find an establishment that has pool tables and look for a man standing near them to play pool. You can even have a second player join in the fun. You can also make a wager to play against the computer.

Game Rules

The game rules are along the lines of standard pool. If you scratch (hit the white ball into one of the pockets), the computer player (or second player) places the cue ball on the table and takes a shot. Scratching on the 8-ball is allowed also in this game.

Aiming Mode

Aim the pool stick left and right to make the break off the cue ball. Press the appropriate button to proceed to Shooting Mode.

Shooting Mode

Strike the cue ball by tilting down and then pushing up. The cue ball hitting gauge appears in the bottom-right corner of the screen. The green dot on the ball indicates the cue's strike location. Move the tip of stick on the cue ball to affect the cue ball's direction. A row of dots plots the ball's trajectory according to the position of the cue.

Score Meter

The score, which appears in the bottom-left corner of the screen, displays the number of the potted balls (balls that have been sunk). If a foul occurs, this scoreboard illustrates the foul, or shows that the scratched ball is in your hand.

The Scratch

A scratch occurs when the cue ball enters a pocket, either directly or after hitting a ball. When a player scratches, the opponent takes a turn. Once the scratched cue ball is in hand, you can place the cue ball anywhere on the table to line up the next shot. Move the ball to the desired position, then continue to play as normal.

Roulette

✓ **Locations:**
Las Venturas Casinos
$ **Maximum Wager:**
$1,000 to $1,000,000 (machine dependent)

Details

The casinos have a few different roulette and blackjack tables from which to choose. As is the case with Blackjack, a higher Gambling skill translates into higher betting limits (Gambling skill is also increased through Lowrider mini-games and other challenges that involve betting).

Roulette follows the standard casino rules. You can lay the standard types of Roulette bets by placing chips on various options on the table, including on-the-line bets. Press the appropriate button to start the roulette wheel spinning.

Slots

- **Locations:**
  Las Venturas Casinos
- **Wager:**
  $1, $10, $20, and $50

Details

Pull the machine's lever (by confirming to play slots) and a graphic of a 3-reeled slot machine appears. All the reels spin and come to a stop one after another. The only combination that pays out is three of a kind and the payout depends upon the type of symbols that match up and the betting amount on the machine you're playing.

Video Poker

- **Locations**
  Some bars (like those in Blueberry, Red County) and Las Venturas Casinos.
- **Wager**
  $50, $100, $150, $200, and $250

Details

To bet, move between the five wagering options. You can bet up to $100 a hand.

Video Poker follows standard poker rules. After placing a bet, you can select Deal and to receive five cards. Hold onto your best cards (using the hold button above the cards), then choose Deal again to get some new cards. You win according to the

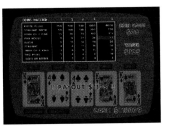

payout scale at the top of the card display. While playing, try to identify all of the GTAIII and Vice City characters on the face cards!

Wheel of Fortune

- **Locations**
  Casinos in Las Venturas.
- **Maximum Wager**
  $100 to $1,000,000 (table dependant)

Details

There are fifty-four potential slots that the wheel can stop on. Twenty-three of them are $1 spots, 15 are $2 spots, eight are $5 spots, four are $10 spots, two are $20 spots, and there is one "star" slot.

Place a bet on the slot that you think the wheel will stop on. After betting, press the appropriate button to proceed. The camera pans to the spinning wheel, then zooms in to show the slot that it stops on.

Girlfriends

One of the most exciting additions to the world of GTA is the girlfriend feature in San Andreas. CJ has the opportunity to date six different girls! There are some real advantages to dating the girls, as CJ will acquire new outfits, acquire new vehicles, and more if he can successfully keep the girls happy. The rest of this section provides an "overview" of the dating process and provides insight on all of the girls..

Meeting the Girls

CJ meets two of the girls during the normal progression of the storyline missions. That leaves four more girls to locate, date, and... well... you know what comes next. Upon first meeting these women, there is a floating blue triangle marker above them (except for Millie). Simply approach them and press the Action button to speak to them. If they're interested, the dating process can begin. To go out on a date, find the Heart icon on the in-game map and see if she is home. Note that the girls are available at only certain times of the day and she will only go out once a day. (Refer to each girl's section for complete details.) When a girl is home, you'll see a pink marker, her vehicle, and a two-player icon outside. Drive into the pink marker to start a date.

If one of the girls thinks CJ isn't quite up to par, she'll provide a hint as to how she likes her man to look. When this occurs, heed the girl's advice and make CJ's appearance resemble that which she desires. If she likes a muscular man, start hitting the gym on a regular basis. If, on the other hand, a girl likes a chunky dude, start chowing down on a bunch of fast food. Either way, head back to the girl until she decides when it's time to date.

To track CJ's dating progress with the girls, pause the game and select the Stats option. From there, choose the Achievements option. Here you will find a percentage completion for each girl. It usually begins at 10% for each one.

The following section indicates where to find the girls (refer to the Odd Jobs map for exact meeting and dating locations).

GIRLFRIEND MEETING LOCATIONS

GIRL	OCCUPATION	LOCATION
Denise Robinson	Gang Girl	Los Santos: Burning apartment in "Burning Desire" mission.
Michelle Cannes	Mechanic	San Fierro: Inside Driving School, near the water cooler.
Helena Goodpoke	Weapons Expert	Blueberry, Red County: Ammu-Nation, exterior shooting range balcony.
Barbara Schternvart	Cop	El Quebrados, Desert: Parking lot of Sheriff's department parking lot.
Katie Nookie	Nurse	Avispa Country Club, San Fierro: At the edge of the golf course, practicing T'ai Chi.
Millie	Caligula's Croupier	Caligula's Palace, Las Venturas: Follow her to her home from Caligula's in "Key to Her Heart" mission.

Getting the Girls' Attention

This is where it gets tricky. Each girl likes her man in a particular state of physical condition (not particularly in the best possible shape). The girls like a man with lots of Sex Appeal and they want him to look good. Get some sexy clothes, a new haircut, some tattoos, lose some fat (for most girls), and work out. Most importantly, get a nice ride! Sex Appeal is seriously boosted when CJ steps out of a nice car (see Wang's Auto Trader for cars with high Sex Appeal). In particular, the game's various sports cars are usually the best choices to raise CJ's Sex Appeal.

A couple of ways to increase CJ's Sex Appeal is to get different haircuts, purchase different clothes, or get cool tattoos. Note that these changes in CJ's appearance do not effect his overall Sex Appeal like a nice car does, but it does add to it a small bit. Refer to the appropriate sections of this guide for specific information on the increases in Sex Appeal for haircuts, clothes, and tattoos.

After locating one of the girls, walk up to her to interact with her. If she says anything besides cracking on CJ's appearance, answer positively and she'll accept a date. After doing so, a heart icon appears on the map. This icon indicates the location of the girl's house where she will be available for a date. The following section summarizes what each girl is looking for in a man.

GIRLFRIENDS' TASTE

GIRL	WHAT SHE'S LOOKING FOR
Denise Robinson	She gets hooked after CJ rescues her from the burning apartment, but don't show up to her house without lots of Sex Appeal.
Michelle Cannes	She likes a man with meat on his bones, so spend some time eating fatty foods. Her guy needs lots of Sex Appeal, too.
Helena Goodpoke	She likes an average man: no fat and less than 50% muscle. (Essentially the way CJ appears at the start of the game). Lots of Sex Appeal is also needed.
Barbara Schternvart	Barbara likes her men big. Do some eating, but make sure CJ looks nice. Lots of Sex Appeal is a must.
Katie Nookie	She likes a muscular guy with lots of Sex Appeal.
Millie	Pose as a Gimp to get a first date with Millie. Also, make sure that CJ shows up for a date with lots of Sex Appeal.

Sexy Cars

It's always a good idea to step out of a car with lots of Sex Appeal before trying to get a girl to go out with CJ. Note that damage to vehicles lowers their Sex Appeal, so drive carefully.

Arranging a Date

Once a girl agrees to go out with CJ, drive to her house (or date location; Barbara stays at the Sheriff's department) and step (or drive) into the red marker. Each girl is available for dates at different times of the day and they may refuse to go out with CJ if he doesn't look a certain way or if his Sex Appeal is too low.

Random phone call dates will also occur and if you continually ignore these requests, the girl will eventually dump CJ and that girl will no longer be available for dating. The following section lists the times that each girl is available for a date.

GIRLFRIENDS' DATING AVAILABILITY

GIRL	TIME SHE'S AVAILABLE
Denise Robertson	00:00 to 06:00
	16:00 to 00:00
Michelle Cannes	00:00 to 12:00
Helena Goodpoke	00:00 to 12:00
	08:00 to 12:00
	14:00 to 00:00
Barbara Schternvart	00:00 to 06:00
	16:00 to 00:00
Katie Nookie	12:00 to 00:00
Millie	12:00 to 22:00

You Don't Bring Me Flowers... Or Other Gifts

Refer to the flower location map to pick up some flowers before a date. Before the date ends, select the flowers (they appear as a selected weapon) and face her. Press the appropriate button to surprise her. There are also "mystery" items that CJ can give his dates. Think hard—and look even harder—to find one of these items!

It's also possible to plant a big kiss after a successful date. To do so, face the girl outside of the red marker (stepping inside ends the date). Then press the appropriate button to plant one on her. Note, however, that doing so will subtract 1% from that girl's date progress meter. "Gifts", on the other hand, add 1% to the girl's date progress meter.

Kinds of Dates

Each girlfriend decides what she wants to do on the date. She will either request a dinner date, a driving date, or a dancing date.

Dinner Date

When dinner is requested, access the in-game map and take note of the new food icons that appear open for dating. There are four food options available: fast food, diner, bar, and restaurant. When dancing is requested, a dance icon appears on the map[md]there's one club in each of San Andreas' three big cities. Each girl likes certain places to eat or drink better than others and it becomes obvious as soon as you sit down. One key indicator is the background music that is played while CJ and his date are in the establishment. If the music is of the romantic kind, you'll know she's enjoying herself. If not, don't expect the rest of the date to go well!

Driving Date

Driving dates are usually fairly simple ones. During such a date, the goal is to max out the girl's Fun meter (it appears in the upper-right portion of the screen). To do so, you must find an area of the city that she enjoys and drive around as the Fun meter rises. Each girl has a particular part of the city that she likes more than other parts of the city. While driving around, she will indicate which areas are to her liking. Simply find one of those locations and start driving around. Note, however, that some girls prefer to go fast, while others want to take a Sunday morning drive. Drive to her taste and the Fun meter will rise; if not, it will fall. Simply max out the meter for a successful date. Let the meter run out and the date will end unsuccessfully.

Dancing Date

Sometimes, a girl will want to hit the town for some excitement and dancing at a local club. During this type of date, locate a dance icon on the in-game map and drive to the nearest club. Once inside, step into the pink marker to start a dancing mini-game. Hit the appropriate button as the icon approaches the circle to score the most points. Just do well enough to impress her (score a lot of points) and the date will go well. Afterwards, just take her back home.

Be hasty. If you don't get the girl to the club or restaurant fast enough, she will get bored and you'll have to take her home[md]or if you fail to max out her fun meter on those "fun" type missions.

"I Don't Like This Area"

You'll notice while driving a girl on a date that she may occasionally say "I don't care for this area," or something similar. Note that this hint only refers to the driving dates. Do not let this affect where you go on an eating or dancing date.

Giving "Gifts"

Like most girls, CJ's ladies like to receive flowers on their dates. To make the date go even better, locate some flowers prior to the date and give them to the girl before entering the pink marker at the end of the date. Stand next to the date and eventually an on-screen prompt will ask if you want to present her with the flowers. Doing so provides a small boost to the date. For a complete list of flower locations, refer to the maps in this guide.

The girls also like another kind of "gift" as well. This non-traditional "gift" isn't as easy to find, but it does result in a similar increase to the overall date. Just use your imagination and it will soon become obvious what this "gift" is...

Giving gifts seems to bring out the romantic side in the girls, as this usually presents an opportunity to kiss them. Do so if you wish, but refer to the following section to see how it affects the overall dating percentage.

The Girls

The following section summarizes each of the girls that CJ can date. It covers her likes and dislikes and other information that reveals the essentials to a successful dating experience.

Denise

Denise, who lives in Los Santos, isn't very far from the Johnson Family home. In fact, she's just a few short blocks away. She doesn't seem to have a particular preference for her men either. She may be one of the wildest girls, as she oftentimes likes to go on drive-by dates!

GENERAL INFORMATION

Where She's Found:
Complete "Burning Desire" mission in main storyline
Dating Requirements: None
Dating Times: 00:00 to 06:00 & 16:00 to 00:00

Denise is a low-maintenance kind of gal, so any fast food joint will suffice on a food date. There's even a bar nearby that she enjoys. Since there's only one dance club in Los Santos, take her there on dancing dates. It's also easy to please her on driving dates, as the area in and around her house is right up her alley.

BENEFITS OF DATING DENISE

UNLOCKABLES	PERCENTAGE COMPLETE
"Coffee"	40%
Hustler vehicle	50%
Pimp Suit	100%

Katie

Katie, who lives in San Fierro, is a nurse with a penchant for some rather odd fixations. During dates with her, sit back and listen to her conversations with CJ—they're quite entertaining!

GENERAL INFORMATION

Where She's Found:
Avispa Country Club, performing tai chi in the grassy area
Dating Requirements: High muscle, high Sex Appeal
Dating Times: 12:00 to 00:00

Katie is particularly fond of diners and there are a couple of them nearby. The closest one is located just around the bend near her home in Paradiso. For a dancing date, take her to the lone club in San Fierro near the Queens district. Katie isn't a speed freak, so drive at a reasonable rate on a driving date. The closest place that she prefers is near the diners close to her home.

One of the cool features while dating Katie is that, since she's a nurse, she'll get CJ out of the hospital for free and he'll get to keep all of his weapons if he gets wasted.

BENEFITS OF DATING KATIE

UNLOCKABLES	PERCENTAGE COMPLETE
"Coffee"	50%
Romero vehicle	50%
Medic Uniform	100%

Michelle

Michelle, who also lives in San Fierro, is a mechanic.

GENERAL INFORMATION

Where She's Found:
Inside the driving school building in San Fierro
Dating Requirements: High fat, high Sex Appeal
Dating Times: 00:00 to 12:00

Look for a martini glass icon during an eating date, as she seems to prefer these places more than others. As with Katie, take her to the lone dance club in the city to get her groove on. As might be expected, since Michelle is a mechanic she likes someone who can drive really fast. The area doesn't seem to matter as much as the overall speed at which you're driving, so put the pedal to the metal!

Special Date

Michelle has a special kind of date, unique to all the other types. During one of these types, Michelle takes the wheel and decides to drive while CJ rides shotgun. The date ends after about two or three in-game hours, at which point she drives back to the garage to end the date. To fail this type of date, make CJ get out of the car and let her drive away.

BENEFITS OF DATING MICHELLE

UNLOCKABLES	PERCENTAGE COMPLETE
"Coffee"	40%
Monster Truck vehicle	50%
Racing Suit	100%

Barbara

This lady makes her appearance outside the police station in the desert town of El Quebrados. One of the best benefits of dating Barbara is that CJ will get out of jail free and retain all of his weapons!

GENERAL INFORMATION

Where She's Found:
Police Station in El Quebrados
Dating Requirements: High fat, high Sex Appeal
Dating Times: 00:00 to 06:00 & 16:00 to 00:00

Barbara is fond of diner food and there's one nearby, so take her there on food dates. When it comes to dancing, prepare to make a long haul to the dance club in Las Venturas (or San Fierro), as there are no dance clubs in the desert. This divorced mother doesn't seem to enjoy fast cars, so drive slowly around the El Quebrados area at slow speeds to get a successful date.

BENEFITS OF DATING BARBARA

UNLOCKABLES	PERCENTAGE COMPLETE
"Coffee"	About 60%
Ranger vehicle	50%
Cop Outfit	100%

Helena

Helena lives on a farm in Blueberry, which is located in Red County. You can find her on the roof of the Ammu-Nation taking target practice. One cool result of dating Helena is that CJ has immediate access to a Chainsaw, a Flamethrower, Movotovs, and a Pistol, plus he can drive her car—a Bandito.

GENERAL INFORMATION

Where She's Found:
On a farm in Blueberry
Dating Requirements: Low muscle, low fat, high Sex Appeal
Dating Times: 00:00 to 02:00, 08:00 to 12:00, & 14:00 to 00:00

One place that Helena likes to eat is in the Rodeo area of Los Santos. This seems to please her quite well, so take her there on food dates. As for dancing, drive her to the club in Los Santos. Note, though, that it's quite a long drive. Lastly, Helena isn't fond of fast speeds, so take it easy on her driving dates.

BENEFITS OF DATING HELENA

UNLOCKABLES	PERCENTAGE COMPLETE
"Coffee"	About 70%
Bandito vehicle	50%
Rural Outfit	100%

Millie

To start dating Millie, simply complete the "Key to Her Heart Mission."

GENERAL INFORMATION

Where She's Found:
Finish the "Key to Her Heart Mission"; she lives in the Prickle Pine district of Las Venturas
Dating Requirements: None
Dating Times: 12:00 to 22:00

Restaurants are Millie's choice for dinner dates and there is one close to her home. For dancing, take her to the club in the southwest portion of Las Venturas and watch her strut her stuff! It doesn't take a fancy driver to impress Millie, so drive at a regular speed in and around her home.

Special Date

To trigger a special date with Mille, make CJ wear the Gimp Suit. By doing so, Millie invites him in right away for "coffee."

BENEFITS OF DATING MILLIE

UNLOCKABLES	PERCENTAGE COMPLETE
"Coffee"	About 40%
Club vehicle	50%
100%	Nothing is unlocked

Relationship Breakdown

As noted previously, a good date results in a percentage increase in the Achievements screen for that girl. On the other hand, a bad date will decrease that statistic. Here's a breakdown of the percentage increases.

REGULAR DATE	PERCENTAGE
Successful	+5%
Failed	-5%
GIFTS	**PERCENTAGE**
Flowers	+1%
"Other"	+1%
TWO-PLAYER	**PERCENTAGE**
After successful date	???
After failed date	???
OTHER	**PERCENTAGE**
Successful kiss	-1%
Failed kiss	-1%
"Coffee"	+5%

Two-Player Dates

When the girls are home, you'll notice a two-player, free roam icon nearby in addition to the pink marker and her vehicle. To start a two-player date, just walk into the icon and press any button on controller two.

During this kind of date, the second player will control the girl while player one will control CJ. This gives both players free roam of the city without fear of affecting the current relationship with the girl.

Mod Garages

Details

Want a customized vehicle? No problem. Drop by one of San Andreas's Mod Garages. There are three varieties: Transfenders, Loco Low Co., and Wheel Arch Angels. Transfenders is actually the biggest company, as it has a chain of stores around the state. To locate a Mod Garage, locate the red Wrench icon on the map or radar once the garages are opened.

 Increased Sex Appeal?

Getting your car modified does not raise its Sex Appeal. See the Auto Trader for Sex Appeal levels on all vehicles.

Details

Transfenders is a mod garage that caters to a wide variety of vehicles. They specialize in servicing up to 65 different vehicle types! Check out the "Vehicle" section of this guide to see which cars can be serviced at Transfenders.

Mod Garages only open their doors for vehicles that they can service. Each vehicle is different and the parts and prices are specific to that vehicle. However, there are certain services and parts offered that are the same for each vehicle. The following section summarizes the services available at Transfenders.

Transfenders

 Prerequisite
Opens upon completion of Cesar Vialpando.

Location
There are three Transfenders locations, one in each major city (Temple, Los Santos; Doherty, San Fierro; Come-a-Lot Las Venturas).

Paint Jobs

These are custom detailed paint jobs offered exclusively to particular types of vehicles. Examples of a custom paint job are flames or murals. Cost: $1000.

⊖ **Pay 'n' Spray**

Taking a customized painted vehicle into a Pay 'n' Spray will wipe out any customized Paint Job. If you want to keep the paint job, stay out of the Pay 'n' Sprays.

Colors

You can change the color of a vehicle for a low price. When "Color" is selected, a panel of colors appears on-screen. Vehicles with stripes or two-tones have two color options: interior and exterior. These are vehicles with the option to change the color of the seats, mostly convertibles.

Vents

This option, which is vehicle specific, enables you to choose hood vents for a vehicle.

Hood

This option only appears if a vehicle can be fitted with optional Hood Scoops. These accessories come in various sizes: small, medium and large.

Exhausts

It's possible to change exhaust types on many cars. Each exhaust type, the offered amount, and pricing is vehicle specific.

Spoilers

Transfenders can install a variety of rear spoilers to a vehicle. This is a vehicle specific offer.

Lights

Some vehicles serviced at Transfenders have the Light option. This is where a different style of headlamp or fog light can be acquired.

Nitro

Each vehicle that Transfenders can service has the Nitro option. Not every vehicle is offered the full menu of Nitrous options (2x, 5x, 10x), though. The more nitrous you choose, the higher the price. The different Nitro options simply reflect the number of times you can use the nitrous speed boost before returning for another installment.

Using Nitro

Press the shoot button + the accelerate button to fire up the Nitro when driving a car with Nitro installed. This causes blue flames to shoot from the exhaust. The nitro lasts as long as the blue flames extend from the exhaust. You can even come to a compete stop and continue with the remainder of the nitro injection by simply accelerating again. There is a cool-down period required between Nitro doses. Wait for the small blue flames from the previous injection to disperse completely before uses the next Nitro dose.

Roof

Certain vehicles have the option of a selection of roofs. This includes hardtop, soft top, open roof, and roof scoops.

Wheels

There are eight different wheel types at Transfenders. All vehicles are offered this option and all of the wheels are the same for each vehicle. The prices range from $620 to $1560.

Car Stereo (Bass Boost; $100)

All vehicles can have an enhancement to their audio system. The Bass Boost customization increases the low-end sound when the radio is turned on. This kicker costs $100.

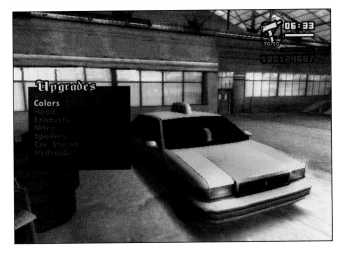

Hydraulics ($1500)

All vehicles have the hydraulics system installation option. The price is $1500.

Loco Low Co.

Prerequisite
Open upon completion of "Cesar Vialpando" mission

Location
There's only one location and it's in Cesar's neighborhood in Willowfield, Los Santos

Loco Low Co. is a small mod garage in Cesar's neighborhood that opens for business after completing the mission, "Cesar Vialpando." This shop only caters to Lowriders, so the garage will only open its door for a lowrider vehicle. The following are the cars that Loco Low Co. accommodates: **Blade, Broadway, Remington, Savanna, Slamvan, Voodoo,** and the **Tornado.**

Loco Low Co. Services

The lowrider mod shop offers a host of customizations. However, the garage only offers certain services for each type of lowrider. The following is a table of all the services and parts that Loco Low Co. offers:

LOCO LOW CO. SERVICE MENU

SERVICE/PART	PRICE	AVAILABILITY
Paint Jobs		
Paint Job 1	$500	Savanna, Remington, Slamvan
Paint Job 2	$500	Savanna, Slamvan
Paint Job 3	$500	Slamvan
Colors		
Color 1	$150	All lowriders
Color 2 (interior)	$150	Savanna, Broadway, Tornado
Roof		
Vinyl Hardtop	$3340	Blade
Convertible Roof	$3250	Blade
Hardtop	$3380	Savanna
Softtop	$3290	Savanna
Roof 1	$3000	Broadway
Roof 2	$2000	Broadway
Front Bumper		
Chromer Bumper	$1000 to $2200*	All lowriders, except Voodoo
Slammin Bumper	$900 to $2180*	All lowriders, except Voodoo
Rear Bumper		
Blade Rear Bumper	$2150	Blade
Chromer Bumper	$500 to $2130*	All lowriders, except Voodoo
Slammin Bumper	$500 to $2095*	All lowriders, except Voodoo and Blade
Exhausts		
Chromer	$500 to $3340*	All lowriders, except Voodoo
Slammin'	$500 to $3250*	All lowriders, except Voodoo

LOCO LOW CO. SERVICE MENU, CONT.

SERVICE/PART	PRICE	AVAILABILITY
Side Skirts		
Wing	$800	Tornado
Chrome Strips	$780 to $1000*	Blade, Savanna, Broadway
Chrome Arches (Flame)	$780	Remington
Chrome Arches (Cover)	$780	Remington
Chrome Trim	$780	Slamvan
Wheelcovers	$940	Slamvan
Other		
Twin Seats	$940 to $990*	Blade, Savanna
Double Seats	$860 to $900*	Blade, Savanna
Chrome Grill (Skull)	$940	Remington
Chrome Bars	$860	Remington
Chrome Lights	$1120	Remington
Front Bullbars 1	$2130	Slamvan
Front Bullbars 2	$2050	Slamvan
Rear Bullbars 1	$1610	Slamvan
Rear Bullbars 2	$1540	Slamvan
Wheels		
Classic	$1620	All lowriders except Voodoo
Dollar	$1560	All lowriders except Voodoo
Twist	$1200	All lowriders
Wires	$1560	All lowriders
Trance	$1350	All lowriders except Voodoo
Cutter	$1030	All lowriders except Voodoo
Rimshine	$980	All lowriders except Voodoo
Virtual	$620	All lowriders
Access	$1140	All lowriders
Car Stereo		
Bass Boost	$100	All lowriders
Hydraulics	$1500	All lowriders
Nitrous		
2x Nitrous	$200	All lowriders
5x Nitrous	$500	All lowriders
10x Nitrous	$1000	All lowriders

Installed Hydraulics

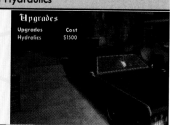

The Hydraulics offered at Loco Low Co. are no different than the Hydraulics that come as standard equipment on some lowriders. Therefore, don't waste any money on a Hydraulic system if your lowrider already has them.

Wheel Arch Angels

⊘ Prerequisite
Open upon completing "Zeroing In" mission.
✴ Location:
There's only one location and it's in Ocean Flats, San Fierro.

Details

Wheel Arch Angles in Ocean Flats is a street racing mod garage that only caters to vehicles that can be converted to street racers. Their two major brands are Alien and the lesser expensive X-Flow products. The vehicles that can be serviced at Wheel Arch Angels are: **Elegy, Flash, Jester, Stratum, Sultan,** and let's not forget **Uranus**.

WHEEL ARCH ANGELS SERVICE MENU		
SERVICE/PART	**PRICE**	**AVAILABILITY**
Paint Jobs		
Paint Job 1	$500	All street racers
Paint Job 2	$500	Jester, Uranus, Stratum, Sultan
Paint Job 3	$500	Jester, Uranus, Stratum, Sultan
Colors		
Color 1	$150	All street racers
Exhausts		
Alien Exhaust	$710 to $850*	Jester
X-Flow Exhaust	$510 to $750*	Jester
Front Bumper		
Alien Front Bumper	$930 to $1090*	All street racers
X-Flow Front Bumper	$840 to $950*	All street racers
Rear Bumper		
Alien Rear Bumper	$950 to $1200*	All street racers
X-Flow Rear Bumper	$510 to $950*	All street racers
Roof		
Alien Roof Vent	$150 to $250*	All street racers
X-Flow Roof Vent	$100 to $200*	All street racers
Spoilers		
Alien Spoiler	$550 to $810*	All street racers
X-Flow Spoiler	$450 to $620*	All street racers
Side Skirts		
Alien Side Skirts	$450 to $670*	All street racers
X-Flow Side Skirts	$350 to $530*	All street racers
Wheels		
Cutter	$1030	All street racers
Rimshine	$980	All street racers
Mega	$1030	All street racers
Grove	$1230	All street racers
Switch	$900	All street racers
Shadow	$1100	All street racers
Classic	$1620	All street racers
Dollar	$1560	All street racers
Import	$820	All street racers
Atomic	$770	All street racers
Car Stereo		
Bass Boost	$100	All street racers
Hydraulics	$1500	All street racers
Nitrous		
2x Nitrous	$200	All street racers
5x Nitrous	$500	All street racers
10x Nitrous	$1000	All street racers

The hot customizations from Wheel Arch Angels are dazzling. You can turn the conservative Stratum into a flashy street racer that will be the envy of all soccer moms! Check out these cool customizations (see pictures).

Jester

Flash

Uranus

Stratum

Sultan

Elegy

Triathlon Races

There are two "Beat The Cock!" triathlon races in Los Santos. The reason this mission has such a peculiar name is because one of the toughest competitors is dressed in a Cluckin' Bell Chicken uniform. You may have seen an advertisement for the event in the Gym— did you? One event takes place on the Santa Maria Beach near the light house and the other is on the small beach near the dock in Fisher's Lagoon (just southwest of Palomino Creek). Step into the red markers that only appear on theses beaches on Saturdays and Sundays. You should only take these challenges once you have a good amount of Stamina and a high Cycling Skill.

Santa Maria Beach: Beat The Cock!

- ✅ **Prerequisite**
  Only available on Saturdays and Sundays.
- ✳ **Location**
  Santa Maria Beach
- Ⓢ **Reward**
  $10000

Details

Enter the red marker on the shoreline of Santa Maria Beach, just east of the lighthouse, to take part in a Triathlon Race. The race is against eight other competitors and CJ's position is illustrated on the race monitor in the bottom-right corner of the screen.

Swimming

Enter the water and swim to the first red marker. Swim as fast as possible through the ocean markers. The checkpoints appear as red blips on the radar, and each red marker has an internal arrow pointing in the direction of the next checkpoint.

Biking

After clearing the last water marker, you have 25 seconds to get on a bike (if not, you're disqualified). Run up the beach and hop onto the Mountain Bike with the blue marker over it. Use the radar while racing up the road through the checkpoints.

The bike portion of the race goes through Back O' Beyond, then off-road through Flint County and into Whetstone and Angel Pine, at which point the race returns to paved roads. You'll pass under Mount Chiliad through the road tunnel and pedal all the way into Missionary Hill, San Fierro.

Just inside San Fierro, ditch the bike before the timer counts down from 25. The next checkpoint up the road to the right will not become active until you ditch the bike.

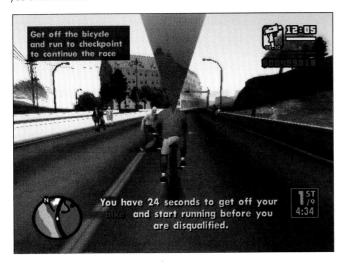

Foot Race

The last portion is a foot race. Run up the road past the Avispa Country Club, then follow the red markers along the winding road of Missionary Hill. The last marker is at the top of the hill under a tower next to the power plant. First prize is $10000!

Fisher's Lagoon: Beat The Cock!

- ✔ **Prerequisite:**
  Only available on Saturdays and Sundays
- ✛ **Location:**
  Fisher's Lagoon near Palomino Creek
- $ **Reward:**
  $10,000

Details

Enter the red marker on Fisher's Lagoon beach that appears east of the dock. There are 8 other competitors including a chicken-man. This race is very similar to the one in Santa Maria beach only it's much, much longer and tougher.

Swim through the 9 water checkpoints and get on the near Mulholland. The competition is in really good shape, so you don't have much time to fall off your bike more than a couple times (depending on your Stamina) during the bike course. The bike course is extremely long (approximately 13 minutes).

The course takes you through Hilltop Farm, Blueberry, past Easter Bay Airport, into San Fierro, through Doherty, Downtown, Calton Heights, across the Gant Bridge, through Tierra Robada, through the desert across the Sherman Bridge, through Bone County, and into Las Venturas.

You cruise the highways of Las Venturas and make your way to Redsands East where you have to lose the bike just past the Burger Shot. With whatever energy you have left, run south along The Strip and pass through the final checkpoint near The Four Dragons Casino. Good luck and get in shape for this one!

chapter 4
The Desert

The stark desert region of San Andreas is beautiful, but also forbidding and mysterious. Part of the mystery for CJ is the unidentified voice that summons him via phone to a ranch in Tierra Robada. Of course, the abandoned aircraft graveyard up north in Verdant Meadows (an ironic name if ever there was one) adds to the intrigue. Then there's that curious stretch of unmarked land in the heart of the region. It seems that only The Truth, true to his name, can shed light on the shadowy secrets buried there in those dunes!

RESTAURANTS

- Cluckin' Bell . . . . Aldea Malvada A2
- Cluckin' Bell . . . . Octane Springs A4

POINTS OF INTEREST

- 24/7 . . . . Fort Carson B3
- Ammu-Nation . . . . El Quebrados A2
- Ammu-Nation . . . . Octane Springs A4
- Hospital . . . . Fort Carson B3
- Hospital . . . . El Quebrados A2
- Bars/Strips
- Safehouses
- Ammu-Nation . . . .'. . . Fort Carson C3

Unique Attractions

UNIQUE STUNT JUMPS

1. **Las Payasadas** • Head east over the tarp-covered dirt pile and jump over the massive chicken. • **A3**
2. **Las Payasadas** • Drive up the steps to the overlook while going south (use the steps near 2-player rampage icon); must successfully land this one. • **A3**
3. **Verdant Meadows** • Speed up the westernmost plane's wing going northeast. This should enable you to clear the plane to the northeast. • **A4**
4. **Arca Del Peste** • Head west along the wooden path and over the canyon river. A motorcycle is the best option here. • **A3**
5. **Valle Ocultado** • Hit the ramp against the wall of the shack with the pier. The jump is a success even if you land in the water; find the nearby beach to exit from the water. • **A3**

OYSTERS

1. **Gant Bridge** • Between the Gant Bridge's northern most support and a cliff. • **A1**
2. **Tierra Robada** • East of the Bayside lighthouse by a rocky outcrop. • **A2**
3. **Tierra Robada** • Hidden from view by a small roadside wall. North of the San Fierro Docks. • **B2**
4. **Valle Ocultado** • End of a pier at the lakeside house. • **A3**
5. **Tierra Robada** • Under wooden bridge to the Northwest of the Sherman dam. • **A3**
6. **Sherman Dam** • Under the west control tower of the Dam. • **A3**
7. **Tierra Robada** • Under the metal bridge just South of Las Barrancas. • **B3**
8. **Tierra Robada** • At the end of a tributary leading into San Fierro Bay, west of Toreno's House. • **C3**
9. **Tierra Robada** • In the water in the boat shed at Toreno's House. • **C3**

Security Services

WEAPONS

1. **Grenades** • Bayside • Alleyway entrance between shops • **A1**
2. **Mystery Weapon** • Bayside • Abandoned lot, behind dumpster • **A1**
3. **Desert Eagle** • Bayside Marina • Far corner of posh house's backyard • **A1**
4. **Katana** • El Quebrados • Behind building amongst mobile homes near northernmost road • **A2**
5. **MP5** • El Quebrados • Behind building two doors west of barber shop • **A2**
6. **Heat Seeking RPG** • Aldea Malvada • Tierra Robada borderline; behind the largest ruined structure • **A2**
7. **Shotgun** • Valle Ocultado • On the lodge's pier • **A3**
8. **Fire Extinguisher** • Valle Ocultado • Next to pumpless gas station • **A3**
9. **AK47** • Tierra Robada • Near front door of camper in small trailer park • **A3**
10. **Brass Knuckles** • Las Payasadas • Behind small building on the corner • **A3**
11. **Parachute** • Arco del Oeste • Inside dilapadated building on top of hill • **A3**
12. **Knife** • El Castilo Del Diablo • Between pens at the snake farm • **A4**
13. **Micro Uzi** • Verdant Meadows • Inside furthest west fuselage at end of runway • **A4**
14. **M4** • Area 69 • Behind southwest guard tower inside Area 69 compound • **A4**
15. **Minigun** • Restricted Area • Inside Area 69 compound • **A4**
16. **Parachute** • Bone County • Walk into building next to comm tower • **B3**
17. **Desert Eagle** • Lil' Probe Inn • Behind the middle solar panel in the trailer park (across the street from bar) • **B4**
18. **9mm** • Tierra Robada • Under west railroad bridge support, hidden from view by the road • **B3**
19. **Molotovs** • Fort Carson • Behind the liquor store • **C3**
20. **Shotgun** • Fort Carson • In front of shanty • **C4**
21. **Shovel** • Hunter Quarry • In front of the packing crate near the mud pile • **C4**
22. **Chainsaw** • Hunter Quarry • On first level of rock crusher machine, hidden behind cylinder • **C4**
23. **Parachute** • Gant Bridge • On top of highest bridge support • **B1**
24. **Thermal Goggles** • The Big Ear • Underneath the satellite dish • **B3**
25. **Night Vision Goggles** • Restricted Area • On top of elevated platform • **B4**
26. **Knife** • Bone County • Near trailer park homes • **B4**

POLICE BRIBES

- **Bayside Marina** • Behind the building on the pier • **A1**
- **Las Payasadas** • In between two buildings • **A1**
- **Bone County** • Northeast of airstrip, out in desolate area • **A4**
- **Bone County** • Far east side of desert, off side of road near Area 69 • **A4**
- **Bone County** • Near windy road • **B3**
- **Bone County** • Just south of Cluckin' Bell in grassy area • **B4**

BODY ARMOR

- **Bayside Tunnel** • On beach • **A1**
- **Valle Ocultado** • Between building near the pier • **A3**
- **Las Payasadas** • Between buildings near the unique stunt jump • **A3**
- **Verdant Meadows** • Inside airplane fuselage near safe house • **A4**
- **Restricted Area** • On top of a guard tower • **B4**

PAY 'N' SPRAY

- **El Quebrados** • **A2**
- **Fort Carson** • **B3**

FLOWERS   (5 of 40)

- **Las Brujas** • In front of headstone. • **A3**
- **Sherman Dam** • In front of monument. • **B3**
- **Tierra Robada** • Next to Gas Station toilets. • **A2**
- **Tierra Robada** • Back of bungalow off the dirt road. • **A2**
- **Bayside** • On front lawn of house. • **A1**

(S) **Cash Available in Strand:**
$22,000

Having had his Crack Syndicate brought to an untimely end, Mike Toreno has done some research on the guy that did the damage. Now he's convinced that CJ might be just the man to do some heavy lifting for him, and he's found a compelling way to buy CJ's skills—using CIA connections to get CJ's brother Sweet out of jail. But first Toreno has to tweak CJ's interest—and make sure he's worthy.

TORENO mission 1

Monster

(🚗) **New Vehicle Introduced:**
Monster Truck

(S) **Cash Gained:**
Up to $5000 (depends on time)

Drive up to Tierra Robada County, following the "?" icon to the sprawling ranch house. When you step into the red marker, a couple of mechanics walk out to work on a monster truck. A voice over a loudspeaker welcomes CJ, challenging him to a driving test "to see what you're made of."

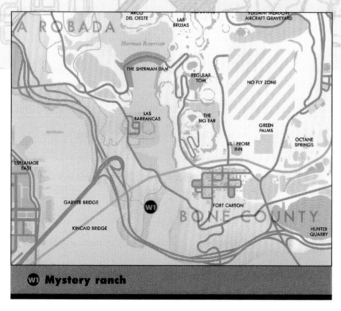

W1 Mystery ranch

A worker brings out another monster truck and explains the challenge:

A timed drive over a course marked by map coordinates. These coordinates, of course, appear as the familiar red column checkpoints. Lose the truck and you fail. You must finish the course of 35 checkpoints within a time limit of 6:30.

Use Your Radar

Remember that the next checkpoint always appears as a red blip on your radar. This is particularly useful on a course that cuts across the terrain without following obvious roadways.

Drive the Course

Get in the monster truck and drive to the first checkpoint, just ahead on the road. Note that each new checkpoint appears as the red blip on your radar. Succeeding checkpoints often appear well off the road, sometimes in rugged terrain.

Go 4-by-4

For tough off-road driving and sharper cornering, hold down the handbrake button to activate 4-wheel steering.

Stay Upright!

Keep an eye out for ravines, arroyos, and gullies along the route. If you turn the truck over, chances are it will catch fire and explode.

When you finally reach the 35th checkpoint in under 6:30, you get ranked. The best time on the list is a smokin' 4:45! You're told the boss will be in touch. We recommend you turn right and use the nearby Save Game disc to save your progress. CJ then gets another phone call from Mystery Man, who promises to explain everything. Go around to the front of the ranch house and step into the red marker to trigger the next mission.

Highjack

Accomplice:
Cesar

Cash Gained:
$7000

The mysterious "boss" introduces himself to CJ. Surprise! It's Mike Toreno. His story is not quite what CJ expected, though. Toreno says he's working for a government agency, battling threats in Latin America "by any means necessary." He claims his drug-dealing is merely a means of gaining money and contacts. He sketches his vision of hell if his work fails: "Communism in Ohio! People sharing! Nobody buying stuff! That kind of bull..." It's hard to imagine a bleaker picture of America.

Toreno says he needs a guy like CJ to do "things I can't get caught doing." He asks him to commandeer a truck being used by a rival agency. It's a two-man job, and Toreno suggests you use Cesar as a partner.

the story

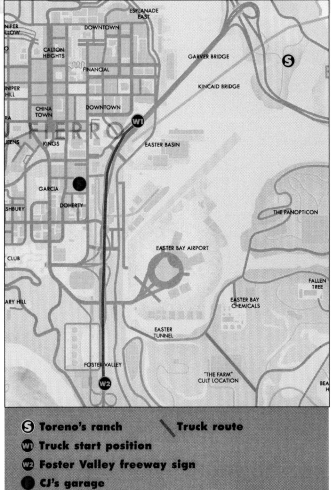

S Toreno's ranch
W1 Truck start position
W2 Foster Valley freeway sign
● CJ's garage
\ Truck route

Directions

Use Bike to Take Cesar to the Truck

Hop aboard the PCJ-600. Cesar climbs on back. The truck (marked by the red radar blip) is on the freeway in San Fierro just across the Garver Bridge, heading south to Foster Valley. Speed north from the ranch to the bridge and race across toward the awesome cityscape in the distance.

Pull Alongside Truck

When you reach the rig, pull up to the cab along its left hand side so Cesar can prepare to jump across onto the trailer. When you get close, hold the bike level and match the truck's speed. (Cesar will give you these directions, too!) As soon as Cesar crouches on the bike, ready to jump, nudge just a bit closer to the truck.

215

Make Jump Before Foster Valley!

If the "Foster Valley" freeway exit sign passes overhead before Cesar makes the jump across to the truck, you fail the mission. If Cesar gets across to the cab in time, he takes control and halts the truck. (Its overhead marker turns from red to blue.)

Drive Truck Back to CJ's Garage

Get into the truck and drive it to your garage in Doherty. When you arrive, save your game, grab a car, and head back to Toreno's ranch— the "**?**" has now changed to a "**T**" on your radar.

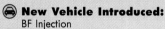

TORENO mission 3

Interdiction

🚗 **New Vehicle Introduced:**
BF Injection
💲 **Cash Gained:**
$1000

the story

CJ walks in on Toreno, who speaks via radio in some sort of bizarre (and amusing) code. Toreno wants a favor, and tells CJ the exact nature of Sweet's current incarceration—up state, D wing, Cell 13, with nasty neighbors on either side. CJ also learns that Tenpenny and Pulaski were responsible for the death of Officer Pendelbury, who was trying to expose their operation. No surprise there.

Toreno's favor requires CJ to take a dune buggy up onto a desert hilltop and set off a flare to guide in a helicopter. The chopper carries, as Toreno puts it, "some precious cargo that needs collecting."

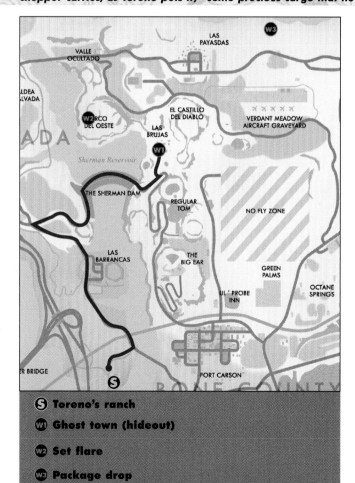

- 🅢 **Toreno's ranch**
- ⓦ¹ **Ghost town (hideout)**
- ⓦ² **Set flare**
- ⓦ³ **Package drop**

Directions

Go to El Castillo del Diablo (Desert)

Take your BF Injection dune buggy and follow the yellow radar blip north through Las Barrancas, clear up to El Quebrados, then east across the bridge. When you reach Valle Ocultado, take a right onto the paved road that veers south and curves around along the red cliffs of El Castillo del Diablo. Next, find the gap in the cliffs on the right hand side of the road where a narrow dirt road runs to the dusty ghost town of Las Brujas.

When you finally arrive, walk into the red marker to get an irritated radio message from Toreno via a transmitter near an old cabin. He tells you to choose a vehicle, grab the provided equipment, and get uphill to the drop zone to wait for the package delivery.

Get Rockets and a Vehicle

Pick up the spinning Rocket Launcher (green blip on your radar) near the front porch, then select the Bandito, the Sanchez, or the Quad. Drive west, following the road out

of town. Track the new yellow radar blip up to the red marker atop a rugged rock arch, the Arco del Oeste.

When you drive into the marker, CJ automatically sets the flare. As the contraband helicopter approaches, two spy agency copters suddenly appear to intercept. Toreno orders CJ to shoot them down and protect the cargo at all costs.

Protect Contraband Helicopter from Spooks

Face the attack copters and wield your Rocket Launcher. The health bar for your contact helicopter appears onscreen. Fire away at the red-marked

spy helicopters, which start to drop agency spooks to the ground! Don't shoot the choppers when they're above you; they'll crash on top of or next to you. Now you face attackers by air and on foot. Stay alert! Two more agency choppers soon join the fray.

Sling rockets to knock the 'copters out of the sky before they can destroy the contraband helicopter. If spooks drop safely, you can hustle to nab the AK-47 in one of the dilapidated shacks on the rounded plateau across the arch. Use it to decimate any enemy ground troops.

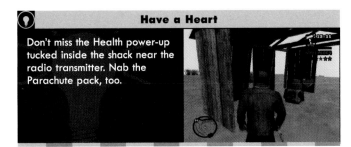
Track Down the Contraband

When the final agency chopper goes down, your contact helicopter swoops in and drops something via parachute. Hop onto your vehicle and follow the green radar blip to find the drop. (You can use the Seasparrow helicopter floating just offshore, too—if you know how to fly it, of course.) To the north of the pickup is a conveniently placed Seasparrow. The search leads you across the desert and through an eerie aircraft graveyard in Verdant Meadows. You find the package lying conveniently next to another radio transmitter in a rocky ravine just north of the graveyard.

Deliver Contraband to Hideout

Grab the package to trigger the last order from Toreno: Get the package back to Las Brujas. Get in your vehicle and follow the yellow blip on the map. This leads you back to Las

Brujas, where you picked your off-road vehicle. Ride into the red marker in the garage to complete the mission. The "T" icon reappears on the map. Follow that back to Toreno's ranch house.

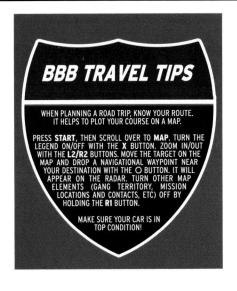

BBB TRAVEL TIPS

WHEN PLANNING A ROAD TRIP, KNOW YOUR ROUTE. IT HELPS TO PLOT YOUR COURSE ON A MAP.

PRESS **START**, THEN SCROLL OVER TO **MAP**. TURN THE LEGEND ON/OFF WITH THE **X** BUTTON. ZOOM IN/OUT WITH THE **L2/R2** BUTTONS. MOVE THE TARGET ON THE MAP AND DROP A NAVIGATIONAL WAYPOINT NEAR YOUR DESTINATION WITH THE **O** BUTTON. IT WILL APPEAR ON THE RADAR. TURN OTHER MAP ELEMENTS (GANG TERRITORY, MISSION LOCATIONS AND CONTACTS, ETC) OFF BY HOLDING THE **R1** BUTTON.

MAKE SURE YOUR CAR IS IN TOP CONDITION!

Verdant Meadows

⬤ **New Property Gained:**
Airstrip

the story

Toreno is impressed with CJ's work. He wants to assign some tougher missions, but CJ needs more flying experience. The government is selling some "property" (an abandoned airstrip) out in the desert; Toreno wants CJ to buy it and start pilot training.

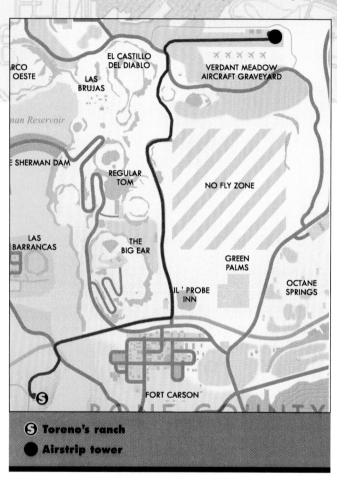

⒮ **Toreno's ranch**

⬤ **Airstrip tower**

Directions

Go to Abandoned Airstrip and Buy It

Drive your vehicle to the property icon (a green house) on the map. It's a long haul. Head east over the bridge and past Fort Carson on your right. Continue northeast through Octane Springs and then north through the open desert of Bone County. When you reach the airstrip, step into the spinning green house icon and purchase the property for $80,000. If you don't have the cash for this, you should try these minigames.

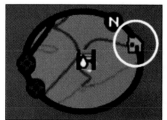

Now you can go through the front door (ground level) into the living quarters (called "Abandoned AC Tower"), where you can use the save game disk.

Walk around back and climb the stairs to the second floor office, where you find a red marker near a TV. Normally, this triggers the training missions of the Pilot School. But the first time you enter the marker, you get a cell phone call from Toreno. He explains that he's set out a series of flight tests that you can access via the TV in the office.

NEW MISSION STRAND OPEN!

Completing the Verdant Meadows mission opens up the Airstrip strand and its first mission, Learning to Fly.

THE AIRSTRIP STRAND

$ Cash Available in Strand:
$15,000

Now that you own an airstrip, you have a base of operations for pilot training. The first time you step into the red marker in the airstrip's upstairs office, CJ gets a cell phone call from Toreno. The boss insists that CJ learn how to fly, especially if he wants his brother free.

AIRSTRIP mission 1

Learning to Fly

New Gameplay Elements Introduced:
Flying planes and helicopters, using a parachute
New Vehicles Introduced:
Rustler, Hunter
 # Respect Gained:
5

PREREQUISITE NEEDED!

✓ This mission is available only after you complete the *Verdant Meadows* mission in which you purchase the airstrip.

After Toreno's first phone call, you can start the pilot training. To access the first flight test, just step into the red marker in front of the TV set. There you can view a demo of each test before you give it a go. Complete a total of 10 tests with Bronze Awards or better to pass the mission.

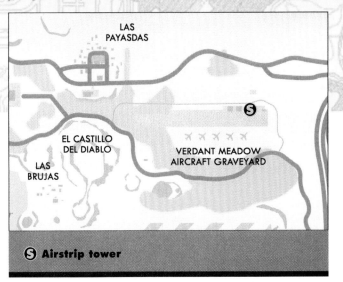

LAS PAYASDAS

EL CASTILLO DEL DIABLO

LAS BRUJAS

✕ ✕ ✕ ✕ ✕
VERDANT MEADOW AIRCRAFT GRAVEYARD

$ Airstrip tower

Use the Left Analog Stick and the Accelerator button to fly through a series of three red coronas (rings) lined up directly ahead of you. If you complete the short course successfully, you get a Certificate Award and gain access to the next training test, Land Plane.

Complete All Nine Remaining Flight Tests

Proceed through the series of tests, following the onscreen instructions as you learn how to land a plane, circle an airstrip, circle an airstrip *and* land, helicopter takeoff, land a

Directions

Complete "Takeoff" Flight Test

The first flight test in the training series is, naturally, learning how to take off. Simply follow the onscreen directions and accelerate down the runway. When the plane's tail rises, start to lift the plane's nose and take off. Don't forget to retract the landing gear.

helicopter, destroy targets with a helicopter, loop the loop with a biplane, barrel roll with a biplane, and finally, parachute onto a target. When you successfully earn certificates for all 10 tests, you pass the mission and become a licensed pilot with full access to all airports.

School in Session

For a review of basic flight controls and more tips on flying, see the **Flight School** section in our **Odd Jobs** chapter. Remember that you can return to the airstrip's Flight School anytime between missions and try for higher scores in any of the flight tests. Complete these tests and you earn enough Flying Skill to get a pilot's license with which you can access all airports.

New Contact Point

After you pass Pilot School, a new airplane icon appears on your radar. It leads you from the airstrip office and down the runway to a red marker in front of the nearest big hangar. That marker is now your contact point for the remaining missions in the Airstrip strand. Step into the red marker to trigger the next mission in the strand.

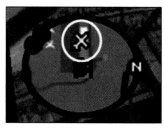

Juank Air

FLYING WITH THE PERSONAL TOUCH

Serving San Andreas and Beyond

FLIGHTS LEAVING HOURLY FROM ALL MAJOR AIRPORTS. REASONABLE PRICES AND PLENTY OF PARACHUTES

PURCHASE TICKETS OUTSIDE OF THE TERMINALS, AND ENJOY YOUR FLIGHT!

Cell Phone Call: Woozie

Soon after you pass all 10 flight tests, Woozie calls with a little business proposition. He invites CJ to come see the setup at the Four Dragons Casino in Las Venturas. When he hangs up, the yellow Four Dragons Casino icon appears on the radar. You are free to go there now if you want, but you still have plenty of desert-based flying fun ahead of you here at the airstrip.

 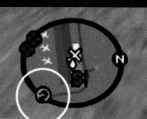

NEW MISSION STRAND OPEN!

*Completing the **Learning to Fly** mission and then receiving the cell phone call from Woozie opens up the Casino mission strand in Las Venturas (see Chapter 5: Las Venturas) and its first mission, **Fender Ketchup**.*

NEW ODD JOBS AVAILABLE!

*Completing **Learning to Fly** opens access to the Pilot School odd jobs. Come back between missions to the upstairs office at the Airstrip to retry the flight tests and improve your skills as a pilot and unlock some airplanes that will spawn in the hangars at the airstrip. For more on this, see the **Pilot School** section of our **Odd Jobs** chapter.*

AIRSTRIP mission 2

N.O.E.

$ Cash Gained:
$15,000

---

the story

After you pass all 10 flight tests in **Learning to Fly**, walk into the red marker in front of the hangar to trigger another surprise "greeting" from Toreno. (He seems to enjoy that, doesn't he?) He gives CJ a new mission. Some of his agency's field operatives are in trouble and need high-tech equipment delivered, pronto. Toreno warns CJ to keep his plane low, under the radar. Get too high and air defenses will respond.

Directions

Fly Low to Angel Pine

Get into the Rustler and take off. Your destination is in Angel Pine. The best way to do this mission is not to follow Toreno's advice. Instead, fly north to the ocean and stay low over the water until you reach Angel Pine (flying west, then south). Turn east to hit the drop-off point, then get back over the water and head north until you're near the airstrip. No obstacles, no muss, no fuss. You have 10 minutes to complete the mission; an onscreen timer starts counting down from 10:00 when you climb aboard. A Visibility indicator bar also appears onscreen. The longer you fly above the radar limit, the more your Visibility bar goes up. If the bar rises to full, enemy radar locks onto your position and triggers an air defense response.

To Drop-off
Back to Airstrip

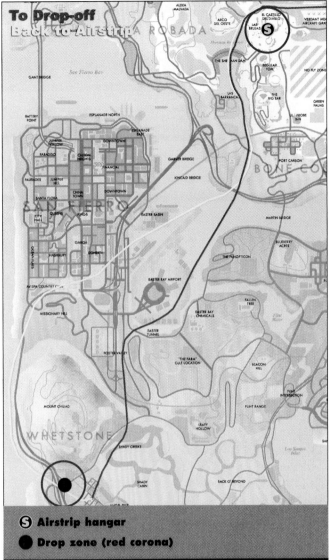

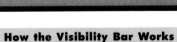

Ⓢ Airstrip hangar

● Drop zone (red corona)

Fly low to avoid radar detection and listen to Toreno's advice: Use the canyon for cover! Right after takeoff, bank slightly left and fly down the narrow canyon to block detection by the nearby radar site, then continue on south by southeast, skimming treetops and rooftops until you approach Angel Pine.

Fly Into Corona to Trigger Drop

Look for the big red ring in the sky above the tiny town and fly through it. This triggers the equipment drop.

Return to Airfield

Return to your airstrip, now marked by the yellow blip on the radar. Practice the same radar-evasion techniques—stay low, follow waterways and canyons, dive under bridge spans, avoid flying over hills and peaks.

Bring Plane to a Stop Anywhere on the Landing Strip

Remember your pilot training? Lower landing gear. Nose down gently onto the runway with the red marker and press Square to brake to a stop.

Stowaway

Weapon Obtained:
Remote Explosives

Cash Gained:
$20,000

the story

Walk into the red marker next to the hangar at the airstrip. CJ hears something approaching and hides as a huge cargo plane lands on the airstrip. Three government trucks drive up and start loading boxes into the plane's cargo hold. Armed guards oversee this work. CJ assumes that Toreno is up to no good, as usual.

But then Toreno himself creeps up to the hiding spot. He blames "traitors from another department" for stealing a consignment of land mines which they plan to offload in the Middle East. He says CJ has clearance from "the Big Guy" to eliminate these guys. Your job: Plant a bomb in the cargo plane.

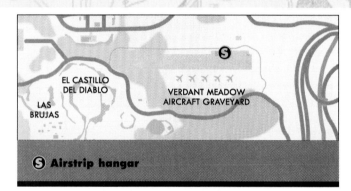

EL CASTILLO
DEL DIABLO

LAS
BRUJAS

VERDANT MEADOW
AIRCRAFT GRAVEYARD

Ⓢ **Airstrip hangar**

Directions

Drive Bike Up Plane's Ramp Before Take-off

Stealth is out of the question. So this situation calls for some creativity. Your directions are to ride the nearby motorbike up the plane's ramp, plant the bomb inside, and get off

the plane safely before it explodes. Sounds crazy, doesn't it? CJ automatically mounts the bike. Accelerate!

A Plane Approach

Stay wide right as you chase down the cargo plane to avoid the boxes tumbling out of its cargo hold. Wait to veer toward and up the hanging ramp until you're nearly even with it.

When the pilot detects your intrusion, he starts his take-off with the cargo ramp still hanging down from the rear of the fuselage. Chase full speed after the plane, dodging the three guards and the boxes that tumble out of the plane's cargo hold. When you catch up to the ramp, zoom straight into the plane.

Riding Technique

Lean slightly forward on the bike to get that extra bit of speed if you're having trouble catching the plane. Using weight-shifting to shift CJ's weight forward makes him more aerodynamic, achieving greater

Once CJ gets aboard, a rolling barrel knocks the motorbike out of the plane. Then a guard issues a challenge, and we see CJ armed with a Satchel Charge!

Kill Guard and Take His Parachute

Of course, you don't want to blow up the plane. You need the armed guard's parachute for escape. Reaching him is tricky, though. Barrels roll down the length of the fuselage

every few seconds. Time your run up the fuselage, ducking into side alcoves when barrels roll, and beating up the plane's crew along the way. When you finally reach the front of the plane, take out the last few crewmen and nab the parachute.

Use the Satchel Charge to Destroy the Plane

Arm yourself with the Satchel Charge and plant it anywhere on the plane. Walk to the very end of the ramp that hangs open at the back of the plane. With the parachute on, jump out of the plane and the satchel charge will automatically detonate. Enjoy the fall for a while as the plane crashes, then open your 'chute and drift down to earth. Head back to your airstrip.

Black Project

New Vehicle Introduced: "Jet Pack"

New Weapon Introduced: Thermal Goggles

Return to the red marker outside the airstrip hangar between 20:00 and 6:00 for this night mission. CJ finds The Truth meditating atop one of the junked aircraft. He upbraids CJ for doing Toreno's (and thus the government's) dirty work. Then The Truth refers to "a place not even on the map" and mentions a train transporting something from a nearby secret research lab. He drags CJ off in the Mothership to investigate.

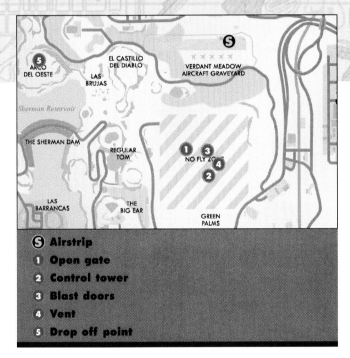

- Ⓢ **Airstrip**
- ❶ **Open gate**
- ❷ **Control tower**
- ❸ **Blast doors**
- ❹ **Vent**
- ❺ **Drop off point**

Body Armor

Look for free Body Armor hidden inside one of the junked fuselages at the aircraft graveyard. Body Armor is also available directly in front of the user after entering the Restricted Area compound.

Directions

Find a Way Into Underground Labs

The Truth gives CJ some Thermal Goggles and drops him off outside the main gate of Area 69, a top-secret military installation out in the desert.

Your ultimate goal is to snatch a "Black Project" item stored in an underground research lab. However, a massive blast door at the bottom of a sunken ramp blocks access to the lab. The blast door switch is in a nearby control tower.

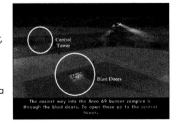

The area is heavily guarded, and multiple spotlights sweep the yard. If you linger in the light too long or shoot out more than two spotlights, you will be spotted. If this happens, the blast doors get locked down and you must find an alternate route into the lab—an air vent. As if all that wasn't enough, you have only until 5:30 to gain entry to the labs!

Radar Red

Use your radar to detect approaching guards—the red blips on the map.

Snipe From the Gate

The yellow radar blip marks the control tower's location on the map. Move toward the complex and stop a short distance from the front gate. Pick off as many guards as you can with your Sniper Rifle. Use your

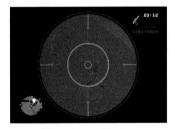

Thermal Goggles to spot hard to see targets. (They glow red in the goggles.) Shoot out the spotlight just above and to the right of the entry gate.

If Spotted...

If a spotlight catches you moving across the yard, the complex goes on "Condition Blue," a heightened state of alert, and the lights go on tracking mode. Duck into shadows for a while until the searchlights stand down from Condition Blue. If the spotlights find you again before the alert ends, the base goes Condition Red and a lockdown disables the control tower.

Snipe From the Guard Tower

Step inside the gate, and turn right. See the guard tower just ahead? Approach it and climb stealthily up the stairs. Knife or gun down the guard on the first landing, then continue up to the top. Whip out your Sniper Rifle and start picking off more patrolling guards. Again, switch to Thermal Goggles to target the bright red blips pacing the complex.

Descend the tower, then crouch and move along inside the perimeter fence to the southwest corner. Turn left and look down the next fence line; you're now facing east and can see the control tower. (This might be a good place to shoot out the light just above you in the southeast corner.) Slink toward the control tower and climb the stairs up into the control room. Don't let the lights catch you!

Get Through the Blast Door

Step into the red marker to see a cinematic of the blast door opening. The door stays open only a short time, so you must hustle to reach it. To do so, exit the control tower and sprint away from the fence around one of the long buildings just north of the tower. Creep into the center of the complex to the concrete area where a recessed ramp leads down into the ground. Hop down onto the ramp and hurry through the open blast door.

If Lockdown Occurs, Find the Vent

If you get spotted and trigger a Condition Red lockdown of the control tower, head toward the east side of the compound and hustle over to the southeast corner of the complex, following the yellow radar blip. Find the vent grate in a slightly raised rectangular box and shoot it open, then drop inside. Follow the vent passage to another grate (and a nice Health power-up). Shoot out the second grate, too, then proceed into the labs.

Find Research Labs

Both entry routes (blast doors or vent grate) lead into the same entry hall. This is the infamous Area 69, a military research facility. The item you seek sits in a lab at the rear of the installation. As you enter, the building goes on Defcon Red Alert, so patrol guards will be wary. The game recommends you use stealth to get past guards and hide in dark areas if spotted, but straightforward violence works, too. Use either approach, depending on your personal style.

Go through the yellow-trimmed door, then move down the corridor into a large room with cranes on ceiling tracks. Turn right and climb the stairs to a platform and nab the Body Armor. Use the platform to gun down the guards below.

Proceed through the exit door and enter the next room, which features red ducts running along the ceiling. Fight across to the opposite doorway, then continue through a side door into a corridor.

Disable SAM Site

Find the defense control room with a red marker in front of a big green radar scope. Wipe out the personnel and step into the marker to disable a Surface to Air Missile (SAM) site outside. (This helps later.) Backtrack to the room with the red ceiling ducts and head down the stairs from there.

Watch out for two guards pacing under a sign that reads **Research Section A**. Climb the stairs under the sign and go around the corner into the laboratory area with hallways lined with aqua floor lights.

Find Keycard

Keep moving and shooting down attackers until you work your way into the central lab. This is where the "Black Project" is being stored. The door to the launch bay won't open without a keycard. Fortunately, there's one nearby. Move through the passage on the left and find the scientist at work. When you approach, he offers you his keycard. Grab it!

Find the "Black Project"

Walk into the red marker that appears across the room to use the keycard in the security door. When you enter the corridor, you trigger a Code Red with all security personnel being called to the launch bay. Time to fight! Shoot your way past numerous guards as you move and roll down the stairs.

At the very bottom of the shaft, in the center of the bay, you see the Black Project—a gleaming jetpack. **Spooky!** Make it your own. CJ automatically straps it on, and guards start pouring into the lab. Fire up the jetpack and ascend vertically through the overhead blast doors.

Meet The Truth at Drop-off Point

Jetpack flying can be fun, but not when a SAM site is slamming rockets into you. (If you didn't disable the site inside the facility, you take some devastating hits before you get out of range.) Fly northwest, following the yellow blip toward the Arco del Oeste. Land in the red marker. The Truth congratulates you, takes the jetpack, and drives away in the Mothership, leaving you stranded in hell. Thanks, man.

Sanchez
There is a Sanchez nearby to help you trek back to the Airstrip.

Cell Phone Call: The Truth
Soon The Truth calls to offer you a date with destiny. He's back at the old airplane graveyard. When CJ hangs up, the airplane icon appears on the map indicating the red marker at the airstrip hangar.

AIRSTRIP mission 5

Green Goo

Cash Gained: $20,000

Step into the red marker by the hangar to see The Truth make an amusing entrance via jetpack. He then presents his plan: Land on the train, kill the guards, then get in and steal the stuff. "What stuff?" you ask. His answer is pure truth: "Steal whatever they least want us to get."

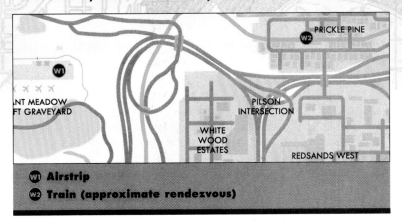

PRICKLE PINE — W2
ANT MEADOW FT GRAVEYARD — W1
PILSON INTERSECTION
WHITE WOOD ESTATES
REDSANDS WEST

W1 **Airstrip**
W2 **Train (approximate rendezvous)**

Take Artifact to The Truth
Time to head home! Fly back to the airstrip by following the yellow blip on the radar. When you arrive, land in the red marker on the runway. CJ presents the jar of green goo to The Truth.

Directions

Fly Jetpack to the Train
Fly east to chase the train, the green blip on your radar. Make haste and you should catch it somewhere around the Prickle Pine district of Las Venturas. Guards atop the train open fire. Hover into range and start gunning them down from above.

Shoot Crates to Find Secret Item
Three crates on the flatbed cars are marked by green overhead cones. As you skirmish with the pesky guards, start shooting at these crates. The first two shatter apart, revealing nothing. The third one contains an alien artifact. Land on the final crate to acquire the artifact.

Asset Acquired
The airstrip property now generates revenue up to a maximum of $10,000. Return regularly and walk through the "$" icon to collect your earnings. Note also that the Jetpack is now available for use near the airstrip control tower, and an enormous hangar is open across the airstrip for saving large aircraft.

MISSION PASS (1 OF 4)
Completing Green Goo gives you one of the four prerequisites needed to open the Saint Mark's Bistro mission later in the Las Venturas chapter.

chapter 5
Las Venturas

Welcome to Las Venturas, city of dreams. A few lucky souls leave town with enough winnings to start a new life. Most leave without their shirts, enriching the wise guys who run the casinos—and who never gamble.

RESTAURANTS

CLOTHING

POINTS OF INTEREST

Mafia interests have run this town for generations, but now Wu Zi Mu and his Triad gang want a piece of the business. The Four Dragons Casino poses a serious threat to the old "corporations" (read: mob families) of Las Venturas. And you can bet they won't take it lightly.

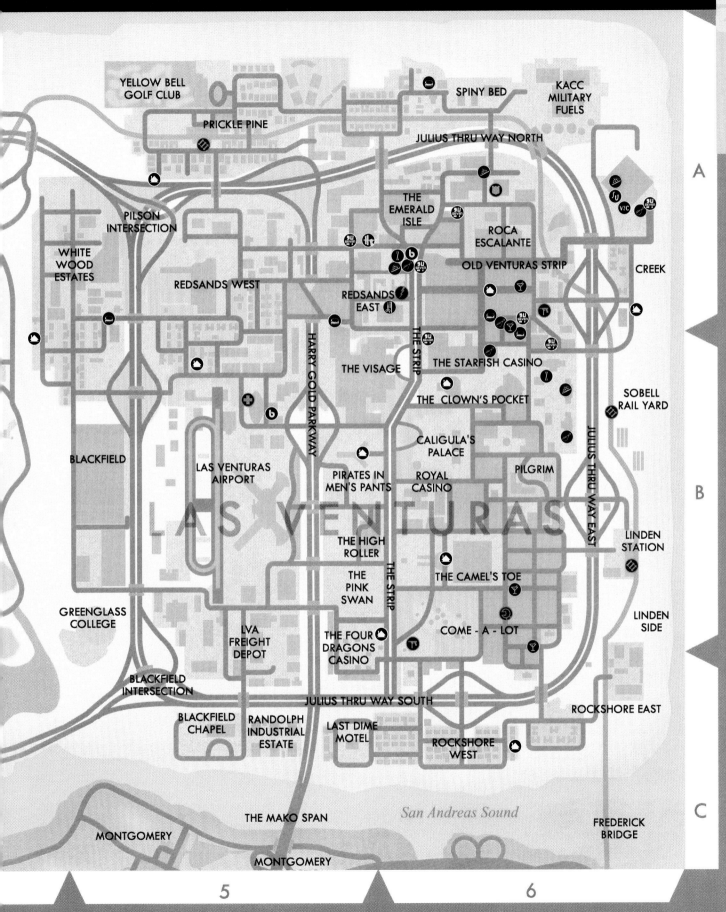

YELLOW BELL
GOLF CLUB

PRICKLE PINE

SPINY BED

KACC
MILITARY
FUELS

JULIUS THRU WAY NORTH

THE
EMERALD
ISLE

ROCA
ESCALANTE

PILSON
INTERSECTION

OLD VENTURAS STRIP

CREEK

WHITE
WOOD
ESTATES

REDSANDS WEST

REDSANDS
EAST

THE STRIP

THE VISAGE

THE STARFISH CASINO

SOBELL
RAIL YARD

THE CLOWN'S POCKET

BLACKFIELD

CALIGULA'S
PALACE

PILGRIM

JULIUS THRU WAY EAST

LAS VENTURAS
AIRPORT

PIRATES IN
MEN'S PANTS

ROYAL
CASINO

LINDEN
STATION

LAS VENTURAS

THE HIGH
ROLLER

THE CAMEL'S TOE

GREENGLASS
COLLEGE

THE
PINK
SWAN

THE STRIP

COME - A - LOT

LINDEN
SIDE

LVA
FREIGHT
DEPOT

THE FOUR
DRAGONS
CASINO

BLACKFIELD
INTERSECTION

JULIUS THRU WAY SOUTH

ROCKSHORE EAST

BLACKFIELD
CHAPEL

RANDOLPH
INDUSTRIAL
ESTATE

LAST DIME
MOTEL

ROCKSHORE
WEST

THE MAKO SPAN

San Andreas Sound

FREDERICK
BRIDGE

MONTGOMERY

MONTGOMERY

A

B

C

5

6

Security Services

WEAPONS

1. **Golf Club** • Yellow Bell Golf Course, on balcony overlooking golf course. • **A5**
2. **Shovel** • Las Venturas, on tennis court at back of apartment complex. • **A5**
3. **Fire Extinguisher** • Spinybed, in between back of Xoomer gas station and car wash. • **A6**
4. **Flame Thrower** • K.A.C.C. Military Fuel, in dark corner behind and underneath overhang of the main building. • **A6**
5. **Tear Gas** • K.A.C.C. Military Fuel, on the ground near the east fence. • **A?**
6. **Cane** • Prickle Pine, behind fence in Yellow Bell Station area. • **A5**
7. **Cane** • Julius Thru Way North, side of house on dead end street. • **A5**
8. **Sniper Rifle** • Julius Thru Way North, partially hidden from road on rooftop of chapel, behind steeple. Climb lower roof in back to reach • **A6**
9. **Heat Seeking RPG** • Pilson Intersection, northeast corner of the top level of car park. • **A5**
10. **Shotgun** • Pilson Intersection, underneath the overpass. • **A5**
11. **Rocket Launcher** • The Emerald Isle, on rooftop (need aircraft to access). • **A6**
12. **Parachute** • The Emerald Isle, on top of tallest skyscraper in Las Venturas; need aircraft to reach it. • **A6**
13. **Rocket Launcher** • The Emerald Isle, on top of Emerald Isle building above parking garage, near helipad. Drive to top of parking garage and take roof access stairs to reach it. • **A6**
14. **Cane** • The Emerald Isle, to the right of the entrance to the building. • **A6**
15. **Night Stick** • Roca Escalante, behind San Andreas Police Department sign on the corner. • **A6**
16. **Minigun** • Roca Escalante, on the bottom level of the parking garage near an elevator. • **A6**
17. **Molotov** • Creek, on rooftop of Cluckin' Bell in strip mall. Park a vehicle next to the building to access the roof. • **A6**
18. **Sawn Off Shotgun** • Whitewood Estates, around back of warehouse. • **A4**
19. **Chainsaw** • Whitewood Estates, on south side of warehouse. • **B5**
20. **Bat** • Redsands West, on baseball diamond. • **A5**
21. **Shovel** • Redsands West, in the dugout on the baseball field. • **A5**
22. **Sawn Off Shotgun** • Redsands West, beyond wooden fenced-in alleyway across from Xoomer gas station (behind dumpster). • **A5**
23. **Molotov** • Harry Gold Parkway, hidden in bushes next to police station, just behind small tree between rocks. • **A5**
24. **Knife** • Las Venturas, near desert area. • **B4**
25. **Micro-Uzi** • Redsands West, in between wall and dumpster underneath power lines. • **B5**
26. **AK-47** • Redsands West, hidden in the bushes on an island in the middle of apartment complex parking lot. • **B5**
27. **MP5** • Starfish Casino, in casino's car park. • **B6**
28. **Bat** • Blackfield, underneath overhang next to stadium. • **B5**
29. **Silenced 9mm** • Blackfield, in the flowerbed underneath the front entrance walkway to Las Venturas Stadium. • **B5**
30. **Tear Gas** • Las Venturas Airport, between control tower building and yellow and white striped ramps. • **B5**
31. **Shovel** • Pirates in Men's Pants, in the rocks and bushes underneath a skull carving. • **B6**
32. **Katana** • Pirates in Men's Pants, on first level deck of the ship near the back. • **B6**
33. **Sniper Rifle** • The Clown's Pocket, on corner of building's rooftop (need aircraft to reach it). • **B6**
34. **Cane** • Pilgrim, in fenced-in area next to sloped rooftop building. • **B6**
35. **M4** • Pilgrim, behind sloped roof on motel nearest the pool. • **B6**
36. **Katana** • Julius Thru Way East, near doors of building with two statues. • **B6**
37. **Spray Can** • Sobell Rail Yards, in between two of the train yard hangars. • **B6**
38. **Rocket Launcher** • Las Venturas Airport, behind southernmost terminal. • **B5**
39. **Sawn Off Shotgun** • Las Venturas Airport, on top of rooftop. • **B5**
40. **Combat Shotgun** • LVA Freight Depot, in the bushes in the flowerbed in the parking lot between Kakagawa and Sumo. • **C5**
41. **AK-47** • The Four Dragons Casino, near secluded north side of the casino's roof (need aircraft to access). • **C5**
42. **Katana** • The Four Dragons Casino, next to bushes and trees. • **C6**
43. **Sniper Rifle** • The Four Dragons Casino, on casino rooftop. • **C6**
44. **MP5** • Come-A-Lot, in little nook around the backside of hotel. • **B6**
45. **Molotov** • Come-A-Lot, on corner of building's rooftop (run and jump from top of doorway structure on adjacent building). • **B6**
46. **Minigun** • Rockshore East, on fifth level of scaffolding. • **C6**
47. **Grenade** • Rockshore East, on warehouse rooftop behind air duct. • **C6**
48. **Pool Cue** • Rockshore East, oehind building next to dumpster. • **C6**
49. **Tec-9** • Red County, underneath bridge leading into Las Venturas. • **C5**

POLICE BRIBES

- **Julius Thru Way East** • Underneath overpass. • **B6**
- **The Emerald Isle** • Between the trees. • **A6**
- **Royale Casino** • Near the powerlines. • **B6**
- **Julius Thru Way South** • Hanging in mid-air on center divider of highway. • **C6**
- **The Camel's Toe** • Underneath the big needle-shaped monument in front of hotel. • **??**
- **Pirates in Men's Pants** • Use a motorcyle to jump off pirate ship's ramp. • **B5**
- **The Four Dragons Casino** • In far corner between two buildings, just off the main road on a brick path. • **C5**
- **Julius Thruway East** • Behind building and next to railroad tracks. • **A6**
- **Redsands East** • In alleyway between two buildings • **A5**
- **Redsands West** • On paved walkway between two houses. • **B5**
- **Las Venturas Airport** • To the west of Harry Gold Parkway. • **B5**
- **LVA Freight Depot** • Just inside fenced-in area next to Waffle shop. • **B5**

BODY ARMOR

- **Redsands East** • In corner of balcony area; run around entire inner section of building). • **A6**
- **Caligula's Palace** • On top of oddly shaped building in middle of lot. • **B6**
- **Rockshore** • To the left of the main entrance to the church, in a corner. • **C6**
- **Come-A-Lot** • Underneath neon archway sign in front of casino. • **C6**
- **LVA Freight Depot** • In far corner next to wooden fence. • **C5**
- **Las Venturas** • In a corner, slightly hidden from the road. • **B5**
- **Greenglass College** • Behind two green dumpsters to the right of the building's main entrance. • **B5**
- **LVA** • In the corner of an airplane hangar (one used in Freefall mission). • **B5**
- **Red County** • At southernmost point of Rockshore West. • **C6**

PAY 'N' SPRAY

- **Redsands East** • **A5**

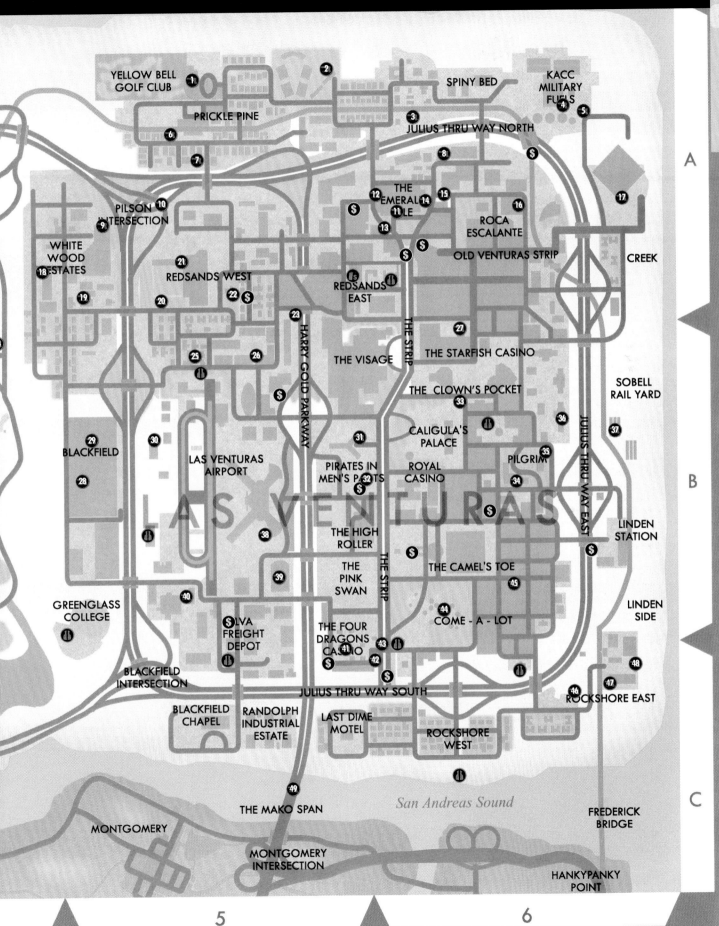

YELLOW BELL
GOLF CLUB 1

2

SPINY BED

KACC
MILITARY
FUELS
4
5

PRICKLE PINE

6

3
JULIUS THRU WAY NORTH

7

8

15

THE
EMERAL 11 LE 12 14

S

16

ROCA
ESCALANTE

PILSON 10
INTERSECTION

9

17

WHITE
WOOD 18
ESTATES

21

REDSANDS WEST

13

S

S

OLD VENTURAS STRIP

CREEK

19

20

22 S

REDSANDS
EAST

S

S

27

23

HARRY GOLD PARKWAY

THE STRIP

THE STARFISH CASINO

SOBELL
RAIL YARD

25

26

THE VISAGE

THE CLOWN'S POCKET

33

36

37

29

30

BLACKFIELD

LAS VENTURAS
AIRPORT

31

CALIGULA'S
PALACE

PILGRIM

35

JULIUS THRU WAY EAST

28

PIRATES IN
MEN'S PANTS 32

ROYAL
CASINO

34

S

LINDEN
STATION

LAS VENTURAS

38

THE HIGH
ROLLER

THE STRIP

THE CAMEL'S TOE

S

LINDEN
SIDE

39

THE
PINK
SWAN

45

40

COME - A - LOT

44

48

GREENGLASS
COLLEGE

SLVA
FREIGHT
DEPOT

THE FOUR
DRAGONS
CASINO 41

43

42

47

46 ROCKSHORE EAST

BLACKFIELD
INTERSECTION

S

S

JULIUS THRU WAY SOUTH

BLACKFIELD
CHAPEL

RANDOLPH
INDUSTRIAL
ESTATE

LAST DIME
MOTEL

ROCKSHORE
WEST

49

THE MAKO SPAN

San Andreas Sound

FREDERICK
BRIDGE

MONTGOMERY

MONTGOMERY
INTERSECTION

HANKYPANKY
POINT

A

B

C

5

6

Unique Attractions

HORSESHOES

1. **Prickle Pine** • In the porch of this house in Las Venturas suburbs. • **A5**
2. **Camel's Toe** • At the very top of the pyramid. • **B6**
3. **Emerald Isle** • On top of gift shop on corner. • **A5**
4. **Roca Escalante** • On top of the Erotic Wedding Chapel. • **A6**
5. **Yellow Bell Golf Course** • On the roof of the golf house in front of a rear window. • **A5**
6. **Rockshore West** • In one of the back yards. • **C5**
7. **The Clown's Pocket** • On top of The Clown's Pocket building. • **B6**
8. **Roca Escalante** • In the middle of the guitar-shaped swimming pool at the VRock Hotel. • **A6**
9. **Rockshore East** • Above a dumpster behind the warehouse. • **C6**
10. **Roca Escalante** • Old Venturas Railway Tunnel. • **A6**
11. **Royal Casino** • In the northwest corner of the parking garage on the third floor. • **B6**
12. **Julius Thruway North** • Hidden in this small garage enclosure. • **A6**
13. **Redsands East** • On top of the roof, across from the 24-Seven. • **A5**
14. **Emerald Isle** • At the very top of the Emerald Isle building. Use the Jetpack or parachute to reach it. • **A5**
15. **Las Venturas Airport** • Behind the main airport building. • **B5**
16. **Blackfield Intersection** • Hidden in a small gap between the warehouse and a wall. • **B5**
17. **Redsands East** • On the back of the Motel on the second floor. • **A5**
18. **The Pirates in Men's Pants** • Hidden in the bushes. • **B5**
19. **Come-A-Lot** • Atop one of the towers at Come-A-Lot. • **B6**
20. **The Four Dragons Casino** • On the roof of The Four Dragons Casino above the garage. • **B5**
21. **Prickle Pine** • In this shallow pool at an apartment complex. • **A5**
22. **Greenglass College** • In middle of the courtyard in front of the college. • **B5**
23. **Creek** • Hidden behind a strip mall on the outskirts of town. • **A6**
24. **Starfish Casino** • On top of the Venturas Steaks Drive-thru. • **A6**
25. **Las Venturas Airport** • Just to the east of the northern section of the runway. • **B5**
26. **The Camel's Toe** • On the east side of the Pyramid on a ledge. • **B6**
27. **Pilson Intersection** • Floating above this wall. • **A5**
28. **Las Venturas Airport** • Just west of the northern tip of the runway. • **B5**
29. **Las Venturas** • Under the "Welcome" sign. • **A4**
30. **Randolph Industrial Estate** • Hidden below a bridge on the way out of town. • **C5**
31. **Come-A-Lot** • At the top of the Come-A-Lot sign. Use the Jetpack to reach it. • **B6**
32. **Julius Thruway East** • On the east side of the Victim billboard. Use the Jetpack. • **B6**
33. **Las Venturas** • On the roof of a wedding chapel. • **C6**
34. **Prickle Pine** • Stashed behind the gate to one of the tennis courts. • **A5**
35. **Emerald Isle** • In a small enclosure near the Emerald Isle. • **A5**
36. **Redsands West** • On the overhang of a Casino next door to the Steakhouse Restaurant. • **A5**
37. **LVA Freight Depot** • At one of the truck docks. • **B5**
38. **Rockshore West** • In a back yard, next to this trash can. • **C6**
39. **Starfish Casino** • On a ledge above the Arts & Crafts shop. • **B6**
40. **Whitewood Estates** • Behind the warehouse. • **A4**
41. **Emerald Isle** • Between gas station and carwash. • **A6**
42. **Emerald Isle** • In the southwest corner outside of the parking garage. • **A5**
43. **Come-A-Lot** • In second story window of red apartment building. • **B6**
44. **Starfish Casino** • In the corner of a dark alleyway. • **B6**
45. **KACC Military Fuels** • In a small, secluded alleyway. • **A6**
46. **Old Venturas Strip** • Inside the S of CASINO. • **A6**
47. **Redsands West** • On top of some packing crates. Use a vehicle to jump on the fence and then up to the Horseshoe. • **A5**
48. **The Visage** • Underneath the waterfall. • **B5**
49. **Whitewood Estates** • In front of this building. • **B4**
50. **Blackfield Chapel** • On the roof of the Chapel. • **C5**

UNIQUE STUNT JUMPS

1. **The Emerald Isle** • Jump south out of the top level of the Emerald Isle multi-story garage and land on the roof of the Souvenir Shop. • **A6**
2. **The Emerald Isle** • Drive up the stairs to the rooftop of the multi-story garage and drive to the adjacent roof. Drop down to the south side of building, then jump the ramp to the east off the ledge. • **A6**
3. **The Camel's Toe** • Jump east from the northeast corner stairs of the Camel's Toe casino, across the street and parking lot, and land on the Pawn Shop rooftop beyond the parking lot. • **B6**
4. **The Camel's Toe** • Adjacent to the steps in the previous jump. Jump north from these steps and land on top of the building directly to the north. • **B6**
5. **Creek** • Jump to the west off this ramp and land on the northbound section of freeway. • **A6**
6. **Redsands West** • Jump north from this ramp and land on a ledge on the building to the north. • **B5**
7. **Julius Thru Way North** • Heading east, use this wooden ramp to make it over the freeway bridge (use one of the faster bikes). • **A6**
8. **Redsands West** • Use the wooden ramp between the storage containers to jump north onto the westbound section of freeway. • **A5**
9. **The Emerald Isle** • Use the ramp to jump east out of multi-story parking garage. • **A6**
10. **Randolph Industrial Estate** • Use rickety ramp to jump north out of the warehouse compound. • **C5**
11. **The Emerald Isle** • Speed west through the wooden poles and use the ramp (go through the Police Bribe) and jump over the street. • **A6**
12. **The Emerald Isle** • This jump is the same as jump #2, but this time jump off the ramp on the north side of the building (the lower ledge). • **A6**

OYSTERS

1. **Bone County** • Bone County beach, North West of Las Venturas. • **A4**
2. **Las Venturas** • The Northeast corner of the map. • **A6**
3. **Roca Escalante** • Under the diving board at the VRock pool. • **A6**
4. **The Strip** • Under a waterfall at The Visage Casino. • **B6**
5. **The Strip** • In front of skull, at the front of the Pirates in Men's Pants Casino. • **B5**
6. **Pilgrim** • In the pool in front of The Pilgrim Hotel. • **B6**
7. **The Strip** • In the Come A Lot Casino moat. • **B6**

FLOWERS

- **Julius Thru Way East** • Crash barrier. • **B6**
- **Las Venturas** • Next to Gas Station doors. • **A6**
- **Near Come-A-Lot** • Outside wedding chapel. • **C6**
- **Julius Thru Way East** • Wedding Tackle front door. • **B6**
- **The Emerald Isle** • In between petrol pumps at Xoomer. • **A6**
- **Royale Casino** • In flowerbed. • **B6**
- **Rockshore West** • In front garden. • **C6**
- **Prickle Pine** • Next to flowerbed. • **A5**
- **Yellow Bell Golf Course** • In front of main sign in flowerbed. • **A5**
- **Redsands West** • In front garden between trees and shrubs. • **B5**

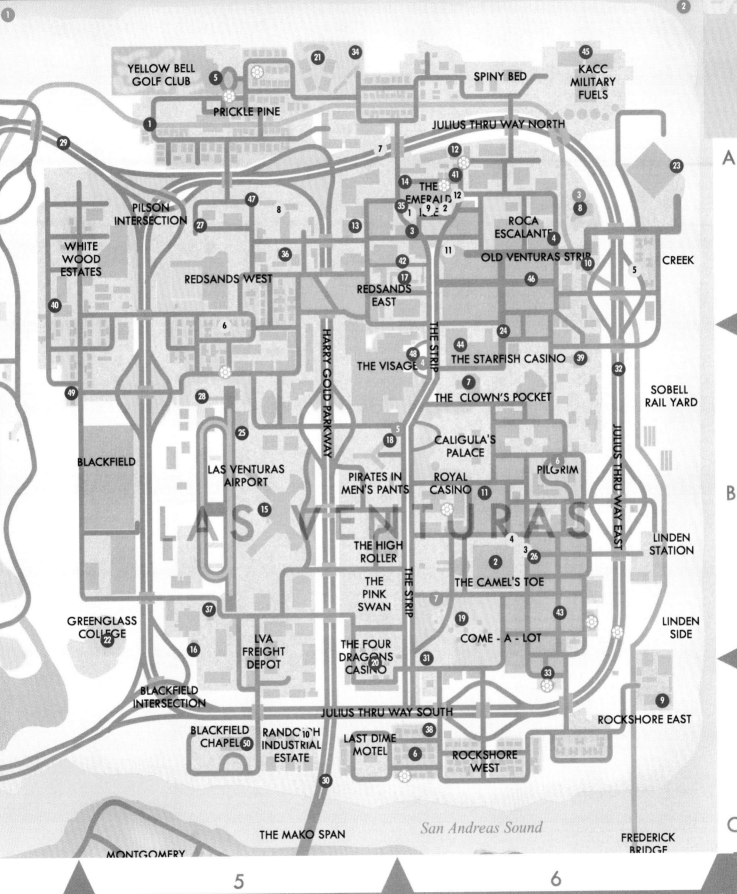

YELLOW BELL
GOLF CLUB

PRICKLE PINE

SPINY BED

KACC
MILITARY
FUELS

JULIUS THRU WAY NORTH

THE
EMERALD
ISLE

ROCA
ESCALANTE

OLD VENTURAS STRIP

CREEK

PILSON
INTERSECTION

WHITE
WOOD
ESTATES

REDSANDS WEST

REDSANDS
EAST

THE VISAGE

THE STARFISH CASINO

SOBELL
RAIL YARD

THE CLOWN'S POCKET

CALIGULA'S
PALACE

PILGRIM

BLACKFIELD

LAS VENTURAS
AIRPORT

PIRATES IN
MEN'S PANTS

ROYAL
CASINO

LINDEN
STATION

L A S   V E N T U R A S

HARRY GOLD PARKWAY

THE STRIP

THE HIGH
ROLLER

THE CAMEL'S TOE

GREENGLASS
COLLEGE

LVA
FREIGHT
DEPOT

THE
PINK
SWAN

THE STRIP

COME - A - LOT

LINDEN
SIDE

BLACKFIELD
INTERSECTION

BLACKFIELD
CHAPEL

RANDOLPH
INDUSTRIAL
ESTATE

THE FOUR
DRAGONS
CASINO

LAST DIME
MOTEL

ROCKSHORE
WEST

ROCKSHORE EAST

JULIUS THRU WAY SOUTH

JULIUS THRU WAY EAST

THE MAKO SPAN

San Andreas Sound

FREDERICK
BRIDGE

MONTGOMERY

A

B

C

1

2

5

6

THE CASINO STRAND

$ Cash Available in Strand: $70,000

 # Total Respect Available in Stra... 60

The Four Dragons Casino is gorgeous, but it's still a work in progress. Woozie's mob enemies are looking to sabotage his efforts. Most of this strand's missions involve your dealings with the rival casino owners.

CASINO mission 1

Fender Ketchup

 # Respect Gained: 10

$ Cash Gained: $5000

the story

When you first enter The Four Dragons Casino, veer left to find the red marker outside Woozie's office. Woozie is agitated. Technical glitches are driving him nuts as he preps for his casino's grand opening. He suspects the Mafia is putting the squeeze on him by planting thugs amongst the local workers. Three mob families, each with a stake in a rival casino called Caligula's Palace, dominate operations in Las Venturas with "some whacked-out lawyer" running the show.

Woozie doesn't know which family is behind his current worker troubles, and he refuses to pay tribute to the Mob in exchange for security. So he offers CJ a share in The Four Dragons in exchange for help in setting things up. Deal! Suddenly, Woozie gets word that his boys caught a thug in the act of smashing deliveries. The boss wants him killed, but CJ has a better idea...

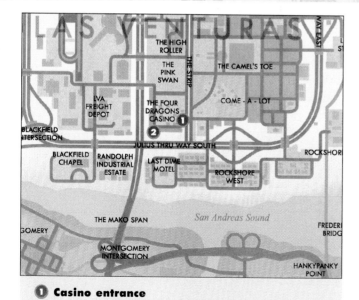

1 **Casino entrance**

2 **Casino garage**

Directions

Drive Fast!

Yes, CJ has the thug tied to the front of a car. The fellow isn't very respectful, given his predicament. CJ gets behind the wheel and a Scare-O-Meter indicator appears onscreen.

Your goal is frighten the guy into squealing about who sent him. As the game suggests, high speeds and screeching hand-brake turns are sure to scare him, as will driving on the wrong side of the road. It's also time for some insane stunts!

Don't take him out onto the Julius Thru Way, even though it's great for good long stretches of high-speed racing. As soon as you get on the freeway, you acquire a Wanted Level, and you don't need the cops involved in this one. Bad collisions can kill your passenger and collisions are guaranteed once the cops get involved.

Dead Men Don't Talk

Yes, insane driving is fun and effective, but don't get too crazy. Slamming headfirst into obstacles at high speed can turn your passenger into "fender ketchup"— and trigger mission failure!

Speed up and down The Strip right outside The Red Dragon in the wrong direction. Head down to the end and turn back on the wrong side. When the Scare-O-Meter finally tops out, the thug cracks and admits he's with the Sindacco Family. But your mission isn't over yet.

Take Thug Back to Casino

Now you must get the Sindacco soldier back to The Four Dragons Casino in one piece. This is easy going unless your insane driving triggered a Wanted Level and cops are swarming. Follow the yellow blip to deliver the car to the casino garage—the red marker around the left side of The Four Dragons complex—then go back inside the casino to Woozie's office.

NEW ODD JOBS AVAILABLE!

Opening the Casino mission strand also opens access to all six of the gambling odd jobs—Video Poker, Blackjack, Roulette, Slot Machines, and the Wheel of Fortune. For details on this, check out the Gambling section in our Odd Jobs chapter.

CASINO mission 2

Explosive Situation

🚗 **New Vehicle Introduced:** Dumper
\# **Respect Gained:** 15
$ **Cash Gained:** $7000

CJ wants to hit the Mafia casino in retaliation for the Sindacco Family's attempts to sabotage The Four Dragons. He's up for a heist, but he needs explosives. Woozie points out an open cast mine to the southwest of Las Venturas, an operation no doubt full of explosives. CJ decides to check it out.

Open for Gambling!

Note the red "$" icon when you enter The Four Dragons casino after Fender Ketchup. This is the casino gambling area, and it's now open for business.

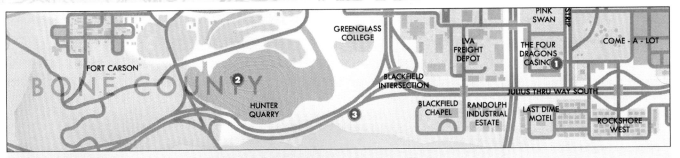

1 Casino office
2 Quarry with dynamite
3 Drop-off point

Go to the Quarry

Jack a car and follow the yellow blip across the map to Hunter Quarry out in Bone County, nearly due west of your starting point at The Four Dragons. When you arrive, drive into the red marker near the hut.

Get Dynamite Before it Detonates

You learn the dynamite is rigged to blow. A Detonation timer appears onscreen, counting down from 2:30. Hurry! Green blips mark the locations on the radar of four dynamite

Get it before the workers destroy it.

crates; each one has a green overhead cone, too. You could run down the quarry ramps to reach the crates, but why do that when you can just hop in your vehicle and make a couple of insane jumps?

 | **Car Hop**

To save time, drive your car over the quarry lip and execute insane jumps down the quarry levels to reach the floor.

Smash Dynamite Crates with Dump Truck

The game says you'll need something "heavy" to smash those crates, and your car won't cut it. Well, we have just the thing for you. Climb into the Dumper dump truck! Smash

through all four dynamite crates (marked by green overhead markers) including the crate carried by the forklift.

Pick Up the Dynamite!

After you smash each crate, the dynamite inside is available for the taking and appears on radar as a red blip. Hop out of the truck and grab the dynamite stick—CJ automatically defuses the detonator—then hop back in and continue to the next crate. Be sure to get all four sticks. Don't miss the one on the moving forklift truck. When you nab the last stick, the timer disappears. Note that the quarry members will put up a fight when you exit the Dumper. Simply ignore them, get back into the vehicle, and move on to the next task.

Get Back Home with the Dynamite

This is easier said than done. Now security teams block the exit at the top of the rock ramp. You'll have to find a different way out. The game gives you a glimpse of a huge conveyor belt that carries rock out of the quarry pit. Say, that might be one way…

Use Dirt Bike and Find Another Way Out

Find the Sanchez dirt bike; to track it down, just follow the blue radar blip. Hop on and speed up the hill right in front of you. Get as close to the quarry wall as possible, then

turn around and gun it toward the red checkpoint column! Hit the checkpoint at full throttle and make the leap across onto the conveyor belt. Brake when you land to avoid overshooting the next checkpoint!

Drop onto the next conveyor belt and turn right. Speed up that one and leap from the end of the belt onto the rock ramp. Watch out! A security guard is posted on the stairs of the next conveyor, and he opens fire the moment you land. Gun him down, then ride up the stairs that lead to the last conveyor.

Take a leisurely ride along the narrow belt, steering carefully so you don't fall. At the next checkpoint, veer right, landing on a rock plateau. Spot the next checkpoint near a chute, then ride along the precarious ledge to reach it. Another security guard waits here to be gunned down.

Charge full throttle up the long chute because you must leap across a hidden gap in your path. After landing, find the next checkpoint. It leads up another chute with an even bigger gap to jump at its end, so take a long approach and hit the chute fast.

You should see a Danger sign on the plateau at the far end of the jump. Speed up the final ramp past the security guards and their armored car, then proceed up the trench through the final checkpoint.

Deliver Dynamite to Drop Point

Follow the yellow blip across the map to the drop point, where one of Woozie's boys waits with a car. Drive into the red marker to complete the mission.

The Four Dragons icon now reappears on your radar, along with a new green "**$**" icon. It's hard to see because the location is actually inside The Four Dragons, so the yellow icon obscures it until you get inside the casino.

Return to The Four Dragons. Inside, follow the yellow Four Dragons icon to Woozie's office to continue the Casino mission strand, or follow the green "**$**" icon to a backroom location within the casino to begin planning for the Caligula's Palace heist. (Remember, the red "**$**" is the gambling area icon.)

NEW MISSION STRAND OPEN!

Completing **Explosive Situation** opens up **The Heist** strand and its first mission, **Architectural Espionage**. This adds a new contact point to your radar map, a green "**$**" icon located inside **The Four Dragons** casino.

NEW ODD JOBS AVAILABLE!

Completing the **Explosive Situation** mission opens access to the **Quarry** odd jobs. For details on this, refer to the **Quarry** section of our **Odd Jobs** chapter.

CASINO mission 3

You've Had Your Chips

Respect Gained:
20
$ Cash Gained:
$10,000

Woozie discovers that someone's been playing counterfeit chips in the casino. The Sindacco Family owns a chip-making plastics factory across town, the obvious source of these forgeries. Woozie wants to destroy it, and CJ offers to do the deed.

Directions

Drive to Factory on Outskirts of Town

Follow the yellow blip northwest to the plastics factory in the Whitewood Estates district. Upon arrival, you learn the mobsters have guards at the main goods entrance.

Try to Enter Factory Unnoticed

Find the main goods entrance, an open garage door near the crane and container stacks. Keep your distance! Two goons sit in a car guarding the entrance.

Drive around to the parking garage on the north side of the factory.

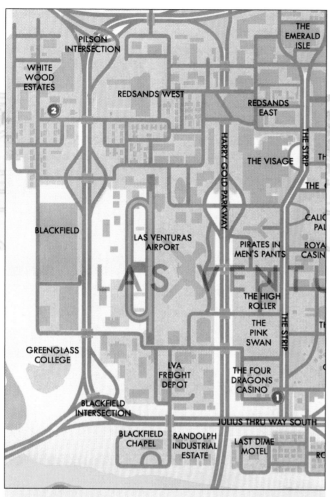

1 **Casino office**
2 **Plastics factory**

Enter the garage and drive up the ramps to the top parking level, then cross to the southwestern edge of the lot overlooking the factory yard.

Get out and drop down into the yard, then circle the factory to the left. Sneak past the crane (nabbing the chainsaw on the way!) and around the corner to the open factory door. Now you can enter, and the unavoidable firefight begins.

Or Just Fight Your Way Inside!

If you attack a guard or get discovered at any point, the factory is alerted and you must get inside quickly. Speed your vehicle right into the open garage door near the crane. Now you must engage in a brutal battle with no fewer than 12 armed crewmen. Plenty of boxes are stacked about the factory floor; use them for cover! Make sure the coast is clear before you destroy the molding machines.

Destroy Injection Molding Machines

Once you clear out the area, turn your attention to the machines. Shoot all 10 of the injection molding machines (marked by green overhead cones) to complete the job. Once you reach the casino complex, drive into the red marker by the garage to complete the mission. A new red marker appears just outside the front doors to The Four Dragons casino.

Strand Choice

Here again, you can choose between mission strands. Inside The Four Dragons, veer left and step into the red marker outside Woozie's office to continue the Casino mission strand. Or veer right following the green "$" icon to the red marker outside the backroom to proceed with the Heist mission strand.

Don Peyote

 # Respect Gained:
5

When you step into the red marker outside the front doors to The Four Dragons, CJ gets a phone call from The Truth, who wants to (as he puts it) "cash in some karma chips." The Truth took a UK band (guess who!) and their manager on a "peyote safari" into the desert a few nights ago, but he got separated from the group and ended up in Los Santos. Now he has no idea where the others are. He tells CJ he took them up Arco del Oeste, a good place to start the search.

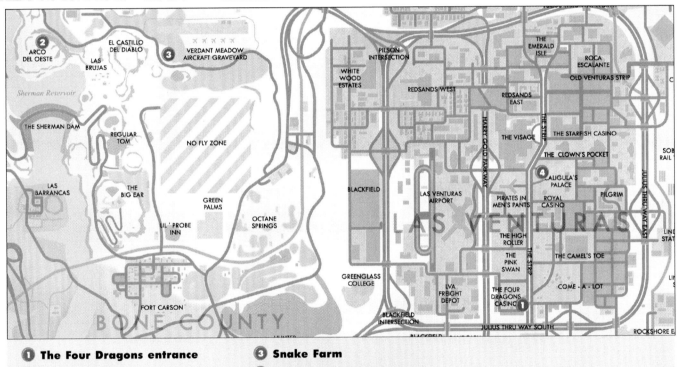

① The Four Dragons entrance
② Paul and Maccer
③ Snake Farm
④ Caligula's Palace entrance

Directions

Find Paul and Maccer

The manager's name is Kent Paul, and the band's lead vocalist is a goofball named Maccer. Vice City players will remember these names well. Grab a four-door car and drive west into the desert, following the blue blip on the map. If you fail to bring a 4-door vehicle, you won't be able to take the guys. This isn't a problem, though. Simply drive to the nearest road and jack one; the guys will wait for you to return. When you finally get up the dirt road leading to the Arco del Oeste, drive into the red marker.

CJ finds Paul and Maccer lying in the dirt, just regaining consciousness. The two are in truly pathetic shape. CJ offers them a ride; Paul knows a guy named Rosie who runs a casino in Las Venturas, and asks to go there.

After the scintillating conversation, get in the car. Paul and Maccer automatically follow. They don't know where the rest of the band is, but Maccer remembers snakes, lots of snakes. CJ knows of a nearby snake farm.

Take Paul and Maccer to Snake Farm

Follow the yellow blip east to the snake farm near El Castillo del Diablo. Along the way, make a quick stop for Paul, who has something he wants to toss. When you arrive, some local rednecks start raising hell with your boys, opening fire. Gun them down!

Kill the Hicks

If you don't kill the hicks right away, they chase you back to the hotel. Once you arrive there, you must fight them on the steps.

Get Back to Rosie's Casino in Las Venturas

Hop back into the car, waiting for both Paul and Maccer to join you, then make your escape, speeding east toward Las Venturas. Paul says Rosie's place is called Caligula's Palace and it's somewhere on the strip. Follow the yellow blip on the map all the way to Caligula's Palace and drive into the red marker.

Meet Rosie and Call Woozie

Paul takes CJ to meet Ken Rosenberg (another familiar name from Vice City), known as Rosie, who seems overjoyed to see them: "My despair is complete." Rosie seems afflicted by his position as a mob lawyer, bemoaning the fact that "every Mafia gorilla from Liberty City to Los Santos" is hassling him. CJ exits and calls Woozie, saying he's figured out a discreet way to scope Caligula's Palace Casino.

Cell Phone Call: Paul

Shortly after you leave Caligula's Palace, Paul calls to ask CJ for some help, saying Rosie's "in a tangle." CJ agrees to stop by the office. A white icon appears on the radar map to mark the location of Ken Rosenberg's office in Caligula's Palace.

CASINO mission 5

Intensive Care

 # Respect Gained:
5
$ Cash Gained:
$5000

the story

Proceed to your new contact point at Caligula's Palace. Enter the casino, cross the lobby, and veer left just before you reach the gaming tables. Step into the red marker by the door to the Managerial Suites to enter the office of Ken Rosenberg, known as Rosie to friends like Kent Paul.

Rosie explains his predicament. He started representing the Liberty City crime families and ended up overseeing their combined operations at Caligula's Palace. But none of the families trust each other to run the casino, so Rosie has been forced into the role of "neutral party"—a nice euphemism for "caught in the crossfire."

Now the Sindacco Family is on the warpath because Johnny Sindacco—the very same guy CJ tied to a car and scared back in the Fender Ketchup mission—is now in a shock-induced coma at the hospital. Rosie believes the Forelli Family will take this opportunity to whack Johnny. If any such hit succeeds, Rosie is a dead man. So CJ offers to help by moving Johnny from the hospital.

Directions

Go to the Hospital

Grab a car and follow the yellow blip east to the Las Venturas Hospital in the airport district. When you arrive and pull into the red marker, CJ tries to pick up Mr. Sindacco. But he learns an ambulance just carted him off! Not good news. Must have been a Mafia pickup.

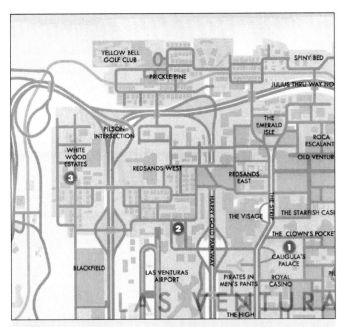

1. **Rosie's office**
2. **Hospital**
3. **Meat factory**

Find Ambulance With Johnny Inside

Three red blips appear inside on your map, indicating ambulances on the streets of Las Venturas. One of them carries Johnny Sindacco and, no doubt, has a mob driver—his reaction will give him away if you ram his vehicle. Ram each ambulance. Unfortunately, if the first one you hit is a real ambulance team, an alert goes out and the Mafia knows you're on the prowl.

Smash Mafia Ambulance Before They Escape!

Speed after the next ambulance. If it's the one hauling Johnny, you get a message saying so. Pursue it! Keep ramming and shooting at the Mafia-driven ambulance to show them you mean business.

Get in Ambulance Before Mafia Backup Arrives

When you finally chase the Mafia driver and his accomplice out of the ambulance, fight them quickly or just hop into their emergency vehicle and drive away.

Drive Johnny to the Meat Factory

Drive the ambulance to the meat factory in Whitewood Estates on the west side of town. Mob backup arrives soon and thug-filled cars hound you en route. Try hard to avoid collisions that allow them to catch you! When you finally arrive at the meat factory, drive into the red marker to complete the mission.

NEW CONTACT POINT OPEN!

Completing the Intensive Care mission opens up the next mission in the Casino strand, The Meat Business. But it also opens a separate, standalone mission called Misappropriation with a new contact point marked by a "C" icon (stands for C.R.A.S.H.) on your map.

Misappropriation

Follow the "C" icon to a house up north in the Prickle Pine suburb. Pull into the red marker in the driveway to find Tenpenny and Pulaski cooking up some barbecue in the back yard. Their little side business is in big trouble, so they're laying low here.

Tenpenny wants CJ to assassinate an agent who has a dossier of incriminating evidence that he plans to pass along to the feds. The handover is taking place in a ghost town called Aldea Malvada, far out in the desert to the west, in Tierra Robada.

239

1 Tenpenny's safe house **2** Meeting location **3** Emerald Isle helipad

Directions

Kill Target and Grab Evidence Dossier

Acquire a vehicle and make the long trek west to Aldea Malvada. We recommend something with good off-road capabilities—an SUV or a motorbike—so you can travel cross-country through the desert. When you arrive, the ghost town is swarming with feds! The inevitable exchange of gunfire tips off the target, who makes a run for it in a waiting helicopter.

Discretion: The Better Part

You are seriously outgunned in Aldea Malvada. We recommend a careful, stealthy approach to the ghost town to get as close to the second helicopter (the one you must take) as possible before opening fire on the federal agents. This way, you can board and escape without engaging in a full-fledged gun battle. Waste enough M4-toting gunmen to avoid being knocked out of the sky as you try to takeoff. Let them gather below CJ at the bottom of the hill and toss some Grenades (or Molotovs) to thin them out.

 Short Cut

It's possible to pick off your target (red marker overhead) in Aldea Malvada with your Sniper Rifle before he even reaches his helicopter for escape! His guards will try to pick up the evidence dossier before you reach it, though, so hurry! If a guard nabs the dossier, a red marker appears over his head.

Don't Let Your Target Get Away!

Fortunately, there's another helicopter nearby (blue marker overhead). Hop aboard this chopper and chase the target's helicopter, which is marked with a red overhead cone.

You can't shoot him down; if you knock your target from the sky, you destroy the evidence dossier, which triggers mission failure. (Tenpenny wants that dossier!) So just stay on his tail as his bird flies southeast over the Sherman Reservoir and Dam, then due east across Bone County to Las Venturas. The target's helicopter eventually lands on a helipad atop The Emerald Isle hotel and casino.

Follow the Target's Lead

You can land on the same helipad, where the target has now abandoned his helicopter. Give chase with guns blazing and try to nail the target on the helipad. If you don't get him right away, however, the target runs downstairs into the multi-leveled parking garage below the helipad. Follow him!

The target may leap from the hotel rooftop and parachute down to the street. Follow suit with your own 'chute and use it to stay on his tail. When you finally get within range, blast the target and quickly nab the evidence dossier (marked by a green overhead cone) he leaves behind.

 **Tenpenny's Call**

If you've already completed the **Freefall** mission, you get a phone call from Tenpenny right after you pass **Misappropriation** to set up a meeting place to hand over the dossier. If not, the call comes after you pass **Freefall** later, as in this walkthrough.

MISSION PASS (1 OF 2)

Completing **Misappropriation** gives you one of the two prerequisites needed to open the **High Noon** mission later.

The Meat Business

Respect Gained:
25
Cash Gained:
$8000

Return to Caligula's Palace and go back to Ken Rosenberg's office. Rosie's happy with CJ's success, but he's not quite out of the woods yet. CJ convinces him to re-assert his managerial control and calm down the Mafia families. They head to the base of the Sindacco Family's smuggling operation, the meat factory in Whitewood Estates.

Unfortunately, Johnny Sindacco has emerged from his coma and is representing his family again. One look at CJ revives his terrors, and he collapses to the floor. His goons waste no time in launching an all-out attack on CJ and Rosie.

① Rosie's office
② Meat factory
③ Woozie's office

Directions

Protect Rosenberg and Kill All Witnesses

Someone throws a firebomb that blocks the meat factory door with flames. Then goons with guns and chainsaws spill out of the factory looking to slaughter both Rosenberg and you. Rosie's no help with the fighting; all he can do at first is cower. A "Rosenberg" health bar appears onscreen, and your job is to keep him alive long enough to escape. You must also eliminate every goon in the factory. No witnesses can survive.

Gun down the first wave of four Mafia goons in the entry hall. As you move toward the flaming doorway, Rosie ducks into another room to find a fire extinguisher. He tells you to take out the goons while he puts out the flames; he also starts up

the meat conveyor, so carcasses on hooks start moving along ceiling tracks in the next room, adding another tactical challenge to the gunfight. Use the metal containers as cover from their gunfire and remember to crouch to make CJ a smaller target.

Don't Get Trapped in the Freezer!

The next room is crawling with armed goons. As the flames die, strafe across the doorway, nailing Mafia gunmen. Then roll into the room, ducking and weaving and

picking off more goons. After you clear the immediate area, Rosie decides to hide in the freezer, the blue-tinted room to the right, just beyond the open metal door. Don't follow him! If you join Rosie in the freezer, a Mafioso type runs up to the door control panel and locks you inside—mission failed!

Body Armor

You can find Body Armor at the far end of the freezer room in the meat factory. However, if you pick it up before all Mafia goons have been eliminated, you could get locked inside the freezer. So if you want it, sprint hard to the Armor and run back out of the freezer or return for it later once the area has been cleared.

Eliminate Goons, Room by Room

Cross the first room, using the moving carcasses for cover as you engage another squad of goons in a small connecting room at the opposite end. Beyond that is another big meat-processing room, crawling with mobsters. Pop up from a window position and pick them off, ducking for cover whenever necessary.

Each time you clean out a room, CJ calls out, "It's clear!" and Rosenberg follows into that room. A storage room full of boxes is off to the right of the meat-processing room. Clear out every last thug! Move along the stacks, watching for gunmen who hide around corners or hide in alcoves formed by boxes above. These guys are sometimes partially hidden from view. You get a message that all witnesses have been eliminated when all of the meat factory rooms are goon-free.

Exit and Drive Rosenberg Back to the Casino

Follow the yellow blip through the stock-house to the exit. Leave the building and hop in a car. Wait for Rosie to join you, and then drive back to Caligula's Palace. On the way, Rosie is sure he's good as dead, but CJ promises to find a way to make the mob merely think Rosie's dead.

Cell Phone Call: Catalina
You receive a phone call from Catalina offering her usual pleasantries. Yeesh!

NEW CONTACT POINT OPEN!

Completing *The Meat Business* mission keeps the Casino strand going, but it also opens up a separate, standalone mission called *Madd Dogg* with a new contact point marked by the "D" icon on the map.

CASINO titled scene

Fish in a Barrel

This isn't an actual "mission," per se, but it is a titled scene. Return to The Four Dragons Casino and go to the red marker outside of Woozie's office. Woozie greets CJ and Ran Fa Li, the Tong representative. He then raises a toast to their new partnership in the casino.

Cell Phone Call: Ken Rosenberg
Rosie is frantic. The Leone Family has made their move. In fact, the head of the family, Salvatore Leone, is at Caligula's Palace right now, taking over the casino. Rosie predicts "war for Venturas. War, war!"

242

Madd Dogg

 # Respect Gained:
10

✓ PREREQUISITES NEEDED!

This mission is available only after you complete The Meat Business.

There's a new "D" icon on your map, so let's go check it out. Follow it to the Royale Casino just south of Caligula's Palace on The Strip. Enter the red marker at the casino door to find some morbid spectators urging someone to jump from a high ledge. CJ finds out the jumper is Madd Dogg, the rapper whose rhyme book you pilfered back in Los Santos! Dogg is despondent about many things (all CJ's fault, by the way), including the success of OG Loc. CJ decides to step in and save the poor fool.

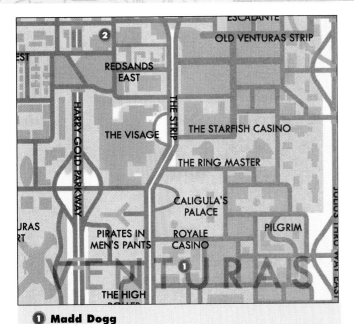

① Madd Dogg
② Mental clinic

Catch Madd Dogg When He Jumps

Now the camera shifts to an overhead view. You can only move your truck side to side under the ledge. Madd Dogg paces back and forth, getting ready to leap. Keep the bed of boxes aligned directly beneath him until he jumps. Keep the vehicle aligned with the arrows on the pavement and do not move closer to the building.

Drive Madd Dogg *Carefully* to the Hospital

If you lined up right, CJ saves the Dogg. Now you must drive Dogg north to the Ivory Towers Drive-thru Mental Clinic up in Redsands East, marked by the yellow blip on the map. A "Madd Dogg" health bar appears onscreen, already depleted by the fall. Drive slowly and carefully. Every bump or collision will drop the rapper's health a bit more.

When you finally arrive, drive into the red marker outside the clinic to complete the mission. Madd Dogg plans to look up CJ when he gets out of rehab. He needs a new manager, since his old manager took an unfortunate drive off the Santa Maria Beach pier.

MISSION PASS (1 OF 4)

Completing Madd Dogg gives you one of the four prerequisites needed to open the Saint Mark's Bistro mission later.

Directions

Use Pickup Truck to Rescue Madd Dogg

Turn around and sprint toward the pickup truck (marked by a blue overhead cone) in the parking lot. The driver stands next to it and will try to get his truck back, so pull away quickly. Drive the short distance to the red marker in the parking lot under Madd Dogg. The truck bed holds a load of soft boxes that would make a nice landing pad for the despondent rapper.

Freefall

 # Respect Gained:
30

$ Cash Gained:
$15,000

the story

Go to the red marker just outside Rosie's office in Caligula's Palace. Ken Rosenberg has a visitor—Salvatore Leone, head of the Leone Family based in Liberty City. Leone is taking control of the casino, and the other families don't like it. In fact, the Forelli mob is sending in a team of assassins to whack Salvatore, flying in this very afternoon disguised as a string quartet. CJ once did business with Leone's son, Joey, so Salvatore gives him the job of hitting the hit men.

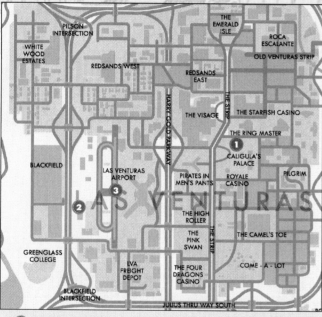

① **Rosie's office**
② **Hangar (steal plane)**
③ **Jet landing**

Hangar Body Armor

Don't miss the Body Armor in the corner of the hangar where you steal the plane.

Intercept Plane Before it Reaches the Airport

Taxi out onto the runway and take off. Use the map and fly due north toward the yellow blip, which is the incoming flight with the Forelli assassins. If the triangle blip is pointing upward, you're too low; if it's pointing downward, lower your altitude until you spot the plane. Once you reach the plane, bank around behind and follow it. Fly into the red corona just above it. When you hit the corona, a cutscene shows CJ bail out of his airplane and freefall. Amazingly, he lands atop the hitmen's private jet!

Directions

Go to the Airport

The Forelli hit men are flying in, so the obvious place to meet them is the airport. Follow the yellow map blip to the airport gate.

Steal Plane in the Hangar

Now follow the blue blip across the tarmac to find the airplane stowed in the hangar. Board it to get the message that the hitmen's flight is scheduled to land soon.

Gun Down the Assassins

Now you switch to first-person shooter perspective. Use the R2 and L2 buttons to duck side to side for cover. When you pop back to the middle of the doorway, be prepared to aim and shoot, then duck sideways again.

Once you nail the fourth hitman, the pilot sneaks up behind you and opens fire. Kill him, and CJ automatically takes control of the jet.

Fly Jet Back to Airport

Follow the yellow blip over the water and across the coastline until you reach the Las Venturas Airport. Land anywhere on the runway to complete the mission.

📞 Cell Phone Call: Tenpenny

Officer Tenpenny checks on the status of that evidence dossier you gathered for him back in the **Misappropriation** mission. (If you haven't yet completed **Misappropriation**, you won't get this phone call yet, obviously.) He wants to meet someplace quiet and "take care of things." He suggests another ghost town, Las Brujas, near "the devil's castle"—El Castilla del Diablo. Sounds like a fun plan.

Completing *Freefall* gives you one of the two prerequisites needed to open the *High Noon* mission later. It also gives you one of the four prerequisites needed to open the *Saint Mark's Bistro* mission later.

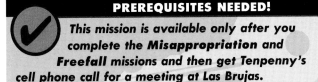

CASINO mission 10

High Noon

🔘 **Respect Gained:**
10

✓ PREREQUISITES NEEDED!

This mission is available only after you complete the *Misappropriation* and *Freefall* missions and then get Tenpenny's cell phone call for a meeting at Las Brujas.

the story

Ready for some face to face with the C.R.A.S.H. boys? It's a long haul to your next contact point, so if you've got an air-craft, use it! (You may have access to a helicopter after *Misappropriation* or a private jet after *Freefall*.) Follow the "C" icon across the map to Bone County and the tiny ghost town of Las Brujas. Walk into the red marker, and a police cruiser pulls up carrying officers Tenpenny, Pulaski, and Hernandez. CJ turns the dossier over to Pulaski.

Suddenly, Tenpenny slams a shovel into Hernandez's head and calls him a snitch. Then Tenpenny gives CJ the shovel and tells him to dig. Looks like CJ's usefulness to the corrupt C.R.A.S.H. crew is finally expended.

Officer Pulaski keeps watch as CJ digs his own grave. But Hernandez isn't dead yet, and manages one last lunge at his patrol partner. Pulaski finishes Hernandez, but the cop's dying fall puts a weapon in CJ's hands. Pulaski, a coward to the end, runs for his car.

🔘 Meet with C.R.A.S.H.

Directions

Kill Pulaski!

You can't gun down Pulaski before he reaches his car, but you can shoot out his tires. When Pulaski gets to his car alive, hop in the nearby Bandito dune buggy and give chase.

Pulaski's car is the red blip on the radar map, and it's marked by a red overhead cone. When you catch up, ram him repeatedly to slow him down, then pull alongside and open up with your MP5. Disable Pulaski's vehicle, then gun him down when he hops out to rush you.

MISSION PASS (1 OF 4)

Completing *High Noon* gives you one of the four prerequisites needed to open the *Saint Mark's Bistro* mission later.

CASINO mission 11

Saint Mark's Bistro

\# **Respect Gained:**
30
$ **Cash Gained:**
$20,000

the story

Head for Caligula's Palace and walk into the red marker outside Rosenberg's office. Salvatore is pleased with CJ's work and wants him to hit the Saint Mark's Bistro in Liberty City next. You ask for backup, so Leone lets you take Paul, Maccer, and Rosie, a motley crew if ever there was one. Outside the casino, CJ sends his "backup" fleeing from Las Venturas to safety.

✓ **PREREQUISITES NEEDED**

This mission is available only after you complete **Green Goo, Madd Dogg, Freefall,** and **High Noon.**

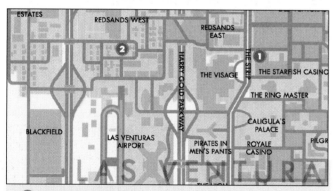

ESTATES
REDSANDS WEST
REDSANDS EAST
THE VISAGE
THE STRIP
THE STARFISH CASINO
THE RING MASTER
HARRY GOLD PARKWAY
CALIGULA'S PALACE
BLACKFIELD
LAS VENTURAS AIRPORT
PIRATES IN MEN'S PANTS
ROYALE CASINO
PILGR
LAS VENTURA

1️⃣ **Rosie's office**
2️⃣ **Jet to Liberty City**

Directions

Get to the Airport

That's right, folks! You're heading to the world of Grand Theft Auto 3. Liberty City or bust! Grab a vehicle and head to the Las Venturas Airport, following the yellow blip to the gates. When you arrive, drive through the gates and follow the blue radar blip to the jet marked by the blue overhead cone at the end of the runway. Board the jet to take its controls.

Fly to Liberty City

Take off and follow the yellow blip east. Once you finally reach it, the scene shifts to Saint Mark's Bistro in Liberty City (a place you never had an opportunity to enter in GTA3! Ahhh… memories). A guard tells CJ

it's a private function, invitation only. CJ explains that Mr. Leone begs to differ, and he bats his way inside.

Kill Forelli and His Bodyguards

Using the planter wall as cover, crouch down and pick off the guards one by one, then move over to the railing and nail any guards you can see downstairs. Watch out for attackers moving up the stairs to your left! Then proceed to the stairs. Having Grenades or Molotov Cocktails for this situation would be great—simply throw them over the balcony to clear the room below.

Careful! More Forelli goons wait for you downstairs at the bar, and we're sorry to say they don't want to buy you a drink. Pause at the top of the stairs and face the room, then inch forward to the railing and pick off the two goons behind the bar. Descend warily. Another goon is posted just around the corner at the bottom of the stairs, tucked into an alcove on the right side of the bar.

Fly Back to LVA

Follow the yellow radar blip back to the Las Venturas Airport and land anywhere on the runway to complete the mission.

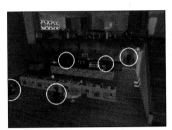

The alcove leads to more stairs, leading down to a kitchen with a black and white tiled floor, then out a back doorway to a courtyard where guards wait by a parked car. When the last Forelli falls, CJ automatically exits Saint Mark's Bistro and ends up back in the jet.

Cell Phone Call: Salvatore Leone

Soon you get one of two possible phone calls from Salvatore Leone:

- If you haven't yet completed The Heist strand and robbed Caligula's Palace (and you haven't if you're following this walkthrough), Mr. Leone calls to congratulate CJ on his stellar performance in Liberty City. CJ protects his friends (Paul, Maccer, and Rosie) by concocting a tale of their deaths. A pleased Leone tells CJ to keep a low profile. From here, you should head to the contact point in The Four Dragons Casino and finish up The Heist strand.

- If you've already finished The Heist strand, Leone has a significantly less friendly message for CJ. Enjoy CJ's taunting reply. It's then time to follow the yellow map blip back to a new contact point at The Four Dragons Casino and wrap up some unfinished business.

MISSION PASS (1 OF 2) AND NEW CHAPTER OPEN!

Completing Saint Mark's Bistro gives you one of the two prerequisites needed to open the Breaking the Bank at Caligula's mission at the end of The Heist strand. It also opens up the final chapter of the game, Return to Los Santos, and its first mission, A Home in the Hills.

THE HEIST STRAND

(S) Cash Available in Strand:
$100,000

(#) Total Respect Available in Strand:
175

After CJ steals the dynamite from Hunter Quarry, he's ready to start planning a big job. CJ and Woozie want to whack the Mafia's bottom line. The plan is to rob the mob casino, Caligula's Palace, and launder the money through The Four Dragons. But it takes a lot of preparation to pull off such a dangerous heist.

HEIST mission 1

Architectural Espionage

(#) Respect Gained:
10

PREREQUISITE NEEDED!

This mission is available only after you complete Explosive Situation, the second mission in the Casino strand.

Enter The Four Dragons and follow the "$" icon on the radar to the Maintenance room where Woozie waits. CJ's excited about having a secret place like this to plan a heist. Woozie suggests CJ get a layout of Caligula's Palace casino, and that's that. Meeting adjourned.

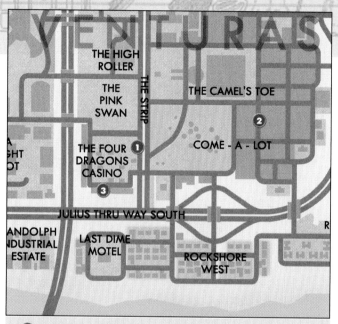

① **Casino maintenance room**

② **City Planning Department**

③ **Casino garage**

Directions

Grab a Tourist's Camera, If Necessary

You need a camera to photograph the casino blueprints. If you don't have one, drive north up the Strip toward the red blip on the map. Several tourists carry cameras near the Pirates in Mens' Pants casino complex on the west side of the Strip. Whack one and grab the camera he drops. You can also check our Las Venturas **Security Services** map for another hidden cameras in the area.

Head to the City Planning Department

Drive to the location marked as a yellow blip on the map. The game warns you that security is strict in the City Planning Department, so don't start any trouble. Okay, whatever. When you arrive, make sure your weapons are holstered before you go inside the marked door, so the security guard leaves you alone.

Approach the front desk. When the girl asks, "Can I help you, sir?" answer positively. CJ asks to look at plans for Caligula's Palace casino. She says okay, but asks if you're aware that reproduction of official blueprints is prohibited. Answer negatively; CJ didn't know that, and asks why. The girl doesn't want to be party to a daring raid. Then respond positively with a load of hooey that mollifies the woman, and she buzzes open the stairwell door to the second floor.

Be Nice to Planners!
Bad behavior is not tolerated at the Planning Department. Don't shoot or hit anyone. If you do, you immediately fail the mission.

Climb Stairwell to Reach the Blueprints

Turn around and go through the door next to the sign on the wall that reads "Plan Library" with an arrow pointing up. A message tells you the blueprints you need to photograph are in the far room on the top floor. Climb the stairs until they stop at the top floor.

ⓞ **Twin Hearts**
If you climb the stairs to the first floor of the Planning Department, you can find some goodies. Enter from the stairs and turn left down the main hallway. The first door on the left holds two spinning Health power-ups.

Create a Diversion in Document Depository

When you reach the top floor, a message warns you that you must divert the guard's attention before you can snap photos of the casino blueprints. Go back down one flight of stairs to the first open doorway, turn right, and walk straight through the doorway ahead labeled "Document Depository."

Find the decrepit old air conditioning units (under green overhead markers) across the room and whack them with a baseball bat or shoot them with any gun. When they explode, a fire alarm goes off. The alarm triggers an evacuation of the building.

The cops can't shut the bottom doors to lock you in because of the fire. Run back down the stairs; armed guards wait on nearly every landing to stop you, with a couple more in the lobby. Use the lobby door as cover and don't forget about the cop behind the front desk. Fight furiously and hurry out the front door.

Photograph Blueprints Pinned to the Wall

Hustle back upstairs and run into the office at the far end of the hall to photograph the blueprint on the wall. When you've snapped a shot of Caligula's blueprint, you get a

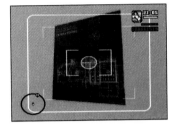

success message and a warning to get out of the building before you're caught. Do it!

Take Camera Film Back to Four Dragons Casino

Hop in your car and rush to your destination, marked by the yellow blip on the map. Your Wanted Level is probably very high now, so drive aggressively. Don't let the cops box

you in! When you reach the casino, drive around the left side to the red marker by the garage area, then pull into the marker to complete the mission.

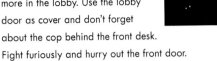

Key to Her Heart

Respect Gained:
15

PREREQUISITES NEEDED!

✓ *This mission is available only after you complete the Misappropriations and Freefall missions and then get Tenpenny's cell phone call for a meeting at Las Brujas.*

Enter The Four Dragons Casino and follow the "$" icon to the red marker. Using maps made from the casino blueprints, CJ lays out the plan for the Caligula's Palace heist. The cash room is on the bottom level of the casino. Naturally, security is tight, including a keycode and several swipe-card access doors. Zero has supplied a security card reader, but you need a card to read first. So one more item is necessary—a contact on the inside.

Directions

Get to Caligula's Palace Casino

CJ has a target in mind. Grab a car and drive north up the Strip to Caligula's. Pull into the circular drive and move into the red marker. A croupier has a keycard and knows the code. She exits the casino and drives away.

Follow the Croupier

Her car is marked by a red overhead cone, and a red blip indicates its location on the map. Follow her, but keep your distance. A Spook-O-Meter appears onscreen. If you get too close, the meter bar rises; drop

back a little to ease her mind. She stops for red lights, so be patient. Eventually she pulls into a strip mall and stops at the XXX Sex Shop.

the story

249

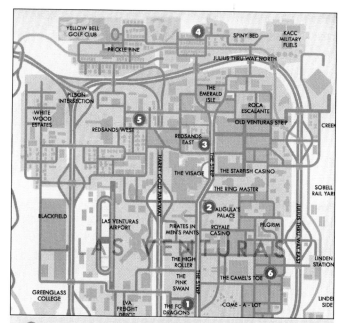

1. Casino maintenance room
2. Caligula's Palace (croupier)
3. Sex Shop
4. Croupier's house
5. Steakhouse
6. Dance club

Follow Croupier into Sex Shop

Park, get out of the car, and hurry into the red marker just outside the Sex Shop. Inside, walk to the back of the store, around the corner and into the red marker. (Hurry! If you don't find her quickly, you'll lose her and fail the mission.) This triggers a scene with the croupier, who tries on an outfit and takes a cell phone call from someone named Benny. She calls Benny "Master" and says she'll meet him at her house.

Get a Gimp Suit and Follow the Croupier Home

Enter the back right dressing room to don a gimp suit, then hurry out of the shop and hop in your vehicle to follow the croupier's car again. Tear out of the parking lot quickly, but keep your distance and keep her Spook-O-Meter low. She gets ahead when she leaves the shop, but then makes some pretty erratic stops and turns. Be both quick and patient.

Park Outside Croupier's House, Intercept Gimp

When the croupier finally arrives at her home, park in the red marker near the house. Now get out of the car, stand in front of the croupier's house, and wait for her gimp to arrive. The shirtless fellow comes slouching down the street soon enough. If he makes it to her house, the mission fails. Gun him down, nab the purple item he drops, and go to the red marker at the croupier's front door. She calls you inside, Master.

Court Millie

After a private interlude, you emerge from the croupier's house (her name is Millie) with a new girlfriend. However, you'll have to wine and dine her a bit before she'll hand over the keycard. Start dating Millie by following the new Girlfriend icon (the red heart) to her house, then show her a good time so you can "make progress." Your goal: Get your "Progress with Millie" bar above 33 percent. A graphic bar appears after every date with Millie, allowing you to estimate your progress. You can check the exact percentage by selecting "Achievements" from the Stats page, then scrolling to the "Progress with Millie" number.

Don't Be a Stalker

If Millie's not home, don't waste time just lurking and waiting until she gets off work at 2:00AM. She likes to dance, so hit the Las Venturas clubs to build up your Dancing skill. Go eat, beef up your stats, do some odd jobs, work out, or try other mission contact points in the Casino or Heist strands if you haven't completed them yet, then visit Millie's house again. For a sure-thing date with Millie, show up wearing the Gimp suit.

If Millie's home, there's a red marker in front of her house. Remember, she works in a casino, so she doesn't get home until about 2:00AM. Step into the marker to trigger her appearance and listen to her needs, then hop in your vehicle and she automatically follows. If Millie's hungry, take her to one of the restaurants, marked on the map by the fork/knife icon. (She's not too fond of burger or pizza places.) We recommend the excellent steakhouse, World of Coq, down in Redsands West. Millie thinks it's fabulous.

the story

Brutal Efficiency

If the dating scene is not your thing, gun down Millie when you meet her for the first date. Wait a while, and then enter her house to find the keycard.

If Millie's tired, take her home. Kill time productively by dancing or finding some flowers, then come back to Millie's after 2:00AM for another date. Give her flowers. If she wants to go dancing, take her to the club at The Camel's Toe casino complex down in southeast Las Venturas. Walk into the red marker on the dance floor to trigger the dancing interface, where you hit each designated controller button as it hits the circle.

Flowers Say It All

Give Millie flowers to pick up some relationship points.

Cell Phone Call: Millie

When your "Progress with Millie" bar (which appears after every date) finally exceeds 33 percent full, CJ gets a cell phone call from Millie. You find out she's not home. After you hang up, go to Millie's house, step into the red marker to enter, and then nab her security keycard.

That's just one more piece of the Heist puzzle. Head back to the maintenance room at The Four Dragons for the next planning step.

HEIST mission 3

Dam and Blast

⊕ Respect Gained:
5

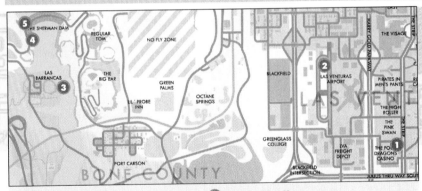

1. **Casino maintenance room**
2. **Airplane**
3. **Jump point**
4. **Quay landing spot**
5. **Generator room entrance**

CJ tries to conduct a briefing for the heist, but the crowd of "insiders" keeps expanding (nice Love Fist poster, CJ!). After a few interruptions, CJ gives up and heads off to the city's power source. His goal is to plant charges on the Sherman Dam hydroelectric generators that can be detonated during the heist, knocking out power to Caligula's Palace Casino.

the story

Directions

Go to the Airport

For this caper, you need an airplane and a parachute so you can drop onto the dam quay. Get a car and drive north up the Strip, then west to Las Venturas Airport. Follow the yellow radar blip to get through the gate.

Need A Parachute?

If you don't have a parachute prior to the start of the mission, don't worry. You automatically get a parachute when you enter the plane.

Get in Plane at the End of the Runway

Drive due west, following the blue radar blip to an airplane at the end of the runway, then board the plane.

Fly Aircraft to Jump Point Over the Dam

Take off and climb to the plane's maximum altitude, heading west toward the Sherman Dam area. The jump point is south of the dam and just east of Las Barrancas, marked by yellow blip on the map. Determine whether the yellow blip is pointing up or down to decide if you need to climb or descend. When you get close, you can see a red corona in the sky. Fly into the corona and jump from the plane.

Land On or Near the Dam Quay

Freefall for a while, guiding yourself toward the landing point on the quay that extends from the dam and is marked by the yellow radar blip. Open your 'chute with plenty of time to spare and continue to guide yourself toward the red marker on the quay. Land in or near the marker.

In the Event of a Water Landing...

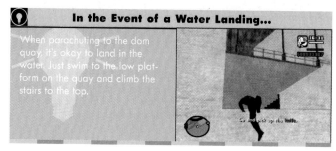

When parachuting to the dam quay, it's okay to land in the water. Just swim to the low platform on the quay and climb the stairs to the top.

Sneak to End of the Quay to Find the Knife

After you land, crouch and sneak down the quay without letting any guards spot you. Follow the green blip to find the knife stashed in front of the red crate, then hop up on the railing and check the moving red blips on your radar. Try to maneuver past them on the ledge or get behind them for stealth kills.

Get Past Guards and Find Entrance to the Generator Room

Follow the yellow blip to the door at the far end of the quay, then step into the red marker. This is the entrance to the generator room.

Guards abound in here; you want to remain silent and practice evasion to avoid setting off a general alarm. A cutscene reveals that security has locked the quay entrance and cops are on the way.

Place a Satchel Charge on Each Generator

Five generators must be rigged with explosives. Each one has a red glowing tip and appears as a yellow blip on your radar. Crouch and move forward, using the shadows in

and around the generators to stay concealed until you can sneak behind patrolling guards for stealth kills. Watch the red blips on the radar, which indicate the guards' positions. When they start to move away from CJ, head for the safety of the generators. Climb the stairs to reach the generator platforms.

When you reach each generator, face it and press the Triangle button to place a charge. When a generator is rigged, its yellow blip disappears from your radar. Once all five generators are rigged with charges, head for the red marker at the far end of the generator room.

Step into the red marker to trigger a cinematic of CJ's wild escape from the Sherman Dam. After the swan dive, swim to the Reefer and pilot the craft to shore, then jack yourself a vehicle and head back to The Four Dragons.

Cop Wheels

🖐 **Accomplice:**
Truck driver
⊞ **Respect Gained:**
20

Enter The Four Dragons and go to the maintenance (heist-planning) room on the right side of the casino. CJ lays out the plan, saying he'll draw the heat while the others grab the green. The mob moves its money out of Caligula's Palace in an armored car escorted by police "outrider" motorbikes. You need both elements to pull off the heist. First up: Gather some "cop wheels."

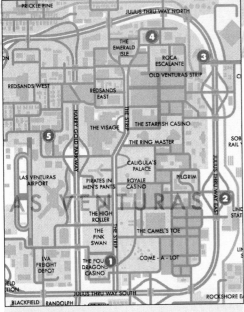

① **Casino maintenance room**

②③④⑤ **Police bikes (start locations)**

Directions

Steal Cop Bikes, Store Them in Packer Truck

A timer appears onscreen, counting down from 12:00. You have exactly 12 minutes to steal four San Andreas Police motorbikes to create the fake cop escort for your heist. Green blips mark the locations of the four targets around town. After you steal each bike, you must ride it to the Packer truck that circles the outskirts of town and drive up the Packer's back ramp. Jack a fast car and hustle to the first motorbike location. You can find one bike apiece at Linden Station, Julius Thruway East, Las Venturas Airport, and Roca Escalante. (Nabbing bikes in this order worked best for us, but you can steal them in any order.) When you get to the first bike, toss the cop off, hop aboard, and hurry away. If a cop is already perched on a bike, ram him with a vehicle to avoid a time-consuming chase.

Ride Bike Onto the Packer Truck

Speed to the Packer! The blue blip on the map marks the truck's location. When you reach it, get behind it and drive right up one of the rear ramps at a steady speed. When the bike attaches, you receive a message to get another police bike for the job.

Repeat Process with the Other Police Bikes

Dismount the bike, hop off the truck, jack the first car behind you on the Thruway, and then hustle toward the next green blip on the map. If the Las Venturas motorcycle takes off, you must chase him and gun him down, drive-by style. This mission gets tougher as you go, because your Wanted Level naturally rises as you steal more police vehicles.

🛑 Star Busters

Check the map for conveniently-placed Police Bribes to lower your Wanted Level.

When you finally get all four bikes onto the Packer within the allotted 10 minutes, CJ sends the truck back to the casino without him. Now you can jack another car at your leisure and head for your next contact point.

Up, Up and Away!

🚗 **New Vehicle Introduced:**
Sky Crane Helicopter
#️⃣ **Respect Gained:**
25

This is a night job, so enter The Four Dragons and go to the heist-planning room on the right side of the casino between 22:00 at night and 6:00 in the morning. CJ's team has the bikes they need, and Woozie's getting the police and security uniforms necessary. But you need still an armored van. Zero suggests using a sky crane helicopter to literally lift a truck. Stealing such an aircraft requires entrance to a local military fuel dump, however.

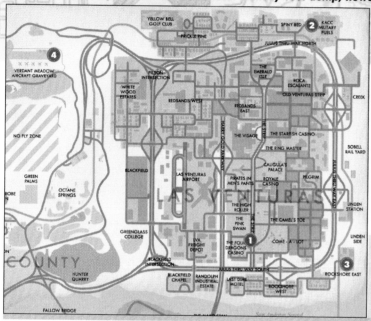

loc∞wn

From the "Pen" to the streets...
get the respect....wear the respect.

Gangsta since 2002

1. **Casino maintenance room**
2. **Military fuels depot**
3. **Van pickup**
4. **Van dropoff**

Directions

Sneak Into Base

Get a car and follow the yellow radar blip due north up the Strip, then work your way northeast to the K.A.C.C. Military Fuels depot. Approach the main gate. You cannot get inside the depot with a civilian vehicle, so wait until the next military vehicle leaves the base. Sneak into the base while the gate opens for the exiting Patriot.

Get Into the Depot

The military guys are well armored so you'd better be packing an AK-47 or an M4. Gun down only the guards around the gate and dash into the open warehouse to the left of the entrance gate. If you were to climb over the fence you would

become a sitting duck; the nearby guards will shoot before you hit the ground on the other side.

High Sentry

If you moved deep into the K.A.C.C. parking lot, watch out for the shooter up on the helipad!

Fight Through the Warehouse

Moving through the loading area lined with crates. Proceed under the big crane and turn right into the warehouse. Carefully fight your way through the stacks of boxes, where at least eight guards are posted in

various positions, both on the ground and on high catwalks.

Get Up to the Roof

Be wary as you exit the warehouse via the far door (opposite side from where you entered); alert guards await your arrival. There's Body Armor to your left, behind some crates as you walk into the open area of the warehouse. Nab it when

the area is cleared. Work your way to the right and find the stairway leading up. Fight your way up two sets of stairs to the building's rooftop.

Man the Gun Emplacement and Fight Two Gunships

Clear the guards from the helipad and run to the far end of the roof and step into the red marker to man the gun emplacement. The perspective switches to first-person, and two gunships attack. Knock them both out of the sky! When the second gunship goes down in flames, you automatically regain control of CJ's movement.

Get to the Chopper and Get Out of Here!

Climb the last set of stairs up to the helipad and board the Sky Crane helicopter. Before you take off, note the onscreen controls for the copter's winch mechanism.

Pick up Bank Van with Winch

Now the armored van location appears as a blue blip on your radar map. Follow it due south to the depot in Rockshore East, down in the far southeast corner of Las Venturas. When you arrive, hover over the van (marked by the blue overhead cone) and lower the magnet to pick it up.

Take Bank Van to Your Airstrip in the Desert

A Van Health meter appears onscreen, so don't slam the van around as you lift it and leave. Avoid slamming the van into buildings as you fly straight toward the yellow radar blip until you reach the airplane graveyard near your airstrip. Take your time! There's no time limit involved. Lower the armored van carefully into the red marker inside the fenced enclosure and release it. Now land the Leviathan in the nearby spot indicated by the red marker. The Leviathan will continuously spawn at the airstrip near the Pilot School building for your flying and lifting pleasure.

Cell Phone Call: Woozie

Woozie calls CJ here, but what he says depends on what else you've accomplished:

- If you haven't wooed the keycard out of Millie (the Caligula's Palace croupier) yet, you need to go back to the Millie's house and make more dating progress. If you kill her on a date, Woozie will call and tell you to break into her house and get the card. Then steal her card. (See the **Key to Her Heart** mission earlier in this strand.)

- If you do have Millie's keycard, an excited Woozie says "You the man!" and asks you to come back to The Four Dragons so you can get on with the Caligula's Palace heist.

MISSION PASS (1 OF 2)

Completing **Up, Up and Away!** gives you one of the two prerequisites needed to open the **Breaking the Bank at Caligula's** mission later.

Breaking the Bank at Caligula's

\# **Respect Gained:**
100
$ **Cash Gained:**
$100,000

Enter The Four Dragons and go to the maintenance room where all the heist-planning has taken place. Dressed as a croupier, CJ gets ready to roll as other team members load up and move out in the disguised armored van. You have some special equipment for the heist, including Gas Grenades and Night-Vision Goggles.

PREREQUISITES NEEDED!

This mission is available only after you gain the keycard from Millie the croupier and complete both **Saint Mark's Bistro** (from the Casino strand) and **Up, Up and Away!** (from the Heist strand).

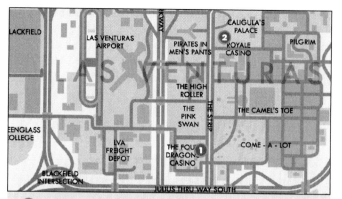

1 **Casino maintenance room**

2 **Heist**

Enter the Mafia Casino

Get a car and drive north up The Strip to Caligula's Palace. Go inside the front doors without brandishing any weapons. Avoid fights or altercations so you don't attract attention or blow your cover. Stay cool! Your entrance triggers a timer that

counts down from 4:00. You now have four minutes to get the team inside.

Open the Keycode Door

Inside Caligula's, follow the yellow radar blip across the casino to the keycode door, which is the staff entrance. Keep your weapons holstered. After a nearby goon asks CJ some questions, approach the securi-

ty door and use Millie's swipe-card to unlock it. Once the door opens, your next step is to find the backup generator room.

Find Generator Room and Gas the Safe Room Guards

Zero guides you down one level. Go downstairs to the first door on the left and saunter casually past the armed goon who stands guard over the generator room.

Zero directs you to the ventilation grills on the back wall. Approach the open grill on the back-left wall and toss a Gas Grenade into the vent.

You see a cinematic of the grenade dropping into the restricted area outside the safe room and the guards falling unconscious to the floor. Zero tells you to find the security door next and use Millie's swipe-card to open it.

Find the Keycard Door

Zero tells you he's hacked the casino's emergency lighting protocols, and then blows the charges you placed at the Sherman Dam. The power goes out and the casino goes dark. Don your Night-Vision

Goggles, exit the generator room, and turn left. Go through the passage marked with the sign that reads "NOTICE: Authorized Personnel Only." At the bottom of the short staircase, turn left. Go down the corridor past the Sprunk! vending machine.

Just around the corner is the keycard door. Approach the swipe panel to the door's right. Use Millie's keycard. When the door opens, enter the room. Your comrades in the van are now at the service bay and need the door opened. Zero tells you to head down to the service bay.

Health Boost

After you enter the security area using the keycard, note the Health power-up down the corridor to the right.

Open the Service Bay Door

Inside the keycard door, follow the new yellow radar blip across the room and through the far door. Proceed along the corridor and around the corner to the next doorway, which leads into the service bay. The power's down, so the service garage door is unlocked. But the door is heavy, so you need mechanical help opening it.

Use Forklift to Open the Roller Door

Find the forklift around the next corner at the far end of the service bay. When you hop aboard, a new yellow blip appears on radar. Follow the blip to the service garage entrance and its big roller door. (Drive straight ahead to the end of the service bay, and then turn right.) Drive the forklift prongs right under the door, then lift the door. Nice work! Your buddies back the armored van into the service bay, and the four-minute timer disappears.

Clear Corridors of Security so Team Can Reach the Vault

Now a new timer appears. You have seven minutes to retrieve the money from the safe and bring it back to the van. Note the multiple red threat blips on your radar. Run interference for Woozie and crew,

gunning down security guards as you move across the service bay, out through the keycard door and downstairs to the security door where the guards still lie unconscious from the Gas Grenade. When you reach the door, Woozie says he'll set the charges while you watch the door.

Destroy Backup Generators

Suddenly, Zero reports that somebody's in the system trying to bring the emergency generators back up! Hustle back upstairs and gun down the guards in the generator room door. Hurry into the generator room and place Satchel Charges on the

both emergency generators, which are marked with overhead cones. Then use the remote control unit to detonate the charges from a safe distance.

After the explosions, head back downstairs to the security doors. Woozie and crew automatically blow them open, and the team goes inside to load up the cash.

Enter the Safe

Go inside the now-open safe. When you do, Zero reports a squad of Mafia gorillas on their way down to the vault! Nab the Body Armor in the safe and hurry back to the doorway to the stairs.

Kill the Mafia While the Team Gets the Cash

Face the doorway and open fire! Several waves of mob goons try to fight their way into the security area. After you cap them, it's time to go!

Lead Your Team Safely Back to the Van

Remember, the seven-minute timer is ticking away! Go upstairs, ready to fight. Your heist team automatically walks the route back to the service bay where the van sits, so stay ahead of them. Protect your guys! Gun down any Mafia thugs who try to stop you. The last doorway leading into the service bay is heavily defended, with two mobsters on each side. Zero's already unloaded the police bikes from the van, so the team is ready to go soon. The onscreen timer disappears.

Don't Get Trigger-Happy!

When you shoot your way through the last doorway into the service bay, Zero stands alone next to the van and motorbikes. Don't gun him down!

Get to the Service Elevator

You're the decoy, so work back through the service bay. Zero's nemesis, Berkley, manages to restore the power, so remove your goggles. Follow the yellow radar blip; it leads you all the way back to the stairs that go up to the casino. Find the red marker and step into it to ride the service elevator up to the top floor of the casino.

Access Casino Roof

After exiting the elevator, turn right and head through the doorway at the end of the hall. (If you go left, you reach a locked door.) Climb the stairs to the top, gunning down any guards on the way up, then go through the marked door onto the casino roof.

Follow Rooftops and Collect the Parachute

A parachute sits atop the casino several roofs to the north. Head north (straight ahead) and hop up onto the rooftop, then climb up the sloped roof. If CJ is too low on health, turn around and pick up the Body Armor directly behind his starting location. A pair of police helicopters dogs your progress and drop SWAT team members onto the roof. Nail both birds with your rocket launcher. When you cross the peak of the first roof, gunmen open fire from below. Wipe them out and continue up the second sloped roof.

Parachute Off and Escape in the Helicopter

When you finally reach the parachute, put it on. A quick cinematic shows a police helicopter sitting on the roof near the Clown's Pocket Casino across the way. Jump off the rooftop and immediately press the Circle button to activate the parachute. Guide yourself over to the helicopter. Gun down the two cops by the copter and hop aboard the Police Maverick. If CJ doesn't make it to the helicopter, don't worry. Simply get down to the street level, jack a car, and drive to the destination. You won't even take any gunfire from the helicopter!

Escape to the Safe House

Now fly through the angry buzz of police pursuit and follow the yellow blip across the map to your airstrip out in the desert at Verdant Meadows. When you finally reach the red marker, watch as Zero admits he told Berkley about the caper. But no matter—the heist is a success, and your bank account now swells with cash

chapter 6

Return to
Los Santos

This final chapter of Grand Theft Auto: San Andreas starts in The Four Dragons Casino back in Las Venturas. Fresh from their triumph over the Mafia families, Woozie and CJ work to make The Four Dragons a success. But CJ grows tired of certain aspects of casino management—i.e., auditioning acts by "people of reduced stature." He longs for a triumphant return home where he can put things right. Then Madd Dogg's release from the rehab facility spurs CJ to make his move.

THE MANSION STRAND

Madd Dogg's magnificent mansion is now headquarters and haven of a drug dealer, Big Poppa. This fact enrages CJ; the home, he feels, belongs in better hands, and would make a good base of operations for a move back into Los Santos.

 # Total Respect Gained Throughout Strand:
130
$ Cash Gained Throughout Strand:
$50,000
◉ Property Available:
Mansion

MANSION mission 1

A Home in the Hills

◉ Respect Gained:
40

the story

Go to Woozie's office in The Four Dragons to see Madd Dogg's return from rehab and CJ's decision to retake Dogg's Mulholland mansion from the drug lord, Big Poppa. Cut to the mission setup: Triad members land via parachute on the mansion helipad. They set some red flares to help guide in CJ and the rest of the team, who parachute down from the transport plane.

Directions

Land on Mansion Roof with the Triads

Guide your parachute on the same trajectory as the four Triads floating below you, descending onto the flare-lit helipad. You land in a hornet's nest, as enemy gunmen now swarm the roof!

◉ Land in Cover

Veer to the right as you glide down onto the mansion helipad. Try to land behind the twin air conditioner units to immediately cut off enemy fire. Crouch as you land and grab the nearby Body Armor.

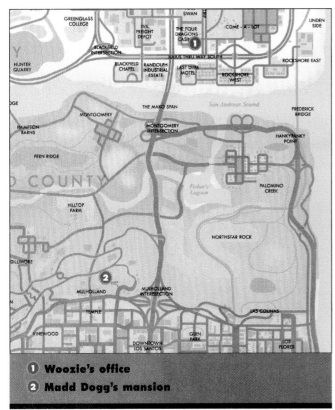

① Woozie's office
② Madd Dogg's mansion

Keep Roof Clear Until Backup Triads Arrive

This is an old-fashioned shootout. Use all of the fighting tactics you've learned so far to survive the vicious helipad combat. Big Poppa's troops (about 30 in all!) pour onto the helipad from left, right, and center in wave after wave. When your Triad backup group is close to arriving, you get a message to protect them when they land.

Lead the Triads Inside the Mansion

Once the Triads arrive, move down the ramp leading from the helipad to the mansion. Proceed across the balcony overlooking the swimming pool. Enter the double doors just around the corner. A Triad member tells CJ you're heavily outnumbered, but calm, cool tactics will prevail. Fine last words from the fellow.

Search for Big Poppa, Kill Anyone Who Gets in Your Way

Avenge the Triad's untimely demise, fending off the five-man ambush (including two hidden in the planter on the left), then go through the next doorway and fight down the hallway hung with the paintings. (It should look familiar from your rhyme-book burglary.)

Watch out for pairs of enemies in every side room as you move down the corridor, and don't miss the Body Armor in the last bedroom on the right. Soon, you get a message telling you where Big Poppa is lurking.

Big Poppa is Downstairs!

When you finally reach the main staircase, crouch and approach the railing. Rain down fire on the enemy in the game room below, using the railing for cover. Killers lurk in both directions in the large front hall at the bottom. (Grab the Health power-up in the large kitchen to the left of the game room.) If you have them, throw Grenades or Molotov Cocktails over the balcony to help thin the numbers below.

Once you clear out the hall, move west past the dining room. Big Poppa (marked by a red overhead marker) appears at the end of the corridor, and yells "You chose the wrong house to rob, fool!" Then he makes a break for it.

Chase Down Big Poppa!

Big Poppa runs down a series of corridors, and his men pop out of rooms to slow your progress. Shoot on the run, keeping after the drug baron. You fight through the TV room, bar, and swimming pool areas before you finally reach the front door. Exit the mansion to see Big Poppa hop in a fast car and try to escape. Fortunately, a hot red sports car is parked nearby, ready to be jacked.

Run Big Poppa Off the Road!

Speed after Big Poppa, chasing the red blip on the radar until you have his car in sight. (It has a red marker overhead.) Keep banging into his rear fender to knock him around the road, then pull alongside and open fire with your MP5. Keep up the pressure until his car finally explodes. Mission passed!

You now own the house, so you can go back and save your game at the disc icon upstairs on the third level. Drive back to the mansion, park by the garages, and get out of the car.

This puts the "CJ" icon on the map, marking the location of your new headquarters at Madd Dogg's mansion. This is your new contact point, as well as your new home.

Go up the brick road that runs beside the mansion, and climb the stone barrier to reach the upper patio of the house. (Or take the long way through the front door and all the way upstairs to the top level.) Find the red marker (your Mansion strand contact point) on the patio just outside the doors at the top level of the house.

MANSION mission 2

Vertical Bird

🚗 **New Vehicle Introduced:**
Hydra Jet

💲 **Cash Gained:**
$50,000

the story

When you step into the red marker on the mansion's upper patio, you trigger a forward time jump—Madd Dogg is now back recording in his studio, with Paul, Maccer, and CJ listening in. Suddenly, Mike Toreno breaks into the frequency and asks CJ for one last favor. He's waiting outside in with a car.

Toreno drives CJ clear up through Red County to the waterfront along The Panopticon, where a speedboat is docked near the shore. According to Toreno, a flotilla of Commie spy ships lurk brazenly off the coast of San Fierro, monitoring transmissions to steal data technology. Toreno suggests that Sweet could be freed this week if CJ will just steal a military jet off a nearby aircraft carrier and use it to destroy the spy boats—"nothing big," says Toreno.

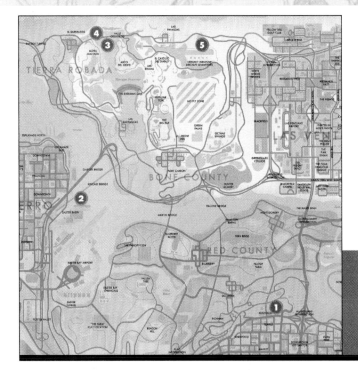

Directions

Take the Speedboat to Aircraft Carrier Near San Fierro

All the gear you need is onboard the Squallo speedboat, including a Knife and a Silenced Pistol. Toreno will brief you via radio earpiece as you go. As you board the speedboat, Toreno tells you the ship you seek is moored in the Easter Basin Naval Base. Follow the yellow blip across the water as you swing out around the long pier to the aircraft carrier at Easter Basin docks. Guide your speedboat around its stern to find an opening to a docking bay inside the big ship.

① **Mansion**
② **Aircraft carrier**
③ **Spy boats (2)**
④ **Spy boats (2)**
⑤ **Airstrip hangar**

Swim in to Avoid Detection

Toreno tells you to sneak in the back without being seen. Pull your boat close to the opening in the big ship, then jump in the water and swim inside.

Crouch and sneak up the ramp from the water, then wait and watch the guards up ahead. Wait until the guards start moving away from you, then hustle through the doorway into the cargo hold.

Move to the boxes on the right side of the cargo hold. Climb and move stealthily over the stacks, pausing to swing the camera around from time to time to keep track of the pacing guards. Eventually, you reach the far end of the hold where you can sneak through a door hatch to exit. Don't let yourself get spotted.

Switch off the SAM Sites

Your ultimate goal is to steal a Hydra Jet, but before you can fly it off the carrier, you must deactivate the SAM (surface to air missile) sites. Climb the first stairway on the next landing.

Don't climb the second staircase; it leads to the top deck, and you don't need to go there. Instead, veer left of the stairs and approach the open hatch. Creep down the corridor to another pair of open hatches, waiting for guards to pop out as you go. Try to be stealthy and use a Silencer Pistol or get them from behind with the Knife. If you trigger the alarm, you'll just have to fight.

Proceed through the hatch on the left into another cargo hold where a forklift drives back and forth. Turn right and move carefully through the crates (another guard hides behind one) until you reach a narrow room with a red marker in front of a console. Step into the marker to deactivate the ship's SAM site. (You see a brief cinematic of this.)

Find a Hydra Jet

Exit the SAM control room and work your way down the length of the hold until you reach several Hydra Jets. There's one on a platform straight ahead. Kill any guards and hop aboard the Hydra. The platform

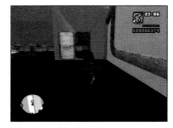

rises to the main deck level. Fire up the jet and go vertical.

Shoot Down the Pursuing Hydra Jets

As you bank away from the carrier, three Hydra Jets launch off the carrier and chase you. These appear as red radar blips behind your position. Turn and engage them one by one, locking on with your missile radar and knocking them out.

Sink the Spy Flotilla

Now you can follow the yellow radar blips to the spy boats at the northernmost tip of the bay, north of the Sherman Dam in Tierra Robada County. Two pairs of enemy spy boats are tucked tightly into the nar-

row bay near the shore, so it's not easy to get a clean shot at them. Get your Hydra Jet to hover nearby, then lock onto a boat, wait for the lock to turn red, and then fire; the boats will be destroyed.

Fly the Hydra Jet to Your Airstrip, Then Home

After you finally destroy all four spy boat targets, Toreno washes his hands of the incident. Thanks, man! Fly the stolen jet to your airstrip up at Verdant Meadow. Land the Hydra

Jet in the red marker on the runway, then taxi into the designated hangar to complete the mission.

 Airplane Dump

When your Hydra reaches the mansion bail out and parachute to the mansion grounds. Save your game. Try to land directly in the red marker (upper patio) to trigger the next mission! Don't worry about losing this fantastic vehicle; one will now continuously spawn at Verdant Meadows Airstrip.

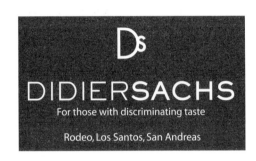

MANSION mission 3

Home Coming

Accomplice:
Sweet
Respect Gained:
40

the story

Back at the Mulholland mansion, Toreno interrupts CJ's phone call with yet another surprise visit. Part of the surprise is a phone call from Sweet. He's out of jail, waiting in Pershing Square, outside the precinct building in Commerce! Toreno says he has one last, little job for CJ: "Go pick up your brother."

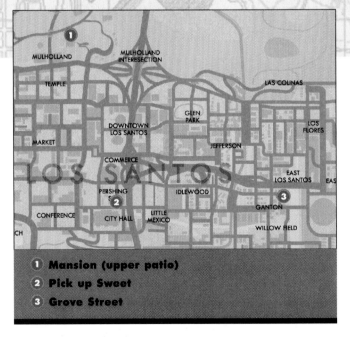

① **Mansion (upper patio)**
② **Pick up Sweet**
③ **Grove Street**

**Directions**

Pick Up Sweet From the Precinct

Drive south to Pershing Square, following the yellow blip on the map to Sweet's location. Drive into the red marker outside the precinct building to trigger a long, bitter

scene between the brothers. CJ tries to get Sweet to join up in his successes, but Sweet is all about the hood.

Drive Sweet to Grove Street

Follow the yellow blip to Ganton. CJ takes Sweet to see how Grove Street is in the grip of base now, with the old gang values literally gone up in smoke. Sweet wants to go to their mother's house. When they arrive, the brothers find the

place is overrun by strung out, crackhead junkies. Sweet wants CJ to help him clean up their house.

Clean Out Local Crack Dealers

The map suddenly fills up with red blips marking the location of drug dealers, and Sweet's health bar appears onscreen. Remember, the dealers are indicated by red markers overhead. If a dealer asks if you want some stuff, reply negatively and open fire. Move down the street and eliminate the dealers one by one. Make sure Sweet keeps following you, and pick up any drug money the dealers drop.

Take Back the Hood From the Ballas

When you've eliminated all the dealers, turn your attention to the Ballas congregating on the streets. Shoot three or four Ballas to provoke a gang war! Attack all purple-clad, red-marked enemies to win back control of Ganton. Stay near Sweet when fighting and keep your brother alive by attacking any gangbanger who attacks him.

Gang War

Remember that when you trigger a gang war, the area under dispute starts flashing red on the map. When you've won the war, the map area turns green.

The Ballas come in waves. Move and shoot, and keep an eye out for Health and Body Armor power-ups in the street. This is a tough fight, because Sweet seems to have a mind of his own sometimes. When you finally regain control of Grove Street, Sweet refuses to go see Kendl, demanding instead that she "come home" to see him. The brothers still disagree on the sanctity of the hood, and Sweet returns to the family home (the Johnson House), CJ's old save house on Grove Street.

Choose a Contact Point

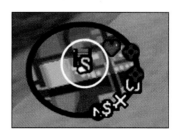

Finishing this mission adds an "S" icon to the map, giving you a second contact point along with the "CJ" back at the Mulholland mansion. The choice is up to you.

NEW MISSION STRAND OPEN!

Completing the Home Coming mission opens up a new contact point marked by an "S" icon, giving you access to the Grove Street strand and its first mission, Beat Down on B-Dup.

MANSION mission 4

Cut Throat Business

🚗 **Vehicles Introduced:**
Vortex hovercraft, Kart go-cart
➕ **Respect Gained:**
40

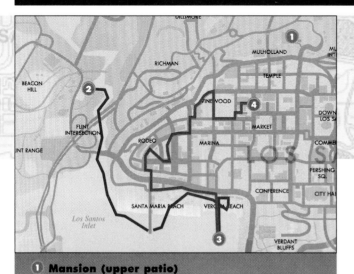

① Mansion (upper patio)
② Video shoot (hovercraft)
③ Switch to go-carts
④ Record producer
╲ Hovercraft chase
╲ Go-cart chase

Madd Dogg is tired of OG Loc's bogus success. Then it hits him—OG Loc's rhymes are very, very familiar. In fact, they came from Dogg's own rhyme book! CJ agrees to make a "cameo appearance" with Madd Dogg on the set where OG Loc is shooting his latest music video.

Directions

Take Madd Dogg to Video Shoot

Get in the car and wait for Madd Dogg to join you. CJ wants to drop in on OG Loc and recoup some royalties for his new man, not to mention the rhyme book. Follow the yellow blip east to the shoot in Flint County, right on the water. When you arrive, you see that OG Loc is being interviewed for TV.

When OG Loc sees CJ and Madd Dogg approach, he hops into a nearby hovercraft and takes off! CJ and Madd Dogg climb in separate hovercrafts to give chase.

Don't let OG Loc Get Away

Follow OG Loc's hovercraft (red overhead marker) as it weaves through bridge struts and boats. You can't catch him, but you can lose him, so don't let him get too far

away. He heads south and then east across the Los Santos Inlet, making a ramp jump right over a small dock off Santa Maria Beach. He then glides under the main pier and guns the hovercraft up the sand and around onto the main pier! Stay on his tail.

Down the pier OG Loc ditches his hovercraft and switches to a Kart. CJ and Dogg make the switch, too.

Close Counts

You can't catch OG Loc's hovercraft or go-cart, so focus on controlled driving rather than taking risks to overtake him. Just stay close and don't lose him to complete the mission successfully.

Chase OG Loc in the Go-cart

Don't lose that fool! He drives up and down stairs, along the beachfront, then up onto the streets and over the freeway into the streets of Rodeo. From there he zigzags east

into Vinewood and down through the alleys of the Market district. Eventually he shoots up a narrow stairway and ducks behind a Los Santos Fashion store.

In the cutscene that follows, CJ and Madd Dogg confront OG Loc in the offices of a record label. Suddenly, a producer named Jimmy Silverman of Blastin' Fools Records appears and offers to talk turkey with the Dogg. CJ steps in as manager while Madd Dogg finally recovers his rhyme book. All is well!

MISSION PASS (1 OF 2)

Completing **Cut Throat Business** gives you one of the two prerequisites needed to open the **Riot** mission later.

THE GROVE STREET STRAND

Sweet's release from prison brings CJ back to the hood to set things right. The Johnson brothers attempt to secure the old neighborhood once and for all in the two missions of this strand.

⬢ **Contact Point:**
The Johnson House
⊕ **Total Respect Gained Throughout Strand:**
80

Beat Down on B-Dup

⬢ **Accomplice:**
Sweet
⊕ **Respect Gained:**
40

1. Sweet's house
2. B-Dup's old place
3. B-Dup's new place
☐ Ballas territory

Back at Sweet's place on Grove Street, one of B-Dup's women tries to sweet-talk Sweet into getting high. He's vulnerable and despondent about the demise of the Families and the power of the crack industry. But just as the pipe goes to his lips, CJ storms in and chases the woman out. Then he rallies Sweet to the cause: taking back the hood, for good.

the story

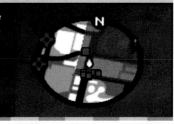
Directions

Get to B-Dup's Place

After a pep talk from CJ, the brothers are ready to take down the pusher man. Hop in the nearby Greenwood, wait for Sweet to join you, and drive up to a couple of Grove boys on the street to recruit them.

Follow the yellow blip to B-Dup's apartment. CJ beats on the door, but a base-head in the hall says B-Dup moved over to Glen Park. Get back in the car.

Go to Glen Park and Take Over the Ballas Territory

Head north to Glen Park, a place Sweet calls "heart of Kilo Trays country." When you arrive (Glen Park is a purple area on the map), start gunning down Ballas dressed

in purple to provoke a gang war. Sweet's health meter appears onscreen, which means one of your tasks in this mission is to protect him. You must defeat all Ballas gang members and win the territory before you can confront B-Dup.

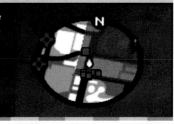

Watch for Purple Blips

Remember that once you provoke a gang war, the enemy gangsters appear on the map as blips that match their gang color—in this case, purple for Ballas. Use your radar to hunt down targets.

Remember to keep an eye on Sweet's health. He can take care of himself pretty well, but stay close to him and watch his back if his health meter drops below 50 percent. The Ballas come in three waves, with little breathing room between each wave. Once you've cleared them all, however, you finally get a crack at the crack palace itself.

Kill B-Dup's Guards!

Use the AK-47 from long-range and try to clear as many of the big platoon of guards surrounding the palatial, well-lit house before getting any closer. Remember to keep Sweet alive! After the palace guard is eliminated, approach the house.

Confront B-Dup

Walk up to the front door to enter the house. Sweet and CJ interrogate B-Dup. He says Big Smoke is paranoid and holed up somewhere, but B-Dup can't say where. Then Big Bear comes out and asks to join

back up with CJ. He's clearly based up and in bad shape. Sweet takes him off to rehab "to get old Bear back." Grab a car and drive back to the house on Grove Street marked by the "**S**" icon on the map.

GROVE STREET mission 2

Grove 4 Life

Accomplice:
Sweet

Respect Gained:
40

Cash Gained:
$10,000

① Sweet's house
② Ballas neighborhoods

Sweet is preaching, and the homies rally behind his call to clean crack out of the lives of the Grove Street Families, once and for all. He and CJ still see things differently about the importance of the hood versus the wider world, but they agree that it's time to put Grove Street back on the map.

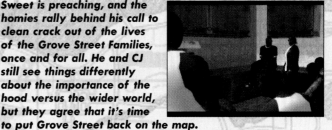

Gather Up the Homies

CJ should have enough Respect by now to assemble a small army of Grove Family homeboys. So first things first—gather up as many green-clad Grove troops as possible. This will be a real war, and the

more troops you can deploy, the better your chances of survival.

Take Over One Neighborhood in Idlewood

Recruit as many Grove Street gang-bangers as you can, then hop in your car and drive (or just jog, leading the pack on foot) into the

Idlewood district, currently controlled by the Ballas gang as indicated by the purple area on the radar map. Start gunning down purple-clad Ballas until you provoke a gang war.

 Know Your Boundaries

Remember that a large district like Idlewood is usually divided into several smaller gang-controlled neighborhoods. When you provoke a gang war in this mission, it affects only one of those smaller neighborhoods, indicated by the flashing red on the map.

Don't forget Sweet! If he dies, you fail the mission. As in the previous Grove strand mission, monitor his onscreen health meter. If it gets too low, you'd better focus on protecting him; follow your brother and pick off nearby attackers until the number of purple blips dwindles on the radar map. You can find buildings with multi-level balconies that are great to get a height advantage over the enemy. Use Grenades or Molotovs from here to thin them out. One in particular has a large fence that prevents enemies from getting at Sweet and your homies.

Take Over a Second Idlewood Neighborhood

Move into another purple neighborhood on the map and repeat the previous steps: provoke a war, hunt down all purple blips. When you gain control of the second neighborhood, your mission is complete. Grove 4 Life, baby!

Take Sweet Back to Grove Street

Grove Street is on the up again. Grab a vehicle and drive up next to Sweet (if he doesn't just follow you into the car). When he gets in, follow the yellow blip, heading east back to Ganton and your house on Grove Street.

MISSION PASS (1 OF 2)

Completing Grove 4 Life gives you one of the two prerequisites needed to open the Riot mission later.

THE RIOTS STRAND

This intense three-pack of missions wraps up *Grand Theft Auto: San Andreas*. The Johnson boys and Grove Street make a stand in the hood as the Los Santos riots rage all around, concluding with a showdown between CJ and his primary antagonist.

Total Respect Gained Throughout Strand:
210

RIOTS mission 1

Riot

Respect Gained:
40

CJ and his extended family gather at Madd Dogg's mansion to watch TV reports of the pending trial of Officers Tenpenny and Pulaski (the latter has recently "disappeared"). But then a bombshell drops—the DA drops all charges! Tenpenny's free!

Within minutes, the Los Santos ghetto erupts in riots. Sweet is determined that nobody will be rioting on Grove Street, but Cesar points out the view from the mansion: "The whole city is going up!" So Sweet and CJ decide to head home and secure the hood.

PREREQUISITES NEEDED!

This mission is available only after you complete the Cut Throat Business and Grove 4 Life missions.

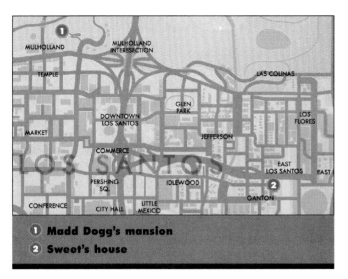

1. Madd Dogg's mansion
2. Sweet's house

Return to Sweet's House

Grab a car from the mansion garage or jack something from the street and start following the yellow blip icon across the map. Stick to the freeway as much as possible to avoid roadblocks, exploding cars, and other confrontations.

When you finally arrive, ignore any chaos out on the street and pull up next to the red marker in the driveway outside Sweet's house. Get out of the car and run into the marker to trigger the next mission.

RIOTS mission 2

Los Desperados

⊕ **Respect Gained:**
60

Sweet's on the phone making security arrangements for the hood, getting things locked down. He then knocks CJ for a while, questioning his brother's dedication to hood and family. Suddenly, Cesar enters and asks for help in his own hood, pushing out the "yay-slinging punks" and getting his old gang back together. CJ agrees to get Cesar's back, but Cesar is low on numbers.

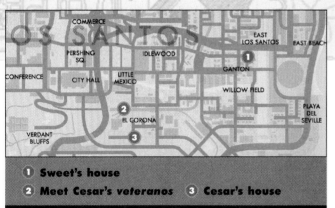

1. Sweet's house
2. Meet Cesar's veteranos   3. Cesar's house

Recruit a Couple of Grove Homies

Cesar's plan is to meet three of his old Varrios Los Aztecas homeboys down at Unity Station. CJ doesn't think three is enough. So recruit two green-clad Grove Street boys, then hop in the Greenwood parked out front, waiting for Cesar and the two homies to join you. (You need a car-load of four to proceed.) Cesar remarks that you don't want to get caught on Ballas turf in this kind of chaos.

Head to Unity Station to Meet Cesar's Veteranos

Follow the yellow blip westward toward Unity Station in El Corona. On the way, Cesar tells CJ he wants to ask Kendl to marry him. CJ's okay with that, but Cesar is worried about Sweet. CJ agrees to talk to him. When you arrive at the station, find the red marker on the platform next to the train tracks. Step into it to see Cesar's Los Aztecas Veteranos (turquoise colors) complain about the Los Santos Vagos (yellow colors).

Help Cesar and the OGs Clear Out the Neighborhood

Note that the neighborhood is yellow on the radar map—the Vagos control it. After you meet the Los Aztecas, Cesar leads you and the others through a Vagos-infested housing project toward his house.

Start icing Vagos. About 30 of them inhabit the project, so be ready for plenty of combat. Follow Cesar's lead as he moves through the buildings; you can spot him from a distance by his blue overhead marker. Move carefully around corners. If

you get lost, follow Cesar's blue blip on the radar map. Cesar will stop at certain points and will not forge onward if there are remaining enemies around. Clear the hidden threats, and Cesar will begin to move again.

Head to the Alleyway

Cesar announces when you've wiped out the last of the Vagos in the housing project, but the area's not clean yet! Follow Cesar toward the yellow radar blip as you move out of the projects and toward the red marker at the head of an alleyway (under a tag that reads "Families"), across the street.

Cesar says you've completed the easy part. Now it gets tough as you move into "the viper's nest." One of the Los Aztecas named Sunny has a little something up his sleeve: a rocket launcher. Up ahead, a squad of yellow-clad Vagos blocks the alley and opens fire.

"Territory Wall"

CJ receives a call from Sweet in which he explains that they need to gain more influence by taking over more territory. You must control 35% of the territory in Los Santos before the final mission will trigger. It is a lot easier to take over gang territory before triggering the riots due to the fact that the number of usable cars during the riots drops significantly, which makes quick escapes almost impossible.

Stay Close to Cesar and Clear Out the Alleyway

Sunny leads off with a rocket volley that explodes the Vagos' car. Lead the way down the alley, ducking and firing, and using the nearby car for cover. Watch out for a couple of Vagos tucked into a garage on the right side.

Early in the fight, one of Cesar's boys named Hazer wanders into the line of fire and takes a bullet. After you clear out the alley, Cesar moves to Hazer, but suddenly more Vagos pour over the fences and walls into the alley! Cesar's trapped out in the open.

Defend Cesar

Fire quickly to keep the Vagos from capping Cesar. Watch out behind you, too, as a couple of Vagos sneak in behind the car you were using for cover. Pass garages with caution; enemies can be hidden within. After you clear out the alley for a

second time, Cesar leads you on to his home. Unfortunately, Cesar's house is crawling with Vagos squatters, including one with a flame-thrower and another atop the roof with a Rocket Launcher.

Finish Off the Last Vagos

Keep your distance on this one, using a longer-range weapon to pick off these targets. Take out the rocket launcher guy quickly. More Vagos attack from up the street to the right, as well. When the battle ends, Cesar thanks CJ for the help and sends him back to the Grove.

RIOTS mission 3

End of the Line

⊕ **Respect Gained:**
40

This is it: Time to face down the enemies of the Grove Street Families. Sweet calls CJ to say Big Smoke's fortress is in Los Flores or East Los Santos. Sweet's call puts the "S" icon back on the map. Go to Sweet's house to see the brothers Johnson united—a powerful force to be sure.

Yes, Big Smoke is going down, but not without a fight. Not even Carl Johnson, original gangster, can bust open Smoke's crack fortress—not without a little help from the Los Santos SWAT team.

PARK

LOS
FLORES

JEFFERSON

SANTOS

EAST
LOS SANTOS   EAST BEACH

IDLEWOOD

GANTON

LITTLE
MEXICO

1 Sweet's house

2 SWAT Tank   **3** Smoke's crack fortress

Directions

Drive to Big Smoke's Crack Fortress

Get in the car with Sweet and head north. On the way, Sweet assures CJ that the crack house is in East Los Santos, on the edge of Los Flores—some old apartments and a warehouse. Follow the yellow radar blip and drive into the red marker.

CJ and Sweet get "heated up," but CJ insists he's going in alone. You learn that the fortress has only one entrance, but it's locked down because of the riots. Looks like you'll have to knock it down. CJ needs a heavy vehicle like, say, a SWAT tank for this job. It just so happens that there's one parked nearby.

Get a SWAT Tank

Head directly downhill, cutting through residential yards as you track the blue radar blip to a police roadblock, where cops exchange gunfire with nearby rioters. You could try a frontal assault up the street through the roadblock—but this is not the best. A smarter tactic is to sneak into the fenced yard closest to the SWAT tank on the blocked street. You can also just hop on the bike by the crackhouse, head south, then west to where the SWAT truck is parked. You'll be approaching the troops from behind, so you can just pull right up to it and hop in.

Creep along the fence as close as possible to the tank before you make your run, thus sparing yourself damage. Gun down the guard next to the tank, then quickly commandeer the big armored vehicle.

Ram SWAT Tank Into Crack Fortress

Drive the tank forward through the road block, then turn right and head back up the hill, following the yellow radar blip. When you reach Big Smoke's fortress, smash right into the green section of wall where the guards stand.

Find Entrance Into First Floor Near Back of Area

Inside, use the water cannon to knock down the gunmen or just run them over. Drive all the way to the end of the area to find the door with the yellow marker. Hop out of the tank and hurry through the door.

Floor 1: Security Area

You learn that Smoke is on the fourth floor in his penthouse suite. Climb the stairs and turn right. Proceed along the corridor, capping the pair of guards, including one who side-rolls out of an alcove.

Move through the gated doorway and fight your way down the next corridor. (Don't miss the Body Armor in the office at the end of the hall.) Then approach the next set of doors.

Get ready! Crouch and burst through the doors into a big warehouse area, then scoot forward to a row of boxes. Numerous gunmen target your position, so pop up for quick shots and drop quickly for cover. Watch out for a pair of high snipers posted on the catwalks above. Stay firmly planted behind your boxes until the room is under control.

Once you clear the main room, look for more thugs in the smaller room through the far door. Terminate them and cross the room, turning around the corner to the next set of stairs. Climb the stairs and nail the guard at the top. Go past the closed double-doors and round the corner to the right to find the Health power-up. Phew!

Return to the double-doors and step through. No guards wait on the other side this time.

Floor 2: Drug Lab

Climb the next set of stairs, but stop and crouch before you reach the top. A gunman waits in the office just ahead. Nail him and grab some more Body Armor, then roll through the double-doors and gun down the guard in the next storage room.

 Explosive Barrels

The crack lab has several barrels of highly explosive materials. Shoot them from the doorway to thin out the guard ranks.

The next set of double-doors opens into the drug lab, a huge crack factory filled with worktables and many armed guards. Clean the scum out of this room, nailing explosive barrels from a distance for quick kills.

Climb the far stairway to another set of doors. These doors are locked, however, so you must follow the raised catwalk all the way around the room. More guards burst onto the catwalk from the doorway on the far side. Plug the explosive barrel next to them on the catwalk to wipe them out.

The office at the end of the catwalk is full of desks with computers. Don't miss the Health power-up at the far end of the room, then proceed through the next set of double-doors.

Floor 3: Ballas Lounge

Climb the stairs, but pause before you reach the top. Crouch and move up a couple more steps, then raise quickly and nail the guard just ahead in the office. Grab the goodies in the office, then move to the next set of doors. Get ready! Two guards stand watch on the other side. Nail them and proceed into the lounge through a handsome set of 8-panel wood doors.

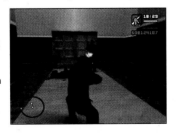

The carpeted, wood-paneled luxury lounge is a nice place for crack dealers to relax after a busy day of killing hope. Add a little excitement to their mix by gunning down anyone you find here. After you decimate the guys right inside the door, hustle over to the mahogany bar and use it for cover. More Ballas pushers wander in from the next room; kill them, then move into that room. Exit via another set of wooden doors.

The next hallway features a statue of Big Smoke. Kill the art lovers gathered nearby, then turn right and follow the hallway to the last door on the right. Before you leave, if you need health and armor, find them in the two stripper rooms on either side of the hall. Gunmen may still be lurking inside with the strippers. Go on through and climb the stairway beyond. At the top, go through the doors to trigger a cutscene.

Go Get Big Smoke

Smoke sits playing a videogame. What a degenerate! After a strong hit of base, he expresses no regrets for what he considers "making something of himself" and pulls a weapon for the final showdown.

Smoke's health bar appears onscreen; you learn he's wearing Body Armor, so aim at other parts of his body to maximize the damage you inflict on him. Hustle over to the bar and get behind it for cover. A few thugs rush in to help Smoke, and he switches off the lights.

Get Thermal Goggles by the Lower Window

You can nail Smoke without the goggles as he rushes around the bar. But it can help significantly to find and wear them. Once Smoke drops, you trigger another scene. Smoke makes his peace... and then the devil himself appears.

Tenpenny tells CJ to fill up his bag with money from Big Smoke's open safe. He says he's "got a fire truck to catch." CJ manages to duck out of sight, but Tenpenny blasts a generator, causing a fire that knocks out the lights. Let's get out of here, fast.

Use Night-vision Goggles to Escape

An onscreen timer starts counting down from 7:00—you have seven minutes to escape! CJ picked up some Night-Vision Goggles from the dying Big Smoke. Select them from inventory and activate them (you can then return to a normal weapon), then cross the room and exit the doors you came in through. Retrace your route back through the Ballas lounge on Floor 3, then downstairs to the drug lab on Floor 2 while fighting reinforcements that have refilled these areas.

Use a Fire Extinguisher to Get Out

Unfortunately, Floor 2 is in flames. Step through the doors and nab the fire extinguisher right in front of you. Then use it to clear a way through the fire to the door on the far wall of the drug lab.

Human Flesh Is Combustible

Don't run through flames! Amazingly enough, CJ will suffer damage if he catches fire. If you completed the Fire Fighter Odd Job, however, CJ will be fireproof!

The goggles make the flames hard to see, so switch them off as you use the extinguisher. Douse the fire on the door leading out to the catwalk overlooking the drug lab, then step out and use the perch to pick off Ballas running around the lab below. Fight through the flames, rush downstairs to the exit door, and extinguish the fire blocking your exit there. Get out!

Take the stairs down to Floor 1, don your goggles again, and fight your way into the big warehouse room. From the doorway, pick off the many guards inside, then take the goggles back off to see fires as you make your way across the warehouse room. Time is running out!

Fight down the last corridor, dousing the flames blocking your path at the hall's end, then hustle down the final staircase and through the marked doorway. Look out! A final squad of goons awaits your appearance. Gun them down and sprint across the

floor to trigger the fiery finale of the crack fortress.

Outside, Tenpenny makes his escape in a fire truck, but Sweet won't let him get away clean. CJ's brother grabs hold of the ladder as the cop drives away. CJ hops in a nearby convertible and gives chase.

Follow That Fire Truck

Follow the fire truck. This is the longest, wildest chase of the game—you don't need to dodge the fire-bombs (they won't hurt your car), but you must avoid police chase vehicles. After a while, one of Tenpenny's cop accomplices moves down the fire truck ladder and stomps on Sweet's fingers! Sweet's grip slowly loosens, as indicated by the "Sweet's Grip" bar onscreen. Drive up underneath him! Eventually, Sweet falls from the ladder. If your car is positioned right, he lands safely next to CJ.

Now Sweet takes the wheel, and it's payback time as you open fire on your enemies. Rotate the targeting reticle over targets. Shoot cops off the seemingly indestructible fire truck, and swivel around to nail police cars and rival gang cars chasing you. Soon enemy motorcycles join the running battle, too.

Eventually, the chase leads past the Los Santos Forum into your home territory of Ganton, and then through a park into Willowfield. More cop cars join the chase, but finally, Tenpenny loses control of his truck and puts it through a guardrail

and off an overpass bridge. Amazingly, Tenpenny emerges briefly from the wreckage—unrepentant to the very end.

Sweet stops CJ from adding a bullet to Tenpenny's self-inflicted demise. The Truth marvels that CJ actually "beat the system." The homey crew muses on how it all went down, and CJ gives his C.R.A.S.H. nemesis one last little nudge, for old time's sake.

Watch the denouement as the gang gathers for some good news from Madd Dogg. The story may be closing, but don't worry…the map is wide open. All of San Andreas is still out there, waiting for a visit from Carl Johnson. Explore!

Official Strategy Guide

By Tim Bogenn & Rick Barba

credits

BradyGAMES Staff

Publisher
David Waybright

Editor-In-Chief
H. Leigh Davis

Director of Marketing
Steve Escalante

Creative Director
Robin Lasek

Licensing Manager
Mike Degler

Assistant Marketing Manager
Susie Nieman

Team Coordinator
Stacey Beheler

Book Credits

Senior Development Editor
David B. Bartley

Title Manager
Tim Fitzpatrick

Editorial Team
Tim Cox
Michael Owen

Lead Designers
Doug Wilkins
Ann-Marie Deets

Production Designer
Tracy Wehmeyer

Brady Acknowledgements

As always, thanks to Terry Donovan, Jenefer Gross, and everyone at Rockstar. Special thanks to Devin Winterbottom for providing great support throughout the entire project, and to Ethan Abeles and Lee Cummings for helping us map everything in San Andreas. Your collective time and expertise have helped make this guide great.

Author's Acknowledgements

Tim Bogenn (the B-OG-enn)
This was the biggest authoring project I've ever been a part of, and without the help of the people I'm about to mention, I would have never been able to accomplish this huge undertaking. To my co-author Rick Barba, it was an honor to work with "the father" of the Strategy Guide—an unforgettable adventure. I would like to thank the following people at RockStar: Devin Winterbottom, Lee Cummings, Jeff Rosa, Ethan Abeles, Scott Peterman, Nick Giovannetti, Gene Overton, Terry Donovan, and Sam Houser. Thank you for all your help and for making feel at home during the two months I lived in your office. Sorry for tagging the wall, I got carried away. I would also like to thank everyone at BradyGames, especially David "we can make it fit" Bartley, Leigh Davis, Mike Degler, David Waybright, Tim Cox, Michael Owen, and Tim Fitzpatrick. Lastly, and most importantly, I would like to thank Jennifer Bogenn for her patience, love, and support.

Author's Warning

Playing video games 12 hours a day for two months raises your Fat stat and lowers Muscle and Stamina. The jury is still out on what it does for your Respect. It's time to visit the 🍔 and hit the 🏋 now.